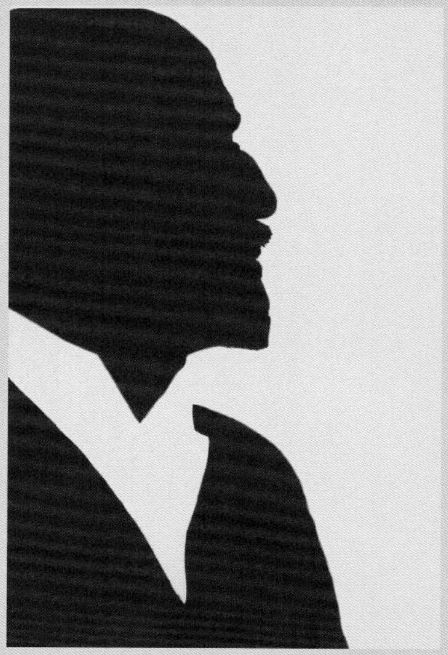

TEN CONTEMPORARY ARTISTS
EXPLORE THE LEGACY OF W.E.B.

Du Bois
In Our Time

RADCLIFFE BAILEY
MARY EVANS
BRENDAN FERNANDES
LATOYA RUBY FRAZIER
JULIE MEHRETU
ANN MESSNER
JEFFERSON PINDER
TIM ROLLINS & K.O.S.
MICKALENE THOMAS
CARRIE MAE WEEMS

University Museum of Contemporary Art
University of Massachusetts Amherst
September 10 – December 8, 2013

This publication is produced in conjunction with the exhibition *Du Bois in Our Time*,
curated by Loretta Yarlow and Eva Fierst, and presented at the University Museum of Contemporary Art.
September 10 – December 8, 2013

University of Massachusetts Amherst
Amherst, Massachusetts 01003
www.umass.edu/umca

Distributed by the University of Massachusetts Press
University of Massachusetts Amherst
Amherst, Massachusetts 01003
http://www.umass.edu/umpress/

ISBN number: 978-1-62534-134-1
Cataloging-in-Publication data on file at the Library of Congress

Editor: Loretta Yarlow
Managing editor: Betsey Wolfson
Copy editor: Chris Jerome
Photo coordinator: Danielle Gagne
All photographs by Stephen Petegorsky, except where noted (page 199)
Appreciation to Tom Adams, Reelife Productions, for video stills for this catalogue
Design by Pam Glaven, Impress, Northampton, Massachusetts
Front cover design adapted from a pamphlet designed by Joseph Krupczynski
Printed by The Studley Press, Dalton, Massachusetts

Front cover image courtesy of Scurlock Studio Records, Archives Center,
National Museum of American History, Behring Center, Smithsonian Institution

CONTENTS

ACKNOWLEDGMENTS

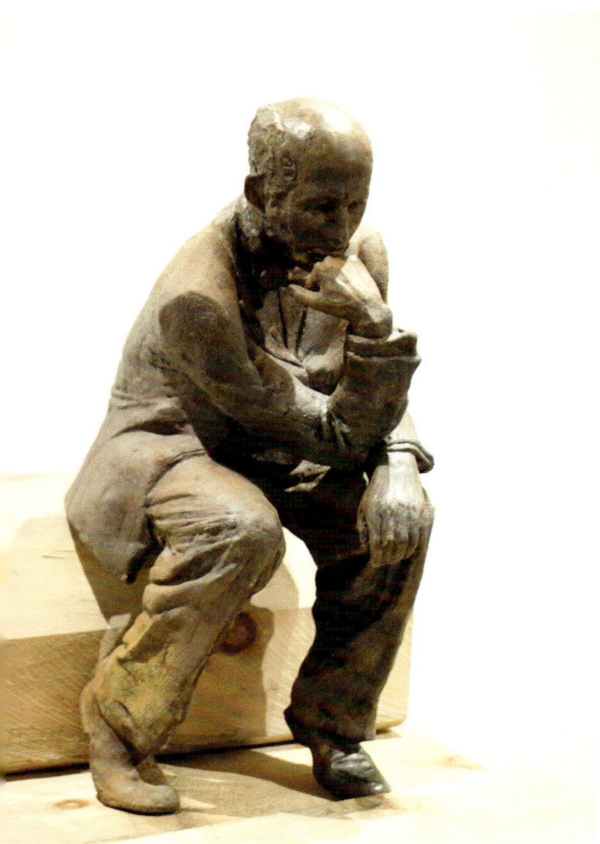

RADCLIFFE BAILEY
Untitled, 2013
Bronze, wood
42″ x 24¼″ x 17″
Courtesy of the artist and Jack Shainman Gallery, New York

THERE WOULD BE NO EXHIBITION or catalogue celebrating W.E.B. Du Bois in our time were it not for the extraordinary contributions of the ten artists who have given so much of their time and hearts to this project. Present and future generations will benefit from their visionary contributions to the examination of Du Bois in the twenty-first century. I want to express my heartfelt thanks to these artists: Radcliffe Bailey, Mary Evans, Brendan Fernandes, LaToya Ruby Frazier, Julie Mehretu, Ann Messner, Jefferson Pinder, Tim Rollins & K.O.S., Mickalene Thomas, and Carrie Mae Weems. It has been an honor to have spent so much time in dialogue and discovery with them. Their passions were contagious, and the enthusiasm and commitment they bestowed on this project will always be a highlight of my personal and professional experience.

We were privileged to have had three Du Bois scholars — James Campbell, Stanford University; Reiland Rabaka, University of Colorado; and Bill Strickland, University of Massachusetts Amherst — collaborating with us on *Du Bois in Our Time*. Their perspectives, which they share with us in this publication, along with the fruitful dialogue they had with the artists, were instrumental in the success of this project. I am deeply appreciative that they made time for this in the midst of their many other academic commitments.

Many colleagues at UMass Amherst were key partners and members of our Steering Committee, and they participated in much of the important decision-making process. Their dedication was critical to fulfilling the promise of the exhibition and its related symposium: Shabazz Amilcar, Afro-American Studies; Whitney Battle-Baptiste, Anthropology; Stephen Clingman, English; Rob Cox, Library Special Collections; Tanya Fernando, English; Eva Fierst, Education Curator, UMCA; David Glassberg, History; Susan Jahoda, Art; Joseph Krupczynski, Architecture and Design; Robert Paynter, Anthropology; Manisha Sinha, Afro-American Studies; and Bill Strickland, Afro-American Studies. My thanks also go to those UMass faculty who served as moderators for the symposium's panel discussions: Shabazz Amilcar, Tanya Fernando, Jim Hicks, Susan Jahoda, and Manisha Sinha.

The symposium was enriched by the presentations made by Nelson Stevens and Mike Thelwell, emeriti professors in the Du Bois Afro-American Studies Program, who broadened our understanding of the UMass connection to Du Bois in the 1970s.

I am particularly grateful to Dr. Johnnetta Betsch Cole, director of the Smithsonian's National Museum of African Art and faculty member at UMass Amherst from 1970 to 1983, who delivered an inspiring keynote address at our symposium. She has graciously consented to allow us to publish her memorable speech here, with the visuals that accompanied her presentation. She deserves special recognition for taking on the epic task of setting the stage for an overarching presentation of W.E.B. Du Bois then and now.

The exhibition would not have come to completion without the tireless dedication of the staff of the UMCA: installation manager Craig Allaben, registrar Justin Griswold, education curator Eva Fierst, and business and communications manager Betsey Wolfson. They wore multiple hats throughout the process and never said no. There are not enough words to thank them.

In particular I offer my deep gratitude to my phenomenal colleague and friend Eva Fierst, who served an essential role in urging us to think of every possible opportunity to extend our educational mission at UMass and beyond. The process of developing and refining this project was supported by her critical feedback and insights.

Joseph Krupczynski, architect/designer and UMass faculty member, was responsible for the superlative design of the exhibition, the accompanying graphics, and our exhibition brochure. He helped ensure that the artists' creations would be seen to their best possible advantage.

Richard Rabinowitz, the leading public historian, championed *Du Bois in Our Time* from our very first interaction. We were extremely fortunate to have had the advice and engagement of someone who so passionately understands the importance of civic engagement as well as the power of art.

We were also fortunate to have had the participation of the Springfield Renaissance School as the site for Tim Rollins and Angel Abreu's workshop in spring 2013. Our appreciation goes to principal Dr. Stephen Mahoney, art teacher Michael Gilane, and the many students involved in the creation of *Darkwater — Of Beauty and Death* (after W.E.B. Du Bois), 2013.

For a series of panel discussions and lectures that took place throughout fall 2013, we are indebted to the following scholars and guest speakers who enriched our understanding of Du Bois's legacy and his contributions to our society: Theaster Gates, Chicago-based social practice installation artist; Chris Tinson, African American Studies, Hampshire College; Bill Strickland, Afro-American Studies, UMass; Jason Irizarry, director of Urban Education, UMass; James Smethurst, Afro-American Studies, UMass; Horace D. Ballard Jr., Ph.D. candidate, Brown University; Kelli Morgan, Ph.D. candidate, UMass; Barbara Krauthamer, Department of History, UMass; Nicholas Bromell, American Studies, UMass; and Preston Smith, Urban Studies, Mount Holyoke College.

Meaningful contributions were made by graduate assistants Brittany Mayo (M.A. Art History 2014), Joe Saphire (M.F.A. Studio Arts 2015), Danielle Gagne (M.A. Art History 2015), and Kelli Morgan (Ph.D. Afro-American Studies, 2014). Their work with Eva Fierst, curator of education, included research, development of didactic materials, and the design of these materials.

I would like to thank graphic designer Pam Glaven for her sensitive design and coordination of this publication. Her close working relationship with the printer, Studley Press, was critically important. Additional thanks must go to copy editor Chris Jerome and to graduate assistant Danielle Gagne for so meticulously bringing together materials for this publication.

I wish to express my gratitude to the following individuals and their galleries for their support and generous sharing of information: Lissa McClure, Marian Goodman Gallery; Stephanie Smith, Lehmann Maupin Gallery; Joeanna Bellorado-Samuels and Elisabeth Sann, Jack Shainman Gallery.

Du Bois in Our Time is the result of a long process, one that could not have occurred or come to fruition without our generous sponsors. I would like to express my profound appreciation to the National Endowment for the Arts, Art Mentor Foundation Lucerne, and the Andy Warhol Foundation for the Visual Arts.

Additional thanks go to the following for their support: Massachusetts Cultural Council; Art Angels (Community Foundation of Western Massachusetts), and Mass Humanities. Support from UMass Amherst comes from: the Class of 1961 Artists Residency Fund; the Office of the Graduate Dean; the Office of the Provost; the W.E.B. Du Bois Library; the Interdisciplinary Studies Institute; and Friends of the Fine Arts Center Residency Fund.

Loretta Yarlow, Director
University Museum of Contemporary Art

REFLECTIONS ON *DU BOIS IN OUR TIME*

DU BOIS IN OUR TIME began as a bold experiment. Can we examine the legacy of W.E.B. Du Bois and his relevance in the twenty-first century through the lens of contemporary art? Can we commission artists to create works of art to help provide a broader understanding of Du Bois, who has been viewed too narrowly as a sociologist and historian rather than as a thinker and a humanist in the richest sense of these words? A further goal of this project was to bring attention to the University of Massachusetts Amherst as the custodian of more than 100,000 of Du Bois's essays, publications, speeches, photographs, and correspondence with noteworthy figures in American and global reform.

Michael Singer, the noted architect, landscape designer, and planner, extended an invitation to me in spring 2010 to attend a workshop at the location of the Du Bois Heritage Sites in Great Barrington, Massachusetts. The Singer Studio had just completed a planning report, and a workshop was about to take place to discuss ways to bridge the Du Bois Center and Archives at UMass Amherst to the heritage sites and the greater community. He recognized the important educational mission of our teaching museum as a multidisciplinary laboratory for the exploration of contemporary art and its intersection with the major issues and ideas of our time. Based on Michael's knowledge of our museum's program, he invited me to participate in the workshop's "think-tank."

I understood the challenge, and saw this as an opportunity for the museum at UMass to offer an untraditional way to link these communities through the visual arts. My proposal was to organize an exhibition based on the UMCA's annual series *Dialogue with a Collection*, in which artists are invited to research the museum's holdings and integrate their own artworks with pieces they select from the collection. This new iteration of *Dialogue with a Collection* would focus exclusively on the Du Bois Archive. I would invite a select group of contemporary artists whose work is socially engaged and research-based to delve into the physical and digital Du Bois archives for ideas and to consult with Du Bois scholars on and off campus to conceive and create new works of art based on the Du Bois legacy and the causes he championed. The premise of the exhibition was that art can encourage us to look at our surroundings in unusual and often profound ways, and that it can elicit insightful dialogue on critical public issues by bringing together a host of people with varying points of view.

Within a few weeks of these first conversations, the concept for *Du Bois in Our Time* was born. I was motivated by the goal of opening the exhibition and hosting a related symposium in fall 2013 to mark the fiftieth year after the death of Du Bois. This timeline also coincided with the fiftieth anniversary of the famous March on Washington, at which the death of Du Bois, then in exile in Ghana, was publicly announced.

For advice on the selection of artists, I called upon a number of notable museum professionals known for their innovative curatorial work and for their wide-ranging thinking about international contemporary art, including Hamza Walker, associate director of the Renaissance Society at the University of Chicago; Trevor Smith, curator of contemporary art at the Peabody Essex Museum in Salem, Massachusetts; and Bisi Silva, independent curator and founder/director of the Centre for Contemporary Art, Lagos. Once a core list of artists had been put together, some of these people recommended other artists they thought would gravitate to the theme of this exhibition and engage with Du Boisian ideas. As a result, *Du Bois in Our Time* brought together ten remarkable artists who work in a wide range of media, are at different stages in their careers, and who bring various personal histories to the project: Radcliffe Bailey, Mary Evans, Brendan Fernandes, LaToya Ruby Frazier, Julie Mehretu, Ann Messner, Jefferson Pinder, Tim Rollins & K.O.S., Mickalene Thomas, and Carrie Mae Weems.

One of our advisors, Bisi Silva, insightfully suggested that *Du Bois in Our Time* would resonate even further with a presence in Africa, thus acknowledging the breadth of Du Bois's influence and his role in the Pan-African movement. She thought Accra, Ghana, would be the logical city to host the project, since it was Du Bois's final home and burial site, and is where the Du Bois Memorial Centre is located. Bisi introduced me to Odile Tevie, director of the Nubuke Foundation, an art center in Accra, and an independent curator from Nigeria, Tayo Ogunbiyi, who she thought could take the lead. Our conversations resulted in their organizing a distinct but related exhibition, *Du Bois in Our Time/Accra*, which premiered in March 2014 at the Nubuke Foundation and the Du Bois Memorial Centre, and was timed to coincide with Ghana's Independence Day celebration. A goal of *Du Bois in Our Time/Accra* is to reintroduce Du Bois to the consciousness of today's West Africa. By engaging African artists, writers, and scholars in dialogue, the aim is to revitalize the legacy of Du Bois and make it more accessible to a wider audience. Programming includes lectures, open discussions, workshops, videos, and a site-specific art installation by the London-based Nigerian artist Mary Evans at the Du Bois Memorial Centre (her site-specific installation at the UMCA furthers our collaboration with our Ghanaian curators). Our interactions and exchanges with the Nubuke Foundation and the Du Bois Memorial Centre can be found on a robust shared website manifesting the process and creating a conversation between the project sites in Amherst and Accra.

I invited a number of key UMass faculty from the departments of Afro-American Studies (Manisha Sinha, Amilcar Shabazz, and Bill Strickland); Anthropology (Whitney Battle-Baptiste and Robert Paynter); Art, Architecture, and Art History (Susan Jahoda and Joseph Krupczynski); English (Stephen Clingman and Tanya Fernando); History (David Glassberg), and the director of the Library's Special Collections (Rob Cox) to form a Steering Committee to provide guidance and advice in developing specific ways to organize and carry out the goals of the exhibition and its symposium. Richard Rabinowitz, one of the nation's leading public historians, whom I met at the Great Barrington workshop in spring 2010, served as an enthusiastic and deeply knowledgeable advisor to the exhibition and symposium from its initial concept to final stages.

We sustained a phenomenal pace in bringing the exhibition and all the related public programs to fruition. A full-day symposium explored the artists' creative process in light of the artworks produced for this exhibition and expanded on its Du Boisian themes. Featured speaker Dr. Johnnetta Betsch Cole, director of the Smithsonian's National Museum of African Art and faculty member at UMass Amherst from 1970 to 1983, offered a profound and moving prologue to the discussions that day. Her keynote speech, *Du Bois in His Time, in Our Time: The Intersection of Public Intellectualism and Socially Engaged Art*, is included in this book. A series of five in-depth panel discussions focusing on various aspects of the Du Bois legacy took place throughout fall 2013. And a provocative public lecture was given by artist/urban planner/entrepreneur Theaster Gates on his remarkable Dorchester Project in Chicago.

As part of *Du Bois in Our Time*, Tim Rollins and Angel Abreu, one of the original members of K.O.S., conducted workshops in Springfield, Massachusetts, in March 2013 with middle school students from the Renaissance School on a project that combined lessons in reading and writing with the production of works of art. For this Springfield project, Rollins selected *Darkwater: Voices from Within the Veil*, a literary work by Du Bois published in 1920 incorporating autobiographical information as well as essays and spirituals that were written by Du Bois. The artworks produced during this collaborative workshop were featured in the exhibition.

Jefferson Pinder, another artist participating in a week-long residency at UMass, thanks to the support of the Class of 1961 Artists Residency Fund, gave faculty and students from across the disciplines insight into his artistic practice and social engagement.

A thirty-minute documentary video on *Du Bois in Our Time* by filmmaker Lynda Kaplan of the American History Workshop, produced by the UMCA and the UMass Du Bois Library, followed the ten artists over the course of a year as they prepared their new work for the exhibition. This documentary introduces people to the exhibition through the power of digital media and is viewable on multiple online platforms.

At the outset, the artists were all familiar with Du Bois's writings and his political activism, but once they began their research and engaged in conversation with our participating Du Bois scholars—James T. Campbell, Saidiya V. Hartman, Reiland Rabaka, and Bill Strickland—they were astounded by the sweep of his intellect and his prescience. The journey of exploration these scholars and artists made is reflected in their essays on the following pages.

The project culminated in a wide range of works, from photography, painting, sculpture, and works on paper to video and installations, as well as a proposal to create a memorial garden in Du Bois's honor. Some artists were inspired by Du Bois's poetic essays, his 1913 *Star of Ethiopia* pageant, some by his early anticipation of the women's rights and environmental movements, and his warnings against nuclear proliferation and other modern afflictions. Others found inspiration in the groundwork he laid for movements in public dissent, while others showed how the problems Du Bois wrote about a century ago are still with us and in certain cases are more urgent than ever. The artists' contributions to this exhibition are all testaments to the inspiration and impact Du Bois has had on their lives and artistic practice. Through the development of this exhibition they helped us think not only about the creative process, but also about the place of art in our world, the interface of art with sociopolitical issues, and the very process of learning itself.

Loretta Yarlow, Director
University Museum of Contemporary Art

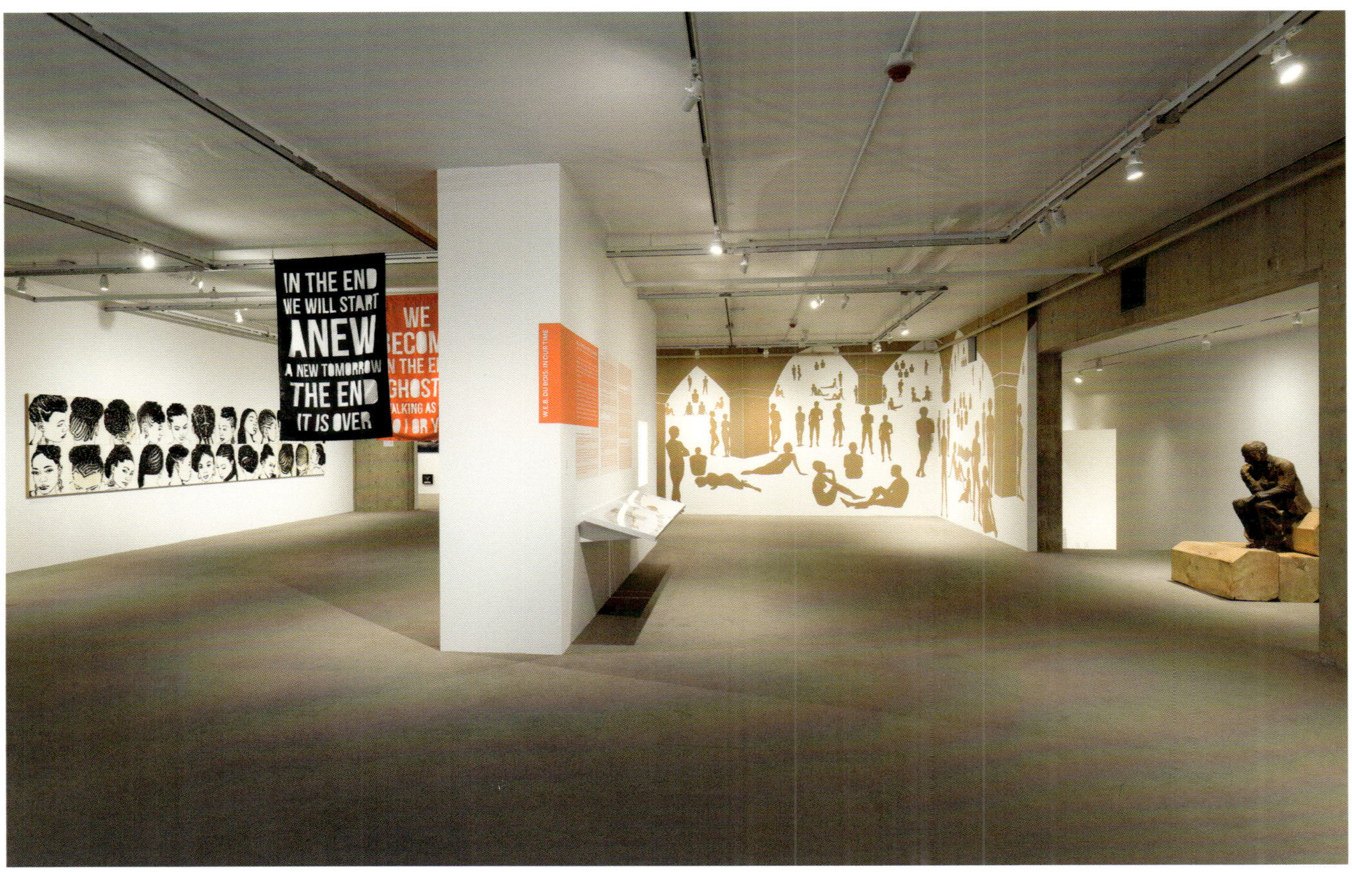

WATCH THE VIDEO produced by the UMass News Office at the exhibition Opening Reception, September 27, 2014
https://www.umass.edu/newsoffice/article/inspiring-du-bois-exhibit

JOHNNETTA BETSCH COLE

DUBOIS IN HIS TIME, IN OUR TIME: THE INTERSECTION OF PUBLIC INTELLECTUALISM AND SOCIALLY ENGAGED ART

September 28, 2013

I WANT TO BEGIN BY GREETING Provost James Saros, other administrators, the faculty, staff, and students of this very special university as well as the folks who live and work throughout this Five College area. I certainly want to acknowledge the scholars and artists who have come from near and far to participate in this symposium. To make sure that I have not excluded anyone, let me say this: My sisters and brothers all, good morning!

And what a great gettin' up morning it is as we gather to celebrate the formidable intellect, courage, moral vision, and principled leadership of the great William Edward Burghardt Du Bois. In hosting us as we celebrate one of the most accomplished thinkers and doers of his time, and indeed of our time, the University of Massachusetts at Amherst proudly affirms its special relationship to the legacy of Dr. Du Bois.

In the vanguard of this exhibition and symposium, the leadership and staff of the University Museum of Contemporary Art is to be especially commended. Loretta Yarlow, you and your colleagues at the museum have earned our gratitude.

Even beyond the specific significance of this occasion, the University of Massachusetts and the Amherst community have and always will command a very special place in my personal and my professional life.

Amherst is the town in which our family raised my three sons. By family I mean that extended community of affection, care, and commitment which came to surround us here. Friendships forged in such circumstances tend to endure forever.

In 1970, I joined this university's Anthropology Department and the W.E.B. Du Bois Afro-American Studies Department. In New Africa House, where Afro-American Studies was housed, Du Boisian Pan-Africanism was alive and well. And the sisters and brothers of that

WATCH THE SYMPOSIUM VIDEOS ONLINE: https://fac.umass.edu/UMCA/Online/DuBoisInOurTimeSympoiumVideos

academic and activist place were bold and bodacious enough to place on the department the distinguished name of W.E.B. Du Bois.

When I, along with two young African scholars, historian Dovi Afesi and art historian Josephus V. Olafemi Richards, joined the new department in its first year, already in residence were an Algerian diplomat, Ambassador Cherif Guelal, and Ben Wambara, a Kenyan teaching Swahili. Holding forth with great brilliance on matters of literature and politics was Jamaica's mighty son, the founding chair of the department Ekwueme Michael Thelwell.

There was a strong presence of artists in the department: Esther Terry and Paul Carter Harrison in theater, Diana Ramos in dance, and AFRICOBRA artist Nelson Stevens in the visual arts. Young historians Ernie Allen and John Bracey came early to the department and have stayed late. Playthell Benjamin, Chet Davis, Ivanhoe Donaldson, Acklyn Lynch, Bill Strickland, and Eugene Terry would also join our righteous band of public intellectuals and socially engaged artists.

In the years that I was here, the vision of an Afro-American Studies department worthy of the name of W.E.B. Du Bois, and a very receptive administration, would attract to the little New England town of Amherst an impressive array of internationally acclaimed activist/intellectuals and artists from the black world: novelists James Baldwin and Chinua Achebe, musicians Max Roach and Archie Shepp; dancer and pioneering Africanist Pearl Primus; and the leading scholarly expert and performer in the Afro-American choral tradition, Horace Clarence Boyer.

Very consequential to our presence here today, Madame Shirley Graham Du Bois was moved to come from her home in Egypt to teach, inspire, and carefully safeguard the legacy of her husband. Her son, David Graham Du Bois, would also serve on the faculty of the department of journalism. The strength of our department was enhanced by the work of kindred souls in other departments such as Sid Kaplan (whom I respectfully and affectionally called Papa Sid), Jules Chametzky, Julius Lester, and Fred Tillis. Let us never forget that whenever we are in this university's Fine Arts Center, we are in the house that Fred Tillis built.

What did it all mean, this list of scintillating names? If that were all it remained, a list of famous names, then I fear it meant very little. But I witnessed a synergy and cultural and artistic cross-fertilization of teaching, scholarship, and performance which transformed this institution and this valley.

There is a strong sense of community among those of us who were a part of the founding and early years of the W.E.B. Du Bois Department of Afro-American Studies. I mean community in the African sense that proclaims: Community consists of the living, the dead, and the yet unborn. How deeply I felt that sense of community when Ekwueme Michael Thelwell and I recently met in Ogidi, Nigeria, to say farewell to our colleague, our brother, the father of African literature, Chinua Achebe.

From what I have described, and it is only the tip of the iceberg, you can see the extent of the cultural ferment within which the university's acquiring of the Du Bois papers was one highly important expression of those amazing and grace-filled times. For example, a number of remarkable black women earned their doctoral degrees here: Maki Mandela, eldest child of President Nelson Mandela; Sister Betty Shabazz, partner in the struggle and wife of Brother Malcolm; Dr. Christie Chinwe Achebe, psychologist and wife of Chinua Achebe; and Camille Cosby, prominent educator and theatrical producer and wife of Bill Cosby.

This university also had a very high political distinction. It was the first American university to divest its portfolio of any shares in companies doing business in apartheid South Africa. My colleagues and I in the W.E.B. Du Bois Afro-American Studies department were proud to be strongly associated with the movement that led to that action.

Of course none of this would have been possible in the face of administrative indifference or hostility, as was much too frequently the case elsewhere in academia. I came to UMass during the last year of the administration of Chancellor Oswald Tippo, when many of these changes were initiated. They were nurtured, developed, and extended by his remarkable successor, Randolph W. "Bill" Bromery. It was Brother Chancellor Bill Bromery who was able to improvise the means to purchase and preserve at this university the literary estate of W.E.B. Du Bois — and to do so without recourse to one penny of state funds.

Let us also lift up the students of that era who stood up and spoke out, who agitated and organized to name this university's library the W.E.B. Du Bois Library. In particular I want to acknowledge two leaders of that mighty effort, both of whom were members of the graduate student senate at UMass: Colin S. Cavell and Shaymala Ivatury. Dr. Cavell is now a professor of political science in a small college in Appalachia. Ms. Ivatury, originally from India, is now the director of analytical sciences at Pearl Therapeutics. Each of these UMass alumni is working in the tradition of education and service that is so closely associated with Dr. Du Bois.

To all of the faculty, staff, students, administrators, and townspeople who struggled to make sure that this university would always be inextricably tied to the legacy of Dr. W.E.B. Du Bois, let us give praise and thanks. As one would say in the southern black community where I grew up: Let the whole church say amen! And as I am fond of adding...a-women too!

I turn now to address the topic: Du Bois in His Time, in Our Time: The Intersection of Public Intellectualism and Socially Engaged Art. As I do so, I want to thank Dr. Ugochukwu-Smooth Nzewi for his considerable assistance with the preparation of this talk. Smooth, as he is called, was a curatorial predoctoral fellow at the National Museum of African Art. And then the day came when he successfully defended his dissertation in art history at Emory University — and predoc Brother Smooth became Dr. Smooth.

My colleagues and I at the National Museum of African Art claim Dr. Smooth as a member of our museum family, and we all exercised bragging rights when he was appointed the first-ever curator of African art at the Hood Museum of Art at Dartmouth College.

Dr. Smooth brought to our discussions about the topic of this address the sensibilities of a practicing artist, the extensive knowledge of an art historian, and insights that come from the "double consciousness" of being a Nigerian who lives and works in the United States.

There is a clear connection between acknowledging the fiftieth anniversary of W.E.B. Du Bois's passing and the hundred and fiftieth anniversary of the Emancipation Proclamation. It is this: Dr. Du Bois brought his extraordinary intellect, and his political acumen, to the ongoing struggle to make real the promises of the Emancipation Proclamation.

Throughout his long and highly productive life, Du Bois was a sociologist, historian, poet, novelist, playwright, cultural critic, public intellectual, and civil rights activist. He spent his life in support of human dignity, civil rights, and social justice. Every interest or issue that he pursued — and there were many — revolved around these three core ideals.

These three core ideals are as relevant today as they were in Du Bois's time. For this reason, the University Museum of Contemporary Art (UMCA) invited ten diverse and dynamic artists to reflect on the life and work of such an amazing personage, and to express their reflections in the mediums in which they do their artistic work. Listen as I do a roll call of the names of these artists:

Radclife Bailey,
Mary Evans,
Brendan Fernandes,
LaToya Ruby Frazier,
Julie Mehretu,
Ann Messner,
Jefferson Pinder,
Tim Rollins & K.O.S.,
Mickalene Thomas,
Carrie Mae Weems.

These women and men have given powerful visual currency to Du Bois's legacy. Together they invite us into conversations about the range and multiplicity of issues and interests that Du Bois cared about and struggled to affect.

My discussion aims to explore Du Bois's legacy through the prism of his role as a public intellectual par excellence and as a man of culture and the arts. I will illuminate this legacy in relation to the works of the ten invited artists who I see as public or socially engaged artists.

The framework of the public artist allows me to think critically about the relationship between public intellectualism, culture, and the artistic process, three areas of great interest to Du Bois. Like public intellectuals, public artists engage with social, political, economic, and cultural issues, and call upon the transcendence of art to elevate public discourse about such issues. They actively create art with the aim of engaging public consciousness. Through their works, as we shall see, they mirror the pulse of our time without compromising the aesthetic experience.

Before exploring the ways in which these ten public artists reflect on Du Bois's legacy, I want to briefly sketch his background. I am aware that many in this gathering are very familiar with Du Bois's work. But for those who are not, here is an ever so brief review of his long, complex, and highly productive life. William Edward Burghardt Du Bois was born on February 23, 1868, in Great Barrington, Massachusetts, a moderately tolerant but mostly European American community. The only child of his parents, Du Bois was raised by his mother, who worked as a housekeeper, but whose earning potential was limited because of a stroke she suffered when he was a boy.

Du Bois was intellectually ambitious. He identified his lifework quite early and set his mind toward actualizing it. After graduating from Fisk University in 1888, he applied to Harvard University to complete his undergraduate studies, and subsequently to pursue a doctorate in political science, with a specialization in political economy. Du Bois clearly understood that a Ph.D. would give him academic legitimacy. But more importantly, it would equip him with the intellectual and social capital he would need in order to effectively play a central role in the struggle for social justice and racial equality.

Du Bois's doctoral dissertation was entitled "The Suppression of the African Slave Trade to the United States of America, 1638–1870." In this pioneering work he systematically analyzed the impact of enslavement on African and African American experiences. He soon followed up with a sociological survey of black urban life in *The Philadelphia Negro*, published in 1899. His other scholarly works included *The Souls of Black Folk* (1903), *The Negro* (1915), *Black Folk Then and Now* (1919), and *Black Reconstruction in America* (1935).

Du Bois wrote several books on Africa and its place in the world. In *The World and Africa*, published in 1947, he examined Africa's contributions to human history while challenging distorted images of Africa's people. In his well-known work *The Souls of Black Folk*, he wrote: "the shadow of a Mighty Negro past flits through the tale of Ethiopia the Shadowy and of Egypt the Sphinx."[1] His prose is flowery but the substance is not lost. Du Bois was mapping an Africa that included Egypt and North Africa, something that was not fashionable to do in the academy at that time.

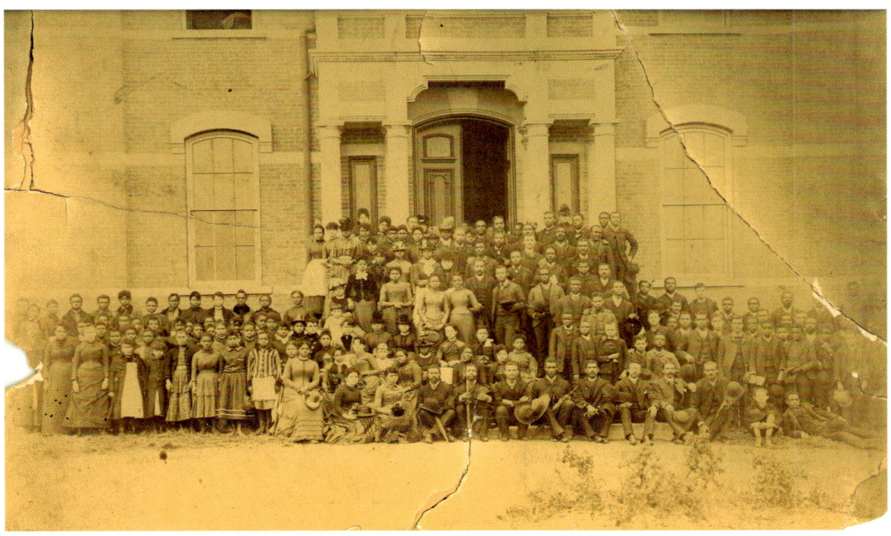

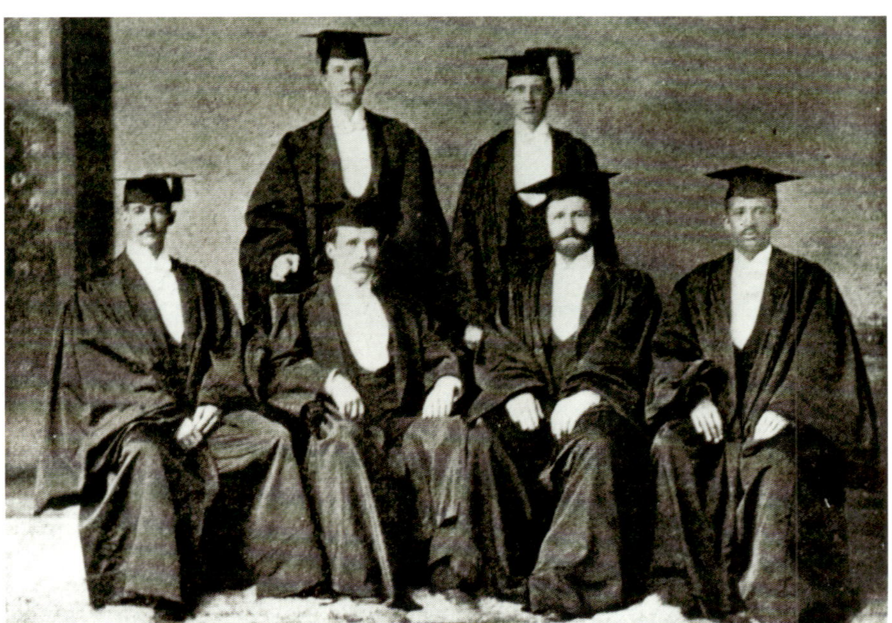

Above
Group portrait of Fisk University faculty and students in front of Jubilee Hall. W.E.B. Du Bois is standing, derby in hand, in top row at far right, 1887
Courtesy of W.E.B. Du Bois Papers, Special Collections and University Archives, University Libraries, University of Massachusetts Amherst

Below
Du Bois in the group of the six speakers at the graduation of 281 Harvard students, 1890
Courtesy of W.E.B. Du Bois Papers, Special Collections and University Archives, University Libraries, University of Massachusetts Amherst

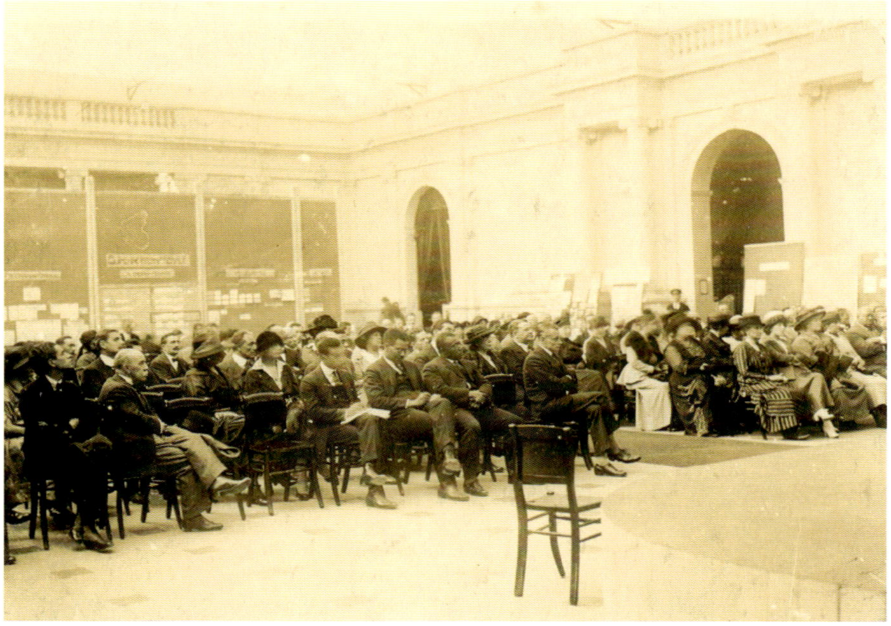

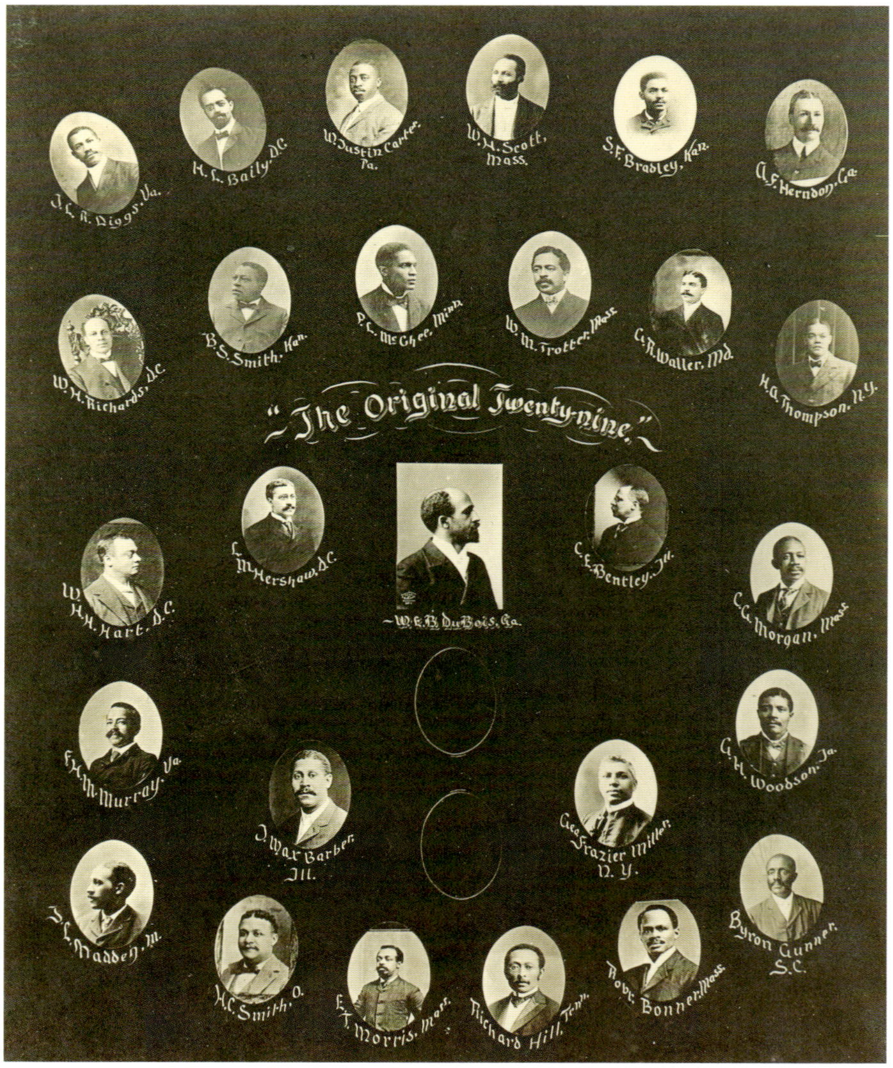

Above
Pan-African Congress, 1921, Brussels
Courtesy of W.E.B. Du Bois Papers, Special Collections and University Archives, University Libraries, University of Massachusetts Amherst

Below
The Original Twenty-Nine who attended the inaugural meeting of the Niagara Movement. The photographs of two members are missing. Du Bois is in the middle.
Courtesy of W.E.B. Du Bois Papers, Special Collections and University Archives, University Libraries, University of Massachusetts Amherst

Opposite Above
Mrs. W. E. B. Du Bois, c. 1910.
Scurlock Studio (Washington, D.C.).
Courtesy of W.E.B. Du Bois Papers, Special Collections and University Archives, University Libraries, University of Massachusetts Amherst

Opposite Below
Announcement for *The Star of Ethiopia*, a pageant, October 1915
Courtesy of W.E.B. Du Bois Papers, Special Collections and University Archives, University Libraries, University of Massachusetts Amherst

Dr. Du Bois taught in several institutions, including Wilberforce University, where he met and married his first wife, Nina Gomer, in May 1896; and Atlanta University, where he taught the longest. But first and foremost, he was a public intellectual who inspired people to engage with the major concerns of his era. The public intellectual, to borrow from Ralph Waldo Emerson, "embodies all dimensions of human potential and actuality."[2] As Barry Gewen puts it, a public intellectual is "deeply committed to the life of the mind and to its impact on the society at large."[3] W.E.B. Du Bois was a public intellectual!

Du Bois had an interest in creating an elite class of public intellectuals. He envisioned a liberal education, capable of producing what he termed the "Talented Tenth," the most intellectually gifted women and men who would provide leadership for black America. His vision clashed with Booker T. Washington's Tuskegee vocational education model. The Tuskegee model produced students with the requisite technical skills to operate in a capitalist economy. This is not to say that Du Bois was against manual training that would enable black entrepreneurship. However, he argued that the struggle for racial equality and political suffrage which would ultimately lead to black economic empowerment needed an elite black middle class with solid liberal education leading the charge. It is important to note that years later, when Du Bois was conducting the research for his book *Black Reconstruction*, he came to the position that it was the oppressed masses that made history through their struggles and not the privileged black middle class.

Du Bois was never shy about confronting the status quo. He not only spoke and wrote about issues of critical importance, he took action, including joining with others to address those issues. And, very importantly, he played a leadership role in the founding of the Niagara Movement and the National Association for the Advancement of Colored People (NAACP).

Du Bois was also the editor of several magazines, including *the Horizon, The Crisis,* and *The Brownies' Book*. These socially engaged organizations and magazines placed him in a position to muld public opinion on a broad range of issues.

As a public intellectual with an international frame of reference, Du Bois was committed to the struggles of those whom he called the "darker race" who lived in the Americas, Africa, Europe, and Asia. From 1900 to 1945, Du Bois was involved in the international Pan-African movement. He believed that racism against African Americans in the United States could not be resolved in isolation from the struggle against racism that oppressed black people in Africa, the Caribbean, and Europe.

After the Pan-African Congress in London in 1900, organized by Henry Sylvester Williams, a West Indian lawyer, Du Bois became a leader of future Pan-African conferences: Paris in 1919, at the end of World War I, London and Brussels in 1921, London and Lisbon in 1923, New York in 1927, and Manchester in 1945, at the end of World War II. As the historian Manning Marable aptly put it: "Leaders are essentially individuals who have the ability to understand their own times, who express or articulate programs or policies that reflect the perceived interests and desires of particular groups, and who devise effective change."[4] Du Bois had a moral gravitas, and influenced people who became extraordinary leaders. One notable example was Kwame Nkrumah, the widely respected Pan-Africanist and first president of independent Ghana. Du Bois spent the last few years of his life, 1958 to 1963, in independent Ghana, secure in the knowledge that colonialism was being defeated in Africa, in spite of the many unresolved challenges on that continent.

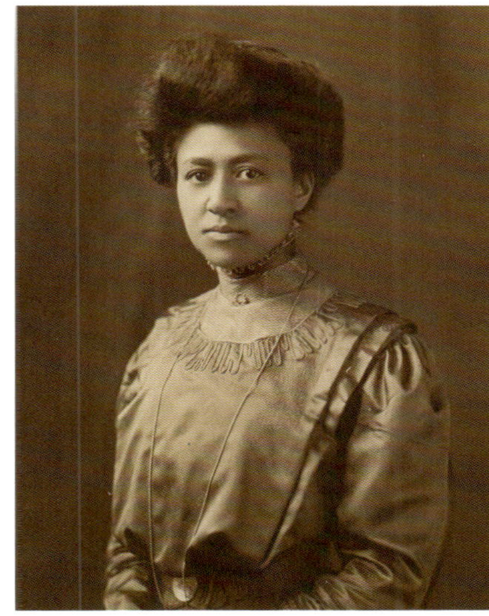

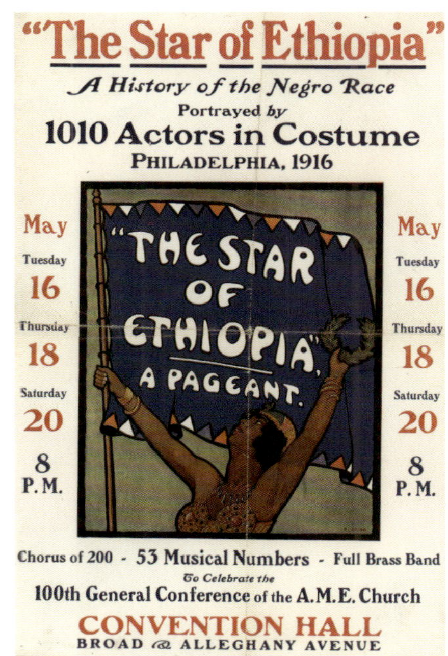

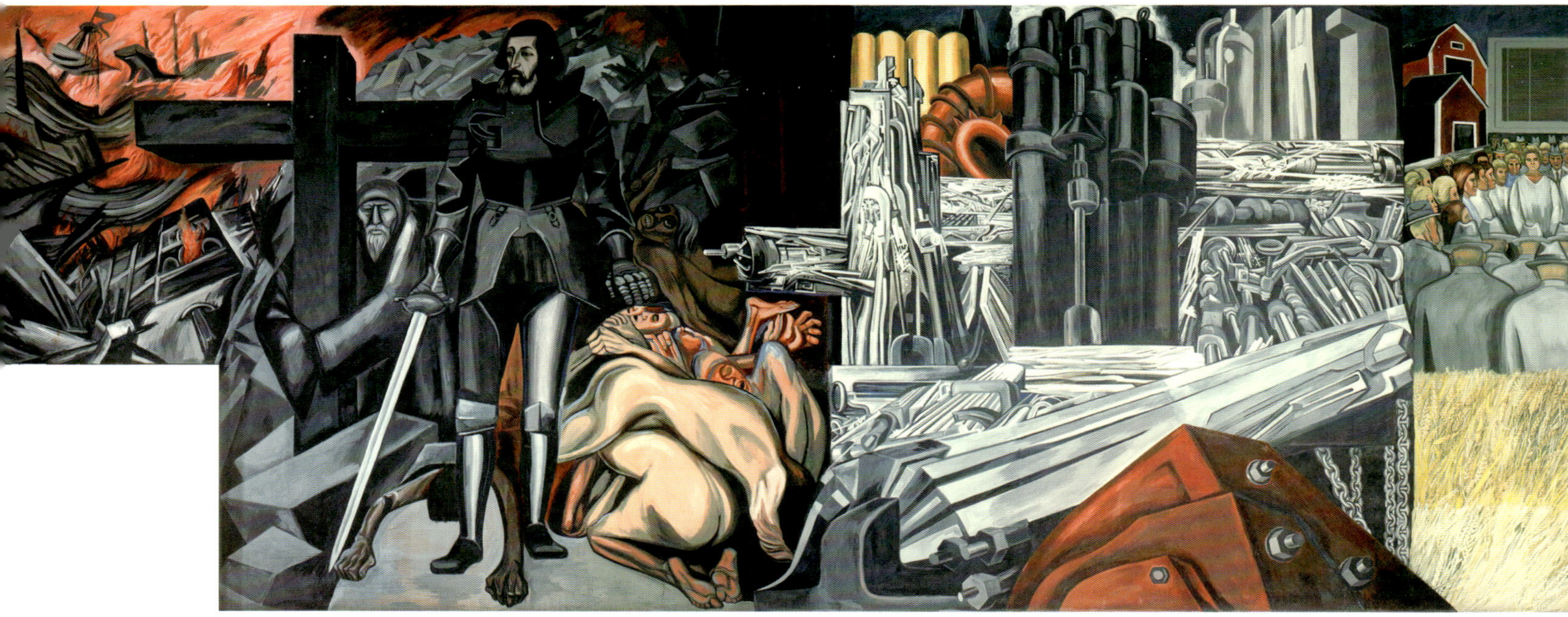

Culture is an important area where Du Bois's role as an activist and public intellectual was quite clear. He viewed culture as a regenerative tool that must be seized to confront the inferiority complex of Black America. Du Bois made this point clearly and emphatically in *The Souls of Black Folk*.[5] Leading by example, he published his own poetry and novels, and was actively involved in theater, producing *The Star of Ethiopia*, and establishing the Krigwa Players in Harlem.[6] The Krigwa Players were very much a part of the New Negro Movement that reached its height in the Harlem Renaissance of the 1920s. Black writers, artists, musicians — and yes, a writer and anthropologist, Zora Neale Hurston — articulated a new black modernism as they drew upon African heritage and African American folk culture. The Harlem Renaissance, inspired other international black modernist movements, such as Négritude in France, Africa, and the Caribbean.

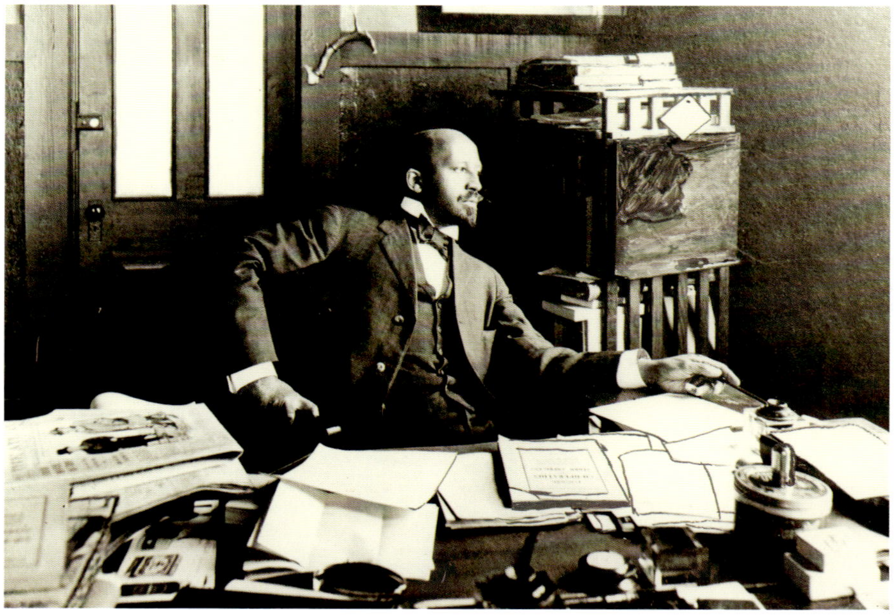

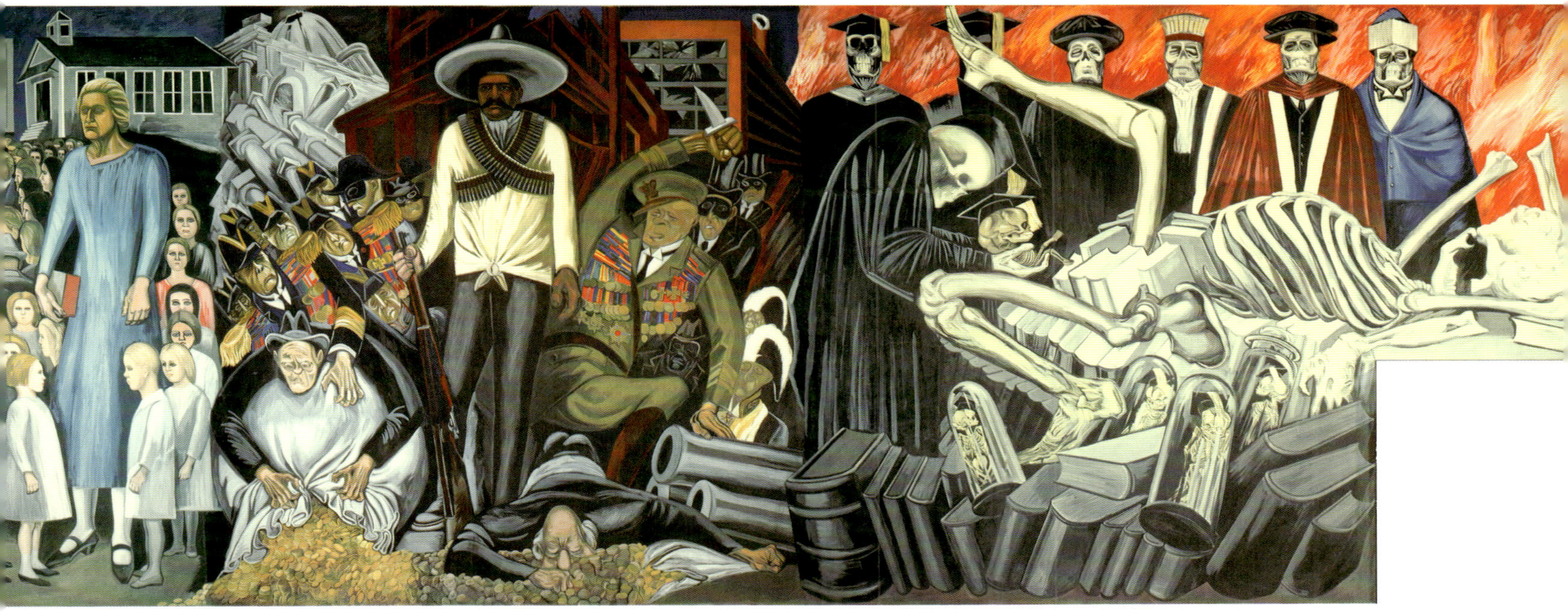

In briefly mentioning the New Negro Movement and the Harlem Renaissance I want to point out the intersection of public intellectualism and socially engaged art in Du Bois's thinking. Writing in 1926, he said this:

> [A work of art] is a creation of beauty, of the preservation of beauty, of the realization of beauty, and we must use in this work all the methods that men have used before. And what have been the tools of the artist in times gone by? First of all, he has used the truth, but as one upon whom truth eternally thrusts itself as the highest handmaid of imagination, as the one great vehicle of universal understanding.[7]

Du Bois spoke of the propagandist value of art, but he firmly believed that art must be socially relevant, without compromising truth, beauty, freedom, and originality. For Du Bois, art should drive cultural freedom, openness, and democracy. He was not only calling upon the raison d'être of art but addressing the role of the public artist.

In Du Bois's time, artists such as Aaron Douglas, José Clemente Orozco, and Pablo Picasso, were socially committed and politically motivated, and thus possessed the qualities of the public artist. Douglas gave a visual face to the New Negro modernism through his graphic illustrations and paintings. In *Aspects of Negro Life: From Slavery to Reconstruction* (1934), he depicts black history and social realities in an uplifting way. The central figure could well be the image of a seer pointing to a future of full civil rights, and plausibly a Barack Obama in the White House. *Aspects of Negro Life* mirrors Du Bois's insistence that black art should be enlisted in the service of racial emancipation. The work is eloquent, and successfully combines visual clarity and a social message.

Orozco's *The Epic of American Civilization* (1932–34) is a gripping historical account that explores migrations and the development of the modern industrialized society in the Americas. The large-scale twenty-four-panel mural painting is one of the most successful works by a politically committed artist who was well known for addressing social and economic inequality, labor issues, and workers' welfare.

Above
JOSÉ CLEMENTE OROZCO
The Epic of American Civilization (left to right: *Cortez and the Cross, The Machine, Anglo-America, Hispano-America, Gods of the Modern World*),1932–1934
Fresco
Overall: 120″ x 74″

Opposite
W. E. B. Du Bois, Atlanta University, 1909
Courtesy of W.E.B. Du Bois Papers, Special Collections and University Archives, University Libraries, University of Massachusetts Amherst

RADCLIFFE BAILEY
Storm at Sea, 2007
Piano keys, African sculpture, model boat, paper, acrylic, glitter, gold leaf
212" x 213"
Courtesy of the artist and Jack Shainman Gallery, New York

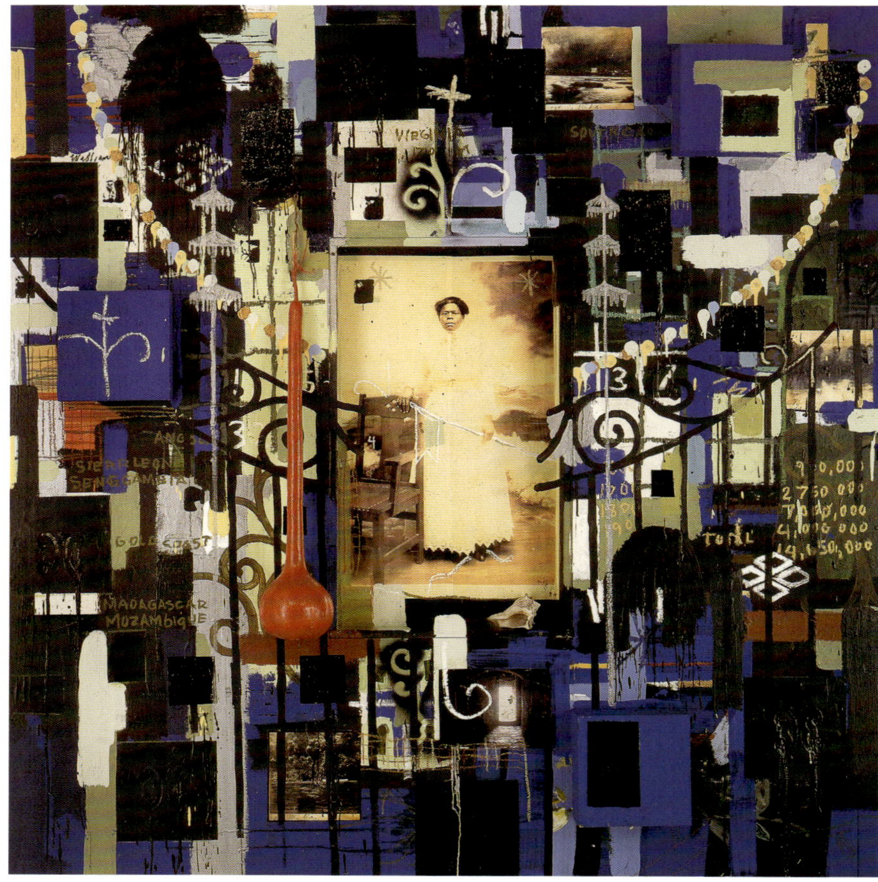

Picasso's famous monochromatic painting *Guernica* (1937) embodies the tragedies of war and reflects the necessity for peace. Picasso was involved in the peace and anticolonial movements, two major issues that preoccupied Du Bois. In narrating the human story, all three works reflect a deep grounding in history, immersed in social justice and a transcendent aesthetic — what Du Bois calls true consciousness.

As is clearly the case with these three eminent artists, the spirit of the public artist surrounds the works of Radcliffe Bailey, Brendan Fernandes, LaToya Ruby Frazier, Julie Mehretu, Ann Messner, Jefferson Pinder, Tim Rollins & K.O.S., Mickalene Thomas, Carrie Mae Weems, and Mary Evans. Public artists are not necessarily artists whose works are in the public domain, such as in museums or public art projects. But they are in the vanguard of addressing critical issues of their time; and through their art they challenge us to consider different ways to relate to each other and to the only earth that we have. Socially engaged artists do all of this while maintaining artistic integrity.

I turn now to note some of the issues these ten artists explore in their art, some of which are reflected in their works that are on view today. I will also note how they approach Du Bois's legacy from different but interconnected perspectives.

Radcliffe Bailey is known for how he explores the intersecting themes of diaspora, memory, and place. He is interested in memory as a process of healing and recovering. In *Storm at Sea* (2006) and *By the River* (1997), he injects new energy into black iconographies and cultural references — piano keys, classical African sculpture, and a family photographic portrait — to explore the historical memory of the Middle Passage as a binding force that

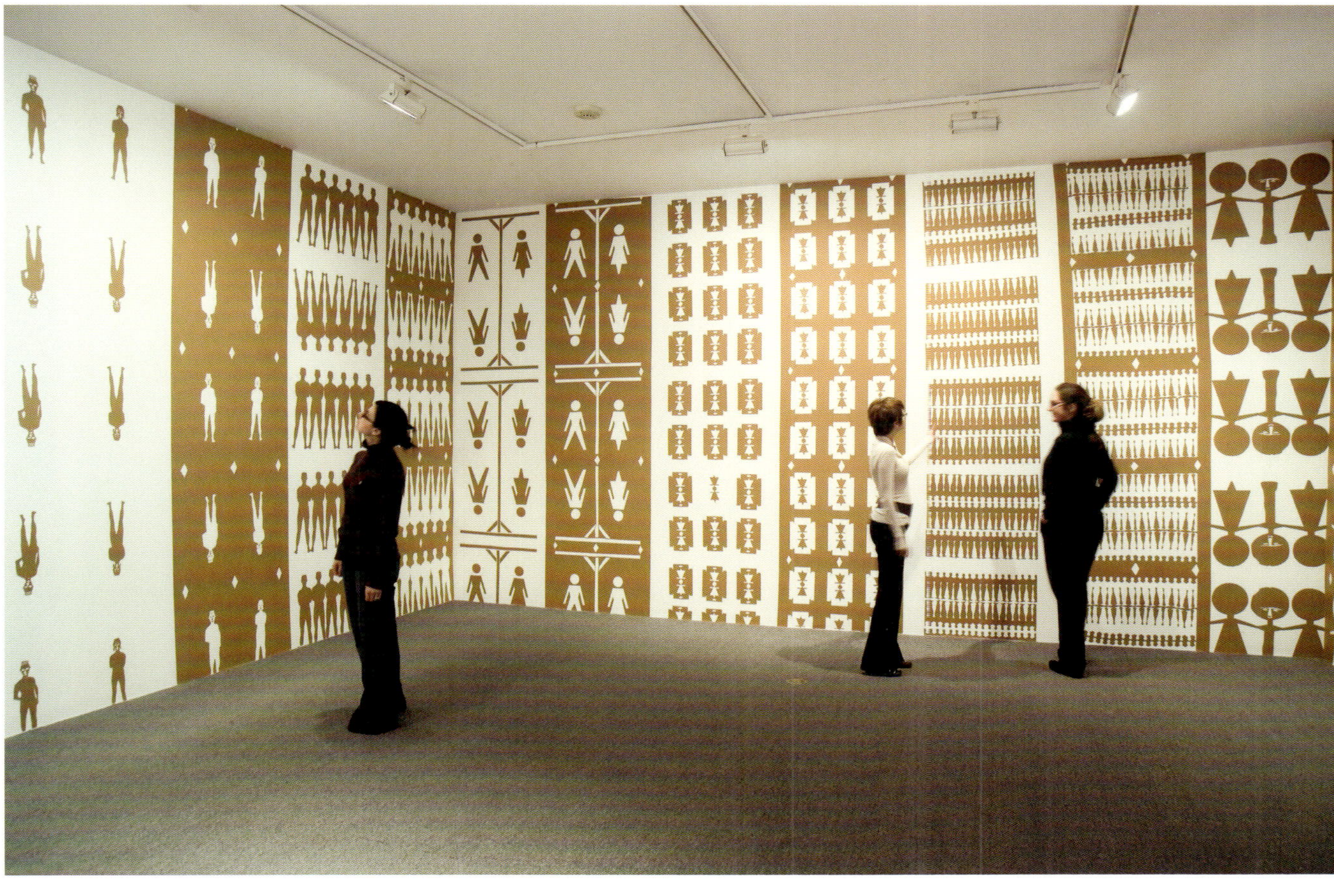

MARY EVANS
Schema, 2008
Kraft paper
452 sq. ft.
Baltimore Museum of Art

connects African Americans either individually or as a group to Africa. Both works emphasize the idea of displacement. This is an idea which, as the sociologist Paul Gilroy has argued, is a crucial leitmotif of the African diasporic experience.[8]

Bailey's abiding interests in the ties that connect the diaspora to the motherland take into account the difficult chapters of black Atlantic history, and the contemporary distance between Africa and its diaspora. In Radcliffe Bailey's work there is a parallel in Du Bois's lifelong interest in Pan-Africanism.

Like Bailey, Mary Evans employs visual symbols charged with cultural references to create large-scale site-specific wall installations from paper cutouts. In *Schema* (2008), for example, we see carefully arranged pictograms deriving from pop culture, classical African objects (Aku'aba fertility figures of the Asante and Lobi people of Ghana), industrially manufactured objects such as razor blades, and tightly packed bodies of enslaved Africans in old slave vessels, a metaphor for the Middle Passage. Evans's work is both historical and sociological, and thus mirrors academic disciplines that defined much of Du Bois's scholarship. She explores the effects of British imperial past in the historical removals, contemporary migrations, and emplacement of peoples of African descent in the New World and Europe. Evans is adroit in her use of positive and negative spaces, signs and significations, to bring history in collision with contemporaneity.

Similarly, Julie Mehretu puts the visual language of signs and symbols to effective use in *Dispersion* (2002). The artist is well known for her large-scale paintings, which combine abstraction and geometric elements. Mehretu conceptually employs layers of human stories as the building blocks of the urban social space — cities in particular. While cities differ in

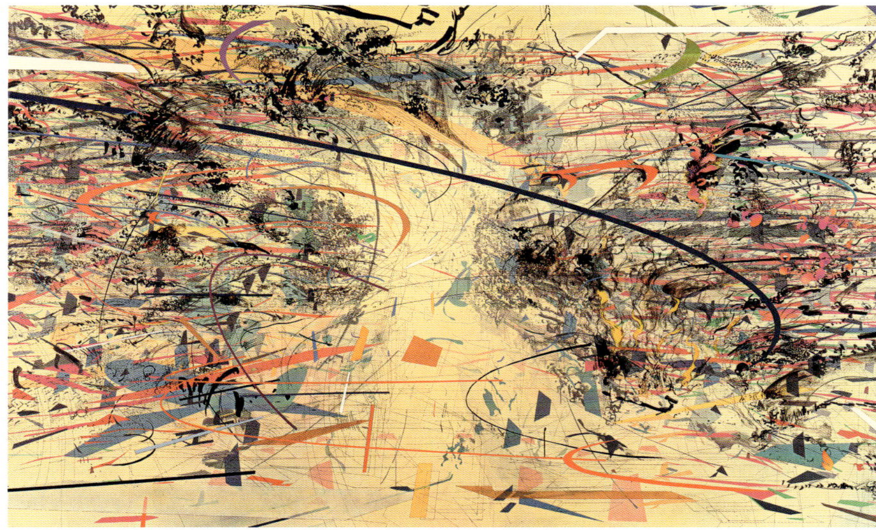

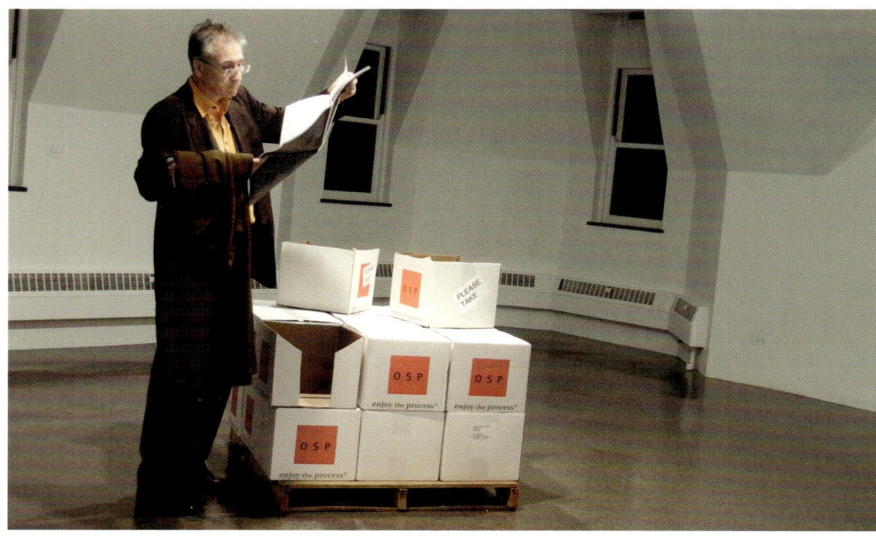

Above
JULIE MEHRETU
Dispersion, 2002
Ink and acrylic on canvas
90″ x 144″

Below
ANN MESSNER
The Disasters of War: Meanwhile in Baghdad
2005–2007
Offset tabloid
Installation of 22 boxes
(45 copies per box); each tabloid
12″ x 18″ (folded)
Two editions of 1,000
The newspaper was delivered to the gallery on the printer's skid and made available to the public free of charge during the exhibitions: *Meanwhile in Baghdad*, curated by Hamza Walker, Renaissance Society, University of Chicago, and *The Disasters of War*, curated by Nina Felshin, Zilkha Gallery, Center for the Arts, Wesleyan University

character, they are all historically, politically, and socially charged by human experiences. These experiences, which include memory, migratory patterns, and globalization, are explored by the artist, who draws from her own experiences of living in several cities on different continents. Mehretu has also explored issues with ethical consequence such as the Iraqi war.

An important issue that preoccupied Du Bois was the connection between war and capitalist exploitation. He believed that wars were waged to exploit human and material resources, and he was an advocate of nuclear disarmament as early as 1904, when it was not fashionable. Writing in the *Independent* of October 15 of the same year, he declared that "War is murder... that armies and navies are at bottom the tinsel and braggadocio of oppression and wrong."[9]

In *The Disasters of War* (2005–07), produced at the height of President Bush's misadventure in Iraq, Ann Messner confronts war situations all over the world. The installation consists of boxes, packed with twenty-eight-page black-and-white newspapers with images and text from different hot spots in the world. The newspapers are made available to the public for free. Messner eschews the wow effect of pushing the messiness of war directly

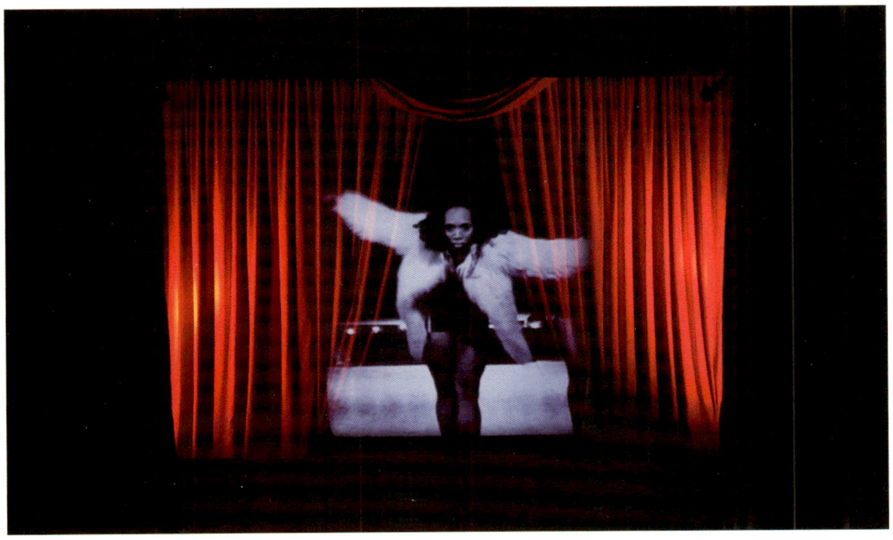

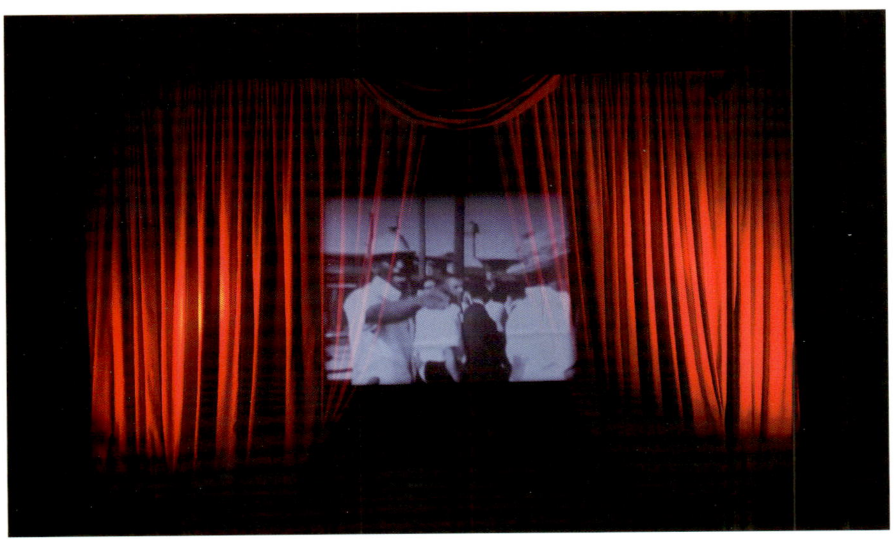

CARRIE MAE WEEMS
Lincoln, Lonnie, and Me – A Story in 5 Parts, 2012
Video

Courtesy of the artist and Jack Shainman Gallery, New York

into the viewer's face. This is neither to trivialize the effects of war on our collective psyche nor the immediacy of visuality. Instead she seeks a more emotive and private interaction between the viewer and the work. The viewer is expected to approach the installation, to pick up one of the newspapers from the boxes, and to spend a quiet moment in a public context, reading and contemplating on what is a major issue of our time. There is nothing beautiful about war, but there is clearly a consideration of aesthetics in Messner's organization of the installation in a gallery space.

In a long career, spanning over three decades, MacArthur "Genius Grant" awardee Carrie Mae Weems has carried out a sustained sociological inquiry into various aspects of black life, the wider American society, and the world at large. She has explored a mosaic of issues that include family relationships, racism and racial stereotypes, gender roles, sexism, wars and violence, social class, history, and politics. Her complex bodies of work are mostly presented as projects, and reflect how she is very much invested in the public. *Lincoln, Lonnie, and Me — A Story in 5 Parts* (2012), a recent video and object installation, brings together several of these issues which she has explored over time. In the installation,

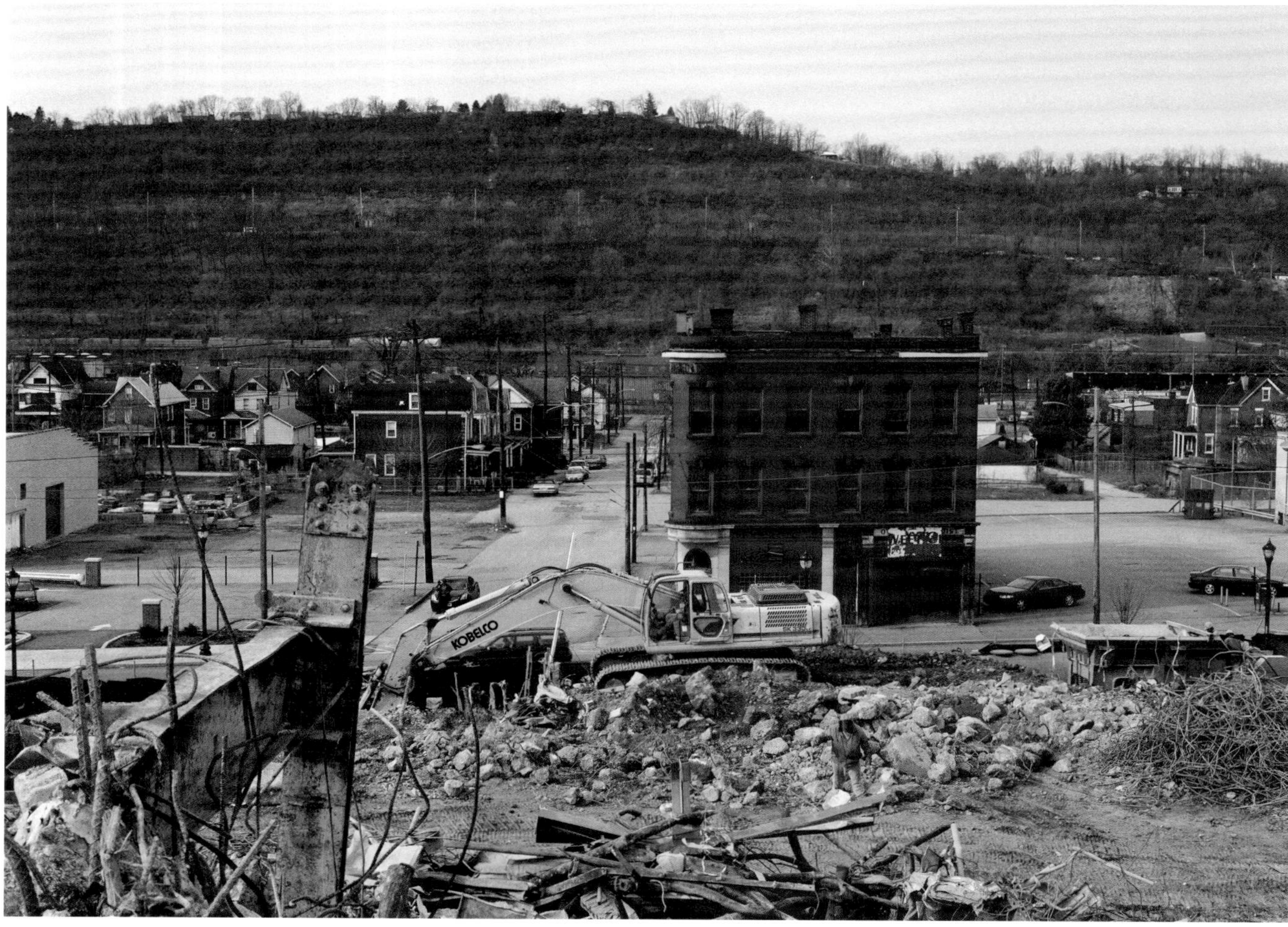

LATOYA RUBY FRAZIER
Fifth Street Tavern and U.P.M.C. Braddock Hospital on Braddock Avenue,
2011
Gelatin Silver Print
20″ x 24″

ghostly characters are invited from the past to retell stories of past struggles. Weems's eclectic interests make her a kindred spirit of Du Bois.

At the height of McCarthyism in the 1950s, Du Bois faced severe persecution by the state apparatus. Citing his involvement in the peace movement and socialist thought in his writings, he was accused of working for the Soviet Union. More significantly these accusations cited Du Bois's distaste for unbridled capitalism — an issue LaToya Ruby Frazier has addressed in her work. Using documentary photography such as in *Fifth Street Tavern and U.P.M.C. Braddock Hospital on Braddock Avenue* (2011), Frazier explores the dark underbelly of corporatization, a byword for capitalism gone amok. She focuses on postindustrial Braddock, a borough located in the eastern suburbs of Pittsburgh, Pennsylvania, where she was born and raised. Factory jobs are no longer available, as they have all been outsourced. The city's population is burdened by ill health arising from the long-term effects of the city's former life as an industrial hub. Health care provision has become a monopoly and unaffordable. Frazier presents the sobering reality of a crumbling city that is struggling with the ghosts of its industrial past and deindustrialized present. The black-and-white photographs are somber and haunting.

Black women are the subject of Mickalene Thomas's *Din, une très belle négresse #2* (2012) and *Qusuquzah, une très belle négresse #3* (2012). The exuberant and evocative portraits are anything but ordinary. They are iconic representations of black and proud women. Thomas

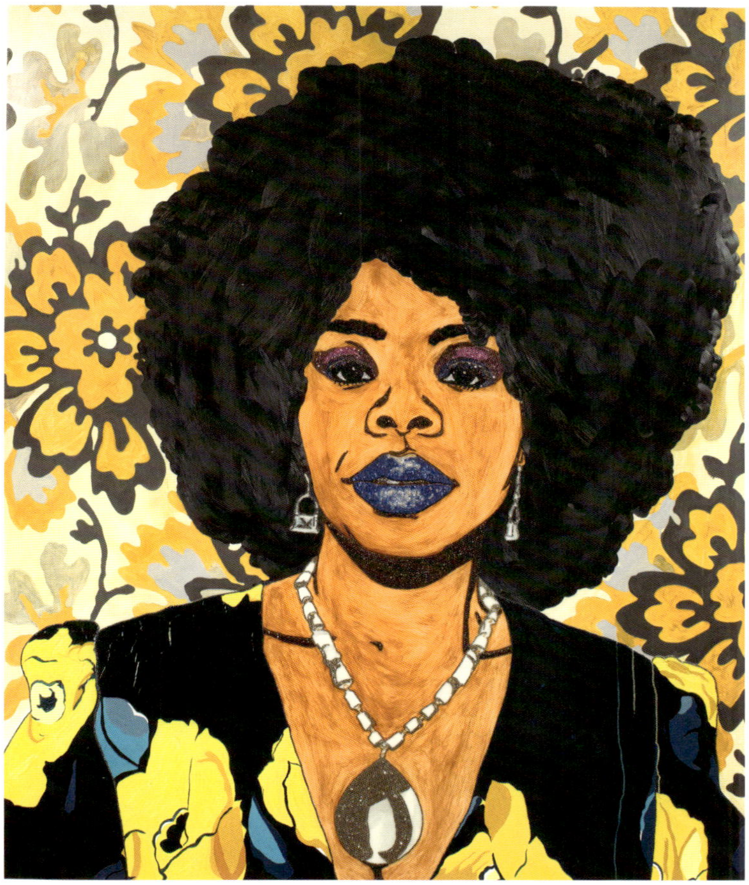

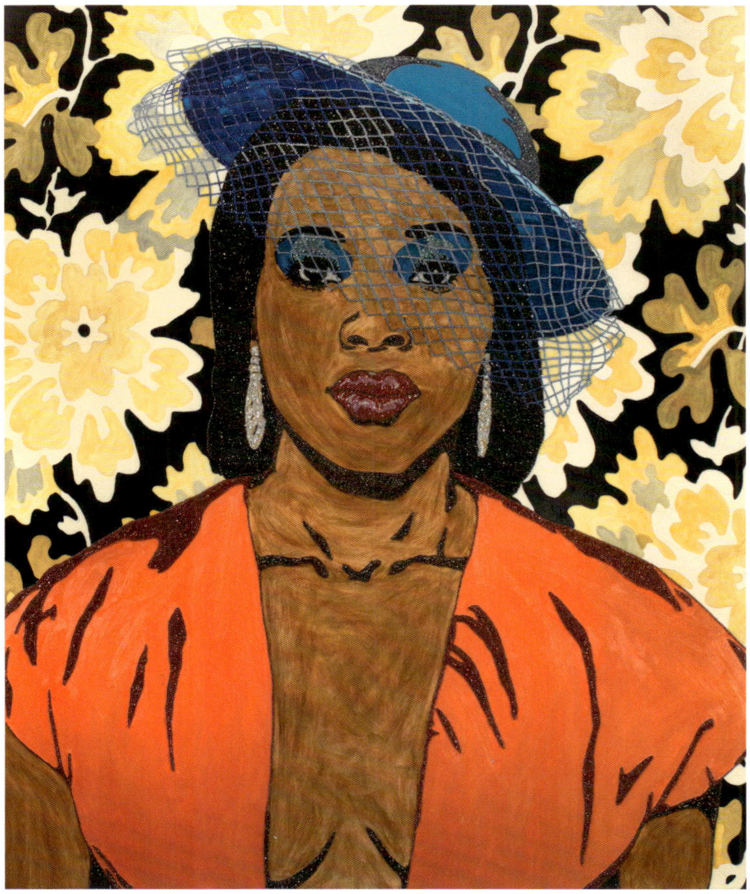

MICKALENE THOMAS
Qusuquzah, une très belle négresse 3, 2012
Rhinestones, acrylic, oil, and enamel on wood panel
96″ x 80″ x 2″
Courtesy of Mickalene Thomas and Lehmann Maupin, New York and Hong Kong

MICKALENE THOMAS
Din, une très belle négresse 1, 2012
Rhinestones, acrylic, oil, and enamel on wood panel
102″ x 84″ x 2″
Courtesy of Mickalene Thomas and Lehmann Maupin, New York and Hong Kong

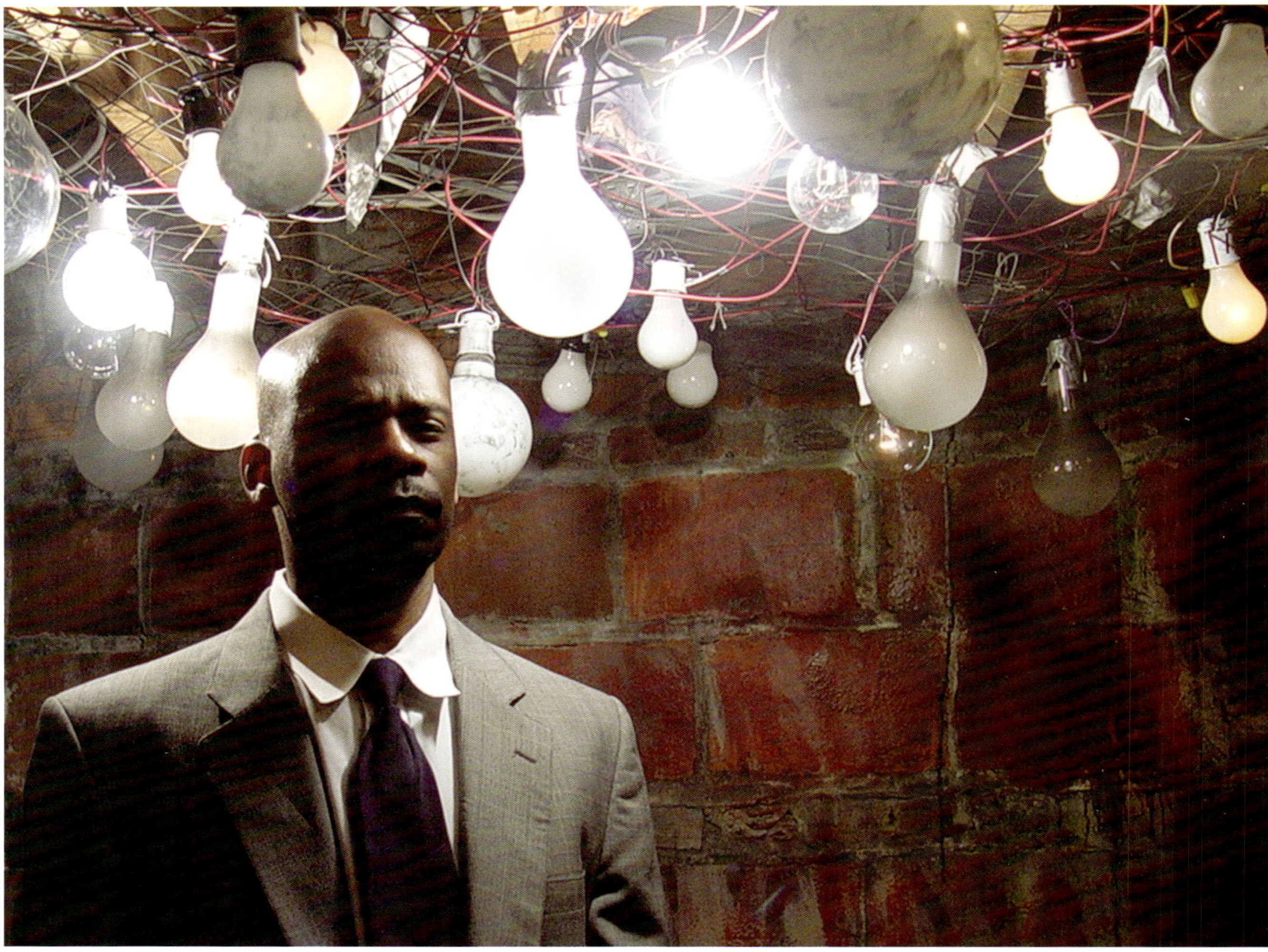

Above
JEFFERSON PINDER
Invisible Man, 2004
Video

Below
TIM ROLLINS & K.O.S.
Invisible Man (after Ralph Ellison), 2008
Matte acrylic and book pages on canvas
24" x 24"
Courtesy of the artists and Lehmann Maupin, New York and Hong Kong

infuses the female portraits with boldness and "sheroism" to convey an ennobling black female presence that has largely been missing in art history. She successfully plays with cultural references drawn from the black church (note the laced hat) and the Black Power movement (check out the large afro puff). In her works, Thomas also explores her interests in civil rights issues, especially the rights of lesbian, gay, bisexual, and transgender people.

Like Thomas, Jefferson Pinder investigates notions of blackness and whiteness from historical, social, and political perspectives. His video work *Invisible Man* (2002) is a visual translation of the first eight pages of Ralph Ellison's novel of the same title. Ellison, who is the protagonist in his novel, talks about how "light," a term that is loaded with meaning, confirms his reality. He narrates how he hangs about 1,300 lightbulbs from his ceiling to represent several hundreds of thousands of black people, whose visibility is confirmed by a white reality. Pinder reenacts this scene. In one continuous unedited shot, the camera lets off light gradually, and the artist, who is in the video, moves from total blackout to total whiteout. The point of visibility in the video process is that gray middle point, where the image, although clearly Pinder, is just a human being, neither black nor white. In moving from blackness to whiteness, Pinder seeks to represent our common humanity, a point that Du Bois always emphasized.

In the poem "Credo" from *Darkwater: Voices from Within the Veil*, a collection of his poems and essays, Du Bois wrote:

> I believe in God who made of one blood all races that dwell on earth. I believe that all men, black and brown and white, are brothers, varying, through Time and Opportunity, in form and gift and feature, but differing in no essential particular, and alike in soul and in the possibility of infinite development.[11]

Pinder aligns himself with these Du Boisian thoughts when he presents his self-portrait to reflect our corporate existence.

Du Bois was passionate in his call for remaking our world into one that recognizes the equality of all races. He debunked falsely held and deeply ingrained assumptions that allowed racism and colonialism to thrive, and he stood in solid opposition to the color line in the United States and in a global context.

Tim Rollins & K.O.S. also explore Ellison's *Invisible Man* (2008), but take an approach that differs from that of Pinder. The painting series was inspired by a newspaper article in the *New York Post* about a massacre in 1993 that involved the murder of fourteen-year-old Christophe Hernandez, who was close to Tim Rollins & K.O.S. members. MURDER VICTIM was the *New York Post's* headline about the massacre. The group cut out the IM and applied it to the ideas explored by Ellison in *The Invisible Man*. They also draw upon the "I AM A MAN" placard held by Memphis sanitation workers after the assassination of Dr. Martin Luther King Jr.

With *Invisible Man*, Tim Rollins & K.O.S. explore a horrific experience, one in which they were personally invested, connecting it to a history of violence in the public domain. As it is with Messner's *Disasters of War*, there is nothing beautiful about violence; however, the graphic-based series, which comprises texts from Ellison's book and bold acrylic lettering on canvas, are supremely successful as artworks.

Like all the artists, Brendan Fernandes gives a visual voice to a range of themes and issues, including history, identities, gender, and migration. He is interested in the threads

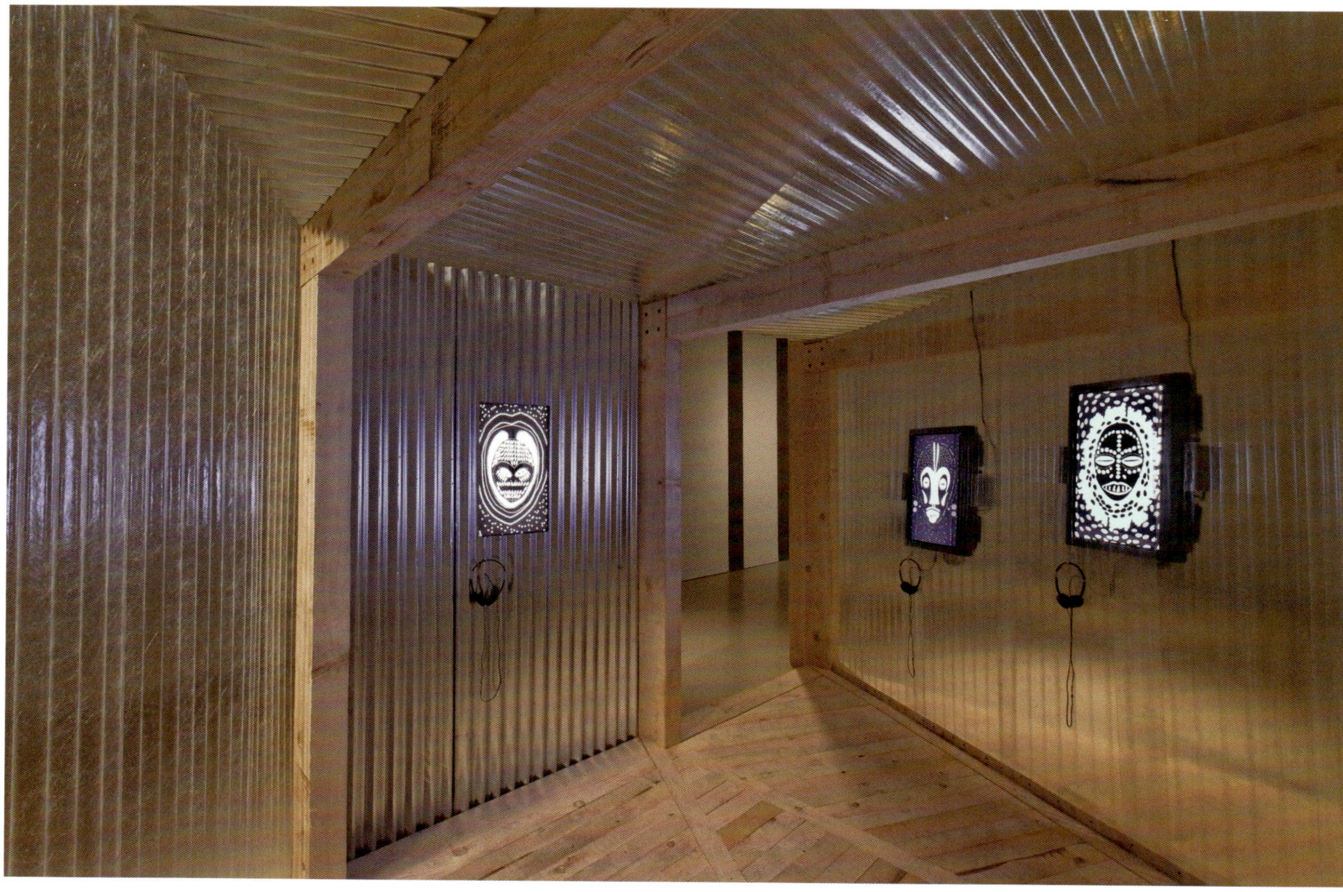

Above
BRENDAN FERNANDES
Voo Doo You Doo Speak, 2010
© Brendan Fernandes

Opposite above
BRENDAN FERNANDES
Dada Afrika Mask III, 2010
© Brendan Fernandes

Opposite below
BRENDAN FERNANDES
Dada Afrika Mask IV, 2010
© Brendan Fernandes

that bind us together beyond racial and cultural subtleties and idiosyncrasies. In *Voo Doo You Doo Speak* (2010), Fernandes explores the cultural perceptions and misconceptions associated with the imaginings of racial and cultural identities of Africa and the African diaspora. His use of technologically animated African masks in the video, sound, and architectural installation lead me to that conclusion. The masks are, however, a veil that allows the artist to play with notions of racial and cultural ambiguities which attend our interconnected world as a result of historical and contemporary movements and migrations.

Fernandes's own biography is very much present in this work and provides the ground for his thinking. He is a Kenyan-born Canadian of Indian descent, living and working between New York and Canada. The installation highlights the fiction of color lines and raises the notion of double consciousness, themes repeatedly addressed by Du Bois.

In all the works that I have discussed, as well as those in the exhibition accompanying this symposium, each of the ten artists successfully combine social activism and aesthetic beauty. Although they are responding to the realities of today's world, the artists speak visual truth to the legacy of Du Bois. This international group of public artists — with multiple ties to several continents (North America, Africa, Europe, and Asia) — represents the global reach and impact of Dr. W.E.B. Du Bois.

My sisters and brothers all, no symposium, no keynote address nor group of artworks, can fully explore the multidimensionality of Dr. Du Bois, whose work was of an unusual magnitude. And is that not why the University of Massachusetts' W.E.B. Du Bois Department of Afro-American Studies and the university's W.E.B. Du Bois Library are so critically important? For they are places, among others in the world, where scholars, artists, and activists can continue to explore, to analyze, and to present some of the many issues and themes in the work of W.E.B. Du Bois.

Dr. Du Bois was a committed humanist who put the community before the individual. In our time, his life of service will remain a constant source of inspiration, challenging all of us to be better humans in that great African spirit of Ubuntu. Ubuntu, the idea that one is a human being because of other human beings. Ubuntu, the declaration that I am because you are, and you are because I am!

In tribute to the Good Dr. W.E.B. Du Bois, let us act on the reality that we are because he is!

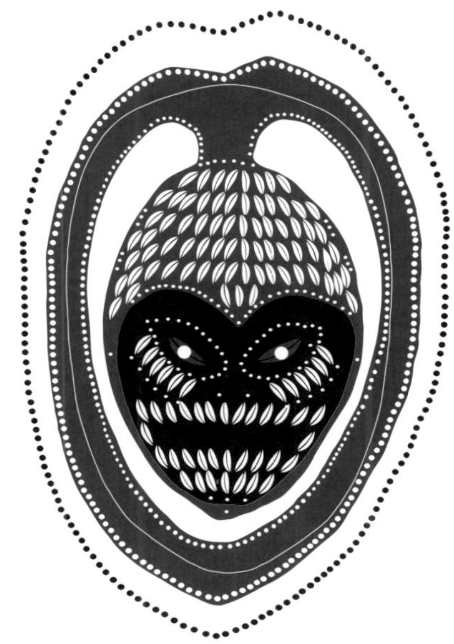

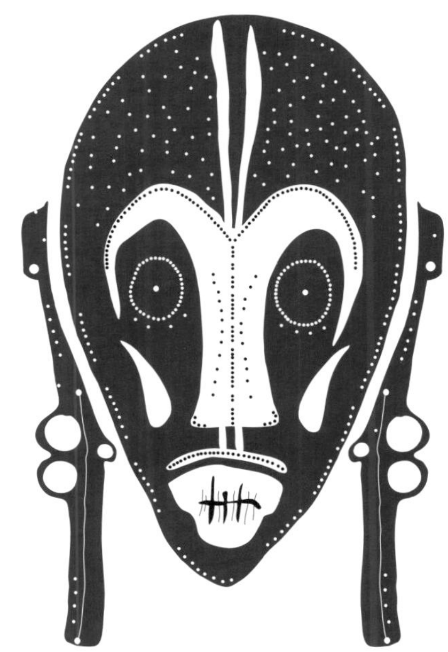

NOTES

[1] W.E.B Du Bois, *The Souls of Black Folk* (London and New York: Penguin Books, 1903 [1989 reprint]), 6.

[2] Ralph Waldo Emerson, quoted in Alan Lightman, "The Role of the Public Intellectual." http://web.mit.edu/comm-forum/papers/lightman.html. Accessed on August 16, 2013.

[3] Barry Gewen, "Who Is a Public Intellectual?" http://artsbeat.blogs.nytimes.com/2008/06/11/who-is-a-public-intellectual/?_r=0. Accessed on August 16, 2013.

[4] Manning Marable, *Black Leadership: Four Great American Leaders and the Struggle for Civil Rights* (New York: Columbia University Press, 1998), xvi.

[5] W.E.B. Dubois, "A Negro Student at Harvard at the End of the Nineteenth Century" [from *Massachusetts Review*, 1 (Spring 1960): 439–458, cited in David Levering Lewis, ed., *W.E.B. Dubois: A Reader* (New York: Henry Holt and Company, 1995), 273].

[6] Marable, 47–51.

[7] W.E.B. Dubois, "Criteria of Negro Art," quoted in Rebecca T. Cureau, "Towards an Aesthetic of Black Folk Expression," in *Alain Locke: Reflections on a Modern Renaissance Man*, edited by Russell J. Linnemann (Baton Rouge: Louisiana State University Press, 1982), 79.

[8] Paul Gilroy, *The Black Atlantic: Modernity and Double Consciousness* (Cambridge, MA: Harvard University Press, 1993).

[9] W.E.B. Du Bois, "Credo," *Independent*, no. 57 (October 15, 1904): 787.

[10] W.E.B. Du Bois, *Darkwater: Voices from Within the Veil* (New York: Harcourt, Brace and Howe, 1920), 164–165.

[11] Ibid., 4.

JAMES T. CAMPBELL

DU BOIS IN THE KINGDOM OF CULTURE

READERS OF A CERTAIN AGE may recall an old Monty Python bit in which contestants on a mock game show were given fifteen seconds to summarize Proust. Scholars studying the life and thought of W.E.B. Du Bois can be forgiven if they sometimes feel a bit like those overwhelmed contestants. Not only was Du Bois a figure of immense depth and complexity, but he also lived an extraordinarily long time. As he himself was fond of noting, he entered history at the dawn of Radical Reconstruction, in February 1868, the very week that Andrew Johnson was impeached. He died in August 1963, the night before the March on Washington, high-water mark of the civil rights movement. For more than eighty of his ninety-five years, Du Bois was actively researching and writing, from his childhood in Great Barrington, Massachusetts, where he established himself as a stringer for the *New York Globe*, to his final days in Kwame Nkrumah's Ghana, where he labored on his unfinished *Encyclopedia Africana*. In the interim, he published some two dozen books, including works of history, sociology, biography, autobiography, and fiction, as well as thousands of articles, speeches, and newspaper columns. He founded and edited four periodicals, most notably *The Crisis*, monthly organ of the National Association for the Advancement of Colored People, which served as his personal broadsheet for a quarter century. He also left nearly a hundred microfilm reels of personal papers, running to a quarter-million pages.

All of these factors — the length of his public career, his astonishing breadth and productivity, the range of different registers in which he wrote — ensure that Du Bois will forever remain a source of fresh discovery and debate. The interpretive challenge is compounded by the sheer immediacy of so much of his writing. As the self-appointed "preceptor of the race" (in biographer David Levering Lewis's felicitous phrase), Du Bois felt compelled not simply to take positions on issues bearing on people of color, but also to instruct those people on the positions they should take. Inevitably, as historical and rhetorical contexts changed, he sometimes found himself adopting positions different from, indeed in stark contradiction to, previous positions. The same Du Bois who thundered that "all Art is propaganda. . . . I do not care a damn for any art that is not used for propaganda" in 1926 had derided that exact position five years before, in a column defending Eugene O'Neill. The problem with black critics, he opined on the earlier occasion, was their insistence that "Art and Propaganda be one," a position that betrayed a "complete misunderstanding of . . . the aim of Art." This is an unusually stark case of self-contradiction, but similar examples abound in Du Bois's work.

The problem is complicated still further by certain signature qualities of Du Bois's mind. From his earliest days, Du Bois exhibited a capacity to hold simultaneously and in tension ideas and convictions that, to less supple minds, might seem contradictory or incommensurable. Every Du Bois scholar has struggled with this problem, trying somehow to reconcile the seemingly irreconcilable in his thought: universalism with racialism; rationalism with Romanticism; robust faith in human progress, under the guidance of an educated elite, with his simultaneous valorization of rural folk; an enduring commitment to empirical social science with what Arnold Rampersad has described as his essentially "poetic" apprehension of the world. Du Bois himself recognized the problem, creating fictional alter egos like Bles in *The Quest of the Silver Fleece*, on whom was "grafted a New England conscience on a tropical heart and — dear me! — but it's a gorgeous misfit."

Gathering all this together, one wonders whether Du Bois might be better introduced by way of Whitman rather than Proust: "Do I contradict myself? Very well, then I contradict myself, I am large, I contain multitudes." And yet Du Bois was not an incoherent thinker. On the contrary, his thought was characterized by both rigor and profound continuity. All of Du Bois's writings, no matter how remote in time and circumstance, were unmistakably products of the same mind and expressions of the same fundamental values: faith in progress; an unswerving commitment to human freedom; and an abiding belief in black folk — a conviction, in his own words, that "Negro blood has a message for the World."

To plumb the depths of Du Bois's thought is to begin to appreciate the challenge faced by contributors to the *Du Bois in Our Time* exhibition. Every artistic commission presents its possibilities and problems, but participants in this exhibition faced a doubly daunting task: not simply to assay the life and legacy of one of American history's most complex, compelling figures, but to translate that legacy into the circumstances of our own very different age. And what a curious age it is, that erects monuments to the civil rights movement while systematically rolling back its accomplishments, that sends a black man to the White House while consigning millions of his brethren to the purgatory of poverty and prison. What are we to make of Du Bois at a time like this?

As one of the consulting historians for the exhibition, I was mercifully exempt from having to solve that riddle. Our role was to supply historical context, to share what we knew of Du Bois's life and times, in hopes that it might help participating artists connect their own imaginations to his. How well we succeeded is for others to judge. What I can say for myself is that the experience of working on this exhibition, of seeing Du Bois conjured back to life through the vision and touch of this extraordinary collection of artists, represents one of the singular joys of my professional life.

In his classic 1903 book, *The Souls of Black Folk*, Du Bois pondered a scene from Booker T. Washington's *Up from Slavery*, an image of a lone black boy sitting in a weed-strewn yard in front of a dilapidated house, poring over a French grammar. For Washington, steeped in the Gilded Age spirit of "triumphant commercialism, and the ideals of material prosperity," the spectacle represented "the acme of absurdities." To which Du Bois replied: "One wonders what Socrates and St. Francis of Assisi would say to this."

A similar question hovered over the opening of the *Du Bois in Our Time* exhibition: What would Du Bois say to this? What would he make of these works of art, inspired by his life and mounted in a university museum just up the road from his boyhood home? Such questions are obviously unanswerable, but they are nonetheless fruitful, for they compel us to consider many of the issues that he himself grappled with in his voluminous writings about art. What are the purposes of art? What is the relationship between art's claim to universality and its role as an expression of racial experience? Are there distinct "criteria of Negro art"? Do artists working on racial subjects labor under any particular political obligations? What is the relationship between "Truth" and "Beauty" — always singular in Du Bois's writing, and usually capitalized — and which has the primary claim on the artist?

Du Bois's reflections on these conundrums were characteristically complex and tension laden. Clearly he believed that black people possessed a distinct artistic temperament, a "tropic nonchalance" that rendered them uniquely susceptible to beauty. It was Du Bois who first declared that the Negro was "primarily an artist," who extolled the Negro's "gift of laughter and song," who insisted that the Sorrow Songs of African American slaves represented "the only true American music," the "most original and beautiful expression of human life and longing yet born on American soil." "The Negro is essentially dramatic," he declared in "The Drama Among Black Folk," an essay published in 1916. "His greatest gift to the world has been and will be a gift of art, of appreciation and realization of beauty."

Thus rendered, Du Bois stands as a prophet of what a later generation, schooled in the ideals of Black Power, would call "the Black Aesthetic." Yet to stop there is to grasp only half the point. Du Bois believed that black people possessed a unique racial endowment, but he also believed in a single, unitary human civilization, a vast "kingdom of culture" that was the creation and the birthright of all people, irrespective of the "Veil" of race. Just as Shakespeare was not the exclusive property of Europeans — "I sit with Shakespeare and he winces not," he famously wrote in *The Souls of Black Folk* — so were the Sorrow Songs not the sole property of one race but a shared human patrimony. Du Bois underscored the point graphically in *Souls*, beginning each chapter with twinned epigrams, one a conventional belletristic epigram from a canonical white writer and the other a few bars of music from an African American spiritual. "Swing Low, Sweet Chariot" and "Steal Away," Byron and Elizabeth Barrett Browning, standing side by side in the pantheon of Civilization.

Given his expostulations about racial gifts and tropical temperaments, Du Bois's own aesthetic tastes remained surprisingly conventional and notably Eurocentric. In a literary age attuned to modernist experimentation and the possibilities of vernacular expression, he preferred the Romantic flights of Byron and Tennyson or of their German antecedents, Goethe and Schiller. His taste in music was likewise classical and conservative. While he appreciated the grandeur of the spirituals, he regarded other popular black forms — blues, jazz, and gospel — as vulgar and demeaning, expressions not of racial character but of racist caricature, ginned up for the amusement of white folks. While contemporaries thrilled to the Duke Ellington Orchestra and Louis Armstrong's Hot Five, Du Bois hearkened to the music of Mendelssohn (to which he listened on the night he died), Beethoven, and Wagner. (One of the most unsettling chapters of David Lewis's two-volume biography depicts a trip to the Wagner festival in Bayreuth, Germany, in 1936, a year after the enactment of the Nuremberg Laws.)

The tensions within Du Bois's thought were abundantly apparent in his creative writing, which explored themes of race and racism but generally did so in highly conventional (and often effusively Romantic) form and language. In contrast to nonfiction books like *The Souls of Black Folk*, *Darkwater*, *Black Reconstruction*, and *Dusk of Dawn*, all of which have achieved classic status, Du Bois's creative work (which included scores of poems and short stories, as well as five novels) is rarely read or remembered today. This has also proved to be the fate of *The Star of Ethiopia*, a sprawling historical pageant that Du Bois regarded as one of his most significant works. First staged in 1913 and briefly revived in 1916, the pageant featured a "crimson-turbaned Herald," who unfolded the history of the Negro — "the Eldest and Strongest of the Races of men whose faces be black" — over the course of three hours, as a thousand costumed actors processed silently across the stage. Logistically and financially unsustainable, the pageant closed after a few performances.

Du Bois articulated his ideas about art not only in his own creative work, but also in his work as editor of *The Crisis*. From his perch at the NAACP's Fifth Avenue headquarters, he pronounced monthly on the state of black art. Perhaps not surprisingly, he lavished particular praise on those who sought to infuse racial themes into classical forms: poet W. S. Braithwaite, whom he later hired as the magazine's first literary editor; the late sculptor Edmonia Lewis, who had chosen a life of European exile in order to pursue her art; Anglo-African composer Samuel Coleridge-Taylor, whose career he chronicled in "The Immortal Child," one of the essays in the 1920 book *Darkwater*. But Du Bois also championed more modern work, especially in the visual arts, reproducing in the pages of *The Crisis* the paintings of Aaron Douglas, doyen of the Harlem Renaissance, and Frank Walts, a now forgotten illustrator whose portraits graced the covers of numerous radical magazines in the 1920s and '30s. In keeping with his belief in the Negro's "essentially dramatic" character, he wrote extensively about theater, reviewing not only black-authored plays but also white-authored plays that treated racial themes. In 1926, he co-founded one of the era's most influential black theatrical companies, the Krigwa Players. (The name, which Du Bois coined himself, was a variant on an acronym for Crisis Guild of Writers and Artists.)

Given his own identity as a writer, Du Bois dedicated particular attention to the state of black literature. He began his career at *The Crisis* by lamenting the state of the field. "We have among ten millions today one poet, one novelist, and two or three recognized writers of articles and essays," he complained. But rather than accept the situation, he proposed to rectify it, promising to produce for the magazine's first anniversary "a matured plan for encouraging young writers." If he did not entirely honor the letter of the pledge, he certainly honored its spirit. He prominently featured the work of black authors in the pages of *The Crisis* and churned out a steady stream of reviews, as well as a monthly "What to Read" column, co-authored with novelist Jessie Fauset. In the aftermath of World War I, as the "New Negro" movement began to gain traction, he and Fauset endeavored to promote and guide it. Langston Hughes's "The Negro Speaks of Rivers," dedicated to Du Bois, was first published in *The Crisis*, and Du Bois was one of the first reviewers to hail the genius of Jean Toomer's *Cane*, even as he confessed bewilderment at the book's modernist form.

As numerous scholars have recounted, the relationship between Du Bois and the New Negro writers would soon sour. The conflict burst into the open in 1926, following publication of Carl Van Vechten's *Nigger Heaven*, a novel championed by young writers like Hughes and Wallace Thurman but loathed by Du Bois, who urged readers to burn the book. But the conflict over Van Vechten's novel was less the cause than the climax of a longer process of mutual disillusionment. Though never mentioned by name, Du Bois was clearly an intended target of *Fire!!*, a journal launched in 1925 by Hughes, Thurman, Zora Neale Hurston, and Richard Bruce Nugent as an *épater le bourgeoisie* against an older generation of black writers and critics. Occasional personal encounters only widened the rift. Claude McKay counted Du Bois as his idol — his celebrated Red Summer sonnet, "If We Must Die," was partially cribbed from an essay Du Bois had written eight years before — but he came away from their first meeting bitterly disappointed. "He seemed possessed of a cold, acid hauteur of spirit, which is not lessened when he vouchsafes a smile," McKay later recalled.

As differences in personality, temperament, and aesthetic values became apparent, Du Bois's enthusiasm for "the Younger Literary Movement" curdled. He accused its members of irresponsible bohemianism, of pandering to white audiences' appetite for black buffoons and criminals while ignoring the rich vein of artistic inspiration to be found in the struggles

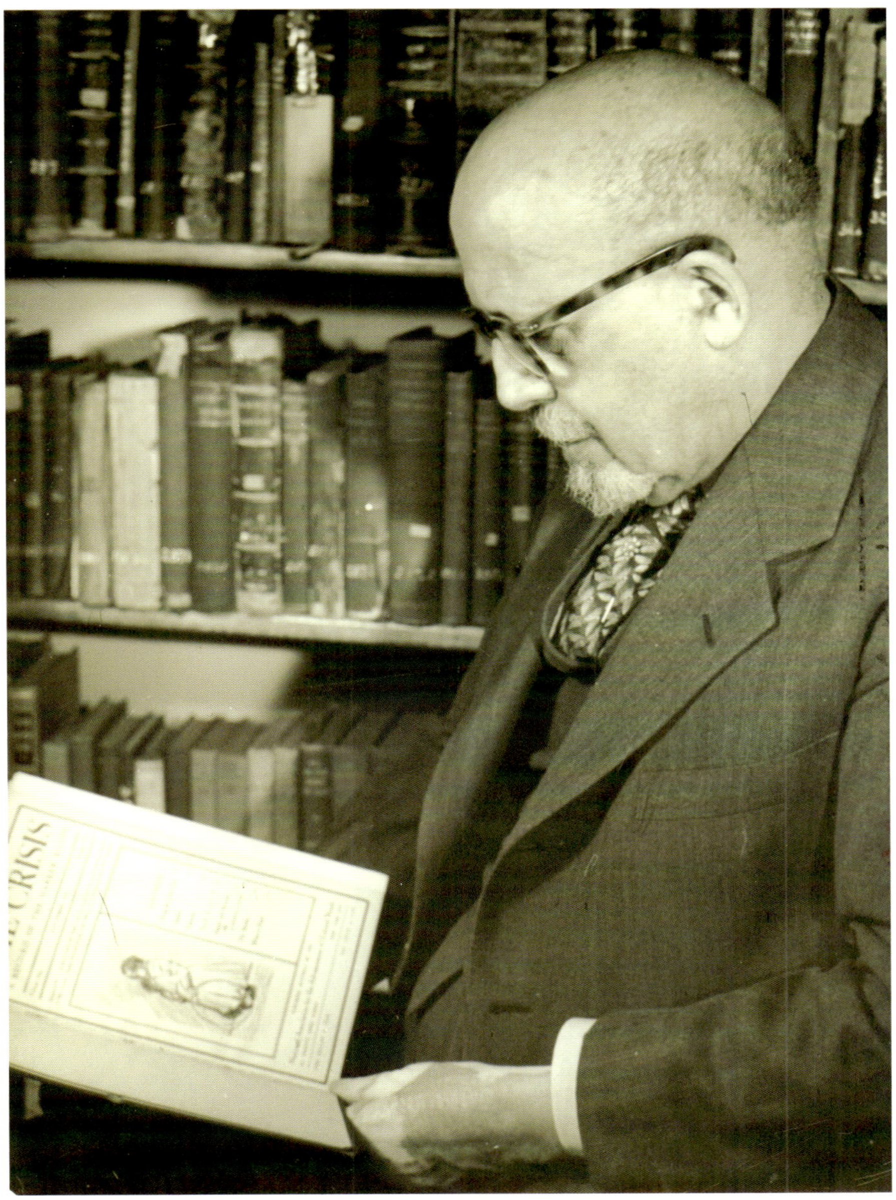

W.E.B. Du Bois in his office, holding the first issue of *The Crisis*, c. 1948
Courtesy of W.E.B. Du Bois Papers, Special Collections and University Archives, University Libraries, University of Massachusetts Amherst

of educated, intelligent Negroes. His reviews in *The Crisis* ranged from disappointed (Langston Hughes's second volume of poetry, *Fine Clothes to the Jew*, contained "extraordinarily beautiful bits," despite its unfortunate focus on "lowly types") to withering (McKay's *Home to Harlem* left him "wanting to take a bath"). It was in this context of paternal rejection and wounded pride that Du Bois penned his oft-quoted statement about not caring "a damn for art that is not Propaganda."

Much more might be said about Du Bois and art — though already an elder statesman during the 1920s, his career had another forty years to run — but the foregoing should be enough to demonstrate the inadequacy of any simple characterization of his views and, by extension, the difficulty of predicting how he would have reacted to the *Du Bois in Our Time* exhibition. Given his penchant for unsparing reviews, we should perhaps count ourselves lucky not to know. No doubt he would have expressed bemusement at some of the works in the show. He may have wished some of the artists to be, if not more didactic, then at least more explicit about the political import of their work. How he would have responded to the sight of himself cast in bronze in the posture of Rodin's *Thinker* or to finding himself the namesake of a new variety of flower is anyone's guess.

And yet I would like to believe — I do believe — that Du Bois would have found much to admire in the exhibition, much that was "Beautiful" and "True." The author of "The

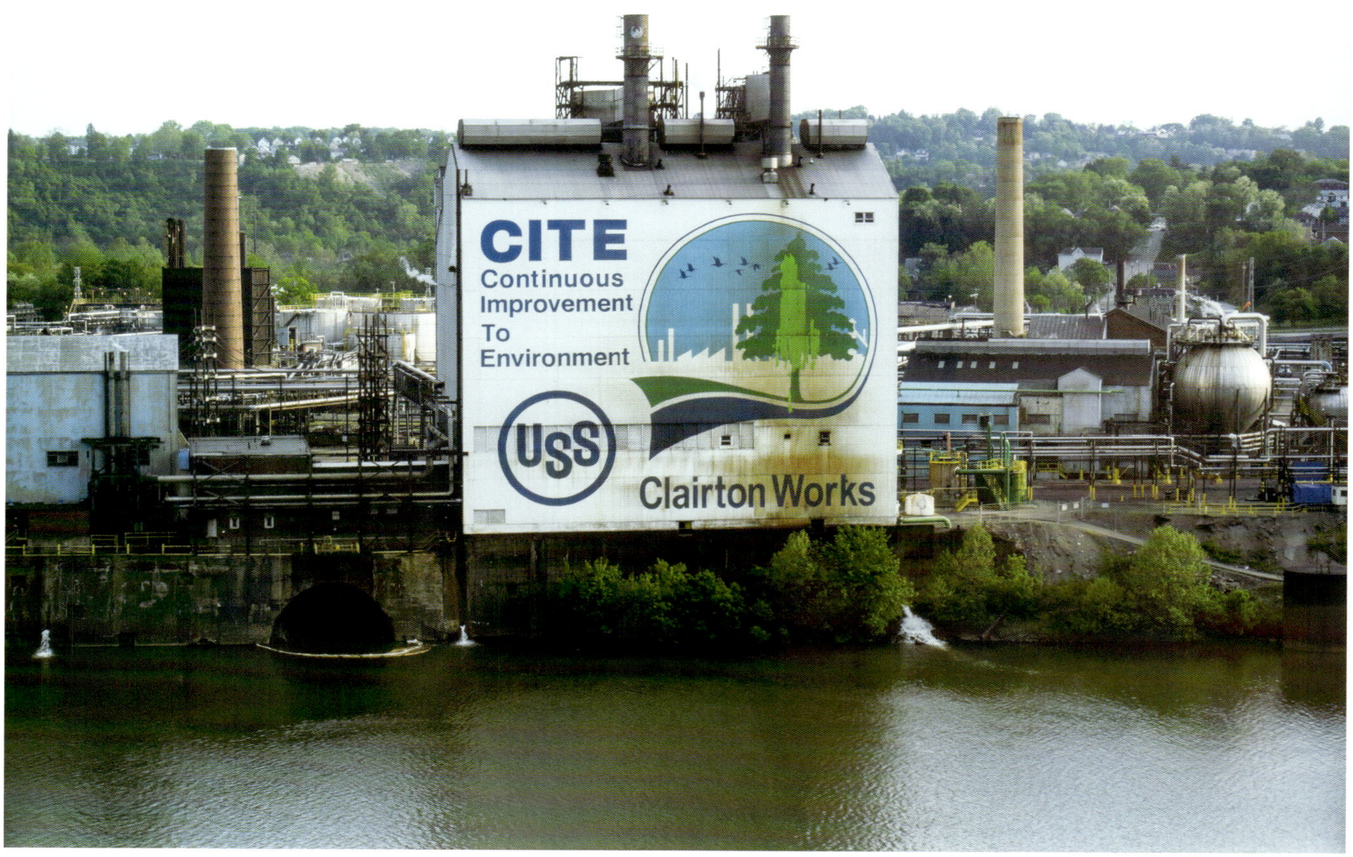

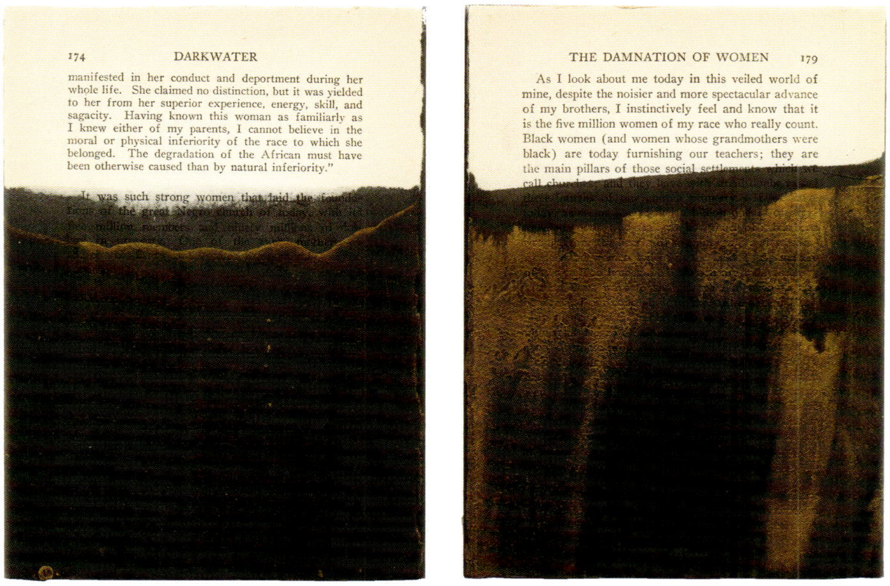

Damnation of Women," a tribute to his own and to all mothers, as well as a searing indictment of his society's cruel degradation of black women, could hardly but respond to Mickalene Thomas's haunting video portrait of her mother. Having witnessed the poisoning of the Housatonic, the "golden river" of his boyhood, he would recognize "A Despoliation of Water," LaToya Ruby Frazier's exploration of the impact of U.S. Steel's Clairton Coke Works on the Monongahela River and on the health of the now mostly poor people who live along it. He would surely be pleased to see the *Encyclopedia Africana* and *The Star of Ethiopia* remembered (though he would almost certainly object to seeing the latter staged in a gritty urban alley), and he would instantly grasp the meaning, if not the form, of Ann Messner's installation of excerpts from his now declassified, severely redacted FBI file: if anyone understood the price we pay when we seek to silence a human voice, it was W.E.B. Du Bois. The fact that the entire exhibition unfolded against the backdrop of Mary Evans's two-dimensional re-creation of the holding pen of a West African slave castle would also move him. Du Bois lived the last years of his life in the shadow of Ghana's Christiansborg Castle, and he often speculated that some of his own ancestors had passed through its portals. In our end is our beginning, and in our beginning is our end. Du Bois understood that too.

But the work I found myself most wishing Du Bois could see was the installation by Tim Rollins & K.O.S. — Kids of Survival — who created original paintings using pages from *Darkwater* as their canvas. "In the treatment of the child the world foreshadows its own future and faith," Du Bois declared in "The Immortal Child," one of the essays in the volume. "All words and all thinking lead to the child, — to that vast immortality and the wide sweep of infinite possibility which the child represents." How furious he would be at this society's casual discarding of its children, particularly of children of color. And how delighted to see some of those same children making art: children from an urban public school not far from his own childhood home, coming of age half a century after the elimination of the last vestiges of legal Jim Crow yet still living in the Shadow of the Veil, creating pigments of black and gold and ceremonially immersing his words in them, baptizing their art and his in a river of time, color, and hope. I think I know what Du Bois would say to that.

Opposite
LATOYA RUBY FRAZIER
from *A Despoliation of Water: From the Housatonic to Monongahela River (1930–2013)*
United States Steel Clairton Coke Works, C.I.T.E. and Monongahela River, 2013
Duratrans, 27¼" x 38¼"

Right
TIM ROLLINS & K.O.S.
DARKWATER (after W.E.B. Du Bois), 2013
Furnace black watercolor, gold acrylic on vintage book pages on panel
24 elements, each 7" x 5"
Courtesy of Studio K.O.S. and Lehmann Maupin, New York and Hong Kong
With students from the Renaissance School, Springfield, Massachusetts

REILAND RABAKA

"TO MAKE A NAME IN SCIENCE, TO MAKE A NAME IN LITERATURE, AND THUS RAISE MY RACE": DU BOIS IN OUR TIME, IN HIS TIME, AND IN THE FUTURE

These are my plans: to make a name in science, to make a name in literature, and thus raise my race.

— *W.E.B. Du Bois*

FROM THE INITIAL INVITATION TO JOIN the *Du Bois in Our Time* project there was something alluring, extremely intriguing, about it for me. At the outset, it seemed to be an opportunity to explore yet another aspect of W.E.B. Du Bois's eventful life and influential legacy. Most of what people know about Du Bois has to do with his pioneering scholarship, or his founding of the National Association for the Advancement of Colored People (NAACP). Relatively few engage Du Bois the aesthete, let alone Du Bois the creative artist — *l'auteur*. Moreover, even Du Bois scholars who rattle off his major accomplishments with uncanny ease frequently fail to mention that Du Bois was also an incomparable literary artist who published five novels and dozens of poems, plays, pageants, vignettes, and short stories. However, Du Bois's literary artistry and penchant for poetics went beyond his creative writing and decidedly seeped into and colored his historical and social scientific writing as well.[1]

Although Du Bois the social scientist has come to almost entirely eclipse Du Bois the literary artist, it is important to recall a telling diary entry Du Bois wrote in celebration of his twenty-fifth birthday, on February 23, 1893, during his student days at Friedrich Wilhelm University (now the University of Berlin). With his youth and enthusiasm on full display in the diary entry, which was posthumously published in *Against Racism: Unpublished Essays, Papers, Addresses, 1887–1961* (1985a), Du Bois declared:

> I am glad I am living. I rejoice as a strong man to run [win?] a race, and I am strong — is it egotism — is it assurance — or is it the silent call of the world spirit that makes me feel that I am royal and that beneath my scepter a world of kings shall bow. The hot dark blood of that black forefather — born king of men — is beating at my heart, and I know that I am either a genius or a fool. O I wonder what I am — I wonder what the world is — I wonder if life is worth the striving — I do not know — perhaps I never shall know: but this I do know: be the Truth what it may I will seek it, on the pure assumption that it is worth seeking and Heaven nor Hell, God nor Devil shall turn me from my purpose till I die.
>
> I will in this second quarter of my life, enter the dark forest of the unknown world for which I have so many years served my apprenticeship — the chart and compass the world furnishes me I have little faith in — yet, I have none better — I will seek till I find — and die. There is a grandeur in the very hopelessness of such a life — life? and is life all? If I strive, shall I live to strive again? I do not know and in spite of the wild *sehnsucht* [longing] for Eternity that makes my heart sick now and then — I shut my teeth and say I do not care. *Carpe Diem!* . . . These are my plans: to make a name in science, to make a name in literature, and thus raise my race. (27–29, all emphasis in original)

It should be observed that for Du Bois, making a name in literature was just as important as making a name in science. With all of the raw energy and passion of a young man at twenty-five, Du Bois set goals for himself that he would spend the rest of his long and storied life striving toward. Sadly, there is a contemporary tendency to overfocus on his scientific contributions at the expense of exploring his aesthetic contributions. But, Du Bois's work — which is to say, his words, *his works of art* — demand that we be true to them, that we not dilute and twist and turn them if, in fact, our desire is to really experience, listen to, and learn from Du Bois, as opposed to merely Du Bois scholars' interpretations of Du Bois.

ALAÀSE: DU BOIS AS LITTÉRATEUR

As I understand it, the *Du Bois in Our Time* exhibition and symposium seek to celebrate Du Bois the prophet *and* the poet, Du Bois the sociologist *and* the novelist, and Du Bois the political economist *and* the belletrist. From my vantage point, a truly comprehensive and authentic understanding of Du Bois simply cannot be gained without engaging him as an artist and, even more, as an artist who was in constant dialogue with, influenced by, and incessantly influencing other artists, especially the radical aesthetes of the Harlem Renaissance such as Jessie Fauset, Alain Locke, Nancy Elizabeth Prophet, Langston Hughes, Zora Neale Hurston, Claude McKay, Countee Cullen, Augusta Savage, Jean Toomer, Meta Vaux Warrick Fuller, James Weldon Johnson, May Howard Jackson, William Edouard Scott, and Aaron Douglas. Within the world of Du Bois studies, however, I am not alone in emphasizing the deep aesthetic dimensions — especially the literary undertones, and sometimes overtones — of Du Bois's oeuvre.[2]

As Arnold Rampersad observed in *The Art and Imagination of W.E.B. Du Bois* (1976), "it is clear to me that his greatest gift was poetic in nature, and that his scholarship, propaganda, and political activism drew their ultimate power from his essentially poetic vision of human experience and from his equally poetic reverence for the word" (ix). This broader, more expansive comprehension of Du Bois as wordsmith "increases rather than lessens the task of judging his achievements and demands more skills than many of us possess." But, Rampersad importantly concluded, "it is the accurate view." Further elaborating on his distinct conception of Du Bois as a littérateur, Rampersad wrote:

> To see him simply as historian or sociologist or propagandist is to overlook the heart of Du Bois's intelligence, just as to underestimate his contribution in each of these areas is to misrepresent the major ways in which his art and imagination functioned. Similarly, one cannot ignore his novels or verse and yet hope to understand or represent the complex gift of a man whose career as a writer covered some eighty of his ninety-five years and whose contribution to Afro-American scholarship, intellectualism, and cultural identity has never been surpassed in scope and quality. (ix)

No matter how daunting many of us may find the polyvocal and multidimensional character of Du Bois's thought and practices, it is important for us to acknowledge and honor the full range and reach of Du Bois's legacy in the twenty-first century — which is to say, *Du Bois in our time*, in our epoch or era. Du Bois has been hailed as a historian, philosopher, sociologist, Marxist, and political activist, but rarely as a literary artist with concrete radical political commitments not simply to African Americans, civil rights, and social justice, but to the multicultural masses, transethnic working classes, women's liberation, and (neo)colonized and/or struggling people worldwide. He has long been praised and criticized by legions of scholars who have interpreted and rigorously reinterpreted his work, often overlooking its deep aesthetic dimensions. The *Du Bois in Our Time* exhibition and symposium offered ten Du Bois–inspired artists and five Du Bois scholars an opportunity to collaborate, revisit, and, in many instances, resuscitate Du Bois the aesthete and literary artist. In fact, whether we turn to works in the exhibition by Jefferson Pinder, Ann Messner, Brendan Fernandes, Mary Evans, Radcliffe Bailey, or Julie Mehretu, what we are viewing and experiencing are translations of Du Bois's literary legacy into contemporary art — which is also to say, *art in the aftermath of many of the major issues that Du Bois sought to grasp and grapple with between the late nineteenth century and the middle of the twentieth century*.

Among the Yoruba people of West Africa (primarily southwestern Nigeria and southern Benin), there is a distinct concept called *àṣẹ*, which essentially means "the power to make things happen and change things." More literal translations of *àṣẹ* render its meaning as "divine power, authority, order, and vital force" (Yai 1996, 26). Hence, through training, experience, and initiation, a person who learns how to use the essential life-force of things to positively bring about change is called an *alaàse*. Undoubtedly, as each of the works of art in the *Du Bois in Our Time* exhibition deftly demonstrates, Du Bois was and remains, however metaphorically and metaphysically, an *alaàse*. He continues to inspire countless intellectuals, artists, and activists, and it has been his ability to raise critical issues and awareness, even from the land of the angels and ancestors, which is to say, in the Yoruba language, from the land of the *Orishas* and the *Egungun*, that helps to highlight why Du Bois's corpus remains relevant in the twenty-first century.[3]

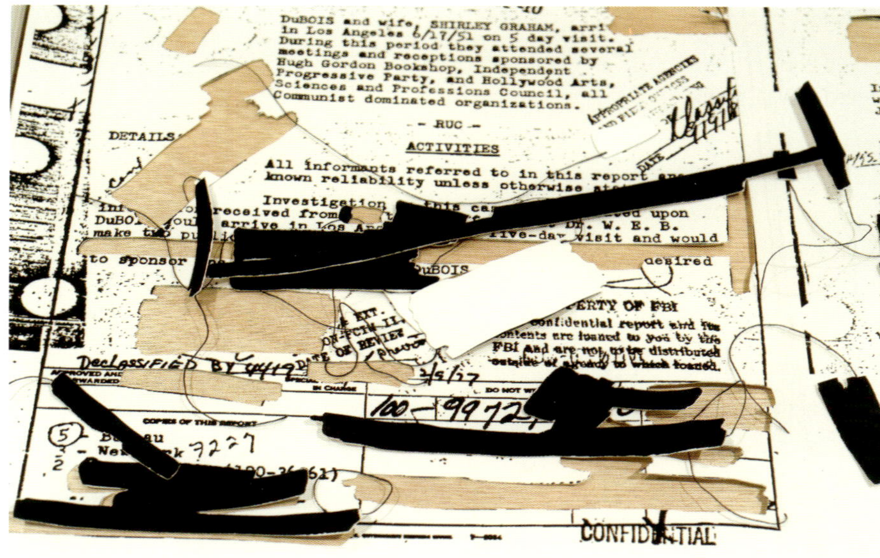

Above
ANN MESSNER
Du Bois: The FBI Files, (detail), 2013
Installation consisting of 447 running foot–incised digital scroll (hand-cut stenciled redaction), printed on Hahnemühle FA paper; 22-foot table inset with 6 in-wall MP5 Niles speakers, CD players, 4 CDs (audio component of the installation)

Above right
BRENDAN FERNANDES
The Encyclopedia Africana, 2013
Hand-bound book, gold foil stamping, and black linen paper
12″ x 9″ x 3″
Collection of the artist and Diaz Contemporary, Toronto

Below right
RADCLIFFE BAILEY
Double Consciousness, 2013
Steel, wax
48″ x 48″ x 17″
Courtesy of Ralph Citino, Philadelphia

One of the most obvious distinctions of the *Du Bois in Our Time* exhibition has much to do with the fact that it is an exhibit in which all of the works of art are grounded in, and grew out of, *the words*, the literary artistry of an iconic African American intellectual-activist. In other words, it is a deeply discursive and textual, if not ultimately *intertextual*, exhibit. One need look no further than Brendan Fernandes's *In The End* and *The Encyclopedia Africana*, or Ann Messner's *Du Bois: The FBI Files*, or Tim Rollins & K.O.S.'s *DARKWATER (after W.E.B. Du Bois)* to get a sense of how profoundly intertextual *Du Bois in Our Time*, both literally and figuratively speaking, was, is, and continues to be. Du Bois's distinct histories, sociologies, paeans, and poetry continue to provide an encomium to, not merely Africa and its diaspora (especially *African* America), but to the "wretched of the earth" (*les damnés de la terre*, as Frantz Fanon famously put it in his 1961 classic) of the twenty-first century.

Each of the works in the *Du Bois in Our Time* exhibit, in the most creative and intertextual manners imaginable, speaks to and comments on both classical and contemporary manifestations of issues that Du Bois engaged during his epoch and which his legacy helps to highlight in the contemporary moment. For instance, it would be difficult to encounter Ann Messner's *Du Bois: The FBI Files* and not think deeply about, and connect, the innumerable abuses of the Federal Bureau of Investigation's Counterintelligence Program (code name: COINTELPRO) between the 1930s and the 1970s with the corrupt character of the National Security Agency's super-surveillance of U.S. citizens' telephone, Internet, and other digital data in our epoch. As his often overlooked classic *In Battle for Peace: The Story of My 83rd Birthday* (1952) demonstrates, Du Bois was no stranger to government repression and harassment, and took a bold and principled stand against efforts to curtail political freedom. Indeed, Du Bois's vision of American democracy was predicated on a distinct conception of participatory democracy that included the most marginalized and oppressed in American society: from women and African Americans (especially African American women) to non-Christian and working-class folk.[4]

Drawing from arguably one of Du Bois's most famous conceptual contributions, "double-consciousness," Radcliffe Bailey's *Double Consciousness* translates and reanimates a key passage from *The Souls of Black Folk* (1903) in which Du Bois audaciously emphasized the quintessential existential ethos that seemingly has been handed down from generation to generation of African Americans since that fateful day in 1619 when the first boatload of enslaved Africans arrived in what would eventually come to be called the United States of America:

> After the Egyptian and Indian, the Greek and Roman, the Teuton and Mongolian, the Negro is a sort of seventh son, born with a veil, and gifted with second-sight in this American world, — a world which yields him no true self-consciousness, but only lets him see himself through the revelation of the other world. It is a peculiar sensation, this double-consciousness, this sense of always looking at one's self through the eyes of others, of measuring one's soul by the tape of a world that looks on in amused contempt and pity. One ever feels his two-ness, — an American, a Negro; two souls, two thoughts, two unreconciled strivings; two warring ideals in one dark body, whose dogged strength alone keeps it from being torn asunder.
>
> The history of the American Negro is the history of this strife, — this longing to attain self-conscious manhood, to merge his double self into a better and truer self. In this merging he wishes neither of the older selves to be lost. He would not Africanize America, for America has too much to teach the world and Africa. He would not bleach his Negro soul in a flood of white Americanism, for he knows that Negro blood has a message for the world. He simply wishes to make it possible for a man to be both a Negro and an American, without being cursed and spit upon by his fellows, without having the doors of Opportunity closed roughly in his face. (3–4) [5]

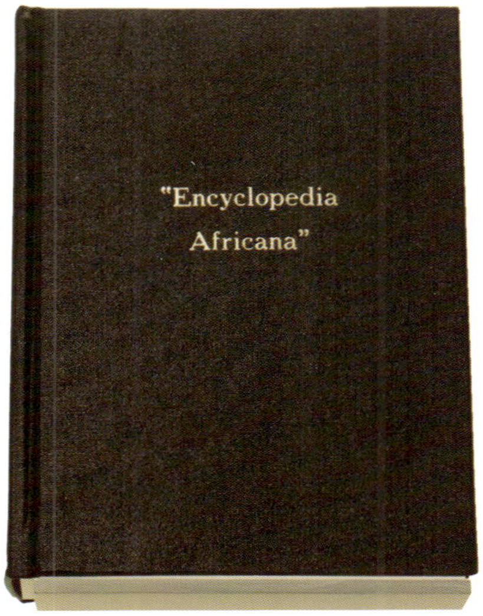

In essence Radcliffe Bailey's work ingeniously inverts Du Bois's double-consciousness, twisting and turning his concept until the angst of "always looking at one's self through the eyes of others" is, in the most uroboric manner imaginable, alleviated as a consequence of continental and diasporan Africans' finally being themselves and freeing themselves from the historical, cultural, and political prison houses that European and American imperialism have long held them in. In this sense, even Bailey's *Untitled* piece, where a life-size Du Bois bronze sculpture is recast as Auguste Rodin's *Le Penseur* (*The Thinker*), disrupts longstanding myths and stereotypes about African Americans being overdetermined by their black bodies, black rage, and black sexuality. Du Bois identified double-consciousness because he understood how important identifying and analyzing forms of oppression and imperialism are for folk of African origin or descent in the aftermath of the African holocaust, African American enslavement, colonization, segregation, apartheid, ongoing economic exploitation, and so on. For Du Bois, as it was for Fanon in *Black Skin, White Masks* and *The Wretched of the Earth*, psychological liberation is inextricable from physical liberation. In other words, in order to really and truly transcend their objectification (i.e., "reification" or "thingification"), continental and diasporan Africans must explore and ultimately embrace forms of radical subjectivity that enable them to continually rupture their relationships with European and American — among other forms of — imperialism.

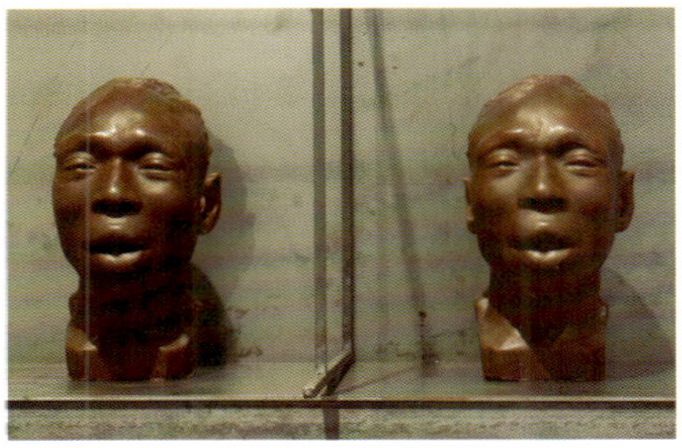

Another pressing issue that Du Bois's life and legacy accented and amplified revolved around women's rights and women's liberation. Although many read him as an archetypal "race man," according to Joy James in *Transcending the Talented Tenth* (1997), Du Bois actually practiced "a politics remarkably progressive for his time and ours" (36).[6] James notes, "Du Bois confronted race, class, and gender oppression while maintaining conceptual and political linkages between the struggles to end racism, sexism, and war" (36–37). His historical, sociological, and political frameworks were dynamic, and constantly integrated diverse elements of what might be termed "feminism" or "womanism," as well as black nationalism, Pan-Africanism, African nationalism, African socialism, Third Worldism, cooperative economics, Marxism, Leninism, Maoism, and pacifism, among others.

In "The Souls of Black Women Folk in the Writings of W.E.B. Du Bois" (1990), Nellie McKay contends: "At a time when black male writers concentrated their efforts on the social, economic, and educational advancement of black men as the 'leaders' of the race, Du Bois is something of an anomaly in his recognition that black women were equal partners in the struggle to claim the human dignity all black people were seeking" (236). Moreover, in *Daughters of Sorrow: Attitudes Toward Black Women, 1880–1920* (1990), Beverly Guy-Sheftall maintains that Du Bois was not only one of "the most passionate defenders of black women," but also one of the "most outspoken [male-] feminists" in African American history and, more generally, American history (13). In fact, in Guy-Sheftall's opinion, Du Bois "devote[d] his life's work to the emancipation of blacks *and* women" (161, emphasis in original).[7]

In *W.E.B. Du Bois: Black Radical Democrat* (1986), Manning Marable echoes Guy-Sheftall's observations, asserting that "[l]ike [Frederick] Douglass, Du Bois was probably the most advanced male leader of his era on the question of gender inequality" and women's suffrage, although he was deeply "troubled by the racism within the white women's movement" (85). Particularly perplexing for Du Bois was the white women's movement's inattention to, and perpetuation of, racism. For instance, Du Bois was bothered by the racial politics of the National American Woman Suffrage Association, whose president, Carrie Chapman Catt, asserted that democratic rights had been granted to African American men "with possibly ill-advised haste," producing "[p]erilous conditions" in U.S. society as it introduced "into the body politic vast numbers of irresponsible citizens." Belle Kearney, a Mississippi suffragist leader, practiced an even more overtly racist politics by advocating that white women's enfranchisement would guarantee, among other things, an "immediate and [more] durable white supremacy" (cited in Marable 1986, 85).[8] Du Bois (1995), in

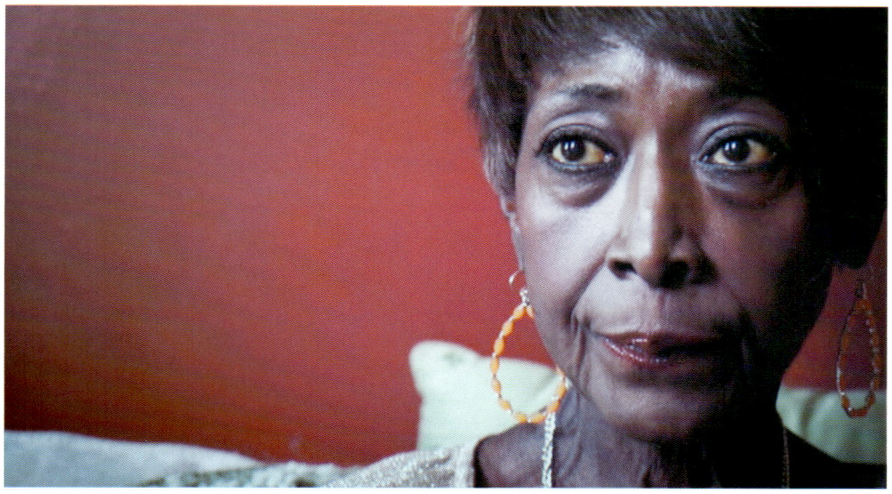

characteristic fashion, shot back: "Every argument for Negro suffrage is an argument for woman's suffrage; every argument for woman's suffrage is an argument for Negro suffrage; both are great movements in democracy" (298).

Ultimately, then, Du Bois placed the critique of sexism and racism right alongside the critique of capitalism, class analysis, and class struggle. In tune with the thinking of many Marxist feminists and socialist feminists, Du Bois was critical of both capitalism and patriarchy.[9] He understood women, in general, to have great potential as agents of social transformation because of their simultaneous experience of capitalist and sexist oppression. However, similar to contemporary black feminists, Du Bois understood women of African descent, in particular, to have even greater potential as agents of radical social change on account of their simultaneous experience of racism, sexism, and economic exploitation, whether under capitalism or colonialism.[10] It is in bearing all of this in mind that the works in the *Du Bois in Our Time* exhibition by Mary Evans, LaToya Ruby Frazier, and Mickalene Thomas, each of which uniquely moves black women from the level of objects to apologetic subjects, conceptually connects with Du Bois's women-centered work, such as "The Work of Negro Women in Society" (1902), "The Black Mother" (1912), "Hail Columbia!" (1913), "Woman Suffrage" (1915), "The Damnation of Women" (1920), and "Sex and Racism" (1957), among others.

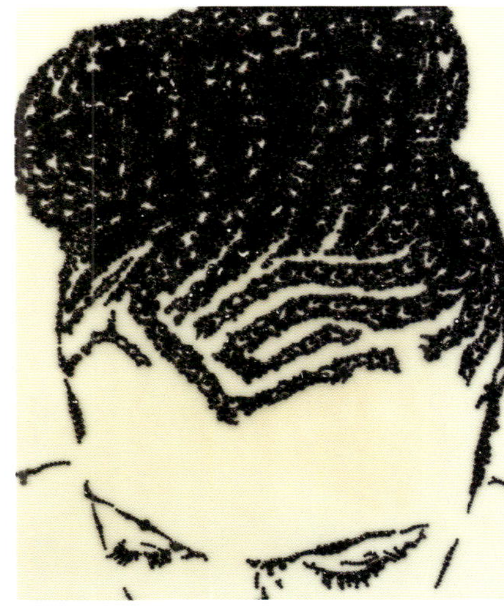

CONCLUSION: "TO THE FEW WHO COULD OR WOULD LISTEN"

Although it would arguably take dozens of exhibits along the lines of *Du Bois in Our Time* to adequately translate Du Bois's polyvocal and polymathic literary legacy into contemporary art, the *Du Bois in Our Time* exhibition and symposium, at the very least, offer us a template. Wedged somewhere between his epoch and ours, Du Bois's thought and texts have come to serve as bridges between the nineteenth, twentieth, and twenty-first centuries. His words — again, his *works of art* — have inspired generation after generation of intellectuals, artists, and activists to come to critical consciousness and rescue and reclaim their humanity, often in the face of seemingly the most insurmountable odds. It is in this sense, then, that Du Bois's life and legacy, as he once prophetically put it, is "significant for all lives of men" — which is to say, for the lives of all human beings who have and will continue to inherit the world his words, his works of art, his *word-art* captured, transfigured, and, truth be told, continues to transform. In a famous passage from *Dusk of Dawn: An Essay Toward an Autobiography of a Race Concept* (1940), Du Bois revealingly wrote:

> In the folds of this European civilization I was born and shall die, imprisoned, conditioned, depressed, exalted and inspired. Integrally a part of it and yet, much more significant, one of its rejected parts; one who expressed in life and action and made vocal to many, a single whirlpool of social entanglement and inner psychological paradox, which always seem to me more significant for the meaning of the world today than other similar and related problems.
>
> Little indeed did I do, or could I conceivably have done, to make this problem or to loose it. Crucified on the vast wheel of time, I flew round and round with the Zeitgeist, waving my pen and lifting faint voices to explain, expound and exhort; to see, foresee and prophesy, to the few who could or

Opposite
MICKALENE THOMAS
Video still from *Happy Birthday to a Beautiful Woman*, 2013

Above
MICKALENE THOMAS
Hair Portraits (detail), 2013
Rhinestones and acrylic on wood panel, 24 panels, each 24" x 20", installation 48" x 240"
Courtesy of Melva Bucksbaum and Raymond Learsy, Mickalene Thomas, and Lehmann Maupin, New York and Hong Kong

> would listen. Thus very evidently to me and to others I did little to create my day or greatly change it; but I did exemplify it and thus for all time my life is significant for all lives of men. (3)

At this point it can be solemnly said that the importance of Du Bois's life, indeed, is "significant for all lives of men." In the American academy, amid the current intellectual trepidation and word-wizardry of many of the more noted academics, Du Bois's discourse on racism, capitalism, colonialism, civil rights, social justice, women's liberation, world peace, and democratic socialism exist furtively in the radical intellectual imagination, stripped of its critical potency, and even mocked by postmodernists and post-Marxists (among many others) who argue that his thought is outdated or old-fashioned. However, for those of us with unquenchable commitments to continuing the fight for freedom, for those of us deeply disturbed by what is going on in our war-torn and global-warming world, and for those of us who desperately search for solutions to our most pressing social and political problems, Du Bois's anti-imperialist ideas and actions, his increasing commitment(s) to gender justice, his radical political vision, and his theory of social change offer a much-needed alternative to, and through, the mazes of postmodernism, postcolonialism, postfeminism, post-Marxism, and neoliberalism, among other contemporary conceptual distractions and disruptions.

If racial colonialism continues to be perfectly pathological, sorely sadistic, and viciously violent — as I understand it to be and as I have argued that it is in all of my work — then we need the insurgent intellectual and radical political resources of what remains one of the most profound and provocative critiques and confrontations not simply of racial colonialism, but also of the ways in which racism and colonialism incessantly overlap, interlock, and intersect with capitalism, sexism, and, even more ironically, humanism — that which acutely occurs throughout the passionate pages of Du Bois's *The Suppression of the African Slave Trade to the United States of America, 1638–1870* (1896), *The Philadelphia Negro* (1899), *The Souls of Black Folk* (1903), *John Brown* (1909), *The Negro* (1915), *Darkwater* (1920), *The Gift of Black Folk* (1924), *Black Reconstruction* (1935), *Black Folk, Then and Now* (1939), *Dusk of Dawn* (1940), *Color and Democracy* (1945), *The World and Africa* (1947), *In Battle for Peace* (1952), and *The Autobiography of W.E.B. Du Bois* (1968), among his other work. It is for these seemingly forgotten reasons that my work not only advocates that authentic Du Boisists solelmnly return to Du Bois, but that I sincerely seek to accent the fact that many of Du Bois's most famous, if not "infamous," theories are more relevant now than they were during his lifetime.

For instance, Du Bois's theory of the sociopathological impact of the simultaneous racialization and colonization of the souls of black folk, his theory of the interconnections and inextricability of colonialism and capitalism, his theory of the dialectic of self-determination and self-defense, his theory of the dialectic of women's decolonization and women's liberation, and his theory of radical humanism are undoubtedly more needed now than ever before. Racial colonial patriarchal capitalist pathology is not simply, as Jürgen Habermas and the Habermasian critical theorists would have it, "colonization of our life-worlds by the capitalist system," although capitalism is most certainly an important aspect of such a pathology, but it also includes the overlapping, interlocking, and intersecting systems of violence, exploitation, and oppression in the guises of racism, sexism, and colonialism as well.[11]

In summary, it must be openly admitted that the aesthetic and theoretic tensions noted in the previous paragraphs point to, and produce an extremely uneasy combination of, criticisms and interpretations that defy simple synopsis or conventional conceptual rules. Consequently, many of Du Bois's critics have heretofore downplayed and diminished the real brilliance and brawn of his work by failing to grasp its antinomies and have, therefore, put forward a divided and distorted Du Bois, who is either, for example, a Pan-Africanist *or* Europhile, a black nationalist *or* radical humanist, a social scientist *or* propagandist, a race man *or* radical women's rights man, a bourgeois individualist *or* dogmatic Marxist communist. Each of the aforementioned superficial ascriptions falls shamefully short of capturing the complex and chameleonic character of Du Bois's discourse and the difficulties involved in interpreting it using one-sided, single-subject theory and/or monodisciplinary devices.

Many dismiss Du Bois and charge his work with being dense because it employs a wide range of theory from several different disciplines, while others, such as those of us involved in the *Du Bois in Our Time* exhibition and symposium, are attracted to his work because it is artistically inspiring, theoretically thick, rich in both radicality and originality, and boldly crosses so many aesthetic, academic, and political boundaries. No matter what one's ultimate attitude toward Du Bois, I believe the fact that his thought and texts continue to cause contemporary controversies, and that his work has been discussed and debated across the arts, humanities, and social sciences for over a century, in some degree points to the multidimensionality and interdisciplinarity of his ideas, which offer enigmatic insights for everyone either to embrace enthusiastically or demur definitively. Hence, the dialectic of attraction and repulsion in Du Bois studies can partly be attributed to the ambiguities inherent in his thought and the monodisciplinary anxieties of many of the interpreters of his work. Suffice it to say that if this is the case, then several previous studies of his thought are seriously flawed because they have sought to grasp and grapple with Du Bois's oeuvre using a monodisciplinary instead of a multidisciplinary model.

Whatever the deficiencies of his thought and the problems with his approach to critical issues confronting African American and other oppressed people, Du Bois forces his readers to think deeply, to criticize thoroughly, and to move beyond the imperialist impulses of the established order. Many critics have made solid criticisms of some aspect of Du Bois's thought, but, when analyzed objectively, his lifework and intellectual legacy is impressive and inspiring, as is his loyalty to the most radical thought and practice traditions in African American and world history. His impact and influence have been widespread, not only cutting across academic disciplines, but setting aglow several social movements, political programs, and artistic initiatives.

Where some theorists dogmatically hold views simply because they are fashionable or politically popular, Du Bois's work draws from a diverse array of often eclectic and enigmatic sources, and therefore offers no closed system or absolute truths. His thought was constantly open and routinely responsive to changing historical and cultural conditions, both nationally and internationally. There are several, sometimes stunning, transformations in his theory that are in most instances attempts to answer conundrums created by changing sociopolitical, historical, and cultural conditions. In conclusion, then, I would like to suggest that it is the openness and consistently nondogmatic radicalism of Du Bois's corpus, the richness and wide range and reach of his ideas, and the absence of any finished system or body of clearly defined truths that can be accepted or rejected at ease, which constitute both the contemporary philosophical fascination with, and continuing critical importance of, W.E.B. Du Bois and his discourse — *in our time and for all time*.

NOTES

[1] I have relied on a number of studies to develop my interpretation of Du Bois's life and legacy, the most noteworthy among them are Andrews (1985), Appiah (2014), Balfour (2011), Bloom (2001), Blum and Young (2009), Broderick (1959, 1974), Durr (2001), Fontenot and Keller (2007), Gooding-Williams (2009), Horne (1986, 2009), Juguo (2001), Kirschke and Sinitiere (2014), Lewis (1993, 2000), Marable (1986), Porter (2010), Reed (1997), Rudwick (1960, 1968, 1982), Shaw (2013), Warren (2011), Wolters (2001), and Zamir (1995, 2008).

[2] For further discussion of works that engage Du Bois's aesthetics and literary legacy, and for the works which influenced my interpretation here, see Aptheker (1989), Bell (1985), Byerman (1994), Du Bois (1985b), Judy (1994), Kirschke (1995, 2007), Kirschke and Sinitiere (2014), Lewis (1993, 2000), Moses (1975, 1978), Posnock (1995), Rampersad (1976, 1979), Smith (2004), and Watts (2001).

[3] For further discussion of Yoruba history, culture, and spirituality, and for the works which influenced my interpretation here, see Akintoye (2010), Bascom (1969, 1970, 1980), Ellis (1964), Falola (1999), Falola and Childs (2004), Falola and Heaton (2008), S. Johnson (2010), Laitin (1986), Olupona and Rey (2008), and Owomoyela (2008).

[4] In brief, COINTELPRO's sole purpose — according to J. Edgar Hoover's many detailed directives to FBI agents between 1956 and 1971 — was to "expose, disrupt, misdirect, discredit, or otherwise neutralize" seditious movements and their leaders. Focusing on individuals and organizations deemed "subversive" by the McCarthyist and post-McCarthyist conservative forces who conceived of themselves as working in the best interest of middle-class and otherwise wealthy white America, the FBI's records indicate that 85 percent of COINTELPRO's work targeted communist and socialist organizations; individuals and organizations associated with the civil rights movement and black power movement, including W.E.B. Du Bois and Martin Luther King as well as other individuals associated with the Southern Christian Leadership Conference, the National Association for the Advancement of Colored People, the Congress of Racial Equality, the Student Nonviolent Coordinating Committee, and several other civil rights organizations; the National of Islam; Elijah Muhammad; Malcolm X; Stokely Carmichael; Angela Davis; the Black Panther Party; the American Indian Movement; a wide range of "New Left" organizations, including Students for a Democratic Society and the Weather Underground; the National Lawyers Guild; individuals and organizations associated with the antiwar movement, the women's liberation movement, the Chicano movement, and the homosexual liberation movement. Tellingly, only 15 percent of COINTELPRO's work was directed at marginalizing and subverting white supremacist and domestic terrorist groups, such as the Ku Klux Klan, various White Citizens Councils, the American Nazi Party, and the National States' Rights Party. For further discussion of the FBI's infamous Counterintelligence Program, especially its assault on African America from the beginning of World War I in 1914 to the end of the Vietnam War in 1975, and for the most noteworthy works that informed my analysis here, see Aronson (2012), Blackstock (1988), Churchill and Wall (1988, 2002), Cunningham (2013), J. K. Davis (1992), Drabble (2004, 2007, 2008), Glick (1989), Haas (2010), Jeffreys-Jones (2007), Medsger (2014), O'Reilly (1983, 1989, 1994), Rosenfeld (2012), and T. Weiner (2012).

[5] Here, with these hallowed words, Du Bois indelibly etched his name into the annals of American literary and cultural history. Although the Veil and the color-line are central tropes in *The Souls of Black Folk*, Du Bois's concept of double-consciousness and its corollary concept of second-sight are simultaneously essential to understanding *The Souls of Black Folk* and, albeit often overlooked by the white sociological fraternity, vital to sociologically comprehending the conundrums and contradictions of racial colonization and racial segregation in a nation, nay, in a world, which pretentiously prides itself on its cultural liberalism and commitment to unfettered democracy. Observe that Du Bois's doubling discourse connected the Veil with second-sight ("the Negro is a sort of seventh son, born with a veil, and gifted with second-sight in this American world"), and America (i.e., the United States), representing the white supremacist capitalist colonial world in deep-seated denial, was to those "born with a veil," "a world which yield[ed] [them] no true self-consciousness, but only lets [them] see [themselves] through the revelation of the other world." Then, as if faithfully harking back to his stated intention at the book's opening — which is to say, to candidly explore the "strange meaning of being black here in the dawning of the Twentieth Century" — Du Bois articulated his own homespun *ontology of black life-worlds and black life-struggles* in a white supremacist capitalist colonial world: "It is a peculiar sensation, this double-consciousness, this sense of always looking at one's self through the eyes of others." Indeed, Du Bois's concept of double-consciousness also seems to have profound implications for a *social psychology of black life-worlds and black life-struggles* in a white supremacist capitalist colonial world. For example, and bearing Frantz Fanon's (1965, 1967, 1968, 1969) watershed work in mind, it might be useful to quickly list some of the psychological concepts and conditions that double-consciousness appears to be conceptually connected to — if not during its day, then certainly currently: schizophrenia; paranoia; dysmorphophobia; inferiority complex; and anxiety disorder, among others. My interpretation of the cultural and social psychological implications of Du Bois's concept of double-consciousness in specific, and *The Souls of Black Folk* in general, has been influenced by Adell (1994), Carroll (2003), A. Davis (1983), Du Bois (2005, 2011), S. O. Gaines (1996), Gaines and Reed (1994), Hubbard (2003), Jennings (1998), T. L. Johnson (2012), Krasner (1997), Mocombe (2008), Shaw (2013), and Wolfenstein (2007). Those readers seeking more detailed discussions of my interpretation of Du Bois and Fanon are encouraged to see Rabaka (2007, 2008, 2009, 2010a, 2010b, 2010c).

[6] Nellie McKay, Gary Lemons, and Hazel Carby each bemoan the fact that there is a longstanding tendency in Du Bois studies to read him primarily as a "race man" and downplay his contributions to "feminist" and/or "womanist" discourse. For instance, in her essay "The Souls of Black Women Folk in the Writings of W.E.B. Du Bois" (1990), McKay claims that Du Bois was one of very few black men who wrote "feminist autobiography": "More than any other black man in our history, his three autobiographies [*Darkwater*, *Dusk of Dawn*, and *The Autobiography of W.E.B. Du Bois*] demonstrate that black women have been central to the development of his intellectual thought" (229, 231). McKay, who is a literary theorist and critic, argues that one of the reasons so many Du Bois scholars read him as a "race man" is because they often overlook his "more creative, less sociological works, where most of his thoughts on women and his own fundamental spirituality are expressed" (230). "Few people, even those who have spent years reading and studying Du Bois," quips

McKay, "know that he wrote five novels and published a volume of poetry" (231). In " 'When and Where [We] Enter': In Search of a Feminist Forefather — Reclaiming the Womanist Legacy of W.E.B. Du Bois" (2001), Gary Lemons laments: Du Bois's "womanist activism remains to be fully claimed by contemporary black men, as he continues to be viewed primarily as a 'race man' " (72). What perplexes Lemons is the fact that the critics who elide and erase Du Bois's women's liberation work do not simply do Du Bois a disservice, but rob contemporary men, especially men of African descent, of a black male *antisexist* role model. According to Lemons, "not only" was Du Bois's "conception of anti-racist resistance feminist-inspired, his worldview was profoundly influenced by black women" (73). Finally, in the first chapter of her book *Race Men* (1998), "The Souls of Black Men," Hazel Carby offers contemporary academics and political activists a deconstruction of Du Bois as "race man" that acknowledges that he "advocated equality for women and consistently supported feminist causes" (12). Carby, who asserts that it is not her intention to claim that Du Bois was "a sexist male individual," is not, however, as concerned with Du Bois's "male-feminist" thought — although she gives it a highly critical treatment — as with many black male intellectuals' erasure and omission of his feminist thought from their discourse on Du Bois and their obsessive concerns with "the reproduction of Race Men" (12, 25). She states: "If, as intellectuals and as activists, we are committed, like Du Bois, to struggles for liberation and democratic egalitarianism, then surely it is not contradictory also to struggle to be critically aware of the ways in which *ideologies of gender* have undermined our egalitarian visions in the past and continue to do so in the present" (12, my emphasis). Carby's caveat, like the cautions of McKay and Lemons, essentially asks that we be cognizant of not only the "ideologies of gender" in the present, but also the "ideologies of gender" of the past, and how this specific species of ideology may have and/or, more than likely, indeed did influence the ways our intellectual ancestors theorized about this or that issue. In other words, we must make ourselves and others critically conscious of sexist sentiment in both classical and contemporary continental and diasporan African liberation thought and practices. My Du Bois studies register as an effort to simultaneously deepen and develop the antisexist aspects of the Africana tradition of critical theory and an attempt to move beyond one-dimensional interpretations of Du Bois which downplay the multidimensionality of his thought and texts. It is important here to note that because of the richness and wide range and reach of Du Bois's thought, within Du Bois studies there are various research areas and agendas — for example, Du Boisist history, philosophy, sociology, anthropology, politics, economics, aesthetics, religion, education, and so forth. Depending on one's intellectual orientation, academic training, and academic discipline, his thought and texts may serve a multiplicity of purposes and may be approached from a wide array of discursive directions. Needless to say, my interpretations of Du Bois have been deeply influenced by my training in, and trek through, African, African American, and Caribbean studies, and specifically continental and diasporan African history, radical politics, and critical social theory. For further discussion, see Rabaka (2007, 2008, 2010a, 2010c).

[7] Some may find Guy-Sheftall's (re)construction of Du Bois as a male-"feminist" troubling. However, as Hazel Carby (1998) contends, it should be held in mind that Du Bois means "many things to many people" (14). He is one of the many male and female "rediscovered ancestors" whose thought and texts are currently being engaged by contemporary

theorists "in response to the needs of various agendas," academic or otherwise (14). Where Guy-Sheftall (1990) and McKay (1990) read Du Bois as a male-"feminist," Joy James (1996, 1997) proffered a "pro-feminist" Du Bois. More recently, Gary Lemons (2001) argued that Du Bois's pro–women's rights and women's suffrage work can actually be read as both "black feminist" *and* "womanist." For further discussion of Du Bois's contributions to gender and women's studies, see Gillman and Weinbaum (2007).

[8] For further discussion of white supremacy and antiblack racism within the women's suffrage movement and what has come to be called "feminist racism," and for the works which informed my interpretation here, see Blee (1991, 2002), Caraway (1991), Ferber (1998, 2004), Green (1997), Newman (1999), Stillion-Southard (2011), Twine and Blee (2001), Ware (1992), and White (1999).

[9] For further discussion of Marxist feminism and socialist feminism, and for the works which informed my interpretation here, see Arruzza (2013), Bhavnani (2001), Eisenstein (1979), Hennessey and Ingraham (1997), Rowbotham, Segal and Wainwright (2013), Sargent (1981), Sayers and Osbourne (1990), Slaughter and Kern (1981), Waters (1994), and Weinbaum (1978).

[10] For further discussion of black feminism, and for the key works which informed my interpretation here, see Bobo (2001), Collins (2000), Guy-Sheftall (1995), hooks (1981, 1984, 1995), Hull, Scott, and Smith (1982), James, Foster, and Guy-Sheftall (2009), James and Sharpley-Whiting (2000), King (1988), Nnaemeka (1998), Oyewumi (1997, 2003, 2005, 2010), and B. Smith (1983).

[11] Habermas, as is well known, asserts the "colonization of the life-world" within capitalist societies thesis in his much-touted magnum opus, *Theory of Communicative Action* (1984, 1987a). However, because of the staggering scope of Habermas's critical theory of contemporary society, several of his other works should also be consulted, as they are in many senses inextricable from, and necessary for, an informed understanding of his distinct discourse. Hence, see also Habermas (1975, 1979, 1986a, 1986b, 1986c, 1987b, 1988, 1989a, 1989b, 1990, 1993, 1995, 1998a, 1998b, 2000, 2006, 2009, 2012).

BILL STRICKLAND

W.E.B. DU BOIS: EDUCATING STILL

As the decades pass, the appreciation of Du Bois will grow.
— *Herbert Aptheker, 1989*

"WE SHALL NOT SEE HIS LIKE AGAIN"

HOW DOES ONE RELATE to a legend? Because Du Bois's accomplishments, and his lifelong commitment to racial, social, and human progress are legendary: i.e., journalist and editor; educator and researcher; historian and sociologist; lecturer and dramatist; political and social activist; and, above all, writer of singular grace and depth; writer of precision — and prophecy — in that his famous prediction, "the problem of the twentieth century is the color line," accurately foretold the racial essence of the era that was only then unfolding. (Many people associate that insight with Du Bois's 1903 classic, *The Souls of Black Folk*. But, in reality, the prediction came even earlier: at the Pan-African Conference in London in 1900 when Du Bois authored the conference's appeal "To the Nations of the World.") But it was not only Du Bois's prediction that came true. Aptheker's did as well.

In the twilight of his life, Du Bois was invited to Ghana by Kwame Nkrumah to continue working on the *Encyclopedia Africana* project that he had originally embarked upon a half century before. After his death, in the late 1960s and early 1970s, limited recognition, in the United States, came in the form of youthful leftist groups who called themselves Du Bois Clubs. Meanwhile, outside America, the city of Berlin commemorated its six hundredth anniversary in 1989 by publishing a monograph entitled *Welcome to Berlin: Das Image Berlins in der englischsprachigen Welt von 1700 bis Heute* (*The Image of Berlin in the English-Speaking World from 1700 till Today*). That monograph contains a chapter on Du Bois, "Die Preussische Lehrjahre eines Schwarz amerikanischen Autor: W.E.B. Du Bois" ("The Prussian Learning Years of the Black American Writer: W.E.B. Du Bois").

The chapter referred to those nineteenth-century years, 1892–1894, when Du Bois studied at the University of Berlin. (It is ironic that a nation in which Du Bois spent only two years of his life — though he visited it five times — esteemed him more highly in the 1980s than did his native land.)

But gradually, as time passed, and as Aptheker had envisioned, to more and more Americans, Du Bois became an accepted — even iconic — figure. And nowhere was this about-face more surprising than in Du Bois's hometown of Great Barrington, which had no reason to doubt the veracity of his constant vilification by the local and national press over his allegedly too-much-akin-to-Russian Cold War politics.

Public opinion was indoctrinated against Du Bois because the U.S. government labeled him a communist "fellow-traveler" in 1949 because he was the U.S. sponsor of the Stockholm Peace Appeal "to banish the atomic bomb." But America called the appeal "a communist trick to disarm the West."[1] Two years later, in 1951, the government indicted Du Bois for working with the Peace Information Center and "not registering as a foreign agent."[2] That was supposed to be a criminal offense because the government had labeled the center "a communist front."

However, because the charge was groundless, the judge dismissed the case. But the government was still not through. Vindictively, it took away Du Bois's passport for seven years to prevent him from going abroad to advocate peace and/or inform the outside world about the continuing — and unsolved — racial problem "in the land of the free."

Race was an issue of great sensitivity to the American government because the Third World in the 1950s was beginning to stir and America's racial contradictions made it fair game for Soviet ridicule. It was no wonder then that Great Barrington, like America at large, succumbed to the anticommunist smears that demonized Du Bois.

But, slowly, after Du Bois's death, the scope of his manifold global contributions began to emerge from the shadows of propaganda to alter people's perception of his life. . . even in Great Barrington.

DU BOIS, GREAT BARRINGTON, AND MASSACHUSETTS' NATIVE SON

This belated embrace assumed many forms. For example, a Friends of Du Bois's Boyhood Site was formed in the 1990s following an archeological field school established at the site in 1982/83 by archeologists of the UMass Amherst Anthropology Department. (It has since excavated some 20,000 artifacts.)

A Du Bois mural was painted near the center of town. And in 2002 a Du Bois River Garden Park was named. There is a "Du Bois in Great Barrington" brochure and a walking tour of fifty Du Bois–connected places that visitors can take with a guide or do themselves. And now there are highway signs leading into Great Barrington that identify it as Du Bois's birthplace. So, as the Bible says, "Truth crushed to earth will rise again."

Moreover, Great Barrington was not the only institution in the state of Massachusetts that belatedly recognized Du Bois's historical worth. Harvard, his alma mater, now has a Du Bois Institute, while UMass Amherst created the W.E.B. Du Bois Department of Afro-American Studies as one of the first Black Studies programs in the nation — and before public recognition of Du Bois's role in black, American, and world history became widespread.

Indeed, one might even say that a unique Du Bois tradition developed at UMass, since the university houses the Du Bois Papers, has renamed its library after Du Bois, and, as mentioned previously, archeologists of its Anthropology Department, through their work on the Du Bois home site, have helped to build a sustaining bond between the university and Du Bois advocates in Great Barrington.

The latest demonstration of that UMass tradition, linking the university to Du Bois, is the exhibition *Du Bois in Our Time* that the Museum of Contemporary Art opened last September to commemorate the fiftieth anniversary of Du Bois's passing in 1963. The exhibition featured ten artists from the United States, Canada, and West Africa who were asked to submit works that they felt were in keeping with Du Bois's legacy. Thus, visual artists, artists in sculpture, photography, public space, and other fields contributed the exhibits that made up *Du Bois in Our Time*.

In the three-month period from September 10 to December 8, 2013, in which the visual exhibits were displayed, the museum also sponsored public events with the artists and Du Bois scholars to further explore the significance of Du Bois's legacy "in our time."

There was, for example, a panel about Du Bois's views on education called "Color Lines of Education," and another on the relation between art and politics that I served on, along with LaToya Ruby Frazier, the Braddock, Pennsylvania, artist-photographer, and Ann Messner, the public-space artist from New York. The panel was moderated by Susan Jahoda of the Art Department, who kicked off our panel discussion by reminding us of Du Bois's own views on art and politics:

> ...All art is propaganda and ever must be despite the whaling [*sic*] of the purists. I stand in utter shamelessness and say that whatever art I have for writing has been used always for propaganda. For gaining the right of black folk to love and enjoy. I do not care a damn for any art that is not used for propaganda. But I do care when propaganda *is confined to one side while the other is strict and silent*.[3] (emphasis mine)

One may conclude, therefore, that Du Bois recognized scant difference between art and prose. Both were to affirm the truth — and reality — of the black condition habitually kept "strict and silent" in America.

"SPEAKING TRUTH TO THE PEOPLE" — THEN AND NOW

This theme of the invisibility of black truth, and the artist's obligation to render it visible, is also the motivation behind one artist in the exhibition, the photographer LaToya Ruby Frazier, who decided to use her camera to lift up the debilitating racial curtain that Du Bois in *The Souls of Black Folk* called "the Veil":

> Herein lie buried many things which if read with patience may show the strange meaning of being black here in the dawning of the Twentieth Century....Leaving then, *the world of the white man, I have stepped within the Veil, raising it that you may view faintly its deeper recesses*...[4] (emphasis mine)

So what Du Bois saw "at the dawn of the twentieth century," LaToya saw — and sees still — in the twenty-first; and she too tries to lift the Veil:

> I'm LaToya Ruby Frazier. I'm an artist and a photographer from Braddock, Pennsylvania. Braddock, Pennsylvania, is an historic steel mill town that is home to Andrew Carnegie's first steel mill, the Edgar Thomson Works, which still operates today.

> When you come from a town like Braddock that's never addressed the historical racism and persecution against working-class people and African Americans...that moves me and concerns me and vexes me [so] *I picked up the camera and began photographing this painful reality... because I was told I didn't exist — I was invisible and it didn't matter.*
>
> *I began to use my camera as a weapon to fight back* against all the things I don't like about America: poverty, discrimination, and racism.[5] (emphasis mine)

LaToya Ruby Frazier uses her camera to fight back against the invisibility to which America has consigned her and the black and white underclass of Braddock, just as Du Bois used his pen and person to shed light upon "the Veil" of his era.

Another similarity is that both focus not on the South but on the North. Each seeks to tell the story of racial and capitalist relations in the same locale: the state of Pennsylvania.

Indeed LaToya Frazier's Braddock story is not all that different, though decades separate them, from Du Bois's story of the black Seventh Ward in his pathbreaking sociological study, *The Philadelphia Negro*:

> I settled in one room in the city over a cafeteria run by a college settlement in the worst part of the Seventh Ward. We lived there a year, in the midst of an atmosphere of dirt, drunkenness, poverty, and crime. Murder sat on our doorsteps, [and] police were our government...[6]

And if black people are still being shunted aside in LaToya Ruby Frazier's time, presumably in the 1980s and 1990s, as they were in the 1890s, when Du Bois wrote *The Philadelphia Negro* (1899), then clearly Du Bois's critique of what was racially astray then is as relevant in our time as it was in his. But deconstructing the American Democratic myth has its own perils.

DU BOIS AND THE STATE THAT CAN DO NO WRONG

In 1988, five years before his death, Du Bois, at the age of ninety, wrote the third version of the autobiography which had been minimally alluded to in *The Souls of Black Folk* (1903) and more substantially addressed in *Dusk of Dawn* (1940). In this final volume Du Bois summed up the conclusions about America that he had reached in those ninety years. His fundamental view was that America seemed incapable of acknowledging its basic flaws but instead sought always to punish its critics:

> America must never be criticized even by honest and sincere men. America must always be praised and extravagantly praised, or you lose your job, or are ostracized or land in jail. Criticism is treason or the hint of treason testified to by hired liars....But honest men may and must criticize America. Describe how she has ruined her democracy, sold out her jury system, and led the seats of justice astray.[7]

Of course Du Bois was himself the archetype of the critic that America would not tolerate, an animosity which is substantiated in Ann Messner's museum exhibit of the FBI's redacted files on Du Bois.

Though heavily censored, the files, which deal with the years 1942 to 1960, give some idea of the wide-ranging and biased nature of the FBI's surveillance of Du Bois. They reveal, for instance, that the FBI monitored his travels nationwide, since there are reports sent to FBI headquarters in Washington from local offices in New York, Atlanta, Chicago, and Washington itself.

Agents covered his talks and appearances and read and commented on his books. With great interest they sought out his thoughts on the international situation. They kept track of whatever news there was about him in the newspapers and recruited informants to spy on him, ad infinitum. And without evidence they passed on hearsay that Du Bois was "a suspected... reputed or concealed communist." (In fact Du Bois did not join the Communist Party until 1961 but did not hide the fact that he favored socialism.) [8]

Every rumor, allegation, or biased opinion was grain for the FBI's anti–Du Bois mill. They even reported on his marriage to Shirley Graham and where the newlyweds were going for their honeymoon! (This absolutely vital information was passed on to all "appropriate agencies" as "a security matter.") [9]

However, what can be gleaned from these extracts of the released, but redacted, FBI files is that they represent only a tad of the FBI's tracking of Du Bois, since as far back as 1919 we know that a new staff member of the General Intelligence Division (forerunner of the FBI), twenty-four-year-old J. Edgar Hoover, submitted a report to Attorney General A. Mitchell Palmer entitled "Radicalism and Sedition Among Negroes as Reflected in Their Publications." Of course Du Bois's *Crisis* magazine was specifically slandered because it "provided Palmer's Department of Justice with abundant and unambiguous evidence of sedition and conspiracy, *or so it would claim*." [10] (emphasis mine)

But although Ann Messner turned the FBI files that she obtained into an accessible narrative for the exhibition, on our panel she pointed out the obfuscatory function of the redactions:

> ...the degree of what's taken out and removed [includes]... what they were doing, how they were following him and what they were saying about him — really speaks to the degree to which they attempted to silence and prevent him [from being effective]. Most of what was written by the FBI was blacked out [and] *we still today are not allowed to see fully what they were doing.* [11] (emphasis mine)

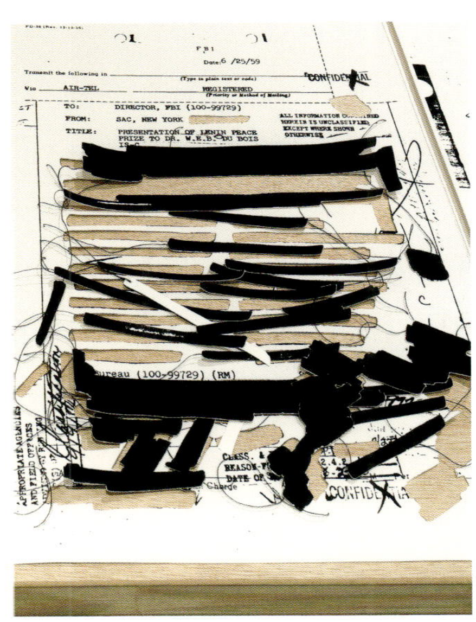

ANN MESSNER
Du Bois: The FBI Files (detail), 2013
Installation consisting of 447 running foot incised digital scroll (handcut stenciled redaction), printed on Hahnemühle FA paper; 22 foot table inset with 6 in-wall MP5 Niles speakers, CD players, 4 CDs (audio component of the installation)

So what has the exhibition taught us? That there are artists today who, like Du Bois, are utilizing their skills to illuminate to the ignored, the exploited, the unknowing, and the honest among us that there are structural and moral flaws in America. Especially in the unfairness visited upon those still made invisible by "the Veil."

EPILOGUE: SO WHAT HAS CHANGED?

Then (1930):

"*Rescue the Housatonic* and clean it as we have never in all the years thought before of cleaning it....Restore its ancient beauty; making it the center of a town, of a valley, and perhaps — Who knows? *Of a new measure of civilized life.*" W.E.B. Du Bois (emphasis mine)

Now (2013):

> The new series of photographs I have on view in the exhibit is called *A Despoliation of Water: From the Housatonic to Monongahela River.*
>
> I went up in a helicopter and flew over the Monongahela River and followed it from Braddock to Pittsburgh; photographing all the industrial waste...
>
> *I'm advertising the end results of capitalism and the destruction of the environment which has destroyed the bodies of the people that are there...*
>
> I'm giving you an X-ray of the decades of debris and degradation of the environment.[12] LaToya Ruby Frazier (emphasis mine)

So what has changed?

The river whose condition Du Bois lamented more than eight decades ago is, according to LaToya, violated still.

And the surveillance that marked the government's umbilical relation to Du Bois, Edward Snowden reveals, is replicated today by the fact that the NSA monitors us all. So our constitutional rights lie shredded in the government's political dumpster...

Julian Assange and Glen Greenwald — of WikiLeaks and *The Guardian* — must flee abroad, and Chelsea (Bradley) Manning is sentenced to thirty-four years in jail for disclosing the military barbarism that treats Afghan lives as meaningless pawns to play with.

And here at home we are told that, in the name of counterterrorism, the government claims the right to take the life of an American citizen anywhere in the world — without due process — and without accountability.

So something has changed. It is no longer the individual Du Boises that the State sees as fair game. It is all of us.

We are now, like Du Bois, the potential prey of the State. That is why we must use every means, including art, to rend the modern concealing "Veil."

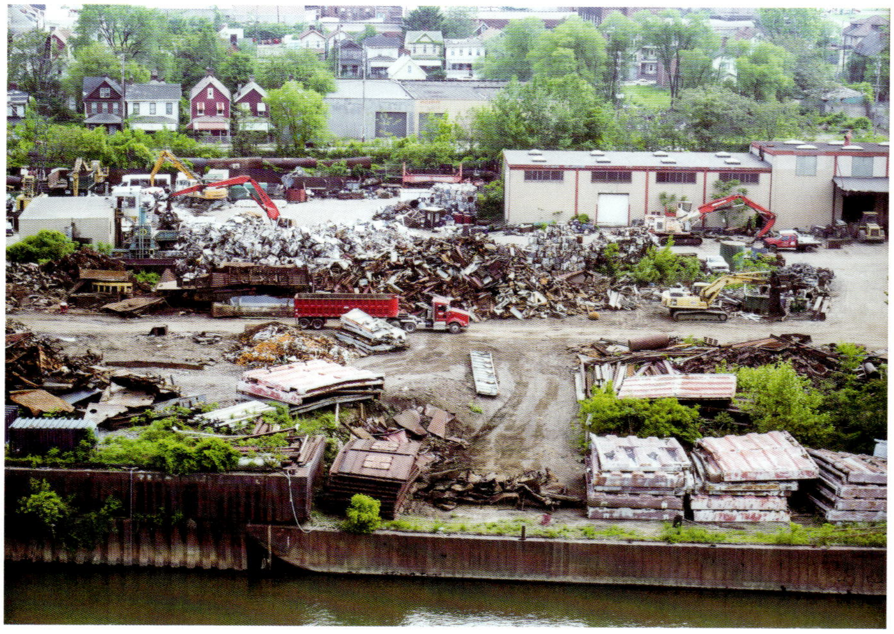

LATOYA RUBY FRAZIER
from *A Despoliation of Water: From the Housatonic to Monongahela River (1930–2013)*
Washington Avenue and Monongahela River, 2013
Duratrans, 27¼" x 38¼"

NOTES

[1] W.E.B. Du Bois, *Autobiography of W.E.B. Du Bois* (New York: International, 1988), p. 20.

[2] David Levering Lewis, *W.E.B. Du Bois: The Fight for Equality and the American Century, 1919–1963,* vol. 2 (New York: Henry Holt, 2001), p. 547.

[3] From Du Bois's lecture "Criteria of Negro Art," given at the 1926 NAACP convention in Chicago; later published in the December 1926 issue of the NAACP's *Crisis* magazine.

[4] "The Forethought," *The Souls of Black Folk* (New York: Vintage, 1990), p. 3.

[5] LaToya Ruby Frazier, exhibition symposium panel "Art and Politics," November 13, 2013.

[6] W.E.B. Du Bois, *Autobiography*, p. 195.

[7] Ibid., p. 417.

[8] "But what is socialism? It is the disciplined economy and political organization in which the first duty of a citizen is to serve the state; and the state is not a selected aristocracy or a group of self-seeking oligarchs who have seized wealth and power. No! The mass of workers with hand and brain are the ones whose collective destiny is the chief object of all effort." Du Bois, *Autobiography*, p. 402.

[9] Ann Messner, exhibition symposium panel "Art and Politics," November 13, 2013.

[10] Lewis, *W.E.B. Du Bois: The Fight for Equality and the American Century*, p. 5.

[11] Exhibition symposium panel "Art and Politics," November 13, 2013.

[12] Ibid.

ARTWORKS

RADCLIFFE BAILEY
MARY EVANS
BRENDAN FERNANDES
LATOYA RUBY FRAZIER
JULIE MEHRETU
ANN MESSNER
JEFFERSON PINDER
TIM ROLLINS & K.O.S.
MICKALENE THOMAS
CARRIE MAE WEEMS

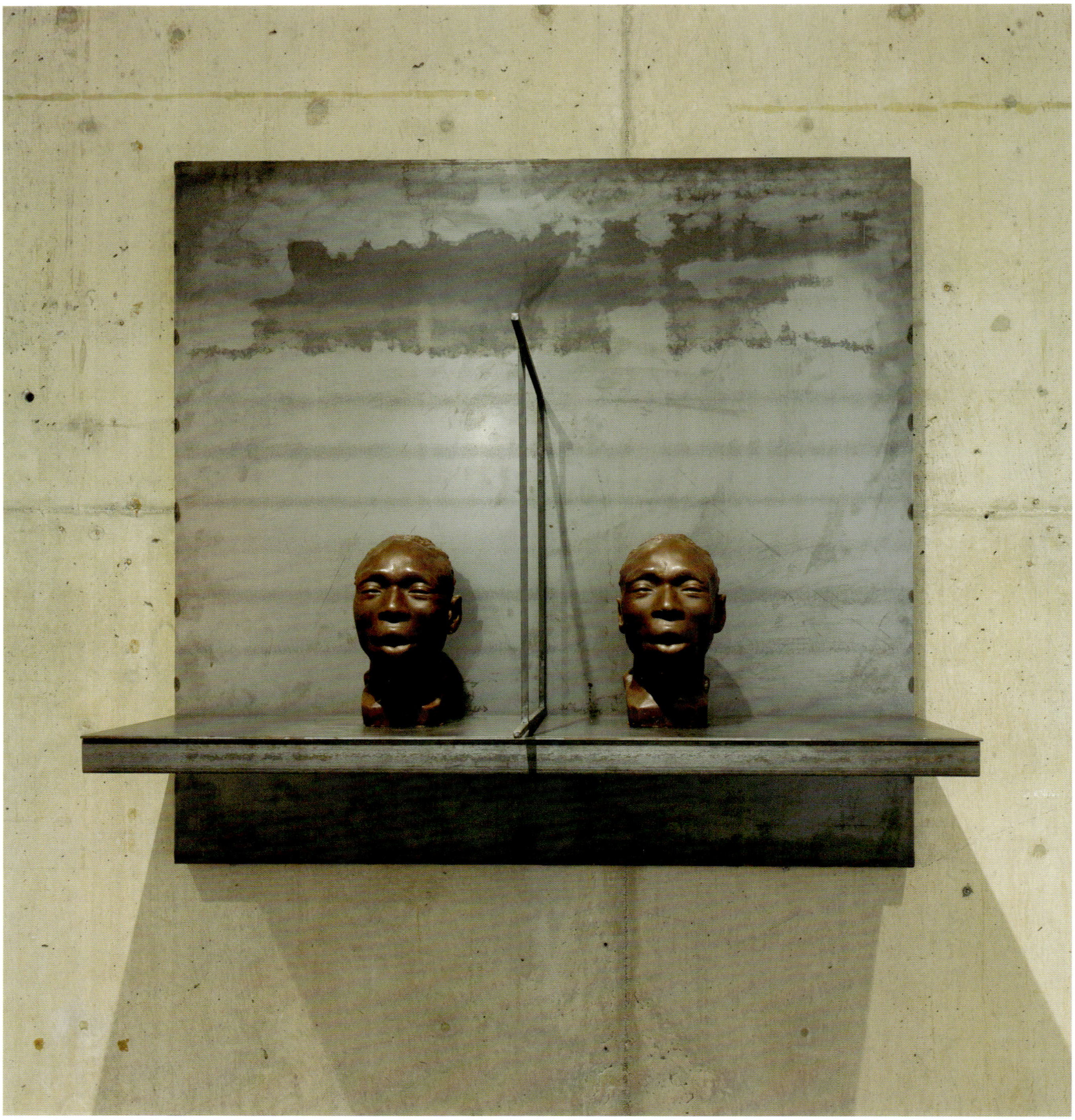

RADCLIFFE BAILEY

Above
RADCLIFFE BAILEY
Untitled, 2013
Bronze, wood
42″ x 24¼″ x 17″
Courtesy of the artist and Jack Shainman Gallery, New York

Opposite
RADCLIFFE BAILEY
Double Consciousness, 2013
Steel, wax
48″ x 48″ x 17″
Courtesy of Ralph Citino, Philadelphia

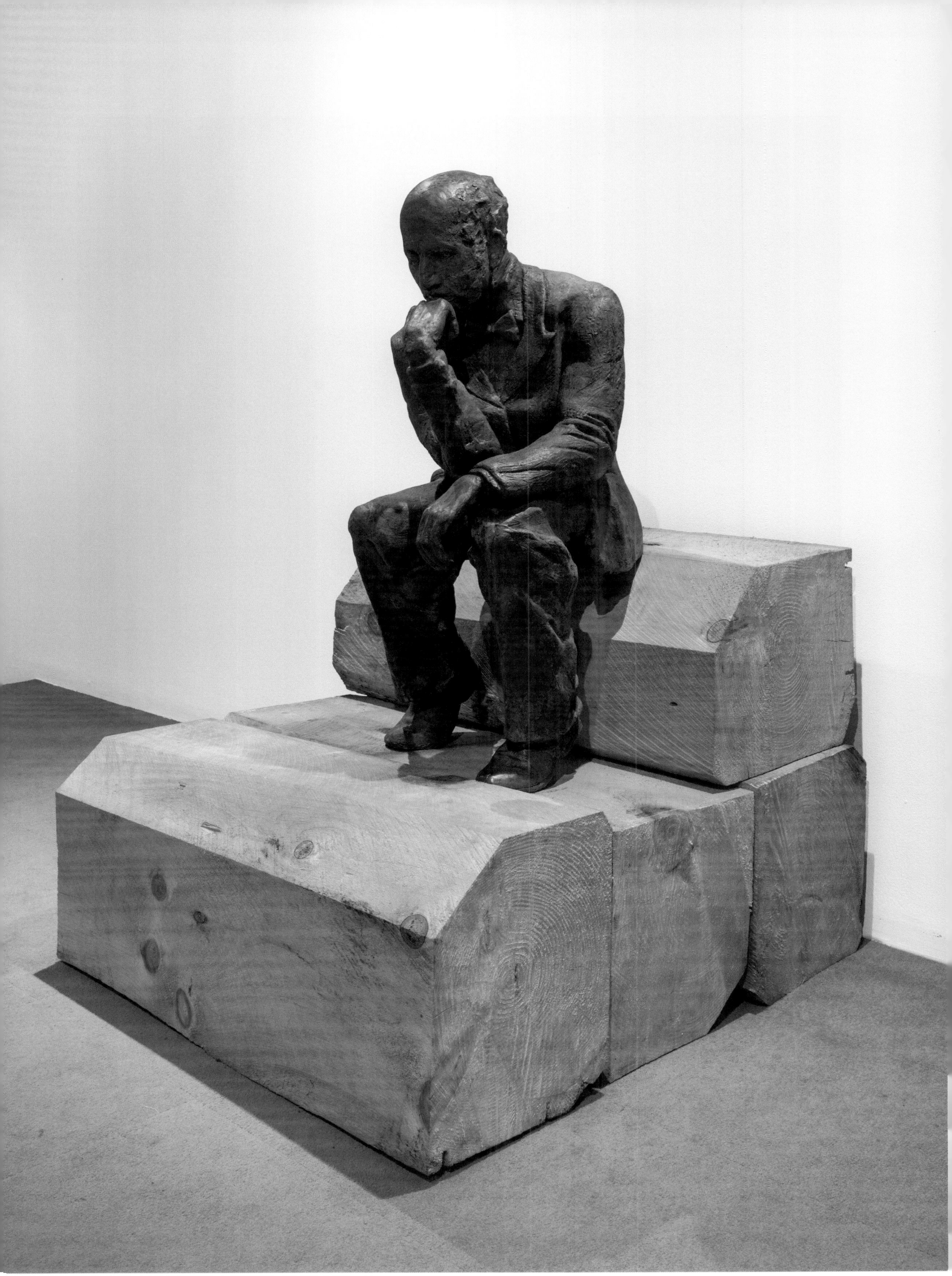

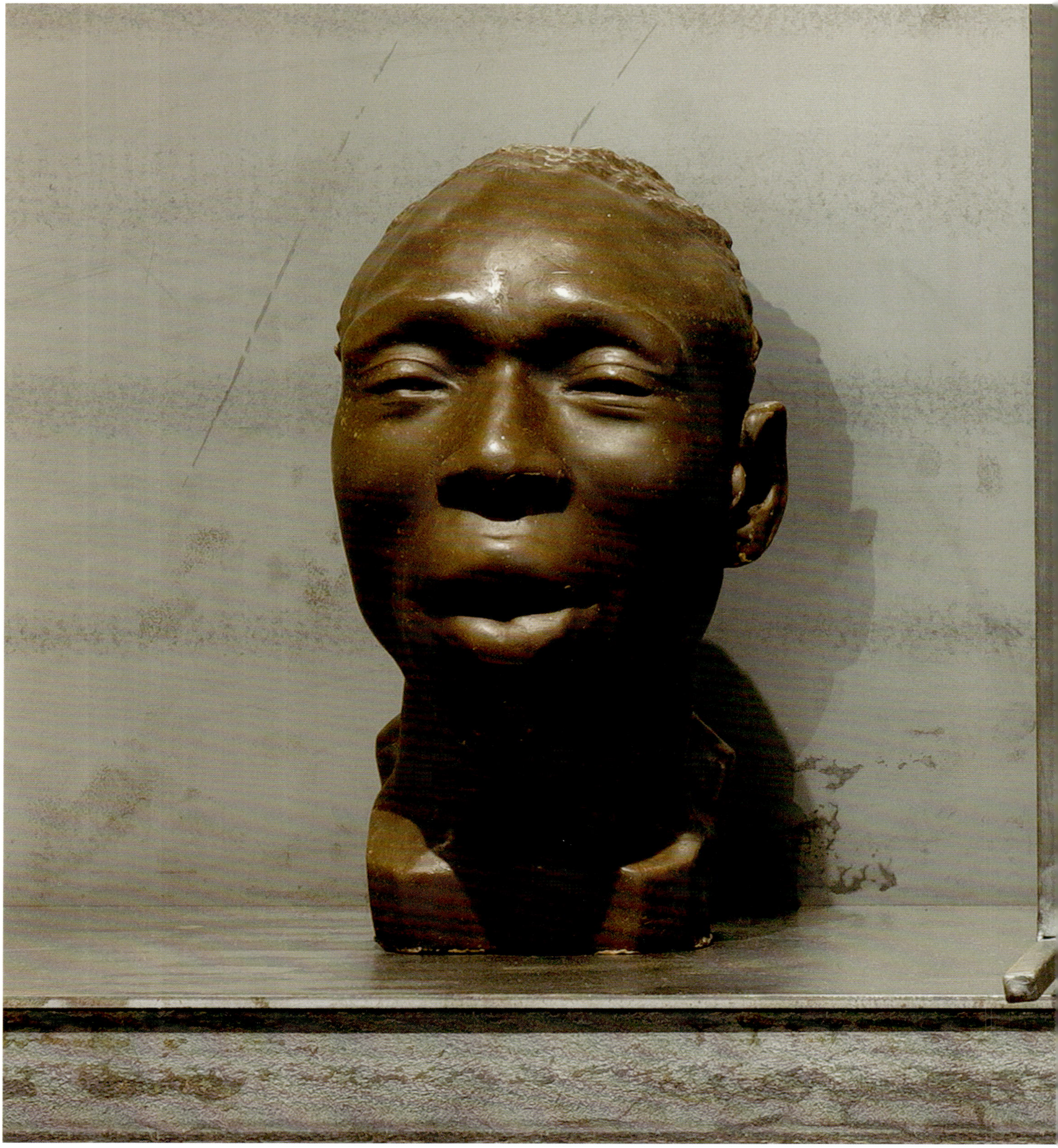

RADCLIFFE BAILEY
Double Consciousness, 2013 *(detail)*
Steel, wax
48″ x 48″ x 17″
Courtesy of Ralph Citino, Philadelphia

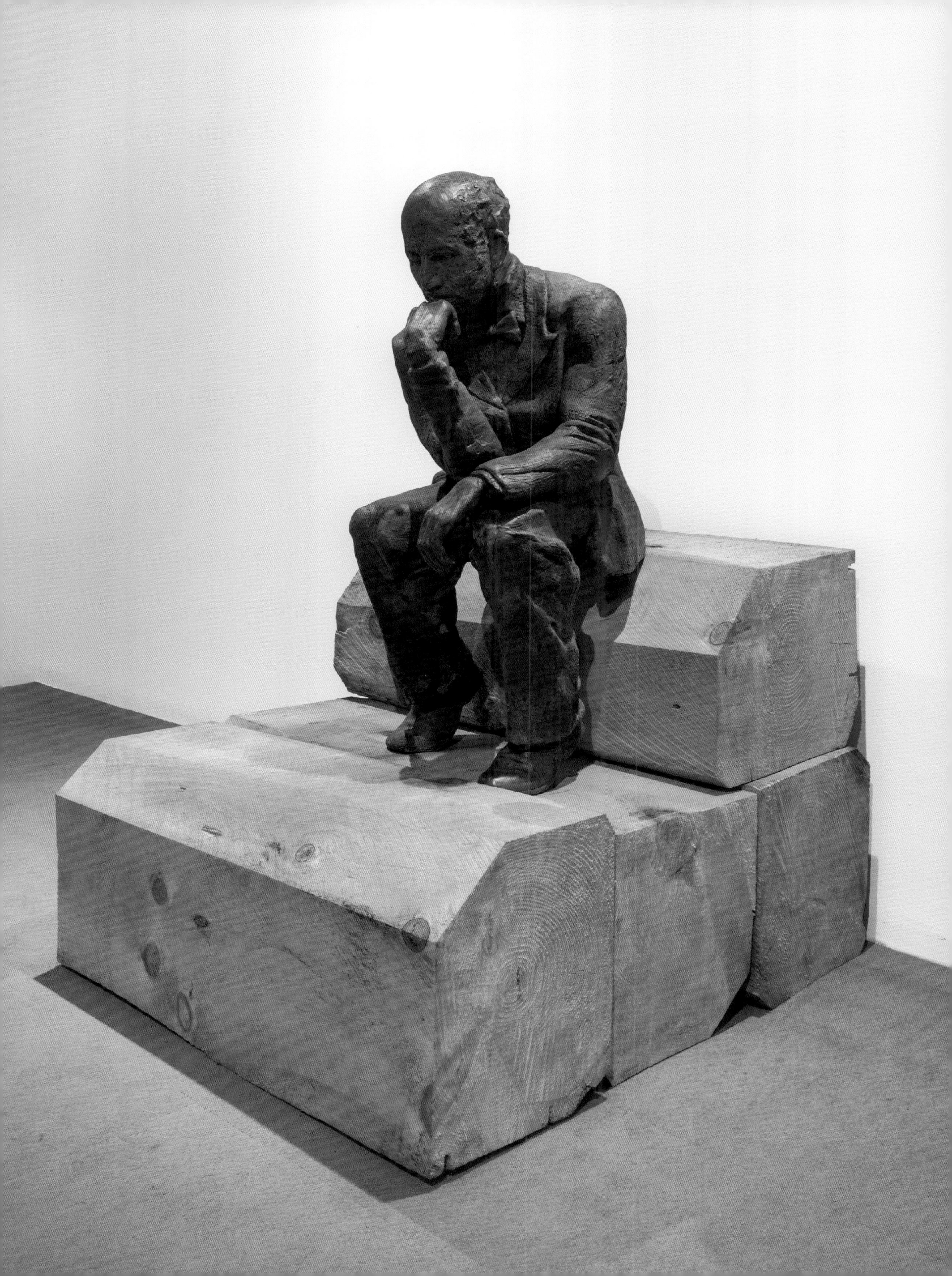

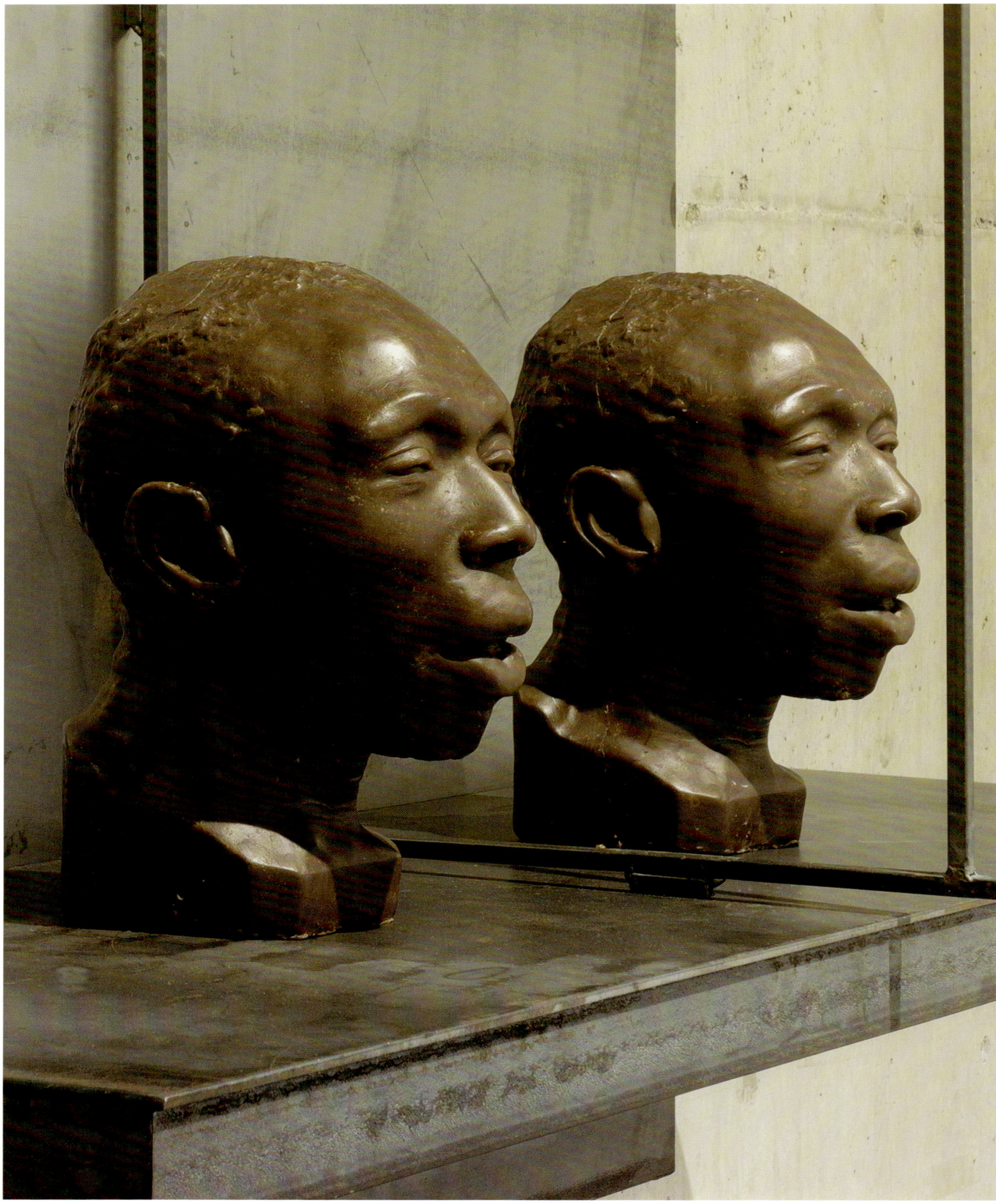

RADCLIFFE BAILEY
Double Consciousness, 2013 *(detail)*
Steel, wax
48″ x 48″ x 17″
Courtesy of Ralph Citino, Philadelphia

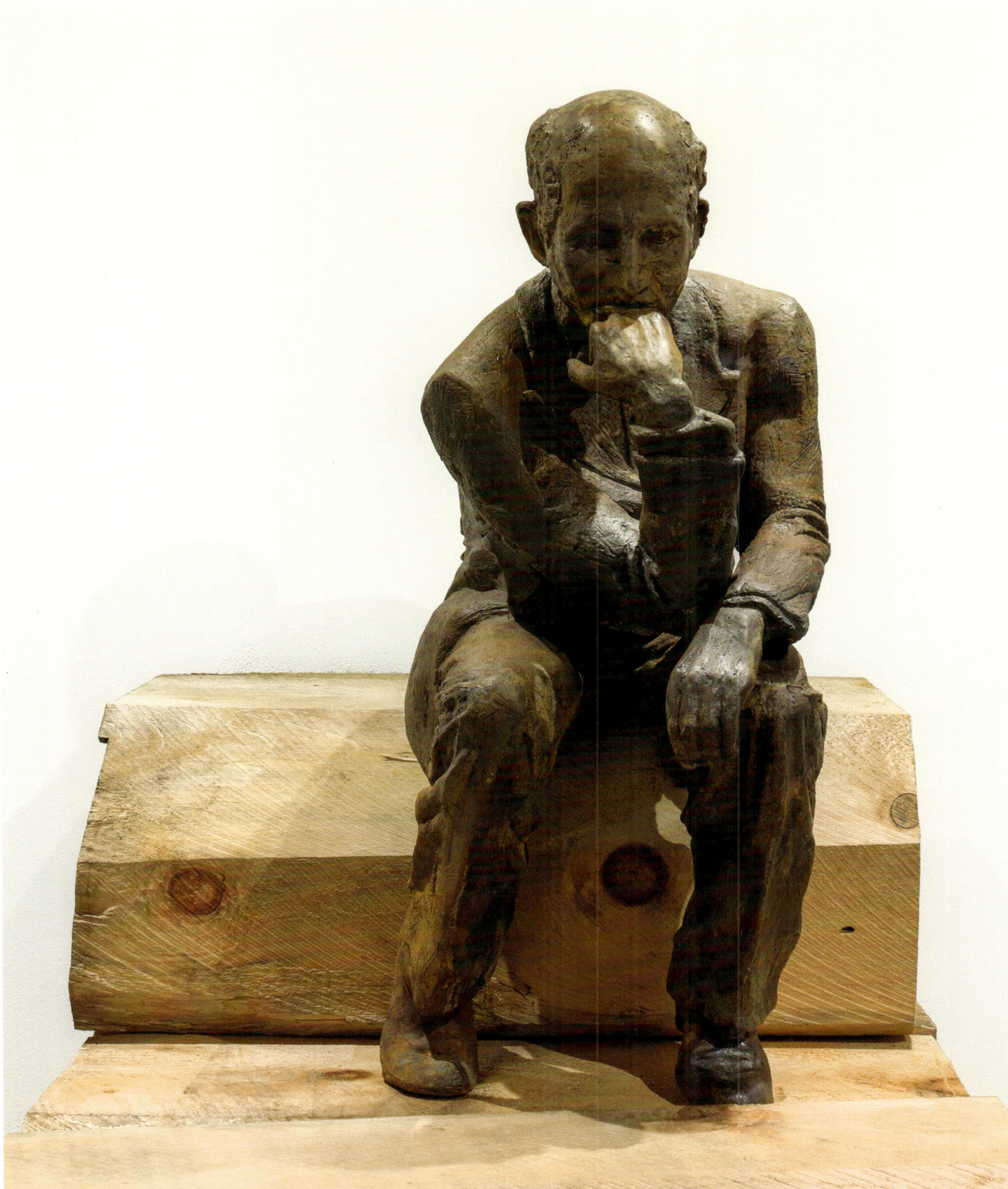

RADCLIFFE BAILEY
Untitled, 2013 *(detail)*
Bronze, wood
42″ x 24¼″ x 17″
Courtesy of the artist and
Jack Shainman Gallery, New York

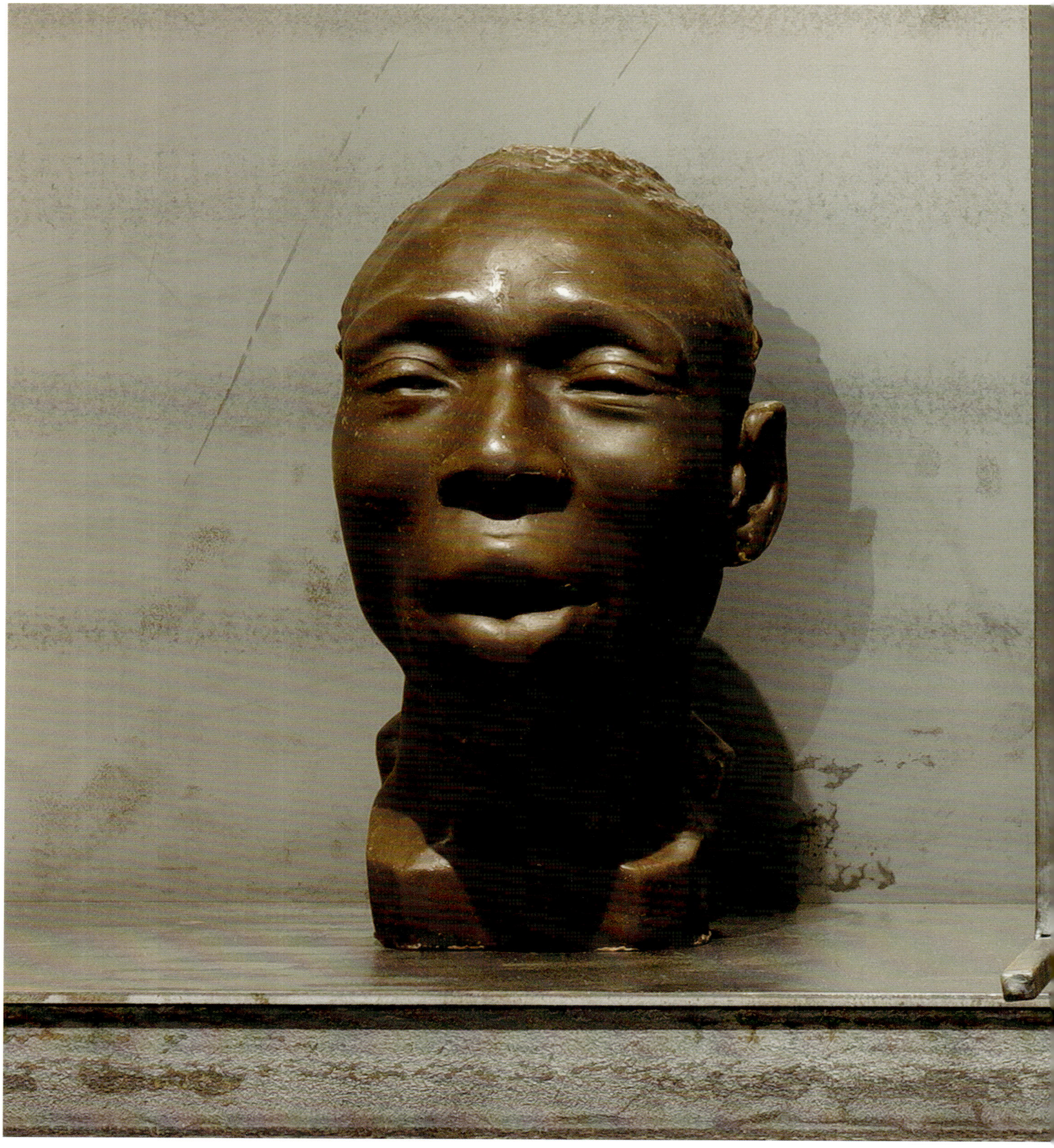

RADCLIFFE BAILEY
Double Consciousness, 2013 *(detail)*
Steel, wax
48″ x 48″ x 17″
Courtesy of Ralph Citino, Philadelphia

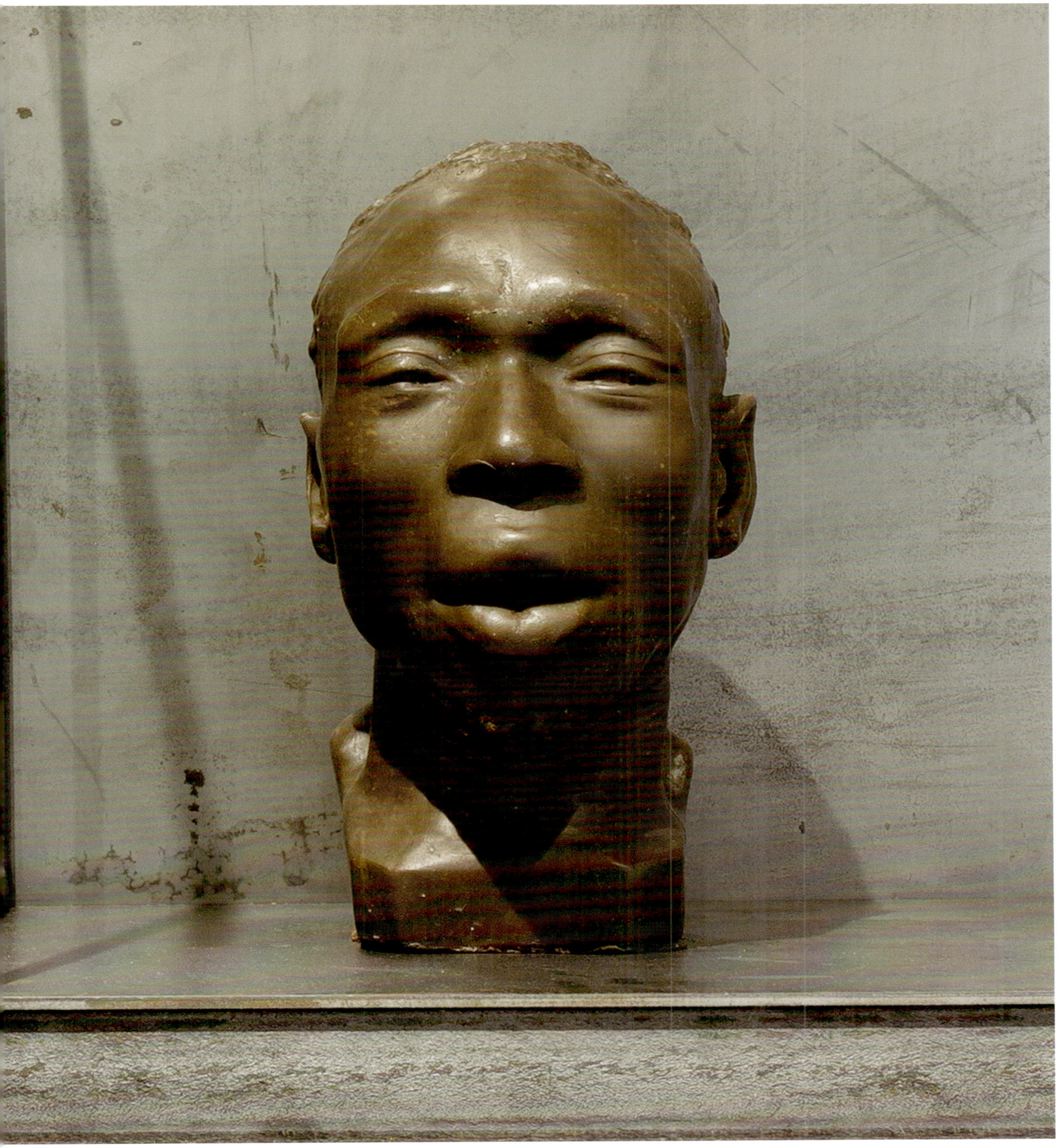

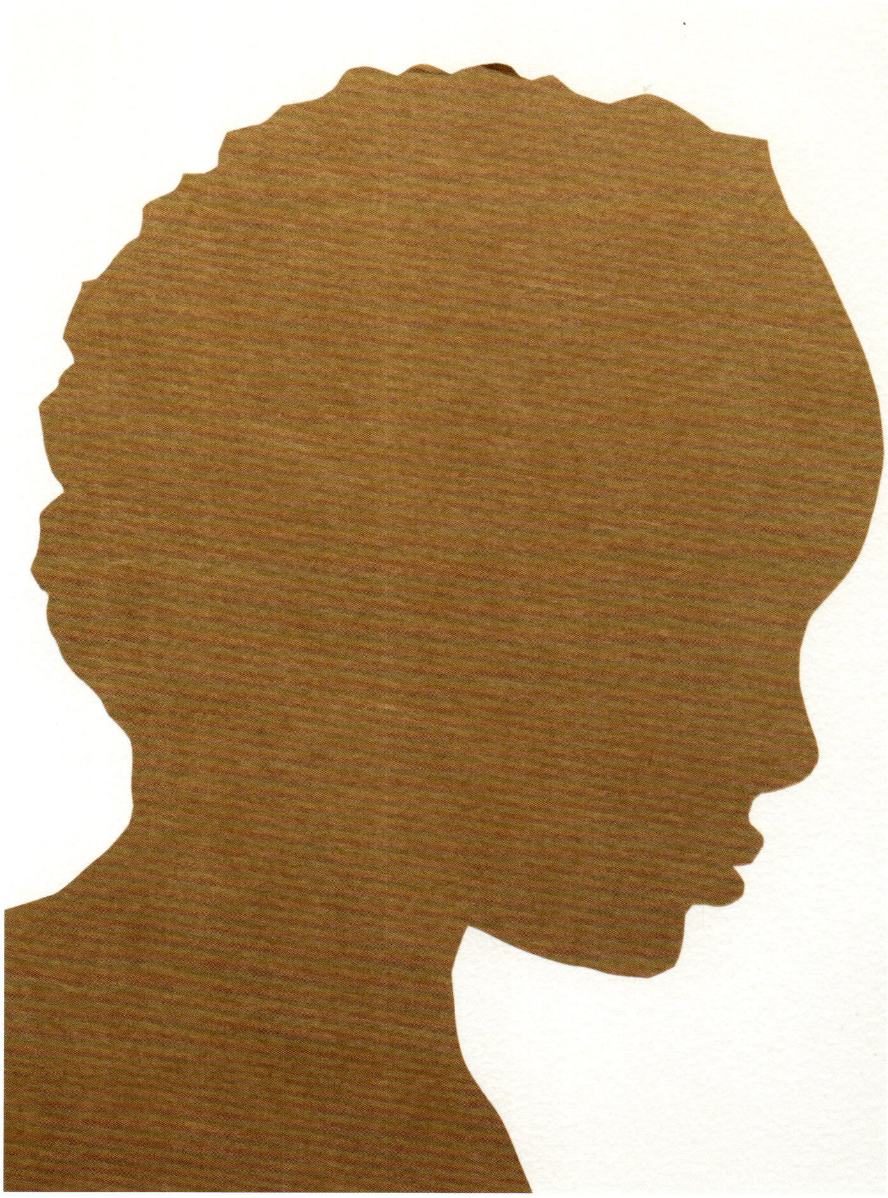

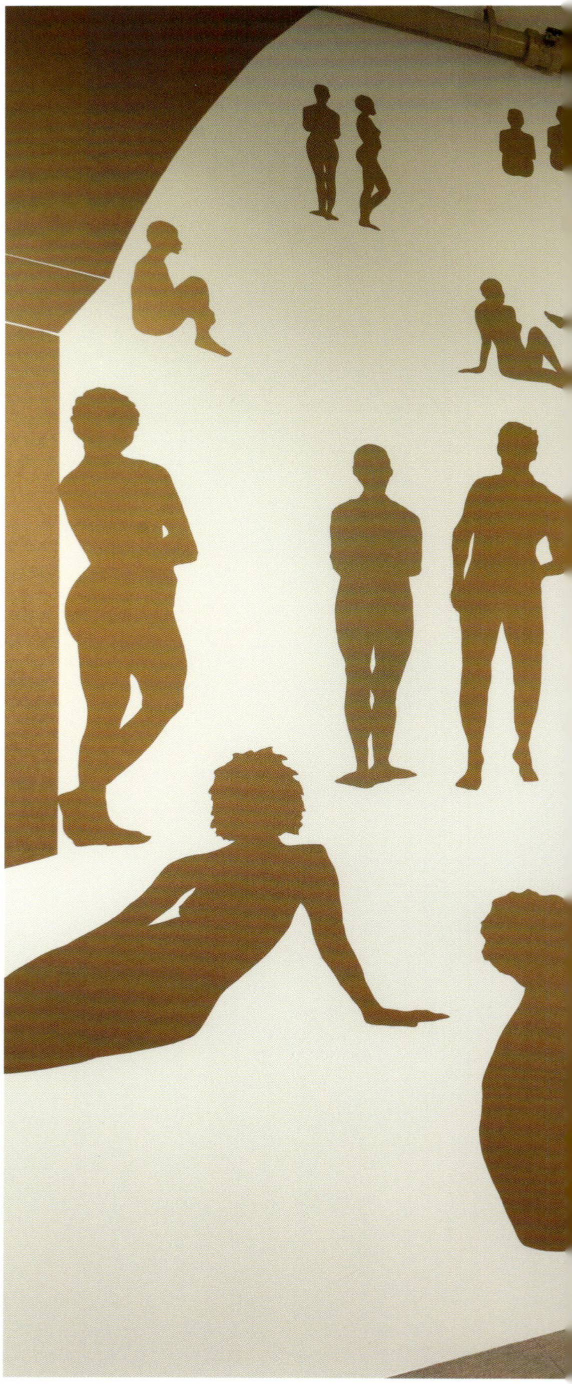

Left
MARY EVANS
Held, February 23, 2013 *(detail)*
Kraft paper
Dimensions variable
Courtesy of the artist

Right
MARY EVANS
Held, February 23, 2013
Kraft paper
Dimensions variable
Courtesy of the artist

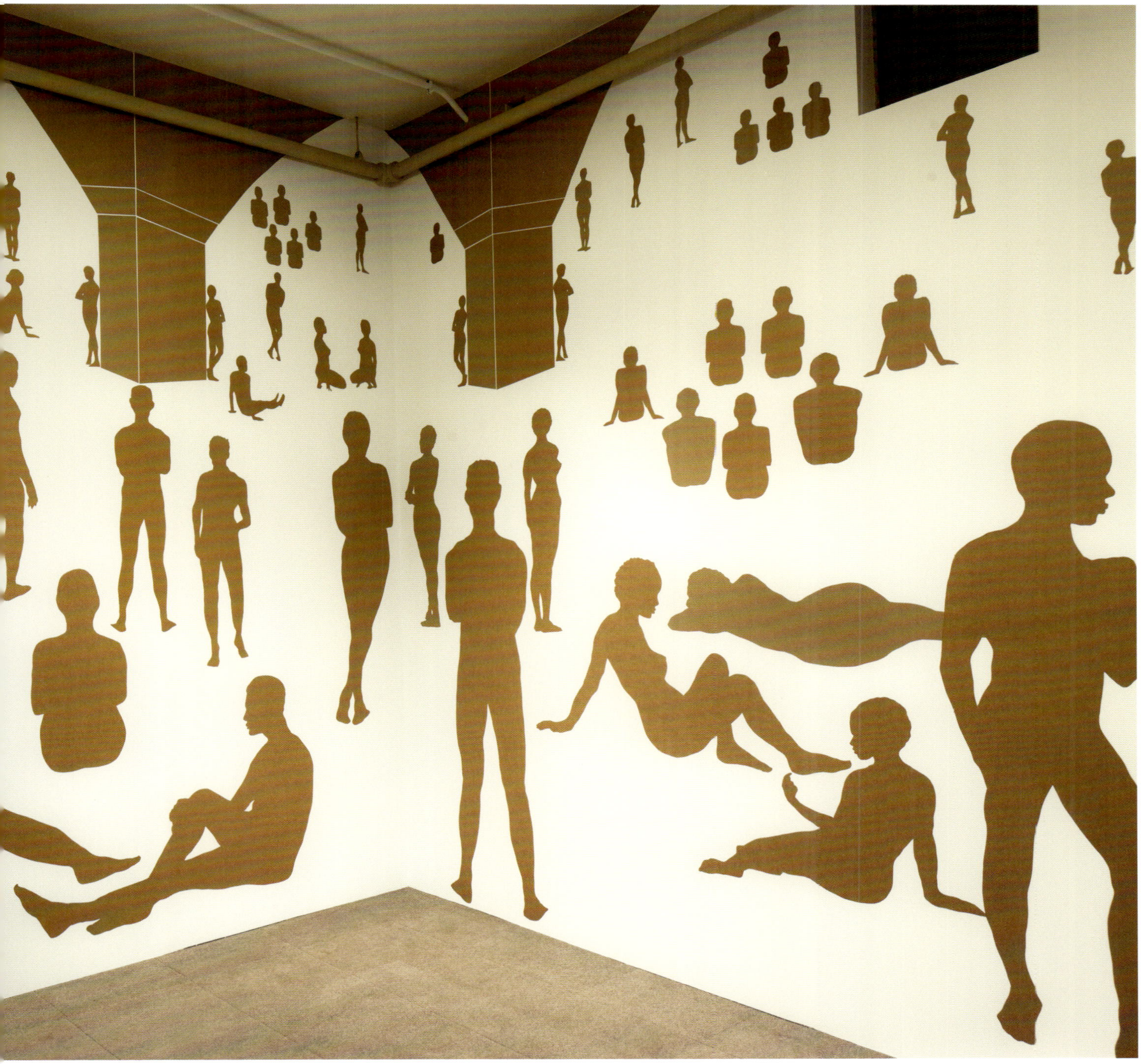

MARY EVANS

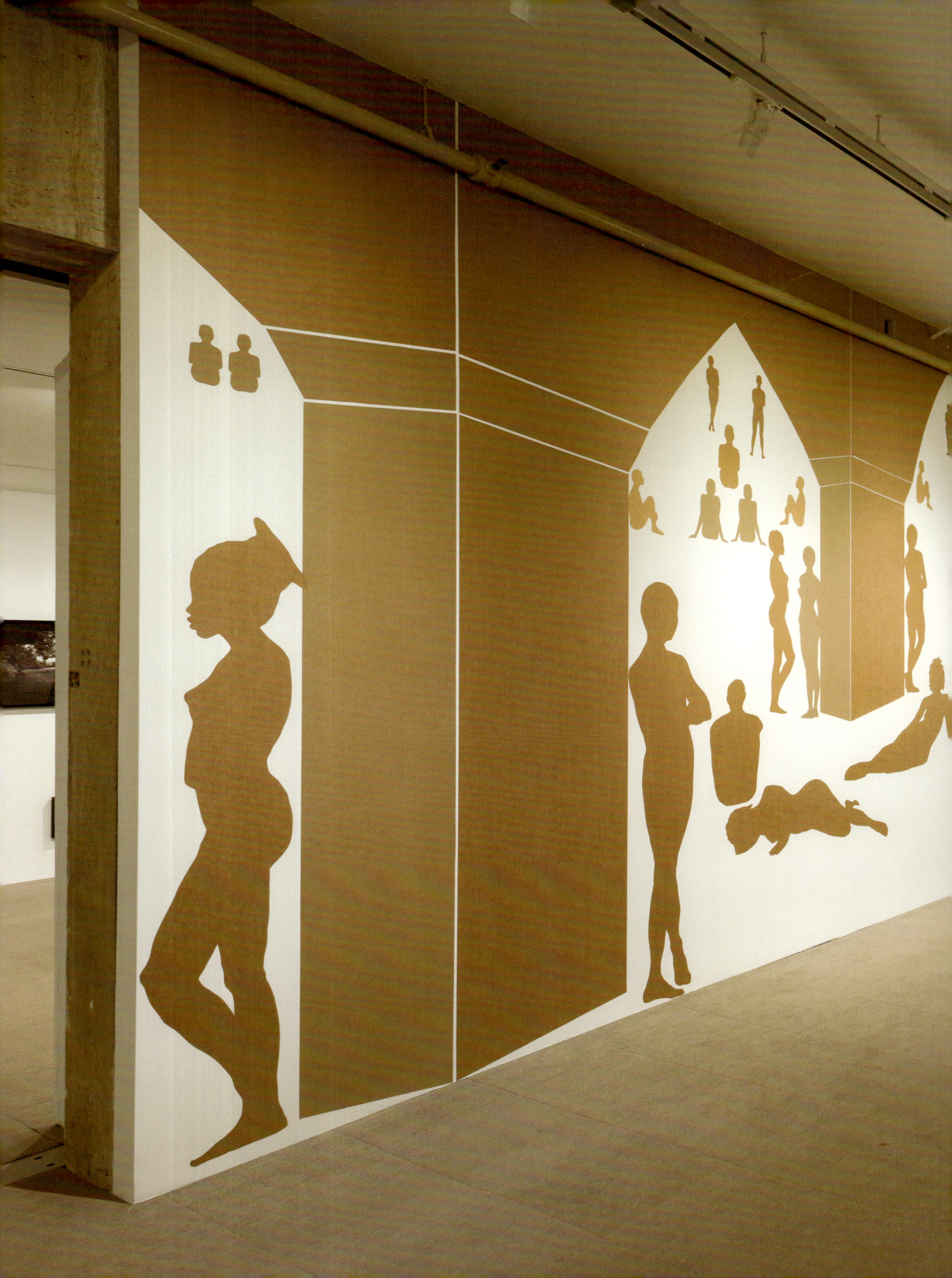

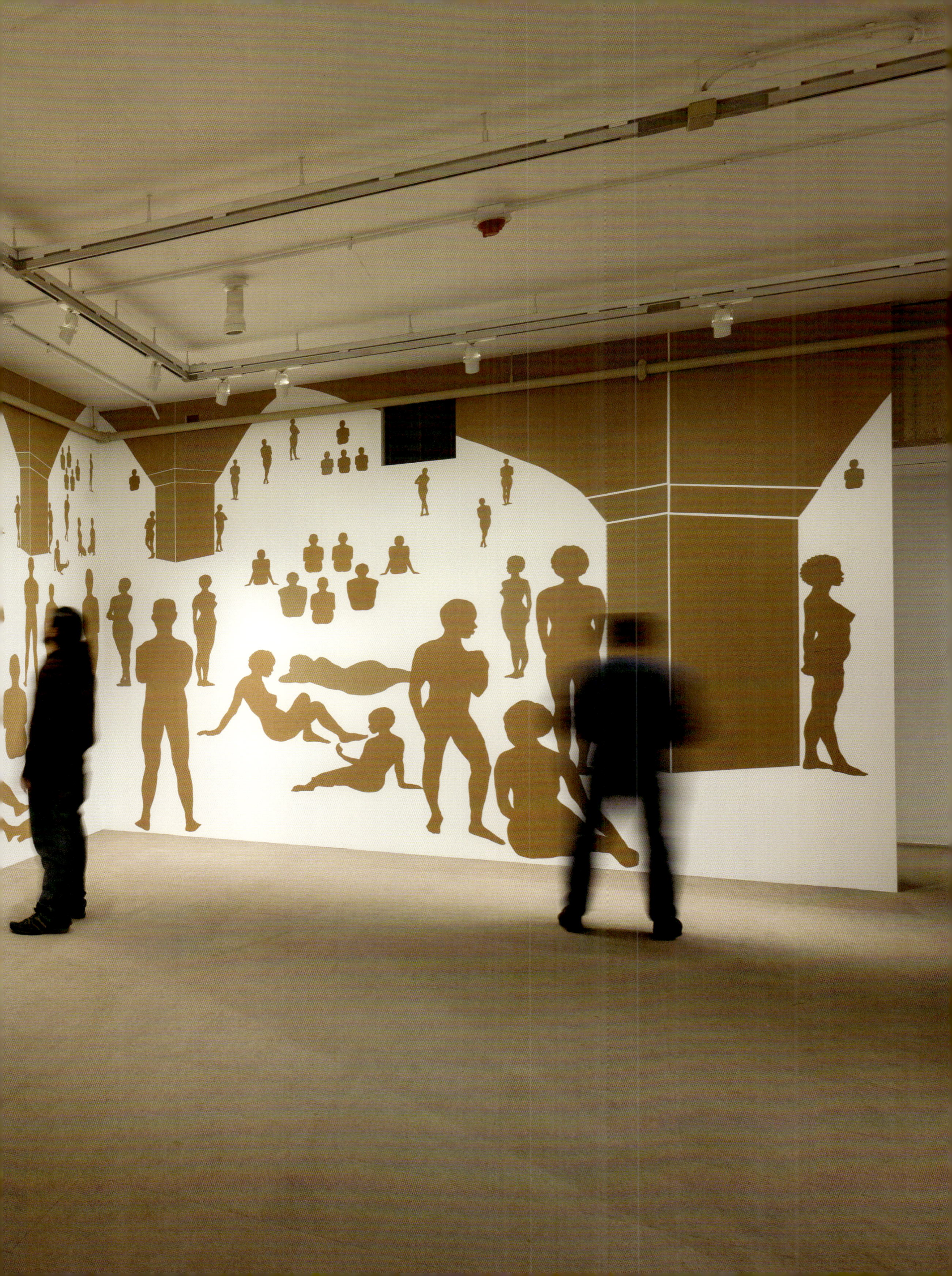

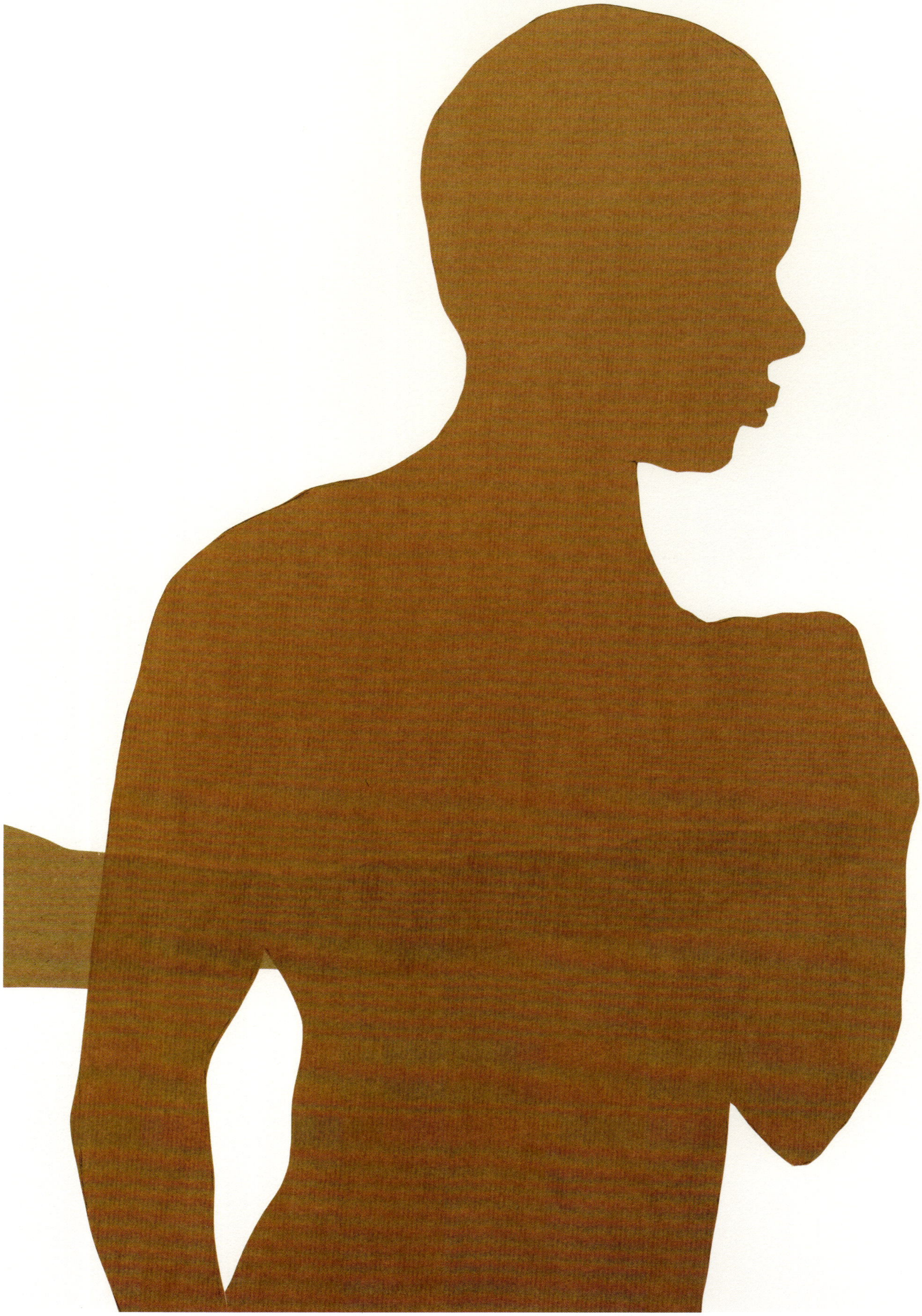

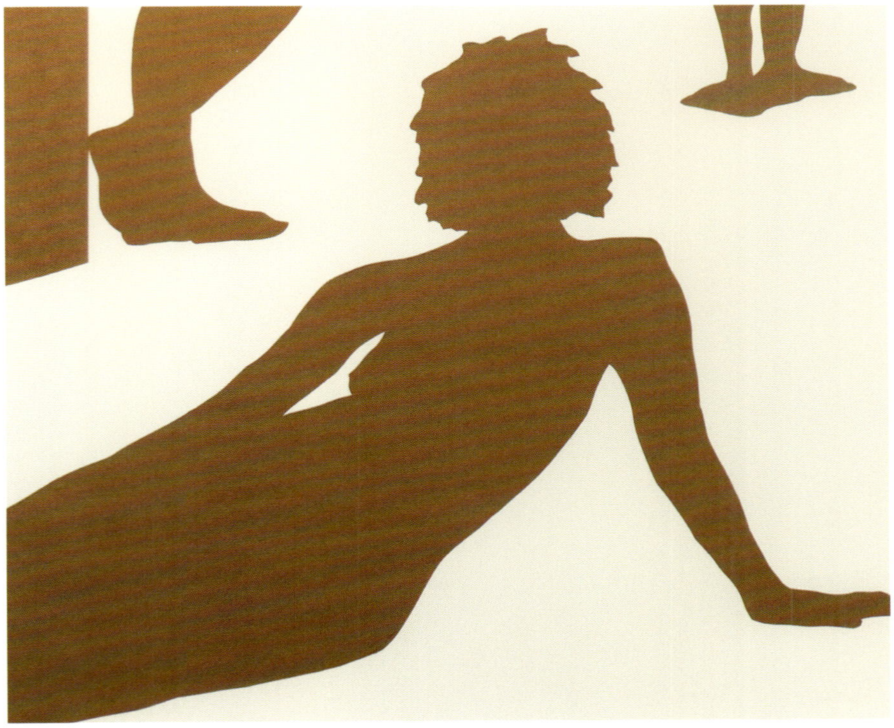

Preceding spread
Installation view

Left and right
MARY EVANS
Held, February 23, 2013
(details)
Kraft paper
Dimensions variable
Courtesy of the artist

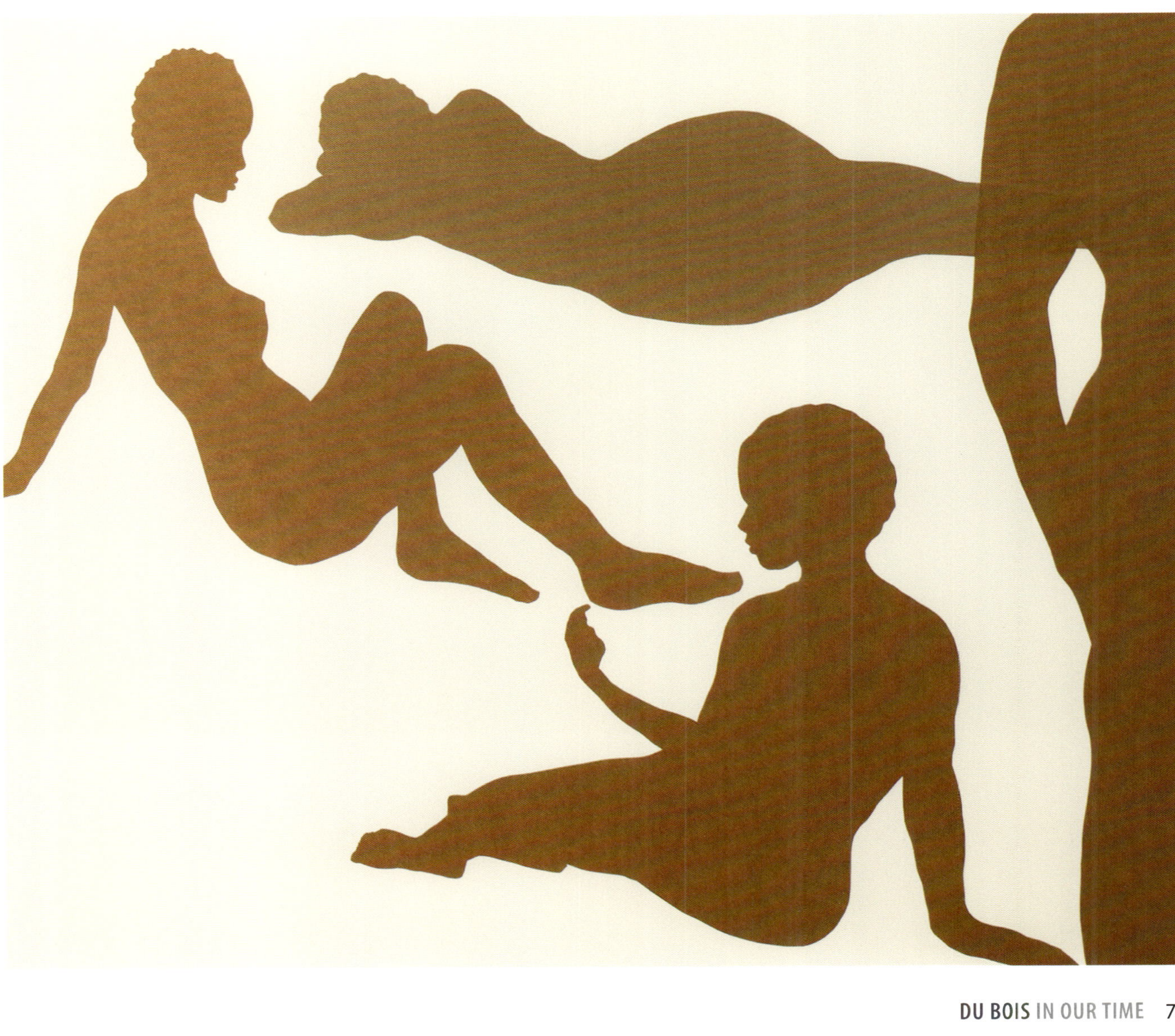

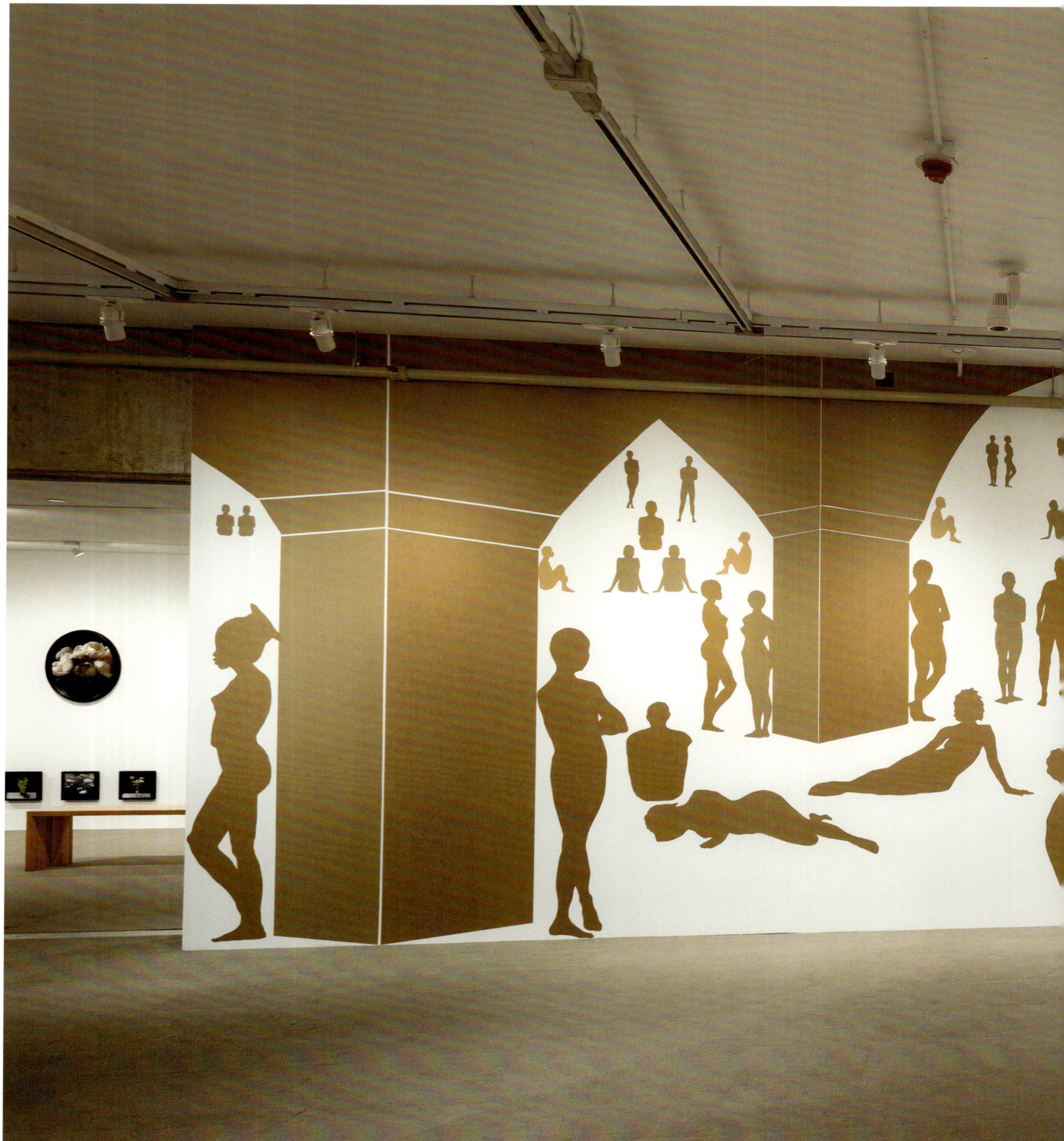

MARY EVANS
Held, February 23, 2013
Installation view
Kraft paper
Dimensions variable
Courtesy of the artist

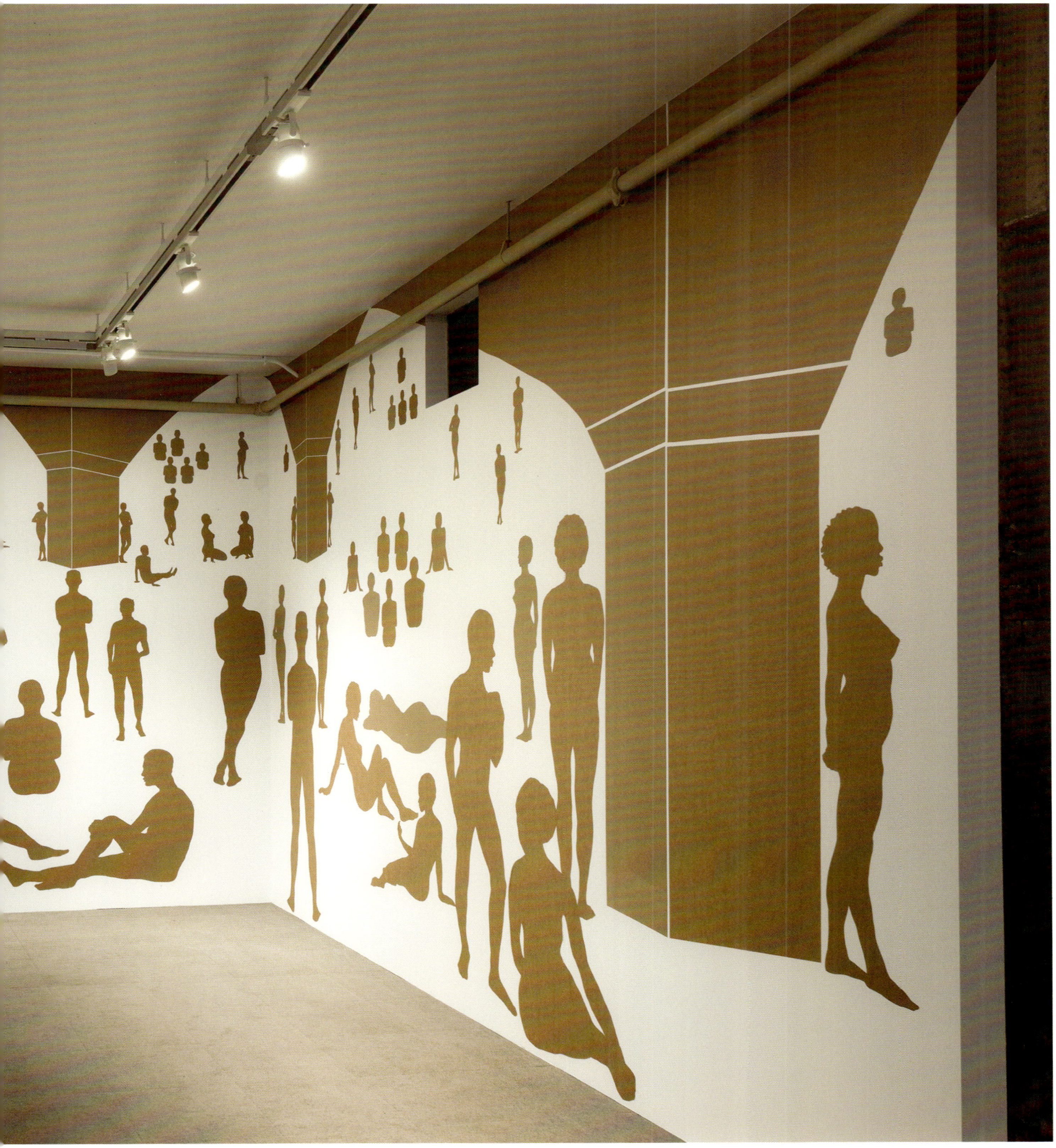

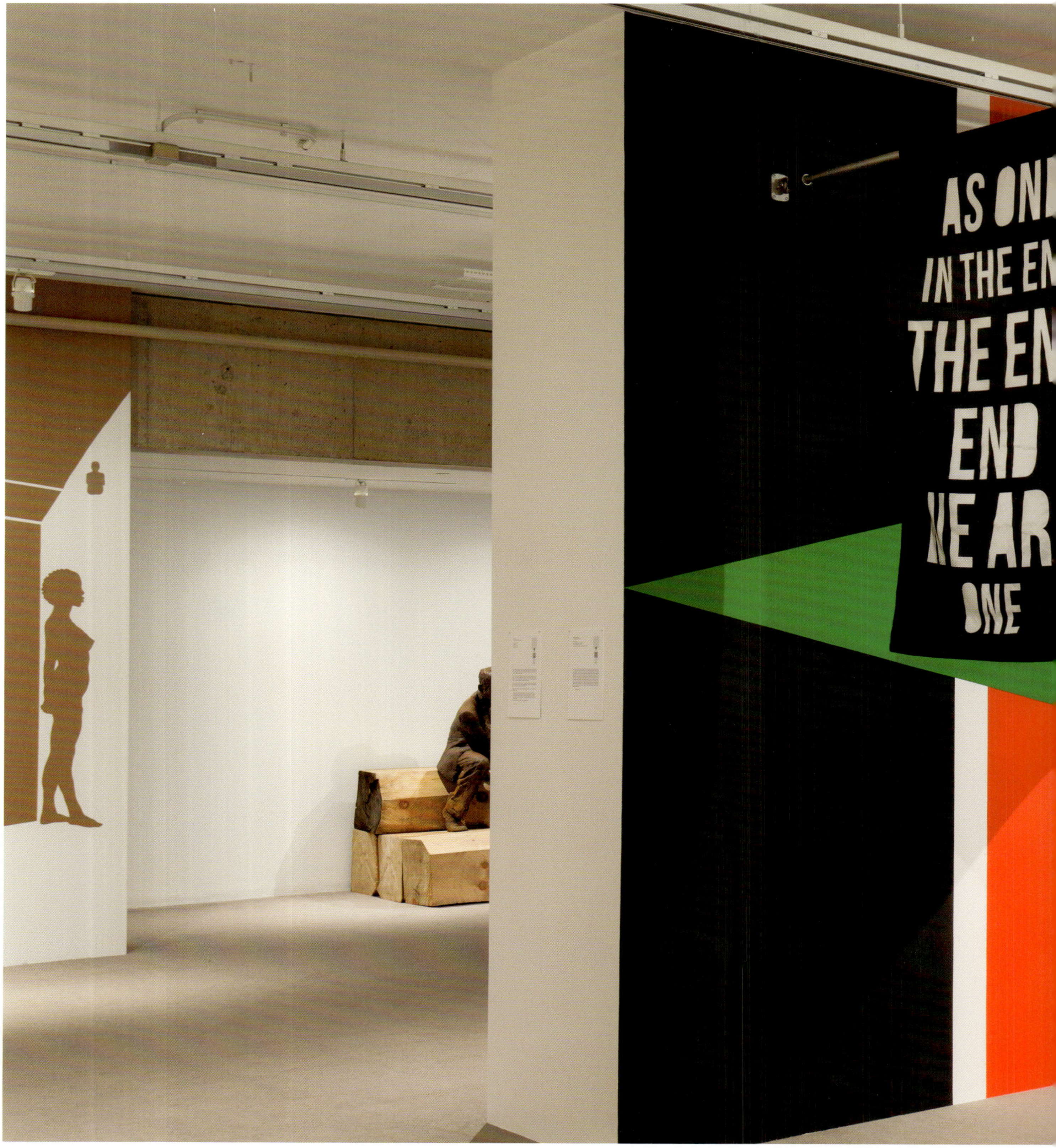

BRENDAN FERNANDES
In The End, 2013
Screen-printed flags, painted wall mural
Flags – 5′ x 3′, Mural – 11′ 4″ x 18′ 5″
Installation view
Collection of the artist and Diaz Contemporary, Toronto

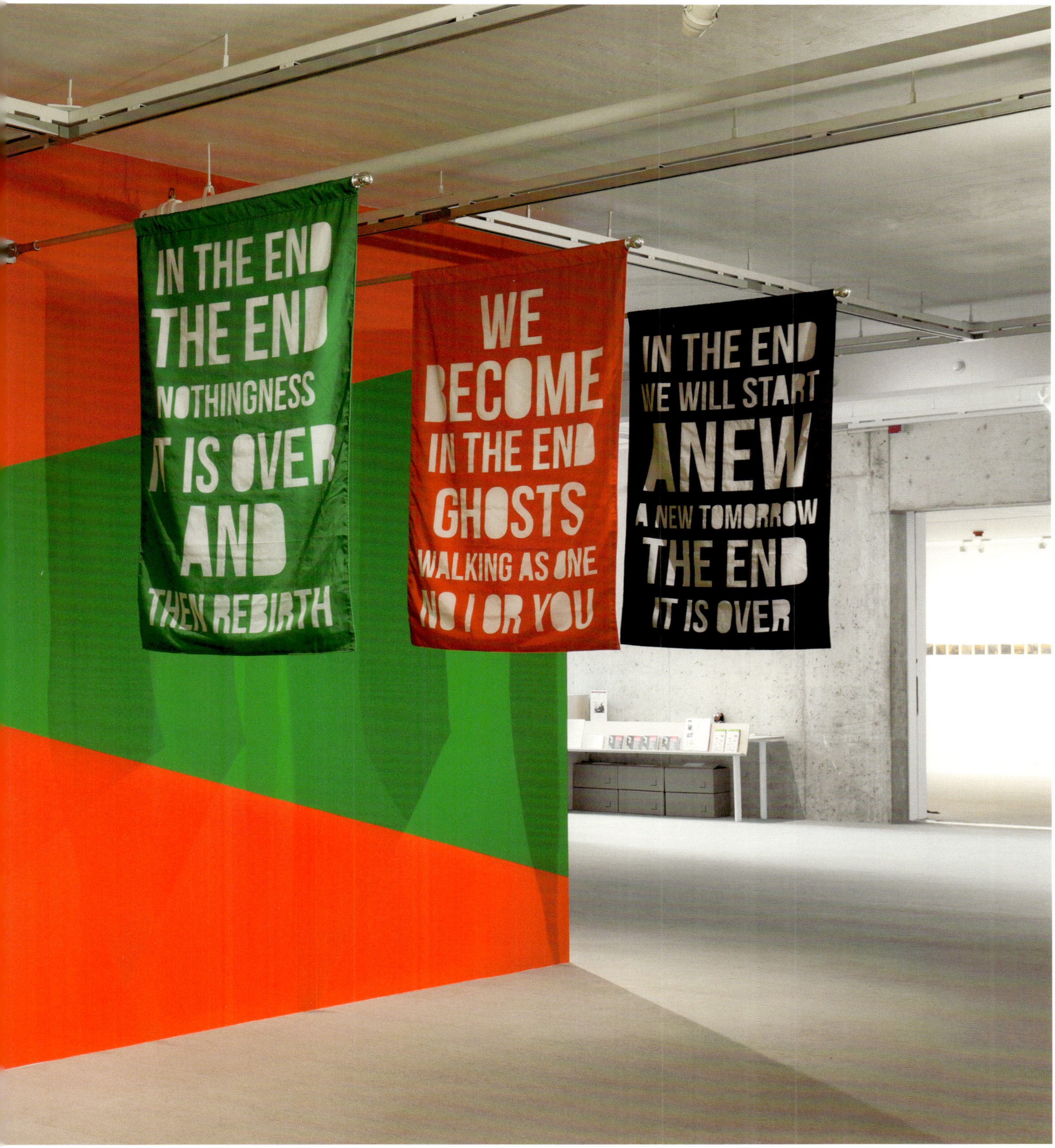

BRENDAN FERNANDES

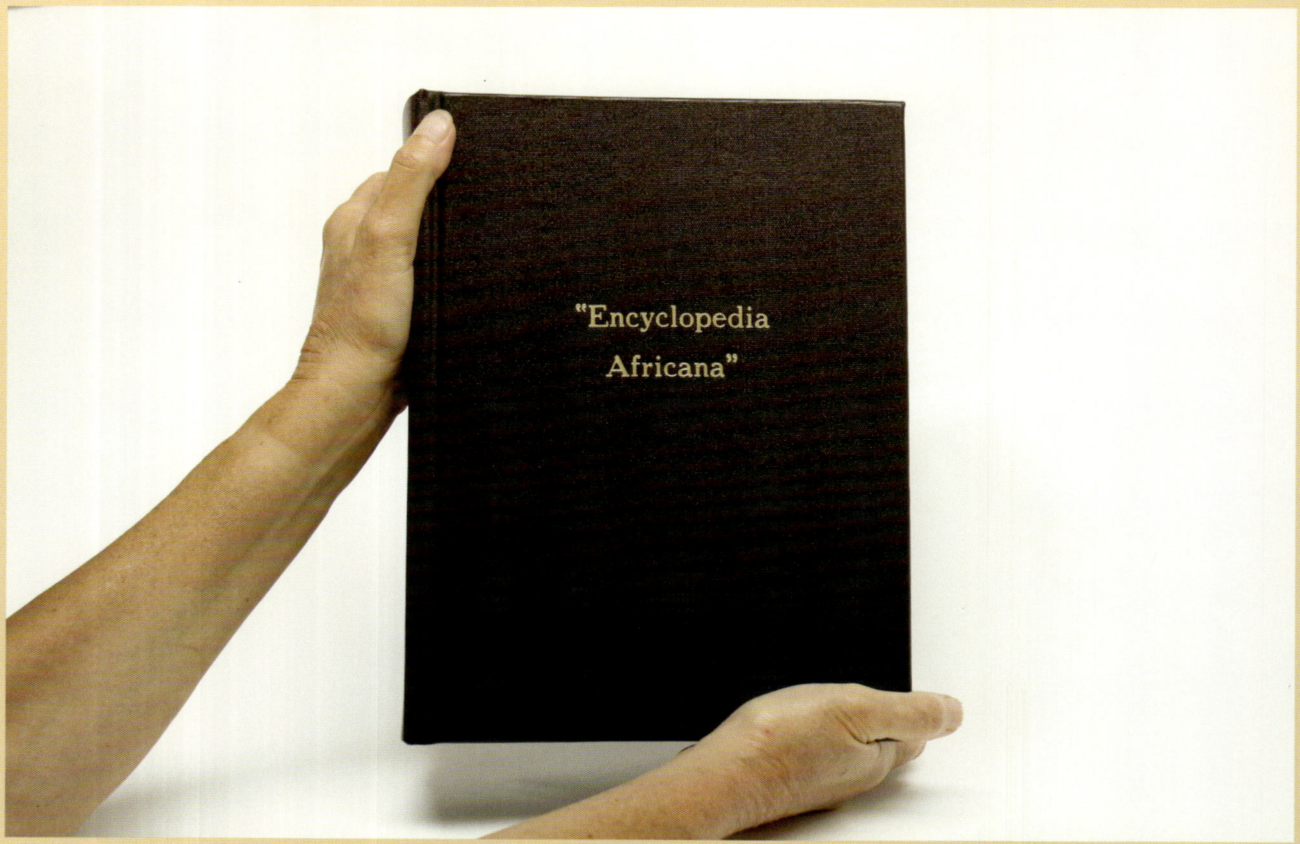

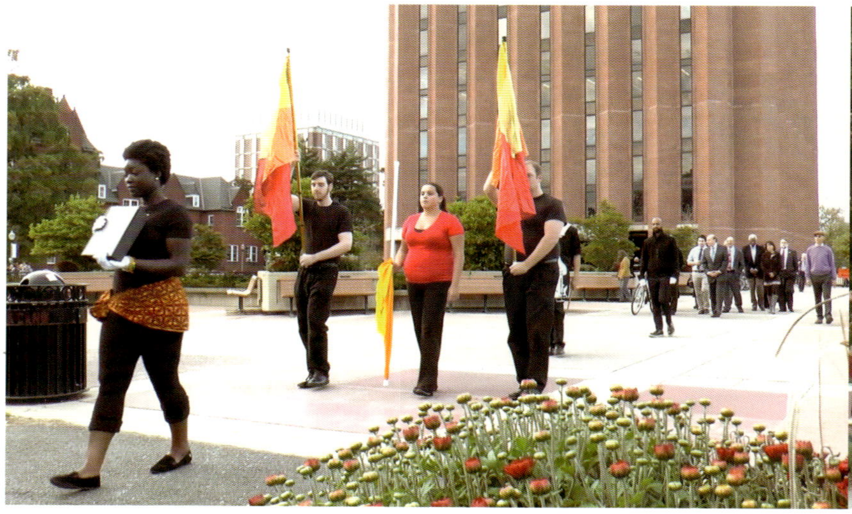

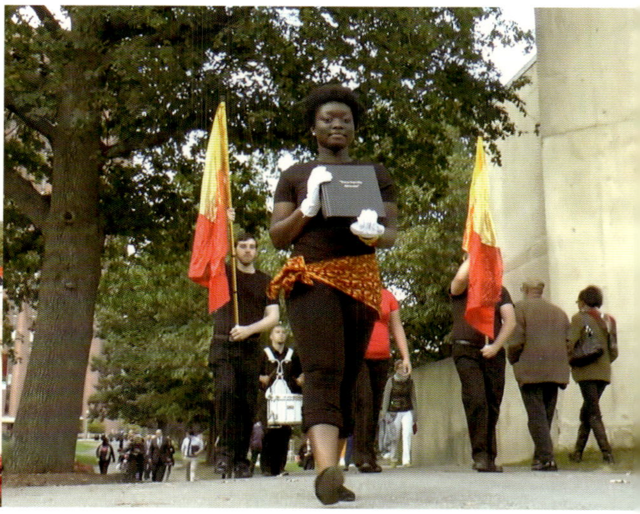

Above left and right
BRENDAN FERNANDES
The Encyclopedia Africana, 2013
Hand-bound book, gold foil stamping, and black linen paper
12″ x 9″ x 3″
Collection of the University Museum of Contemporary Art, University of Massachusetts, Amherst

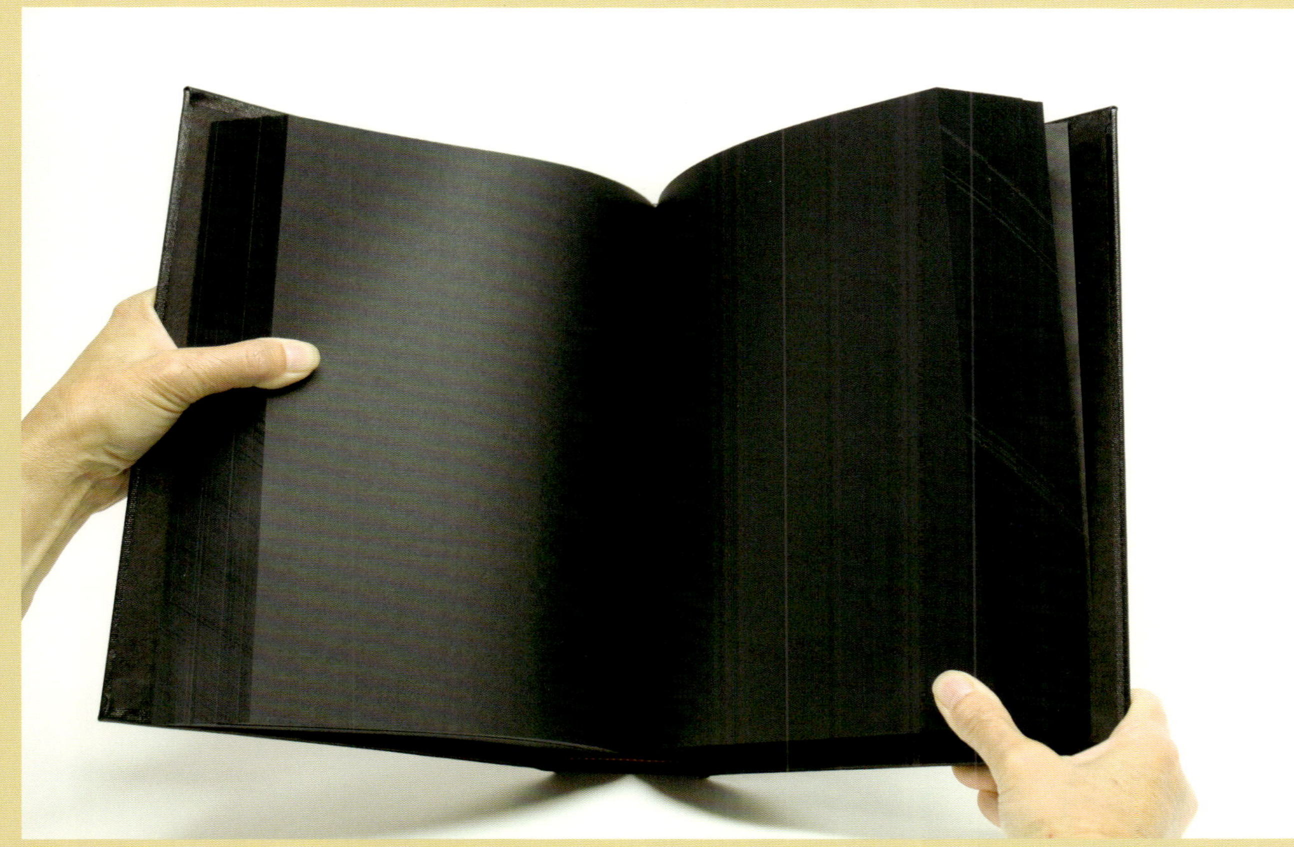

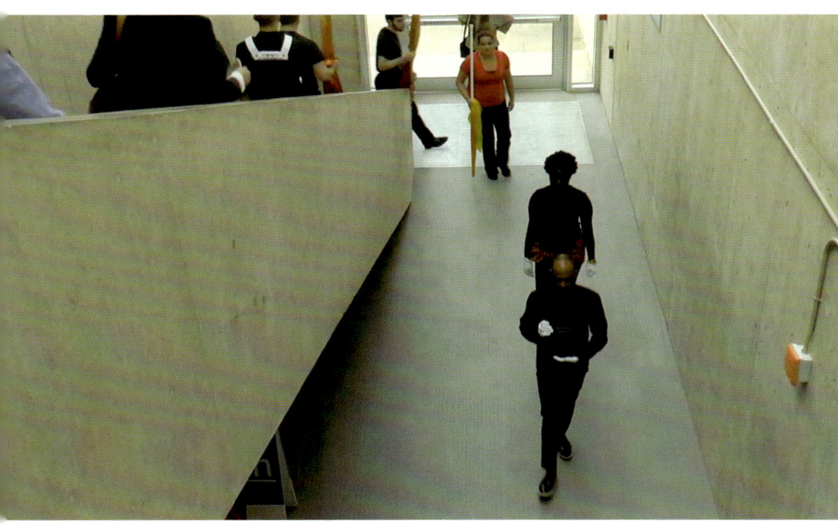

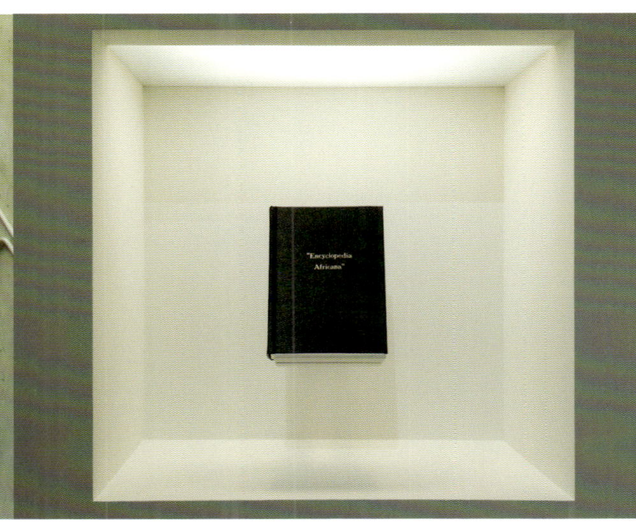

Below, left to right
BRENDAN FERNANDES
Du Bois in Our Time, Encyclopedia Africana Performance
Performance piece by Brendan Fernandes at the UMass campus as part of the symposium and exhibition *Du Bois in Our Time*. The *Encyclopedia Africana* is carried in a procession with the UMass Amherst Color Guard from the W.E.B. Du Bois Library to the University Museum of Contemporary Art, where it is placed in a niche. The book is part of the exhibition.

WATCH THE VIDEO https://vimeo.com/93380324

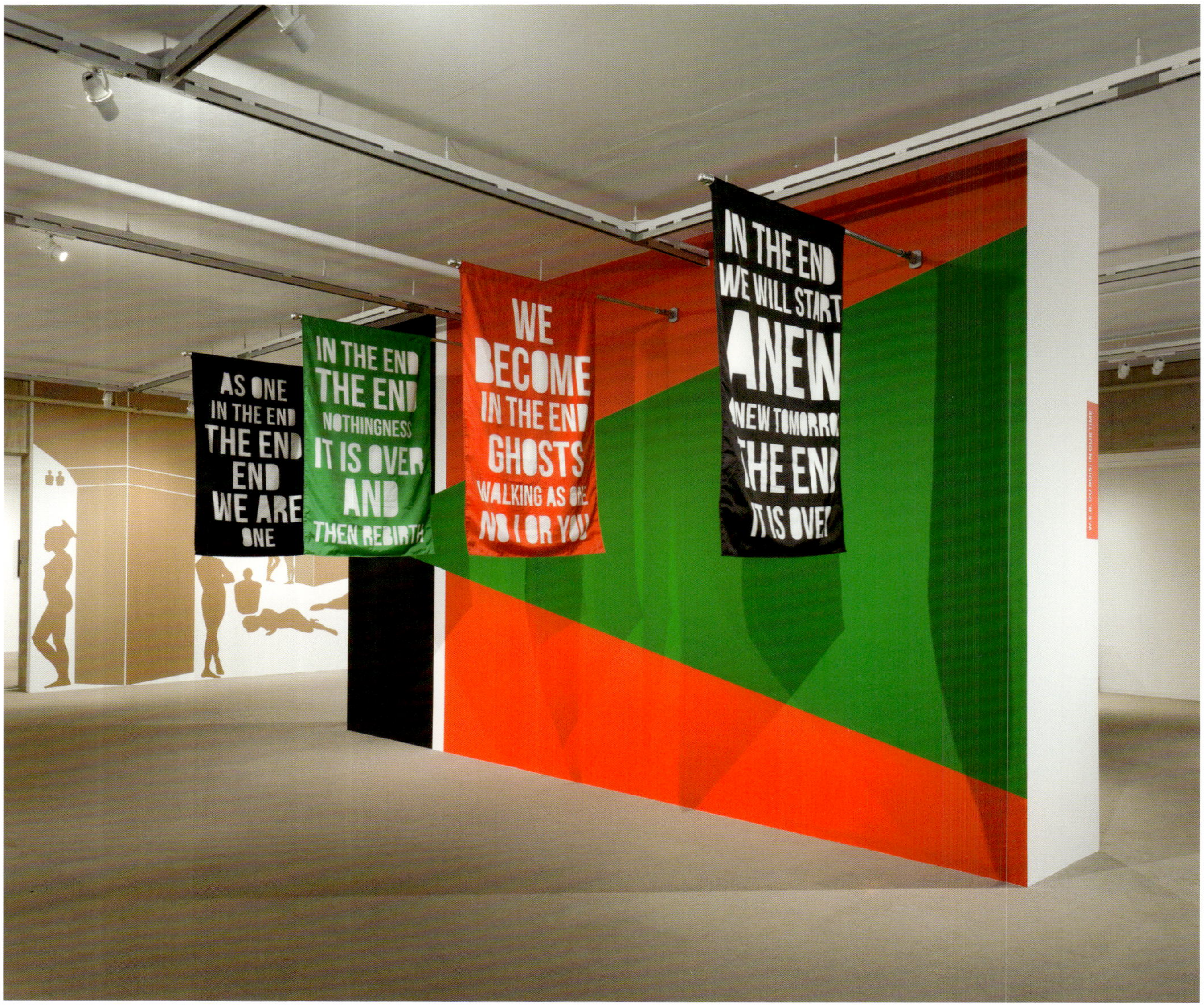

Left
BRENDAN FERNANDES
In The End, 2013
Screen-printed flags, painted wall mural
Flags – 5′ x 3′, Mural – 11′ 4″ x 18′ 5″
Installation view
Collection of the artist and Diaz Contemporary, Toronto

Right
(detail)

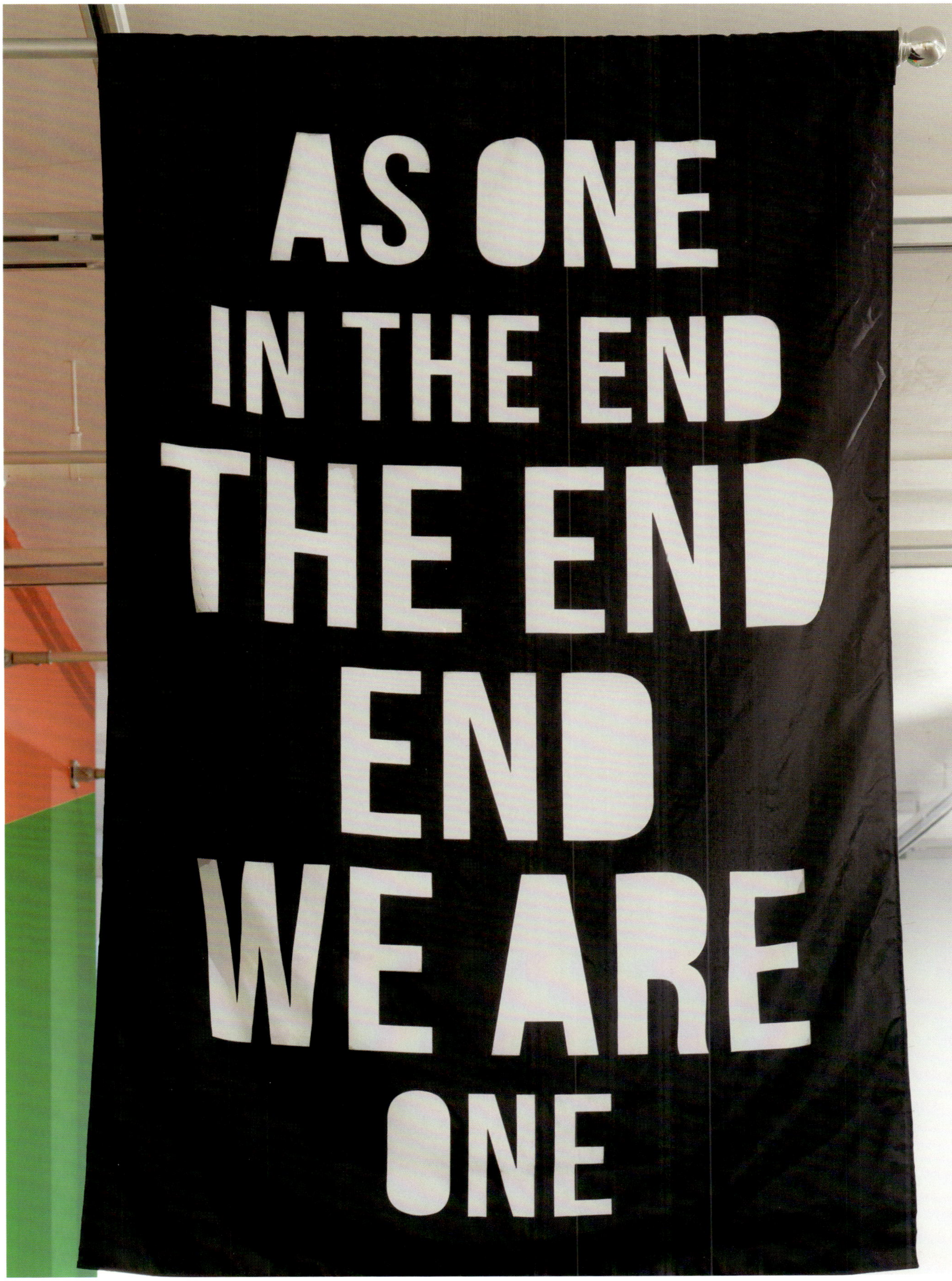
AS ONE
IN THE END
THE END
END
WE ARE
ONE

LATOYA RUBY FRAZIER

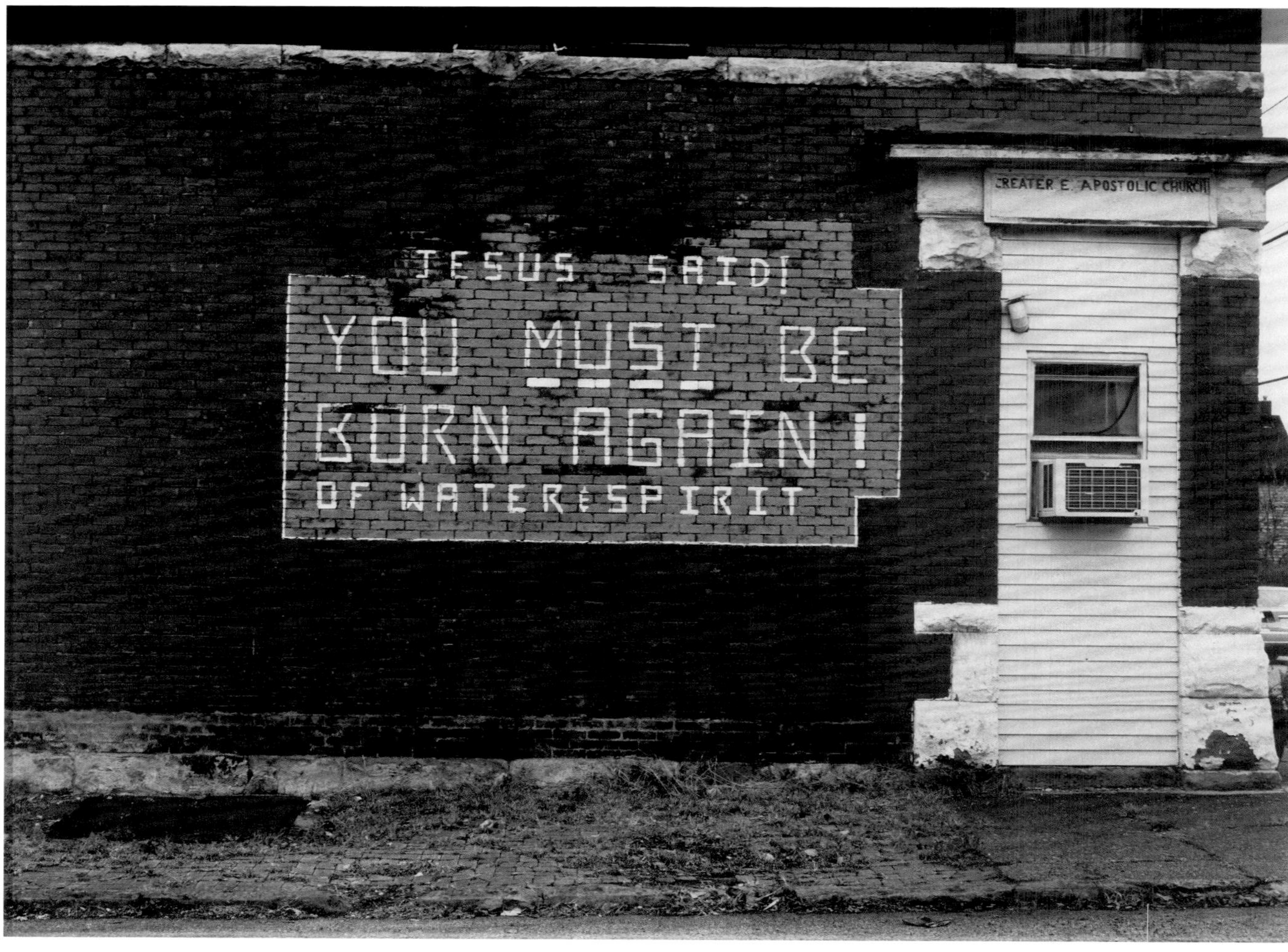

LATOYA RUBY FRAZIER
A Despoliation of Water:
From the Housatonic to Monongahela River
(1930–2013)
Above
Born by Water and Spirit, Ninth and
Washington Avenue, 2009
Gelatin silver print, 30″ x 40″

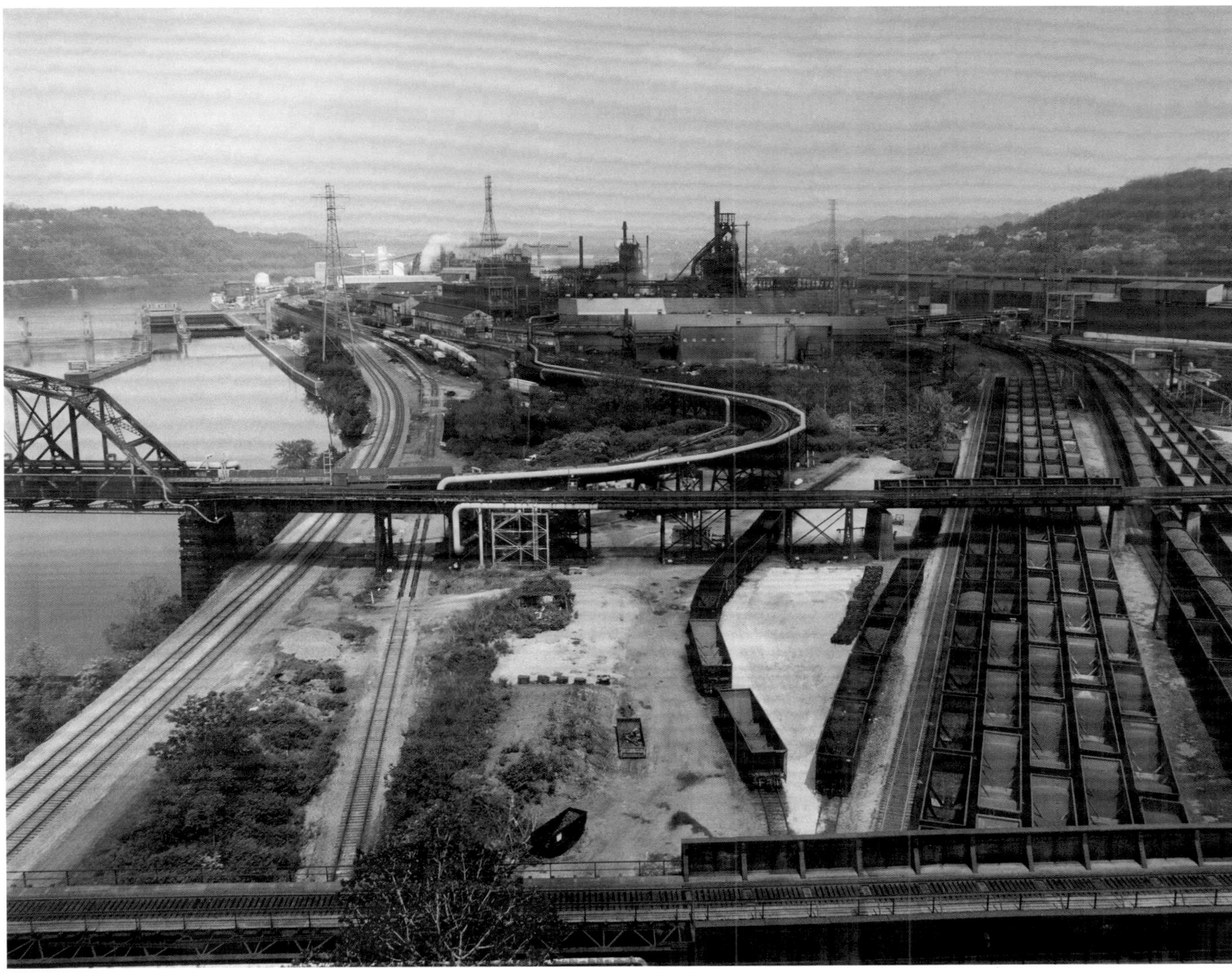

LATOYA RUBY FRAZIER
United States Steel Edgar Thomson Steel Works and Monongahela River, 2013
Gelatin silver print, 48″ x 58″

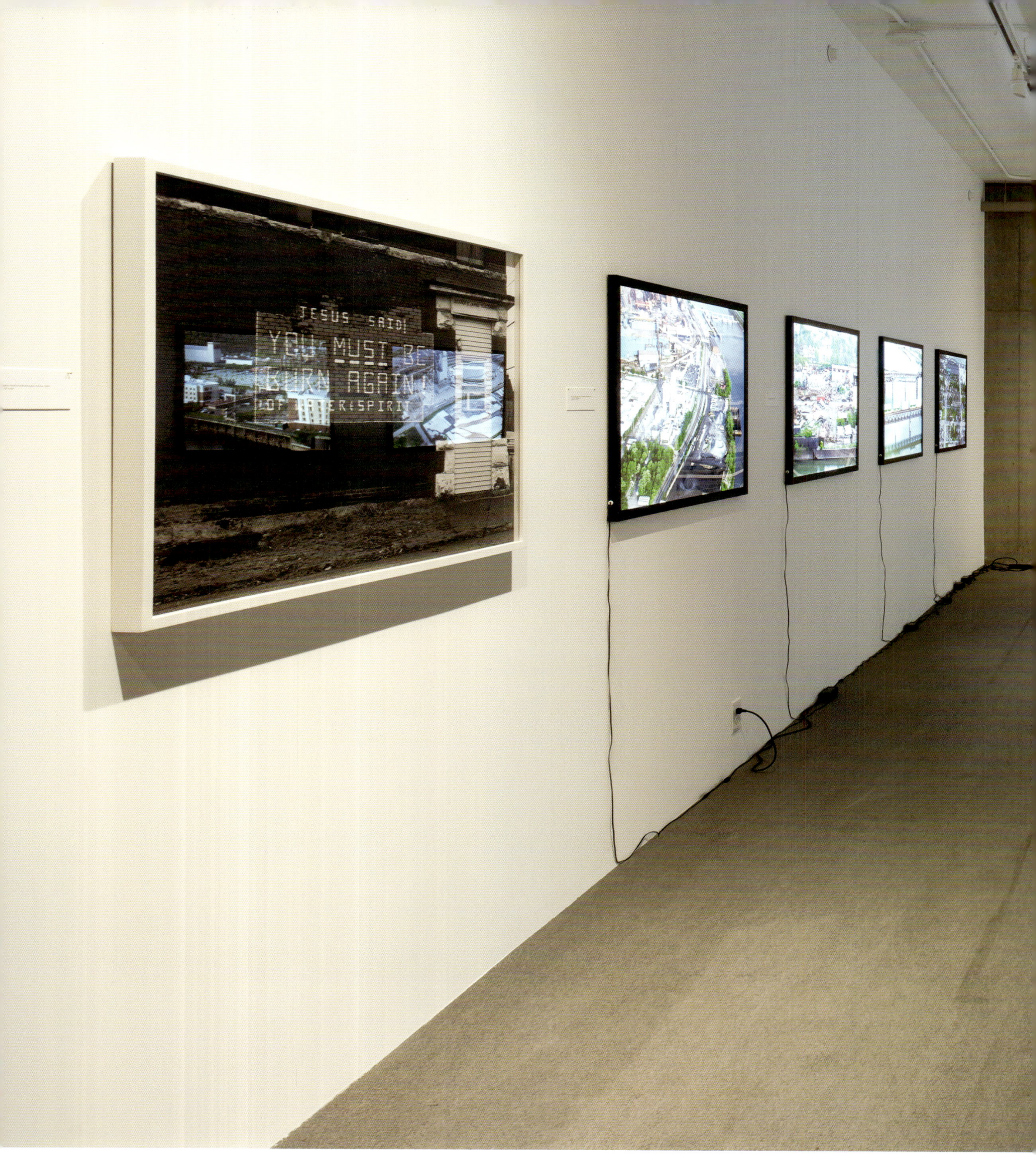

LATOYA RUBY FRAZIER
A Despoliation of Water:
From the Housatonic to Monongahela River (1930–2013)
Installation view

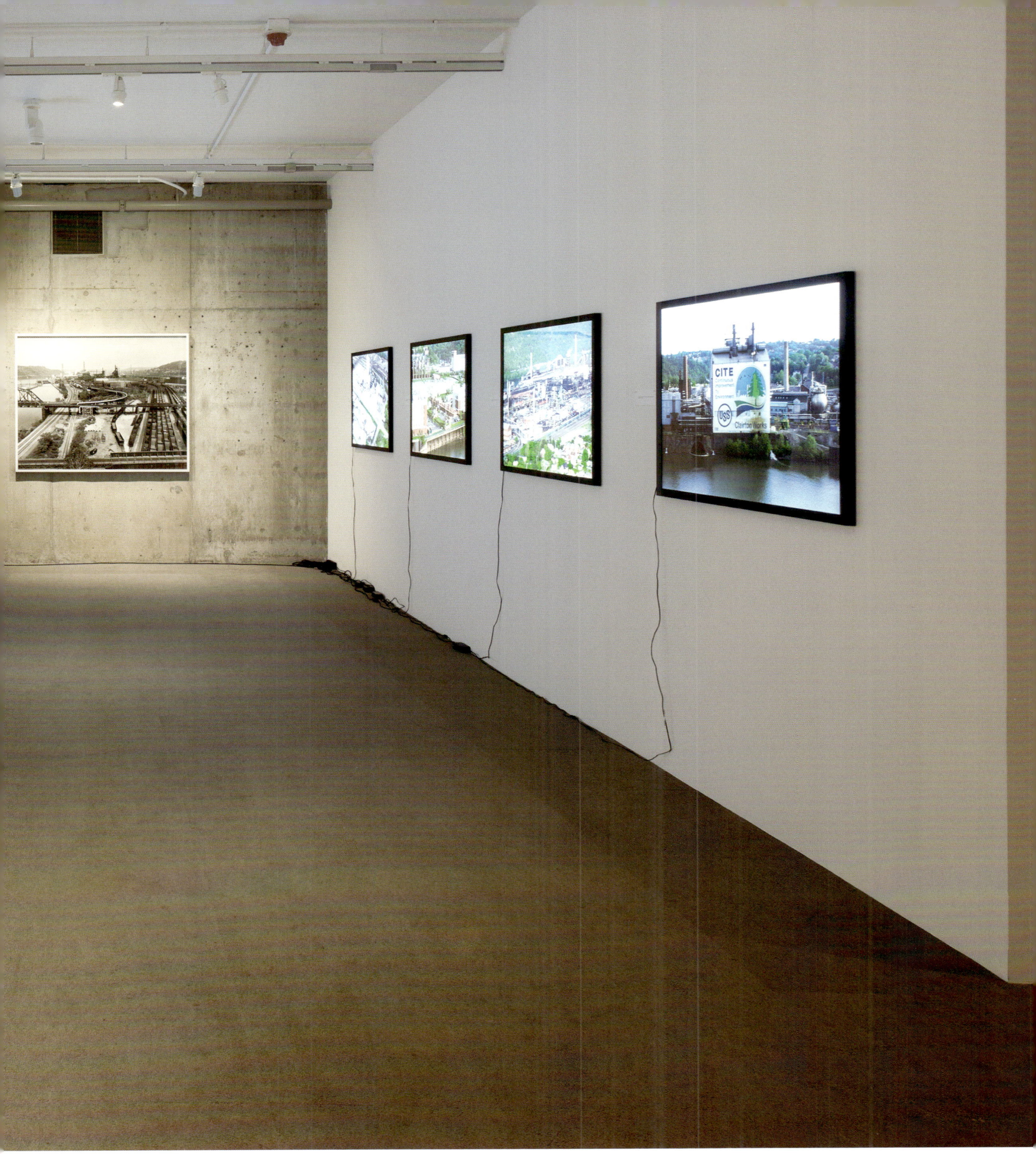
CITE
Clairton Works

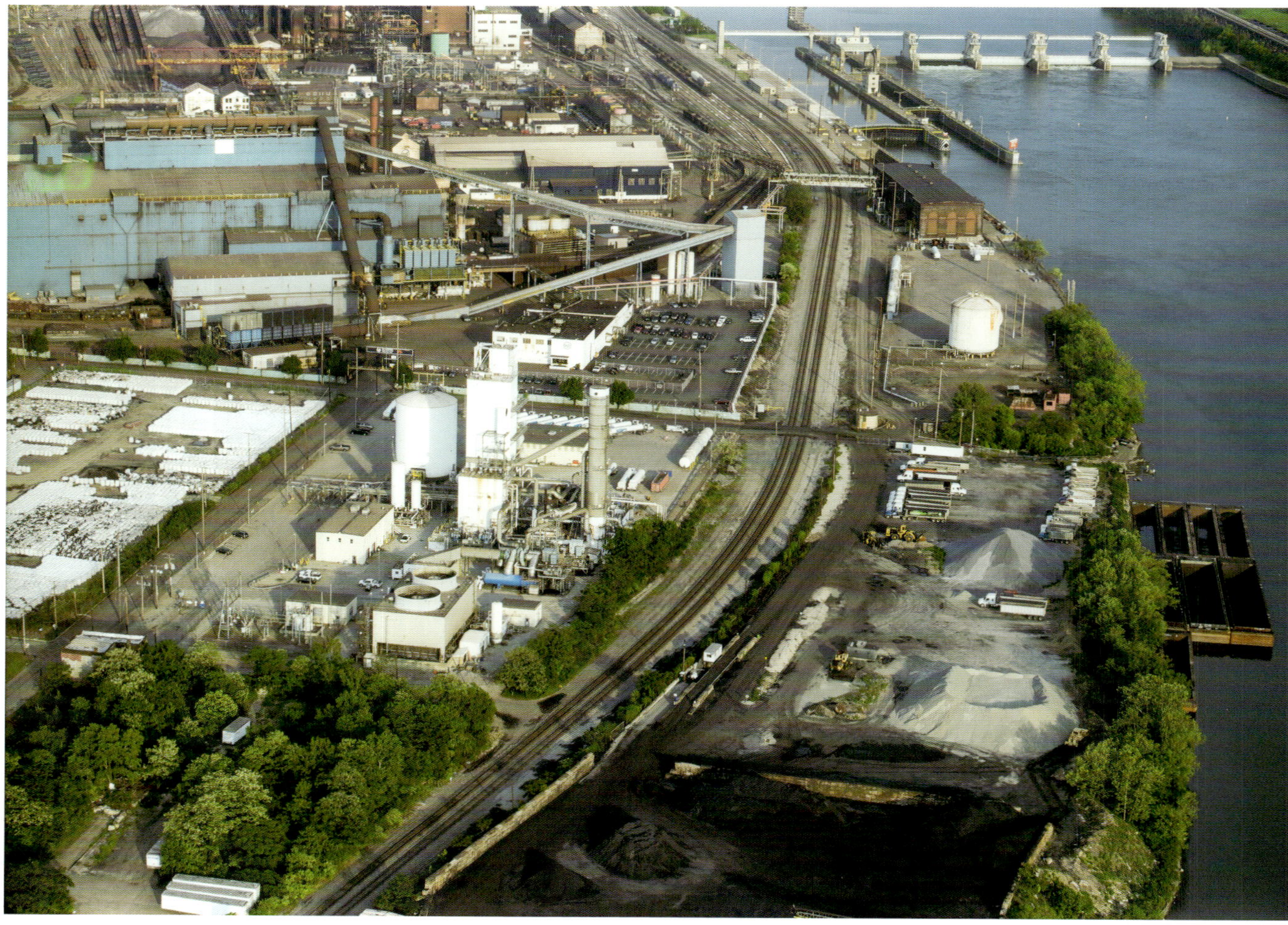

LATOYA RUBY FRAZIER
United States Steel Edgar Thomson Steel Works, Monongahela River and 1755 Battle of the Wilderness, 2013
Duratrans, 27¼" x 38¼"

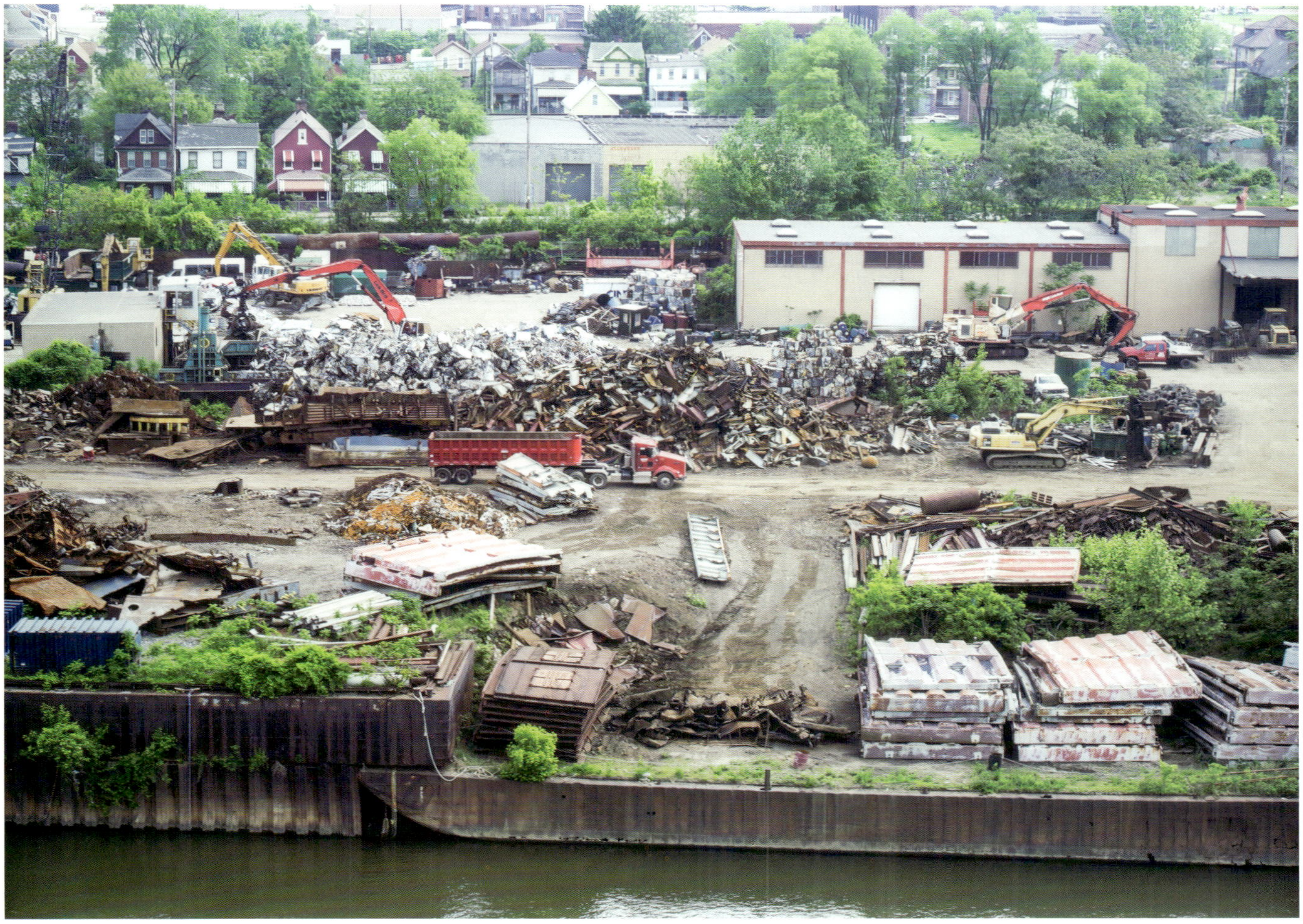

LATOYA RUBY FRAZIER
Washington Avenue and Monongahela River, 2013
Duratrans, 27¼" x 38¼"

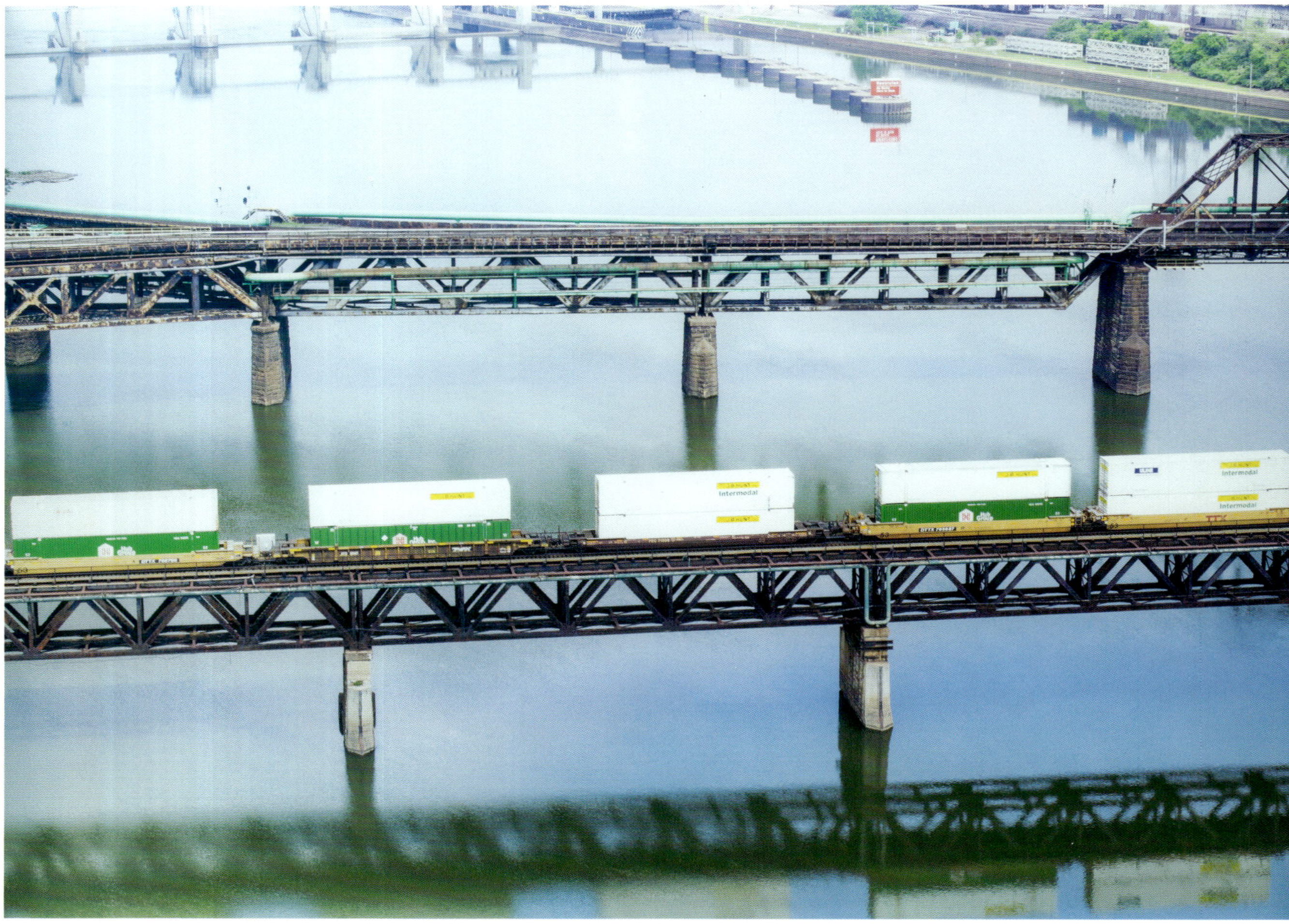

LATOYA RUBY FRAZIER
Monongahela River, bridges and shipping containers, 2013
Duratrans, 27¼" x 38¼"

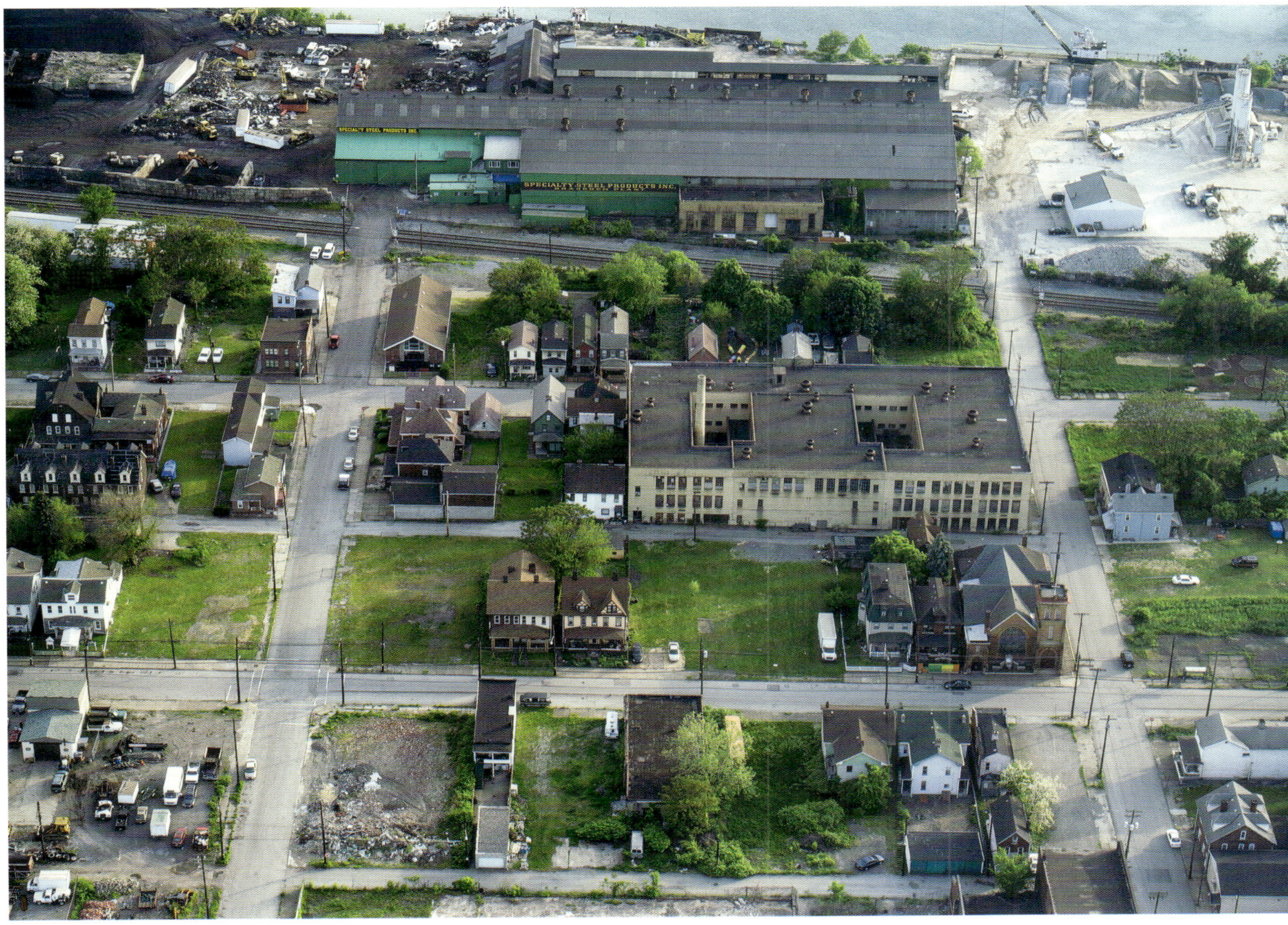

LATOYA RUBY FRAZIER
Eighth and Washington Avenue, Specialty Steel Production Inc. Braddock Plant and My Childhood Home, 805 Washington Avenue, 2013
Duratrans, 27¼" x 38¼"

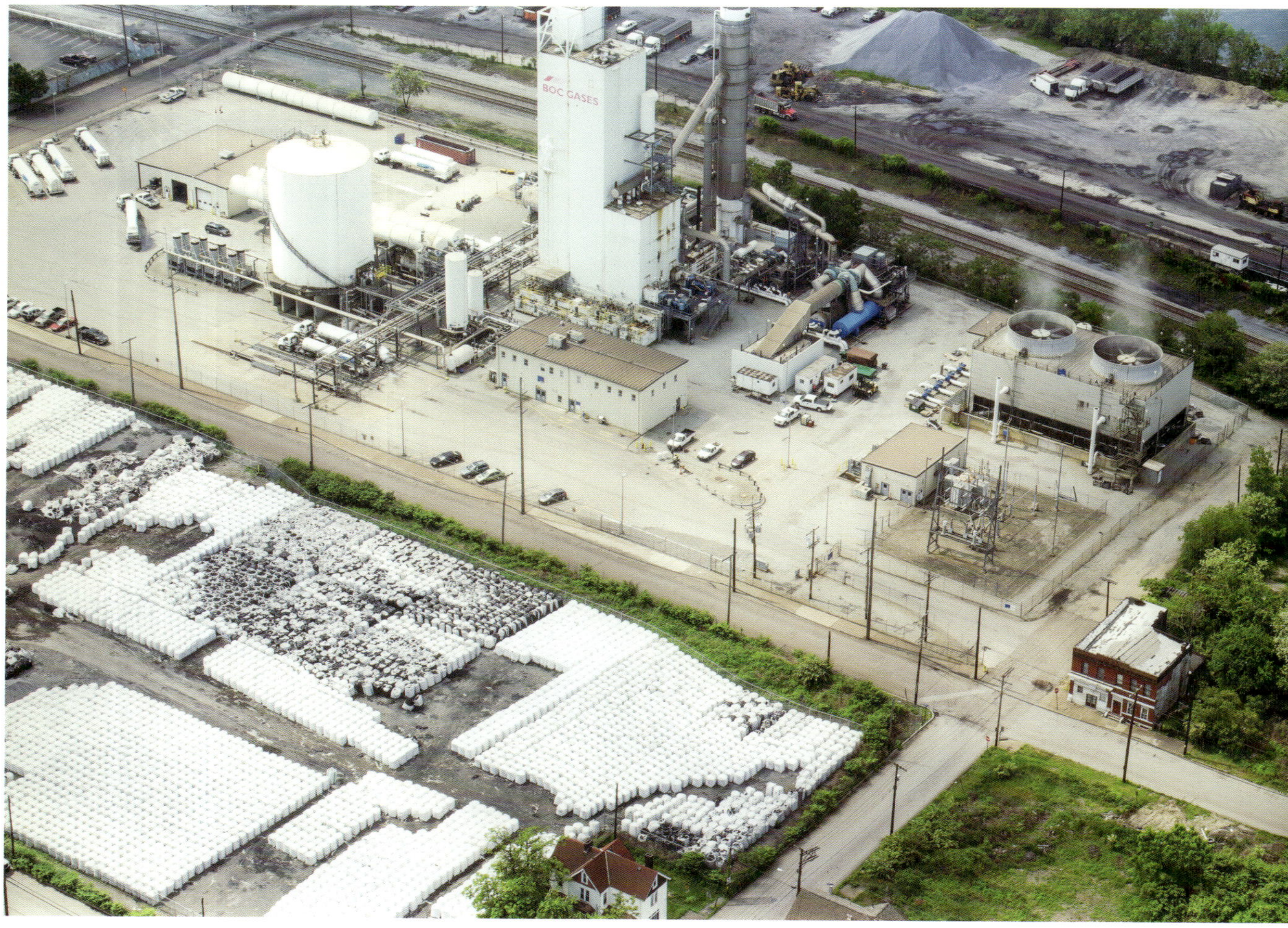

LATOYA RUBY FRAZIER
Ninth and Talbot, BOC Gases, Talbot Towers,
The Bottom and The Bunn
Family House, 2013
Duratrans, 27¼" x 38¼"

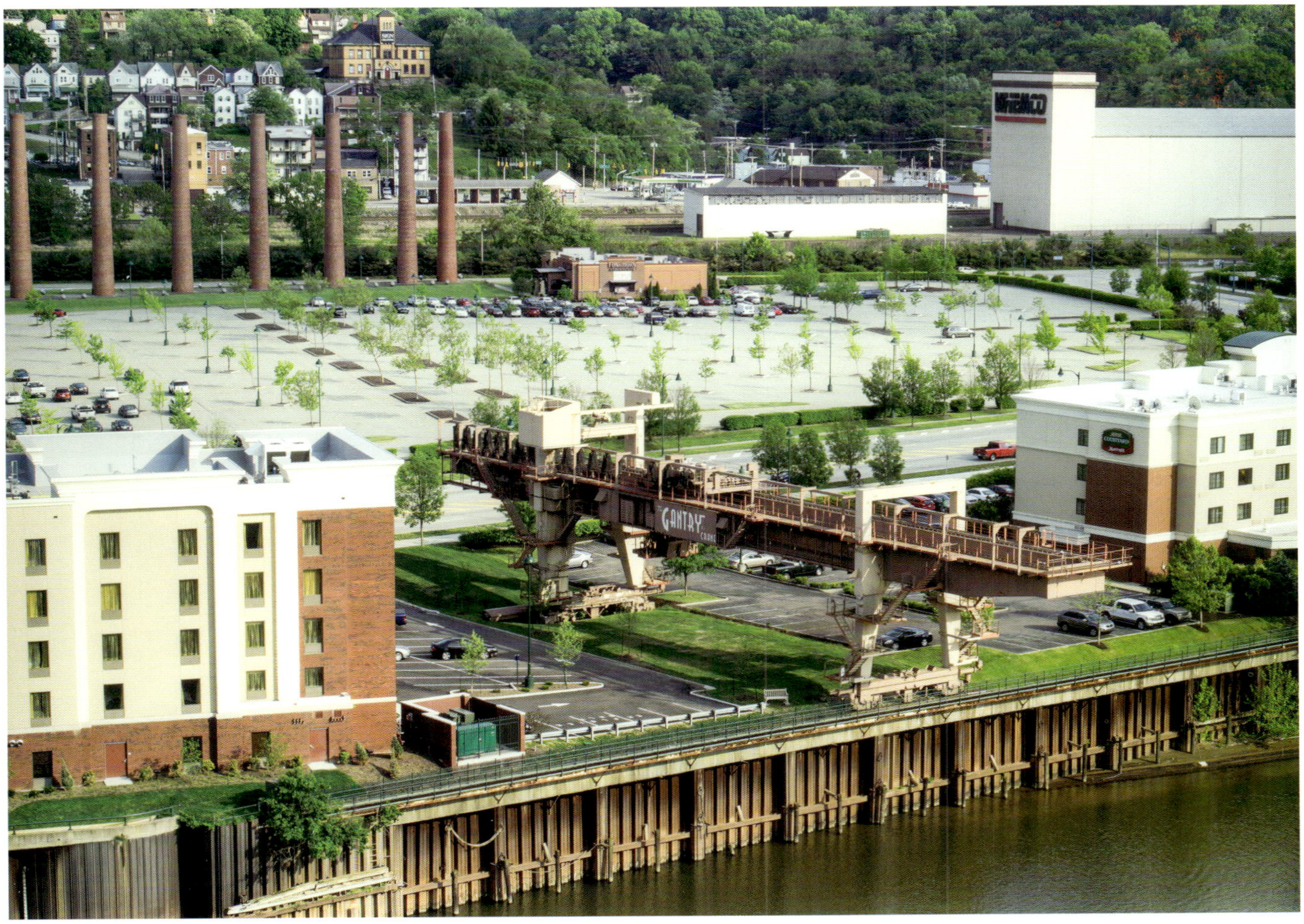

LATOYA RUBY FRAZIER
The Waterfront and Courtyard Marriott, Homestead Steel Works and 1892 Homestead Steel Strike, 2013
Duratrans, 27¼" x 38¼"

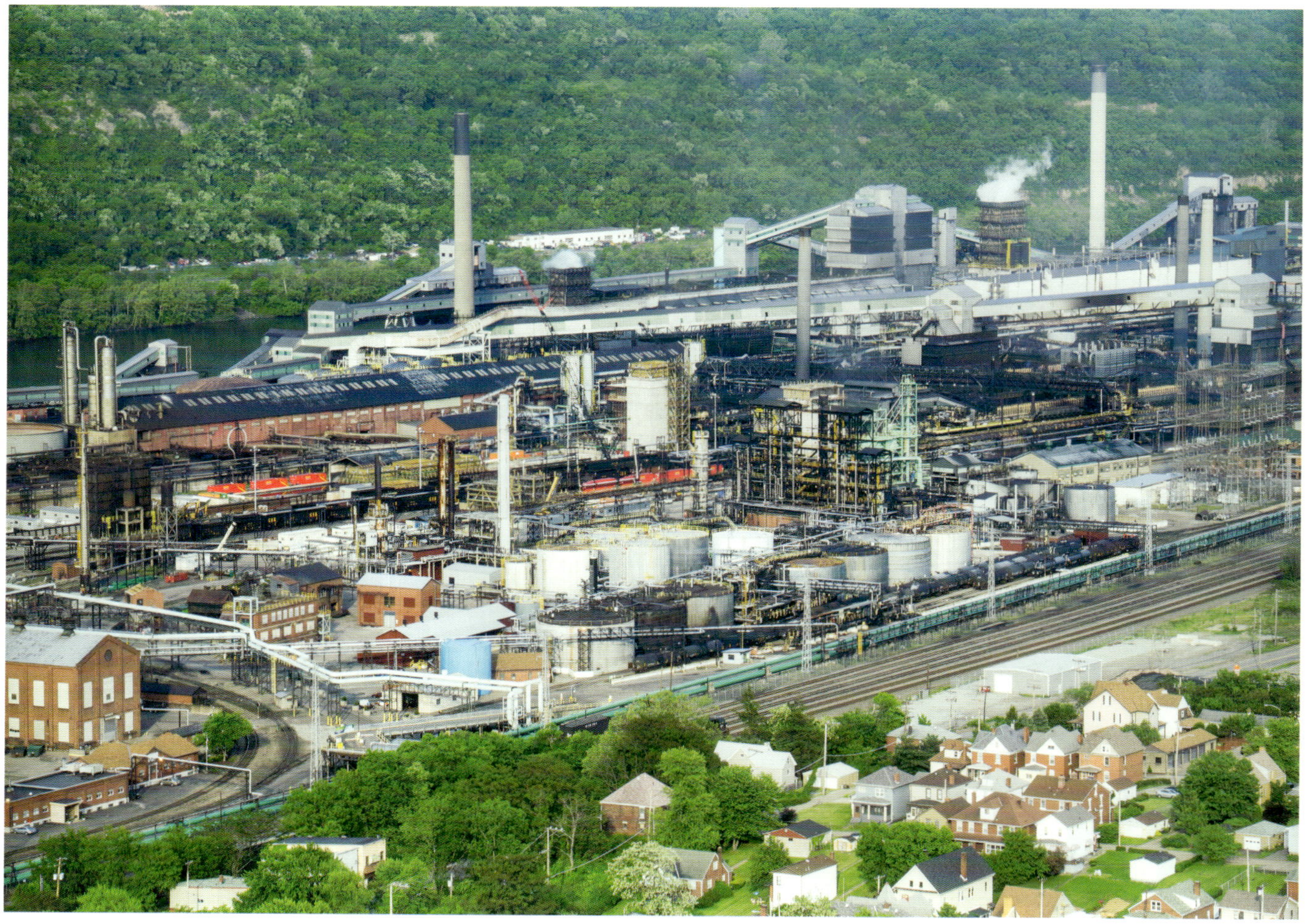

LATOYA RUBY FRAZIER
United States Steel Clairton Coke Works and Clairton, PA, homes, 2013
Duratrans, 27¼" x 38¼"

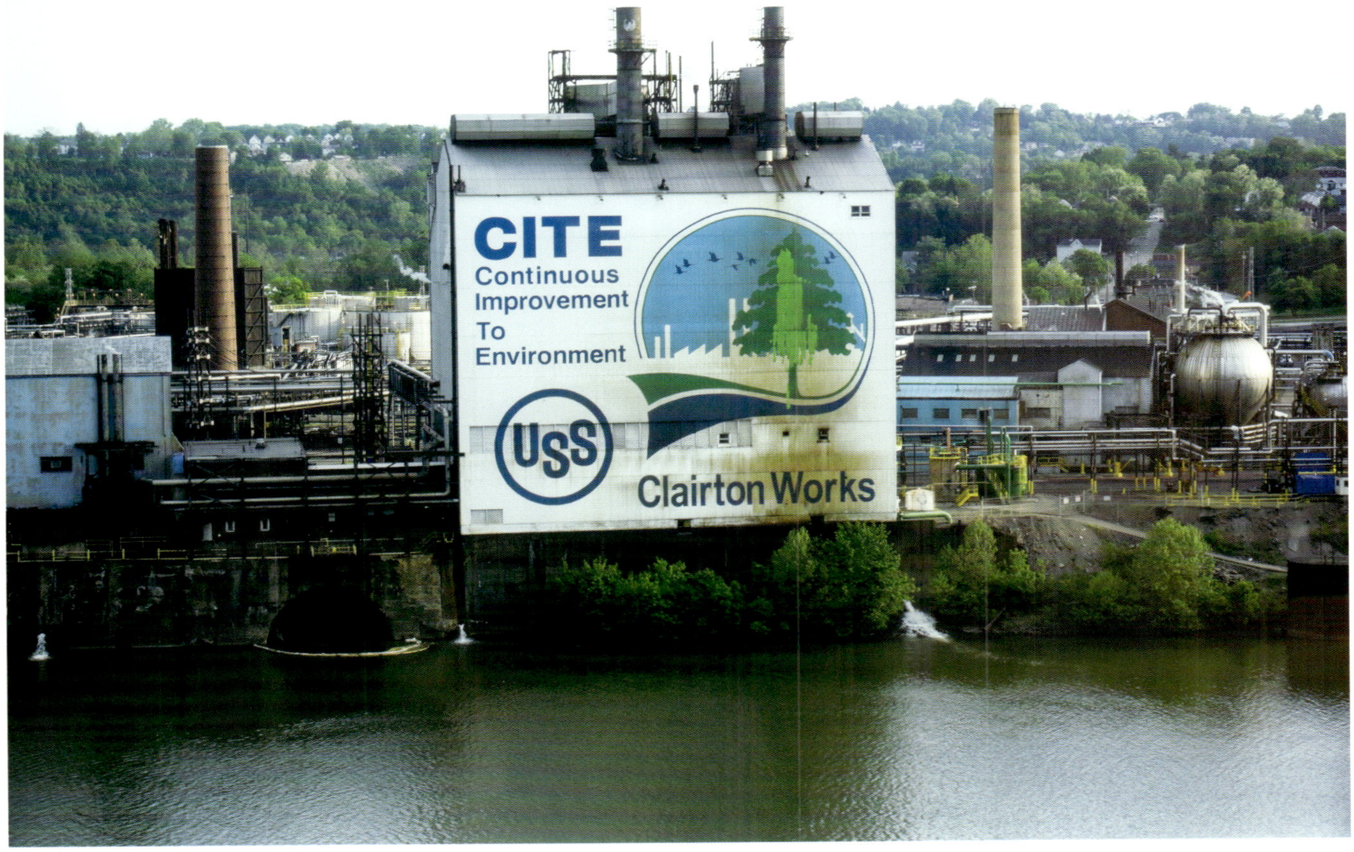

LATOYA RUBY FRAZIER
United States Steel Clairton Coke Works,
C.I.T.E. and Monongahela River, 2013
Duratrans, 27¼″ x 38¼″

JULIE MEHRETU

JULIE MEHRETU
Untitled, 2012
Graphite and acrylic on canvas
25″ x 36″ x 2″
Courtesy of the artist and
Marian Goodman Gallery,
New York and Paris

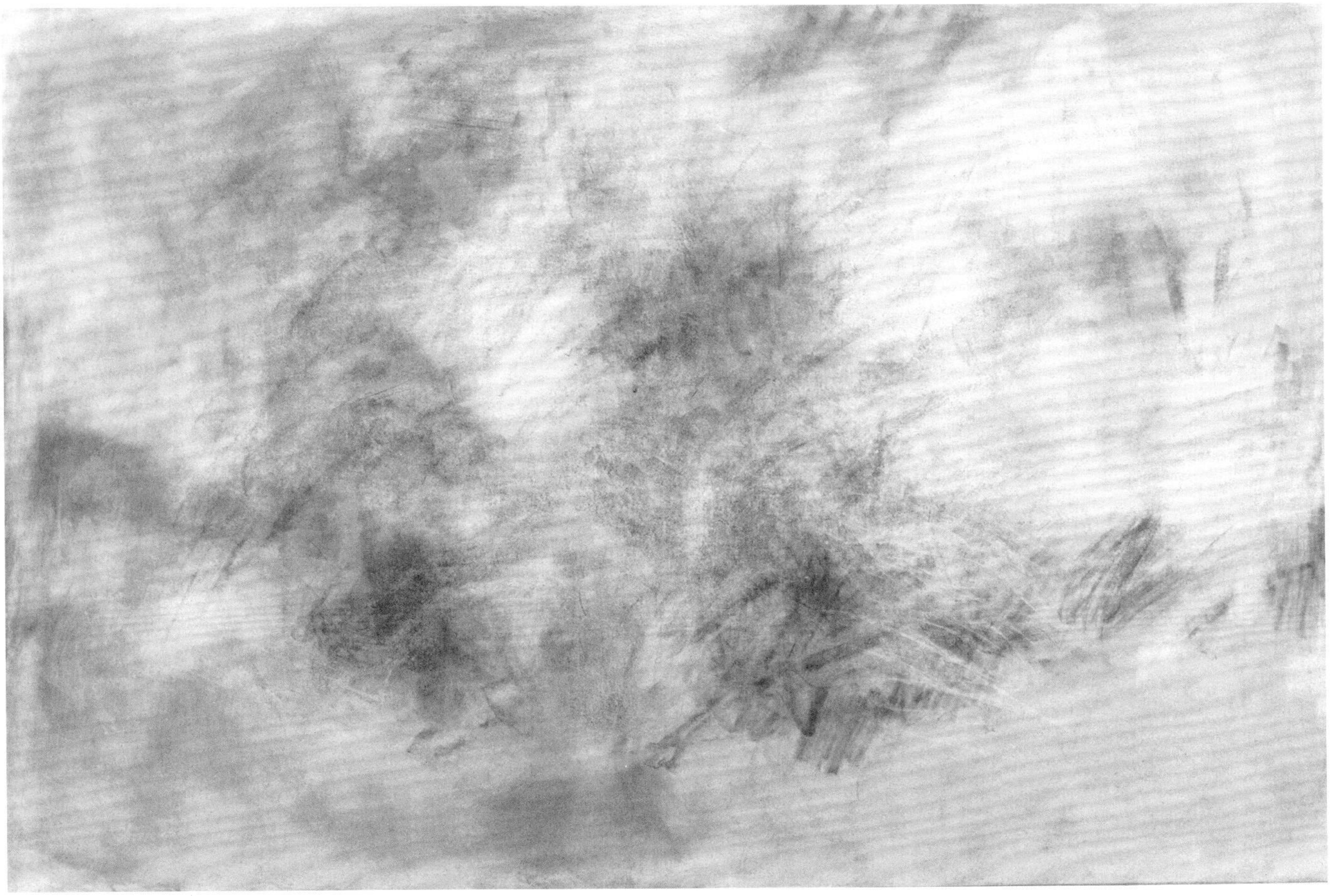

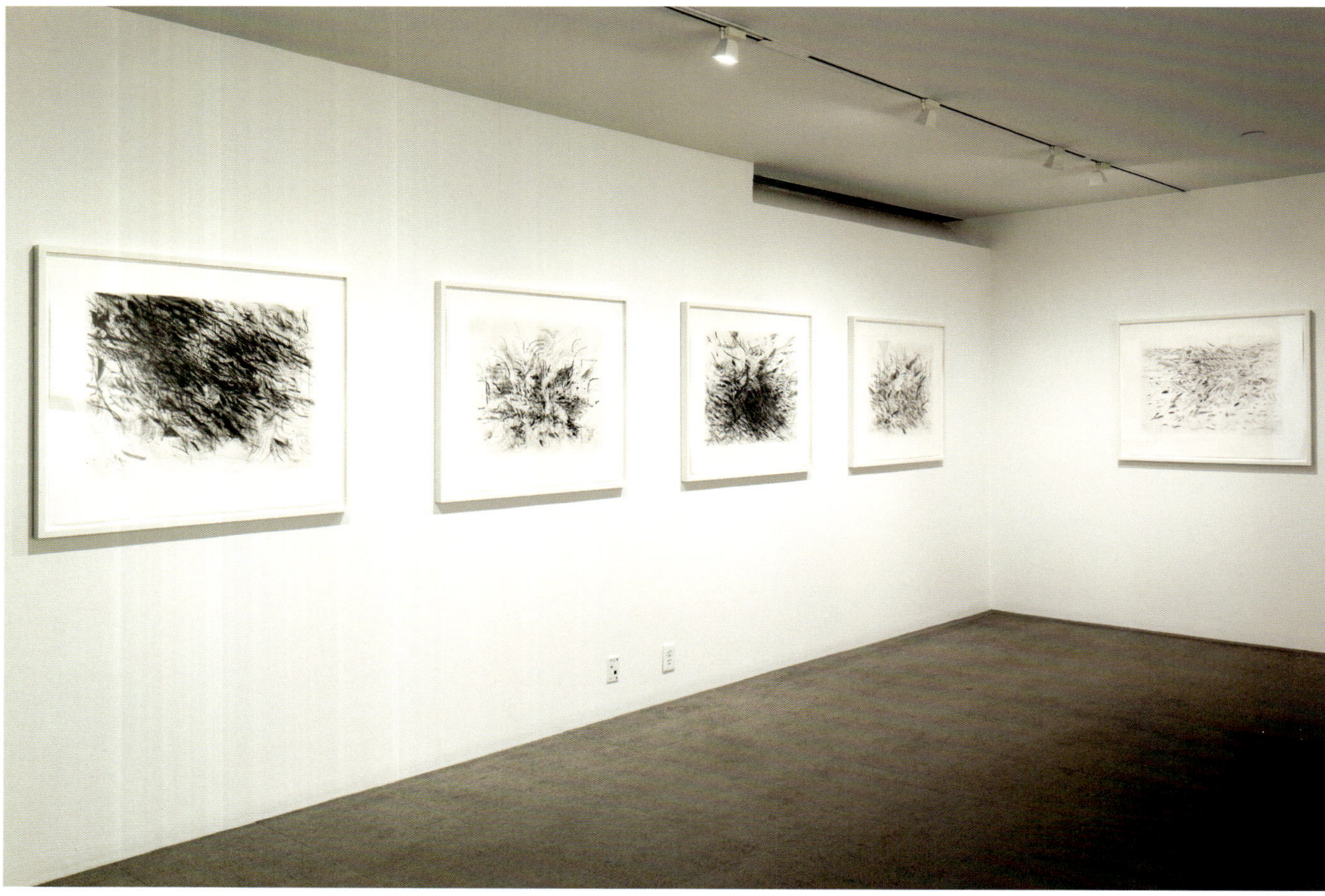

JULIE MEHRETU
Above
Installation view

Opposite
Algorithms, Apparitions and Translations, 2013
from a series of five multiplate etchings with aquatint, spit bite, soft ground, hard ground, drypoint, and engraving, printed on Hahnemühle copperplate paper in an edition of 35, bon à tirer
Plate size 23" x 30", paper size, 31¼" x 37¼"
Courtesy of the artist and
Gregory Burnet collection

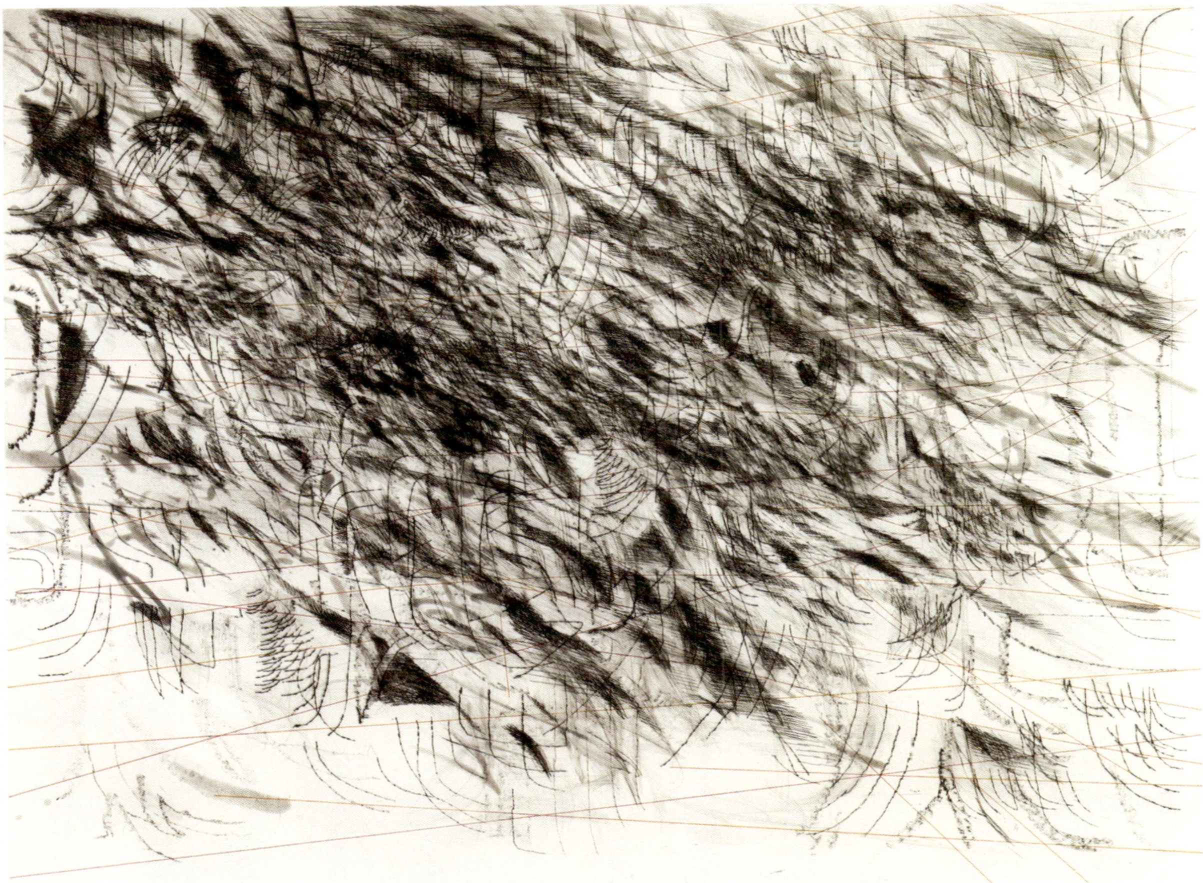

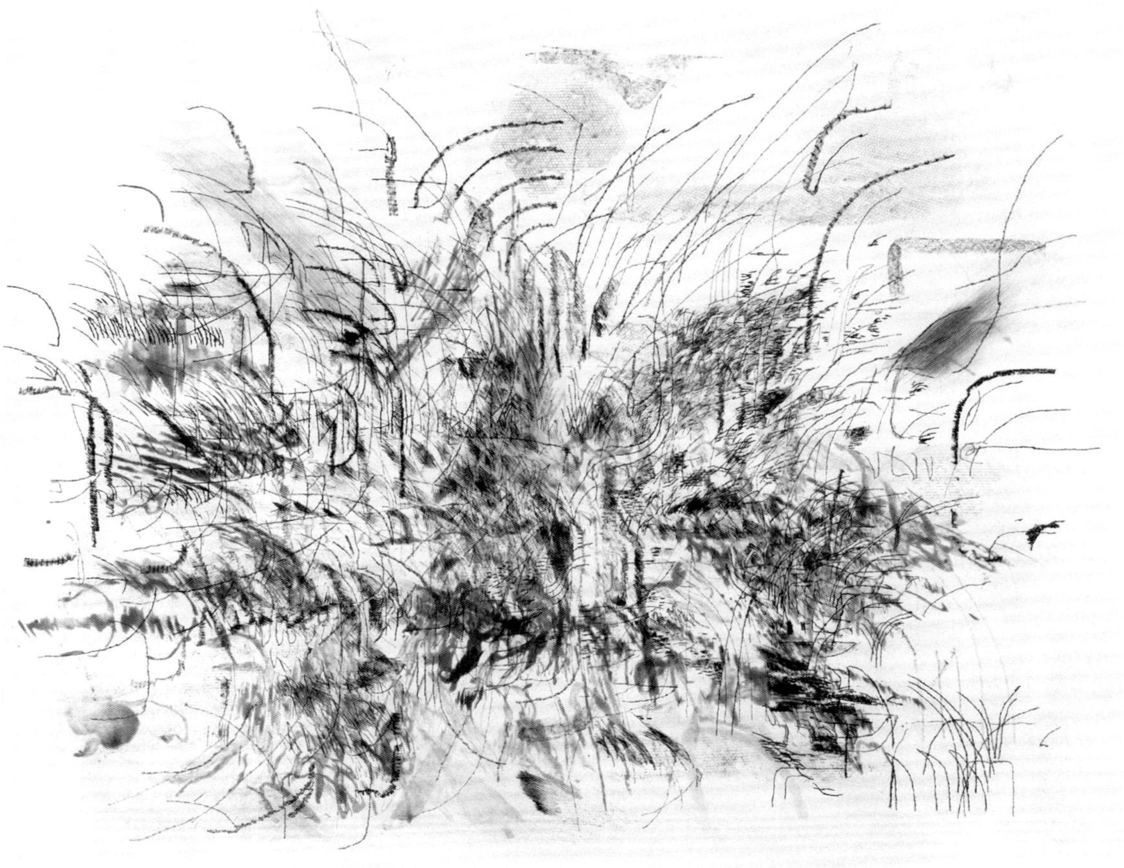

JULIE MEHRETU
Left and right
Algorithms, Apparitions and Translations, 2013
from a series of five multiplate etchings with aquatint, spit bite, soft ground, hard ground, drypoint, and engraving, printed on Hahnemühle copperplate paper in an edition of 35, bon à tirer
Plate size 23" x 30", paper size, 31¼" x 37¼"
Courtesy of the artist and Gregory Burnet collection

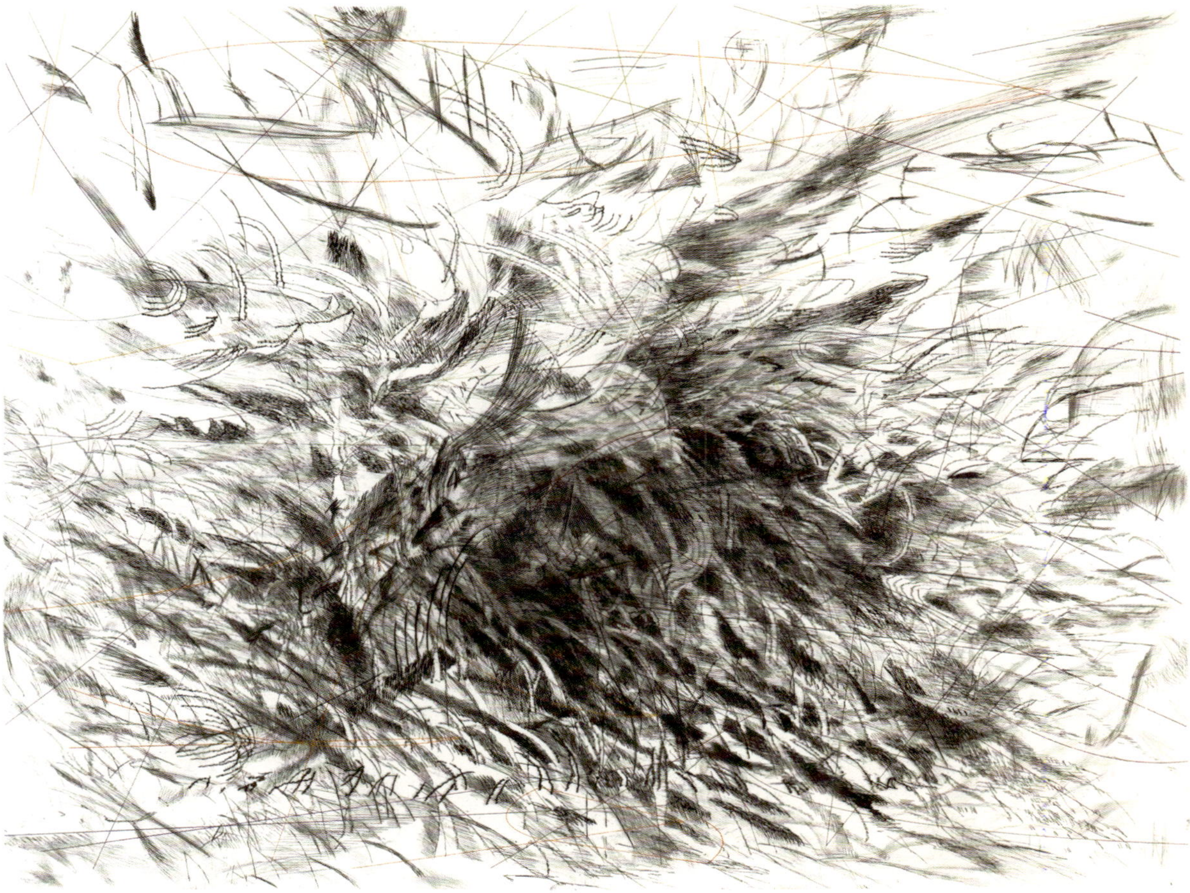

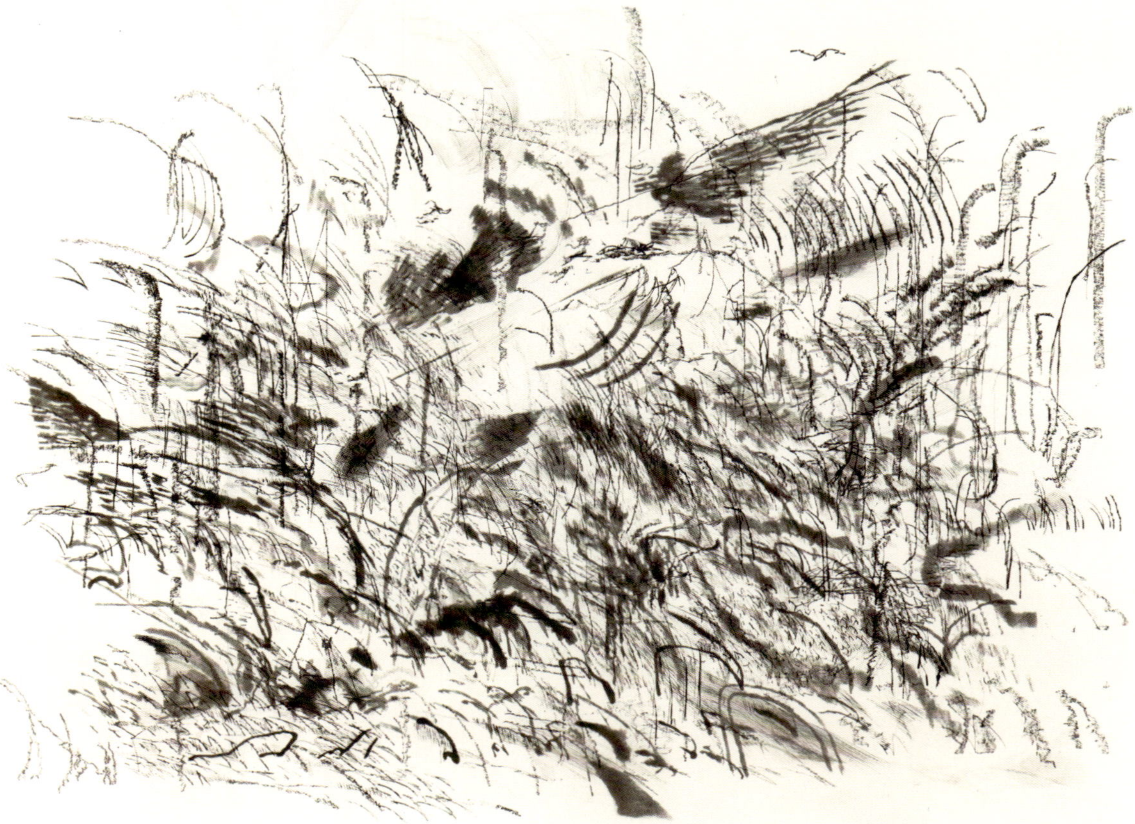

JULIE MEHRETU
Left and right
Algorithms, Apparitions and Translations, 2013
from a series of five multiplate etchings with aquatint, spit bite, soft ground, hard ground, drypoint, and engraving, printed on Hahnemühle copperplate paper in an edition of 35, bon à tirer
Plate size 23″ x 30″, paper size, 31¼ ″ x 37¼ ″
Courtesy of the artist and
Gregory Burnet collection

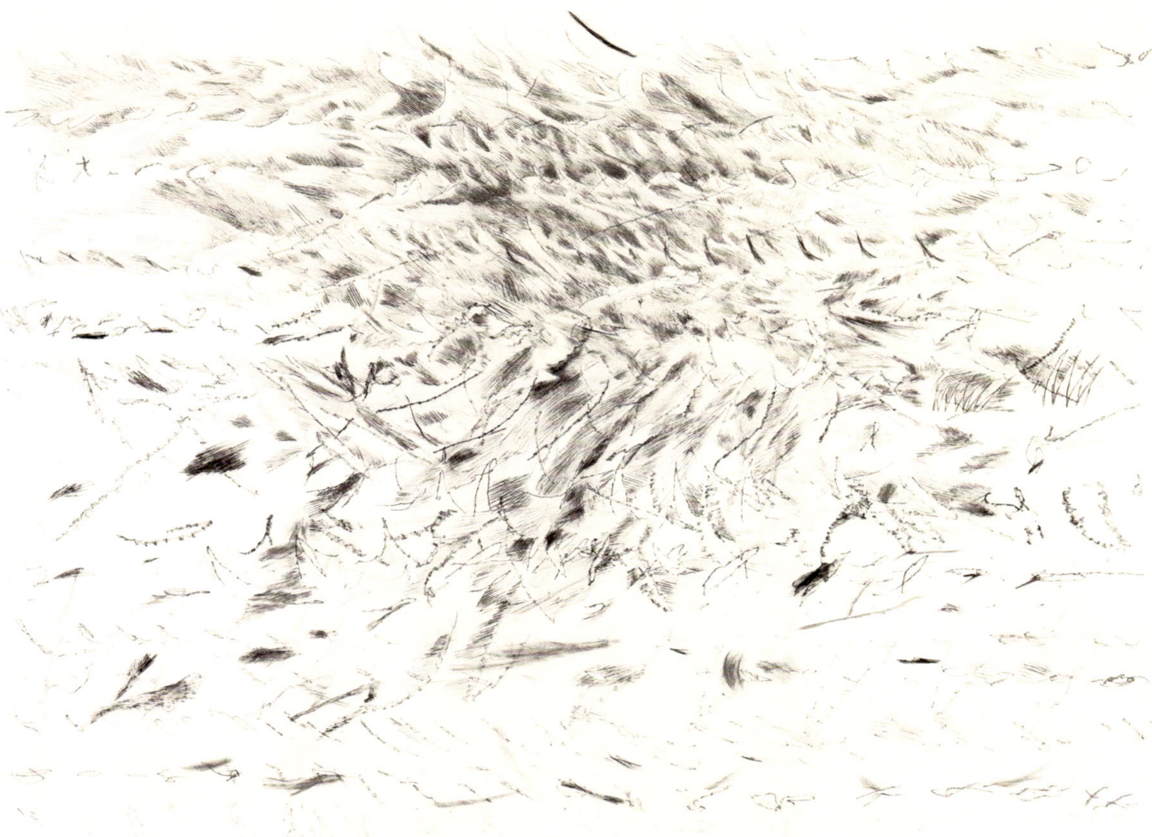

ANN MESSNER

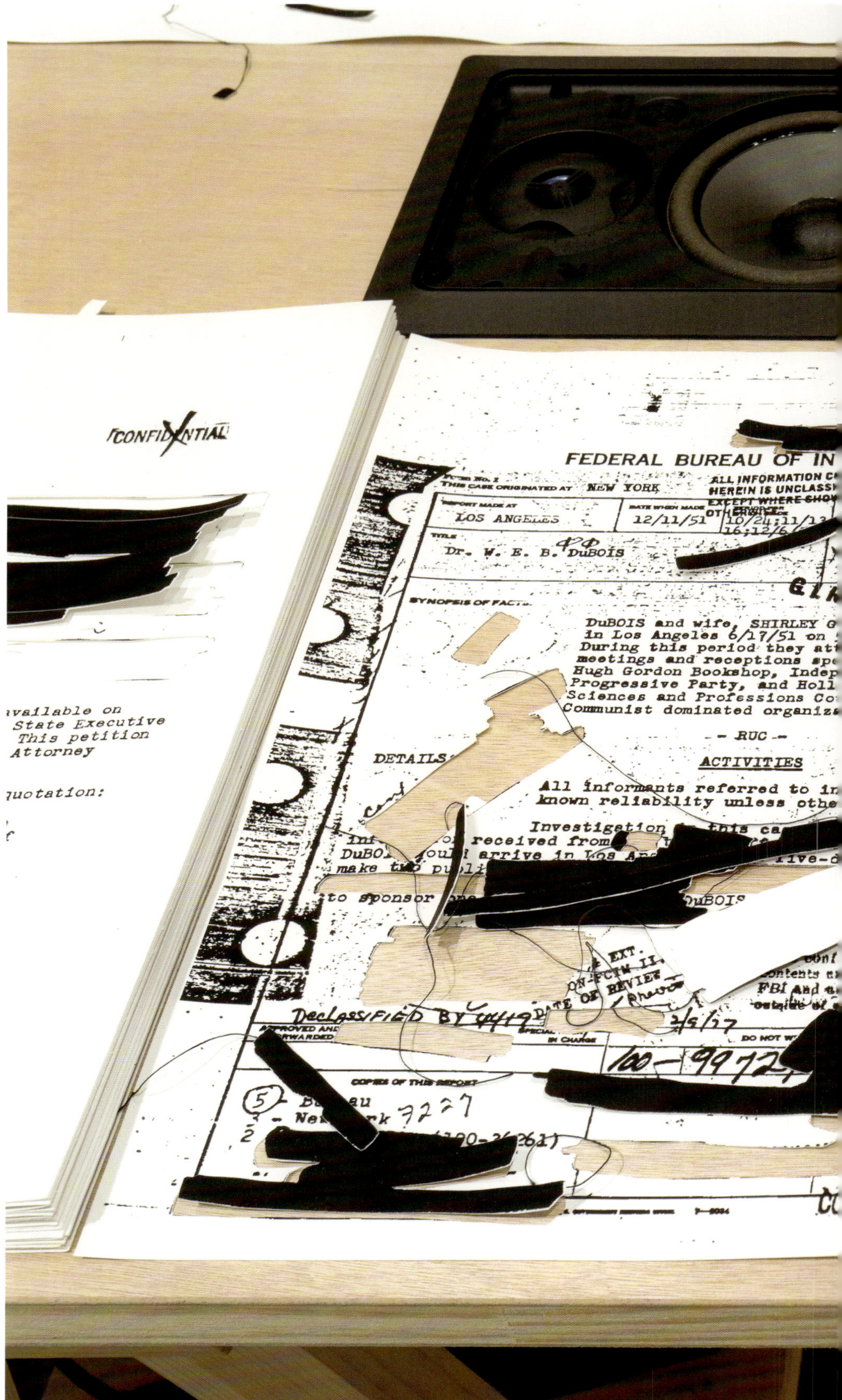

ANN MESSNER
Du Bois: The FBI Files (detail), 2013
Installation consisting of 447 running foot–incised digital scroll (hand-cut stenciled redaction), printed on Hahnemühle FA paper; 22-foot table inset with 6 in-wall MP5 Niles speakers, CD players, 4 CDs (audio component of the installation)

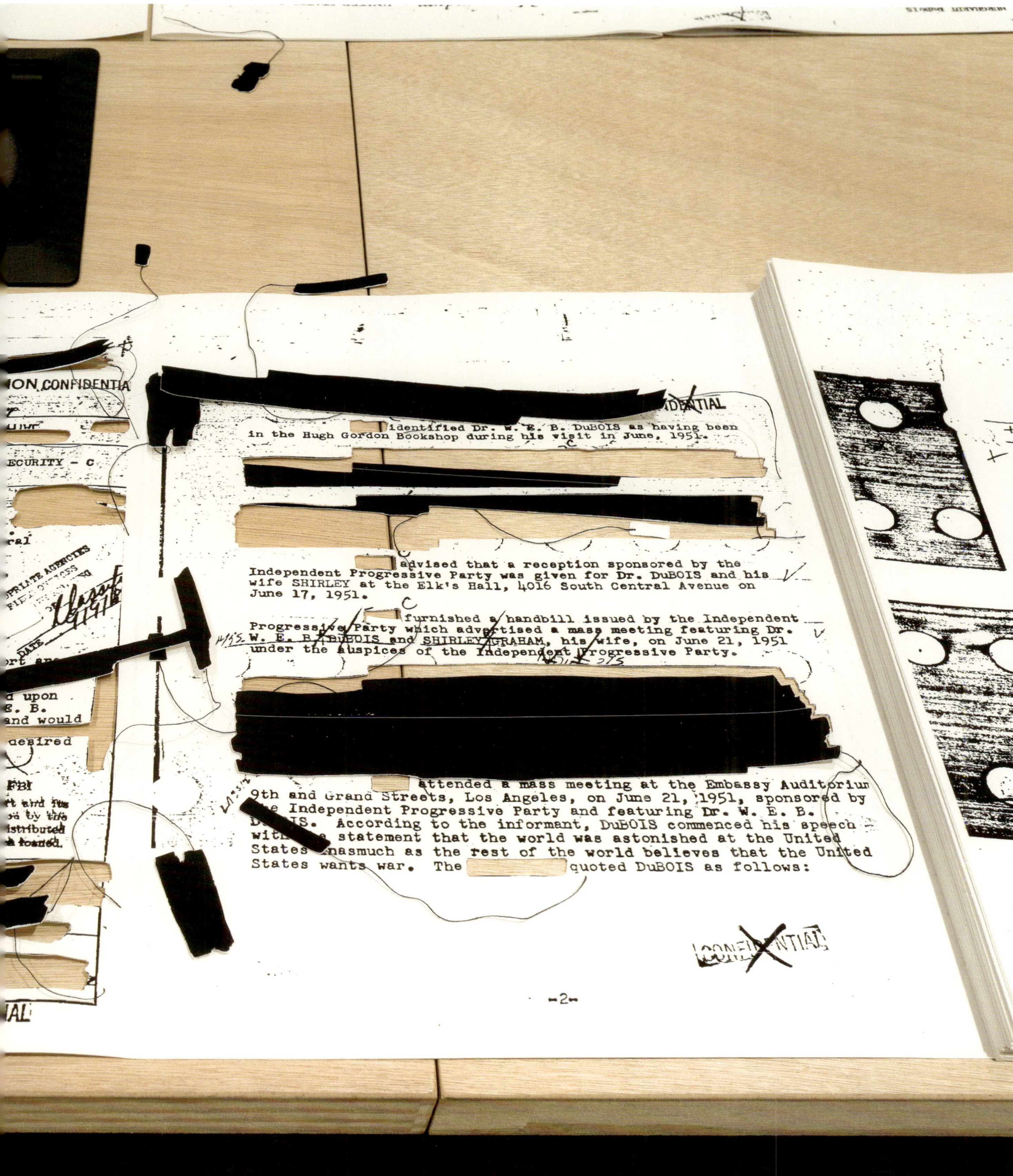
ON CONFIDENTIA
identified Dr. W. E. B. DuBOIS as having been
in the Hugh Gordon Bookshop during his visit in June, 1951.
advised that a reception sponsored by the
Independent Progressive Party was given for Dr. DuBOIS and his
wife SHIRLEY at the Elk's Hall, 4016 South Central Avenue on
June 17, 1951.
furnished a handbill issued by the Independent
Progressive Party which advertised a mass meeting featuring Dr.
under the auspices of the Independent Progressive Party.
attended a mass meeting at the Embassy Auditorium
9th and Grand Streets, Los Angeles, on June 21, 1951, sponsored by
According to the informant, DuBOIS commenced his speech
statement that the world was astonished at the United
inasmuch as the rest of the world believes that the United
States wants war. The
quoted DuBOIS as follows:
-2-

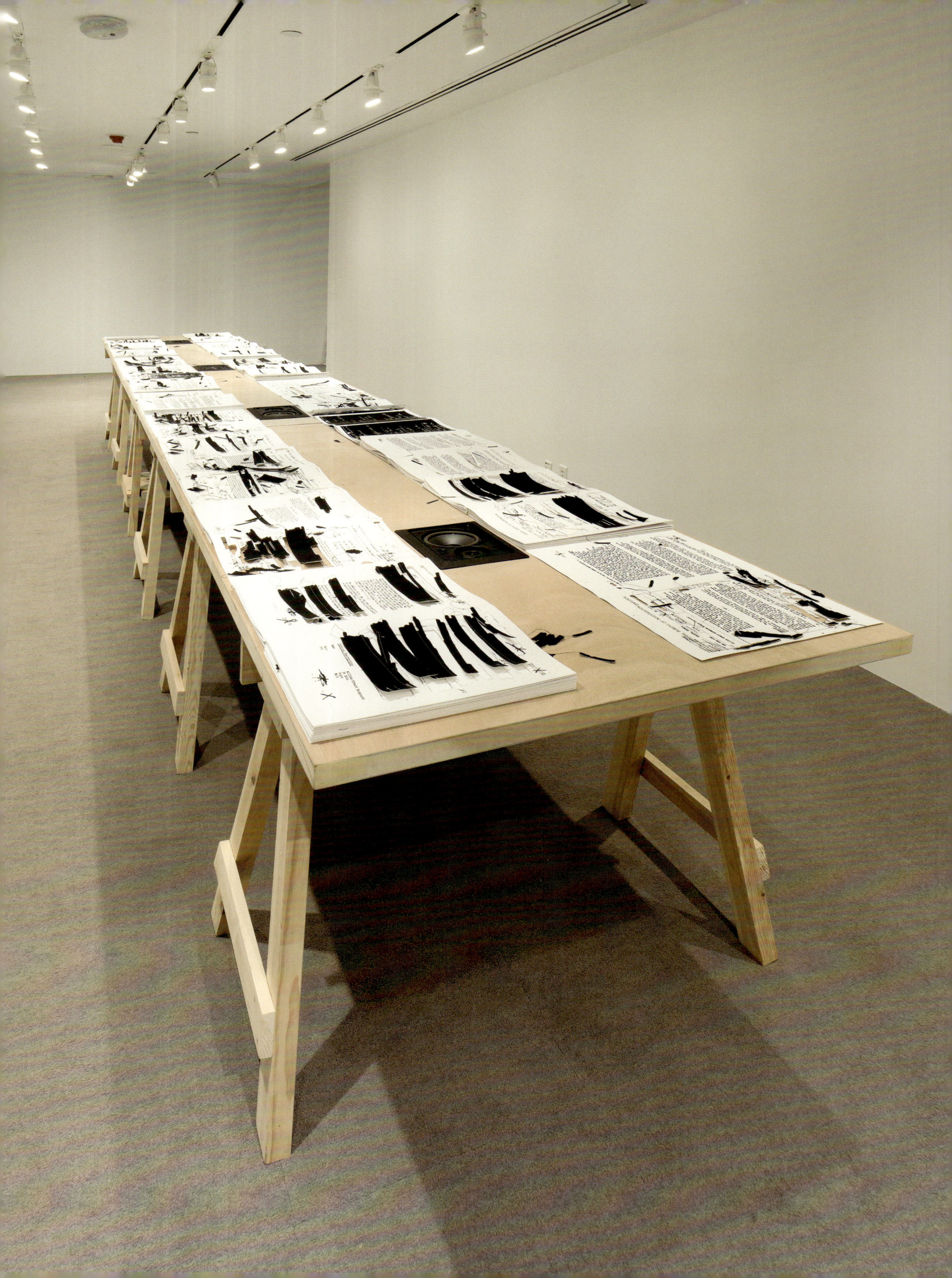

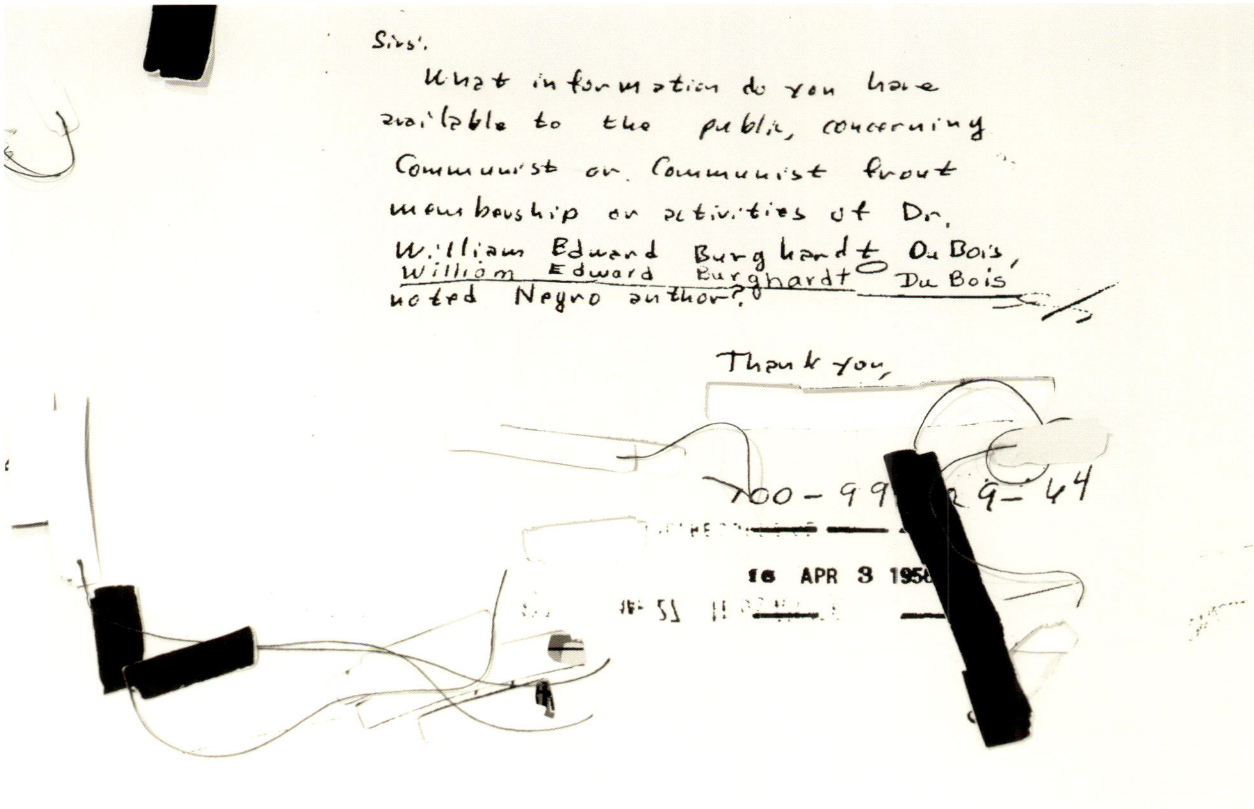

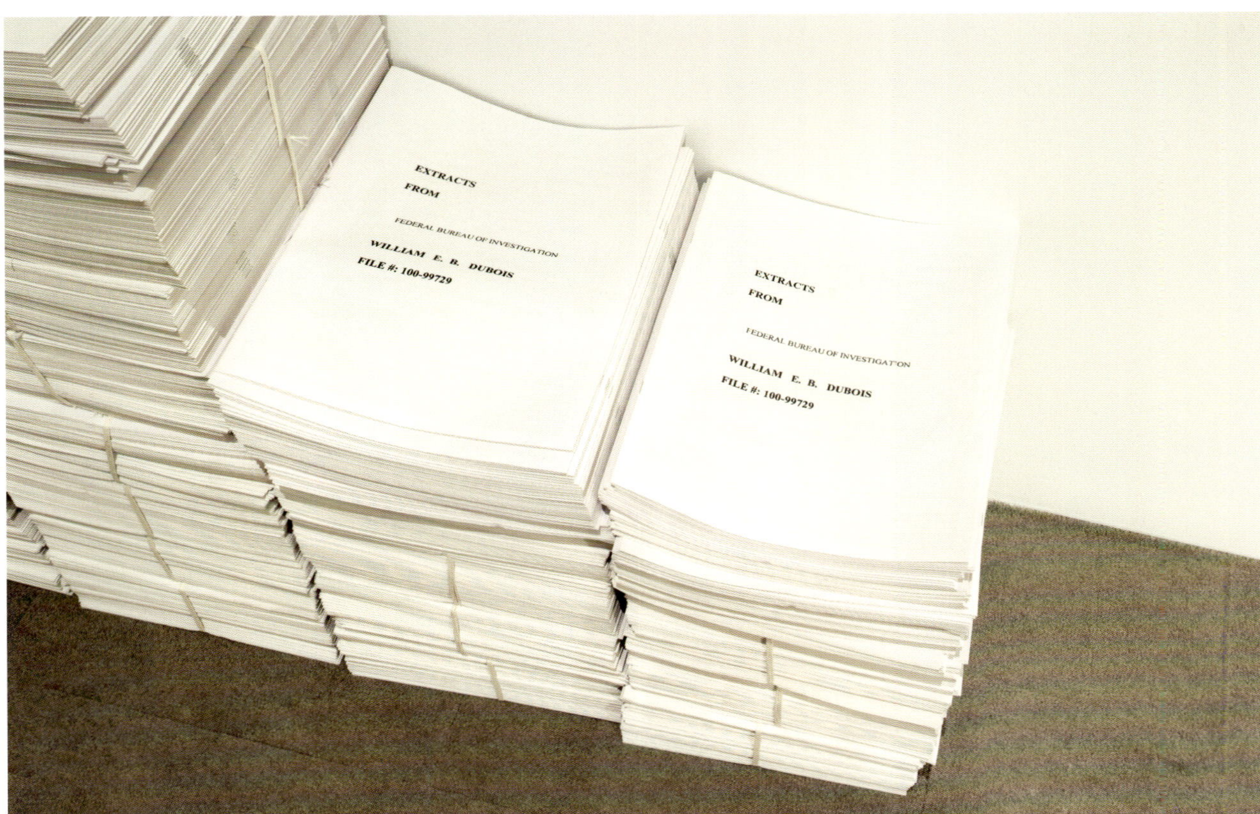

ANN MESSNER
Du Bois: The FBI Files, 2013
Left: Installation view, *Above right: (detail); Below right:* Installation accompanied by 44-page tabloid, edition of 5,000, distributed free throughout campus

AUDIO SCRIPT

Nina Simone, "Strange Fruit," written by Abel Meeropol, 1937

Paul Robeson, HUAC (House Committee on Un-American Activities), June 12, 1956

Randall Robinson, "Memory is the Active Agent of Collective Social Progress," *Democracy Now!* January 13, 2012

Interlude

Henry "Jimpson" Wallace, "No More, My Lord" (Mississippi State Penitentiary, Parchman), February 1948, Alan Lomax Recordings

Malcolm X and James Baldwin in conversation, April 25, 1961

Newscast, 1968 Olympics Men's 200m Final; Winners: 1st, Tommie Smith (USA),

2nd, Peter Norman (AUS), 3rd, John Carlos (USA)

1968 Olympics: *The Black Power Salute*, Tigerlily Films, 2008

John Carlos, 1968 Olympic U.S. Medalist, on the "Sports Moment That Changed the World," *Democracy Now!* with Dave Zirin, October 12, 2011

Fannie Lou Hamer, Pacifica Radio Archive, 1965

Interlude

John Coltrane, "Alabama"

Angela Davis, interview in San Rafael County Prison with Bo Holmström, 1972

Angela Davis, interview in California Prison with Barry Callaghan, 1970

Excerpts from *Prisons on Fire: The Attica Rebellion*, The Freedom Archives

Interlude (brief)

John Coltrane, "Alabama"

Mumia Abu Jamal, Final Boots interview, June 13, 2008

Interlude

Ali Farka Touré with Ry Cooder, "Ai Du," *Talking Timbuktu*, 1994

REPEATS

ANN MESSNER
Du Bois: The FBI Files, 2013
Above: audio script

Right: (detail)

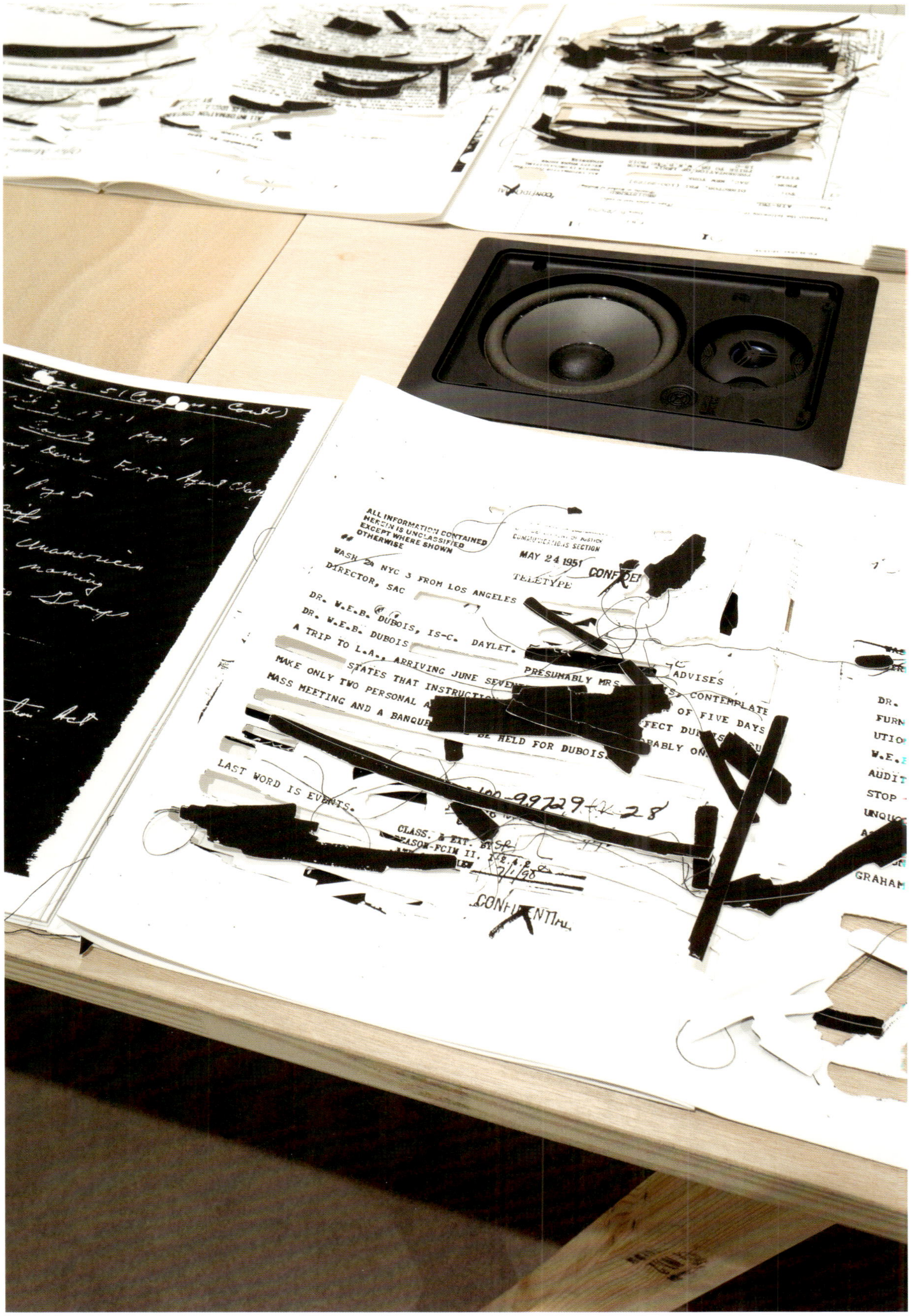
ALL INFORMATION CONTAINED
HEREIN IS UNCLASSIFIED
EXCEPT WHERE SHOWN
OTHERWISE
COMMUNICATIONS SECTION
MAY 24 1951
TELETYPE
WASH 2A NYC 3 FROM LOS ANGELES
DIRECTOR, SAC
DR. W.E.B. DUBOIS, IS-C. DAYLET.
A TRIP TO L.A., ARRIVING JUNE SEVEN
STATES THAT INSTRUCTI
MAKE ONLY TWO PERSONAL A
MASS MEETING AND A BANQU
BE HELD FOR DUBOIS
PRESUMABLY MRS.
ADVISES
CONTEMPLATE
OF FIVE DAYS
LAST WORD IS EVENTS.
CLASS. & EXT. BY
GRAHAM

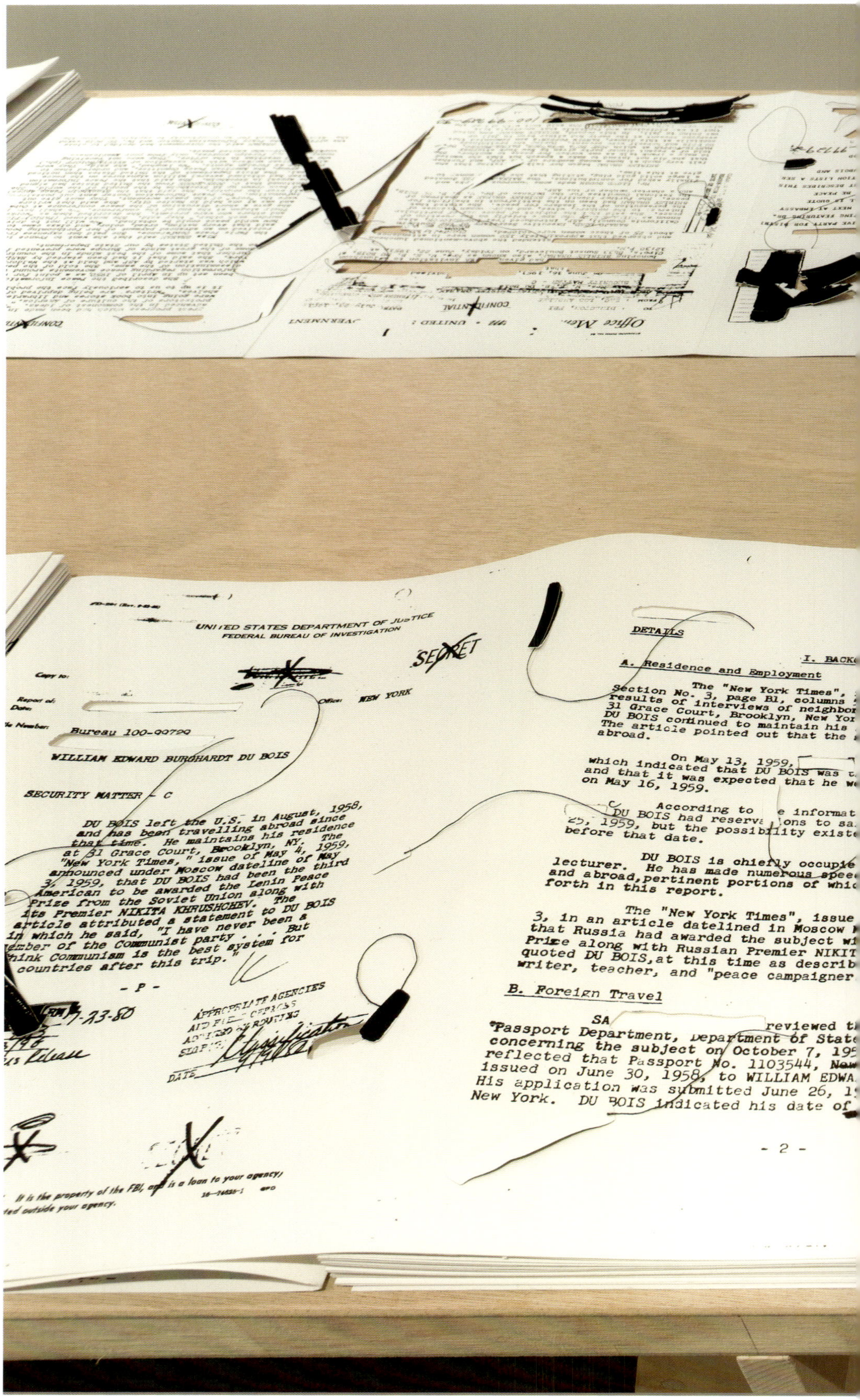

ANN MESSNER
Du Bois: The FBI Files, 2013 *(detail)*

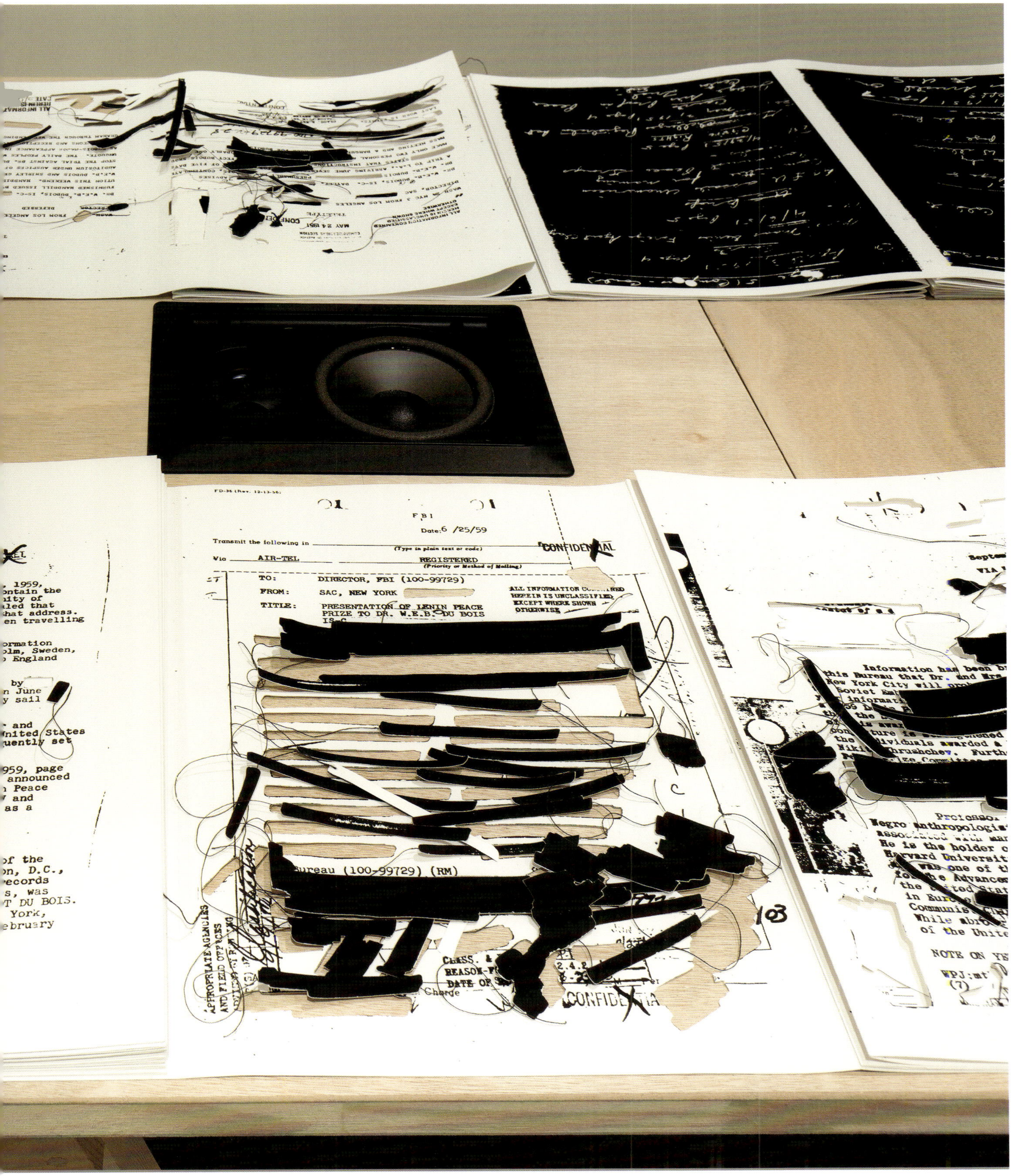

JEFFERSON PINDER

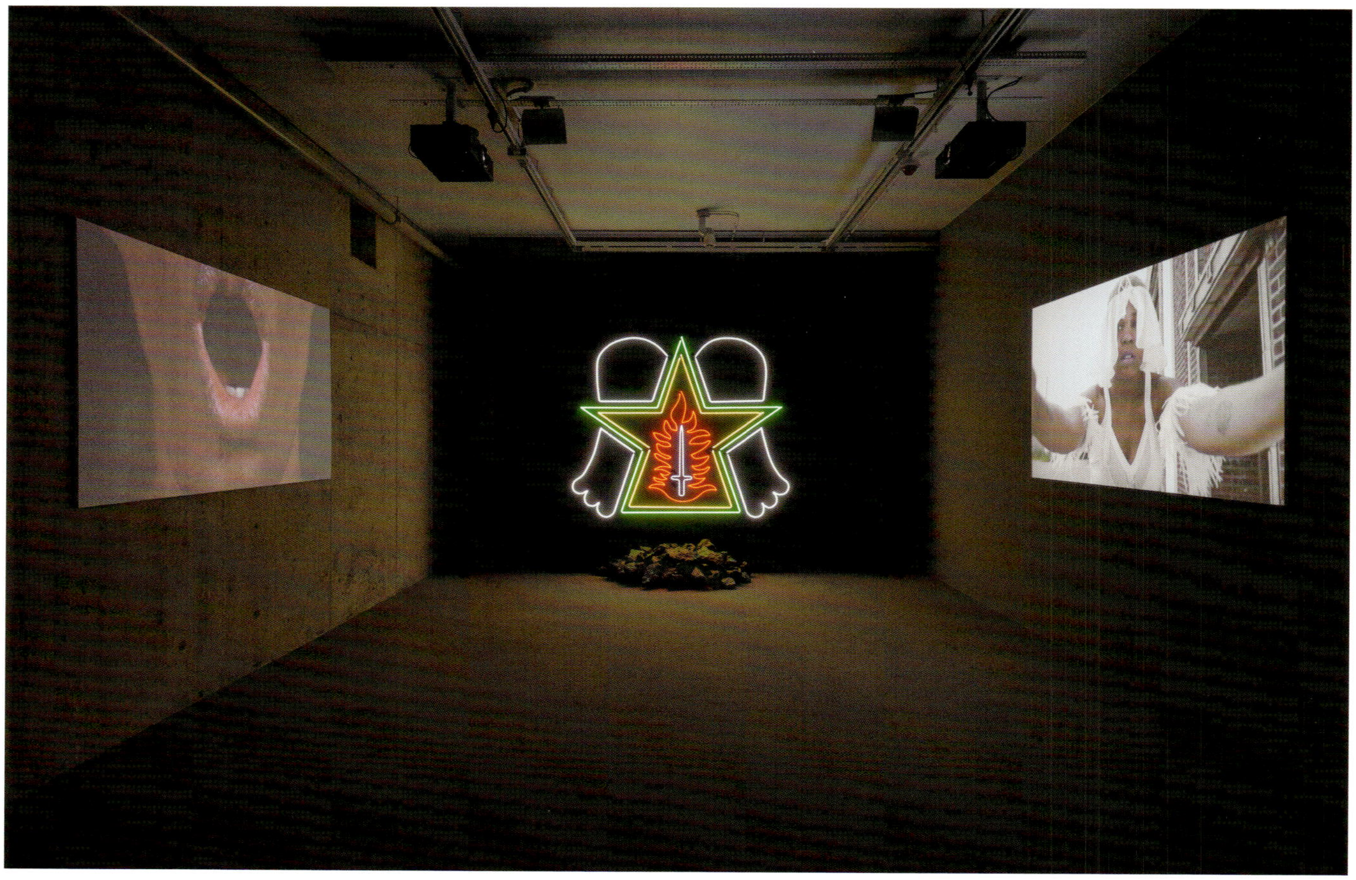

Above
JEFFERSON PINDER
Star of Ethiopia, 2013
Neon, basalt stone
72″ x 84¼″ x ⅝″

Opposite
JEFFERSON PINDER
Overture, 2013
Video, 2-channel projection; 8 minutes
Video stills

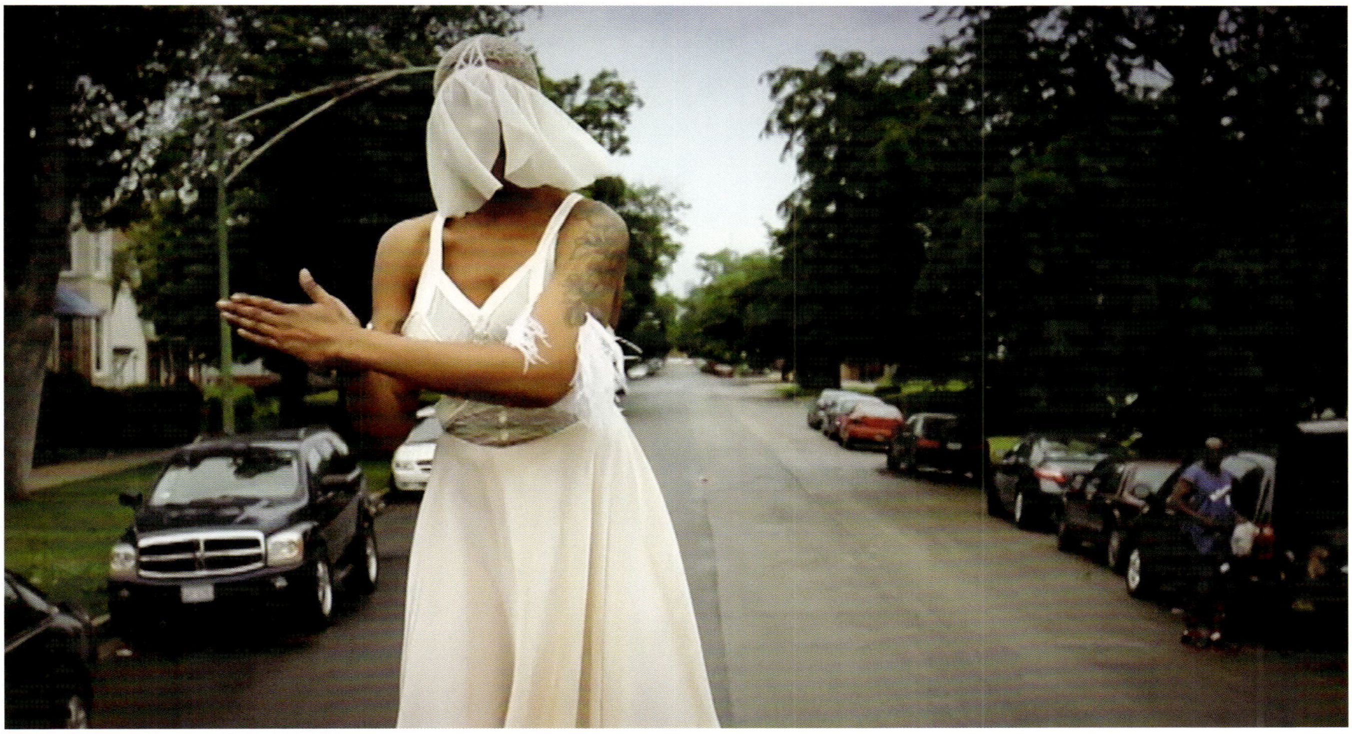

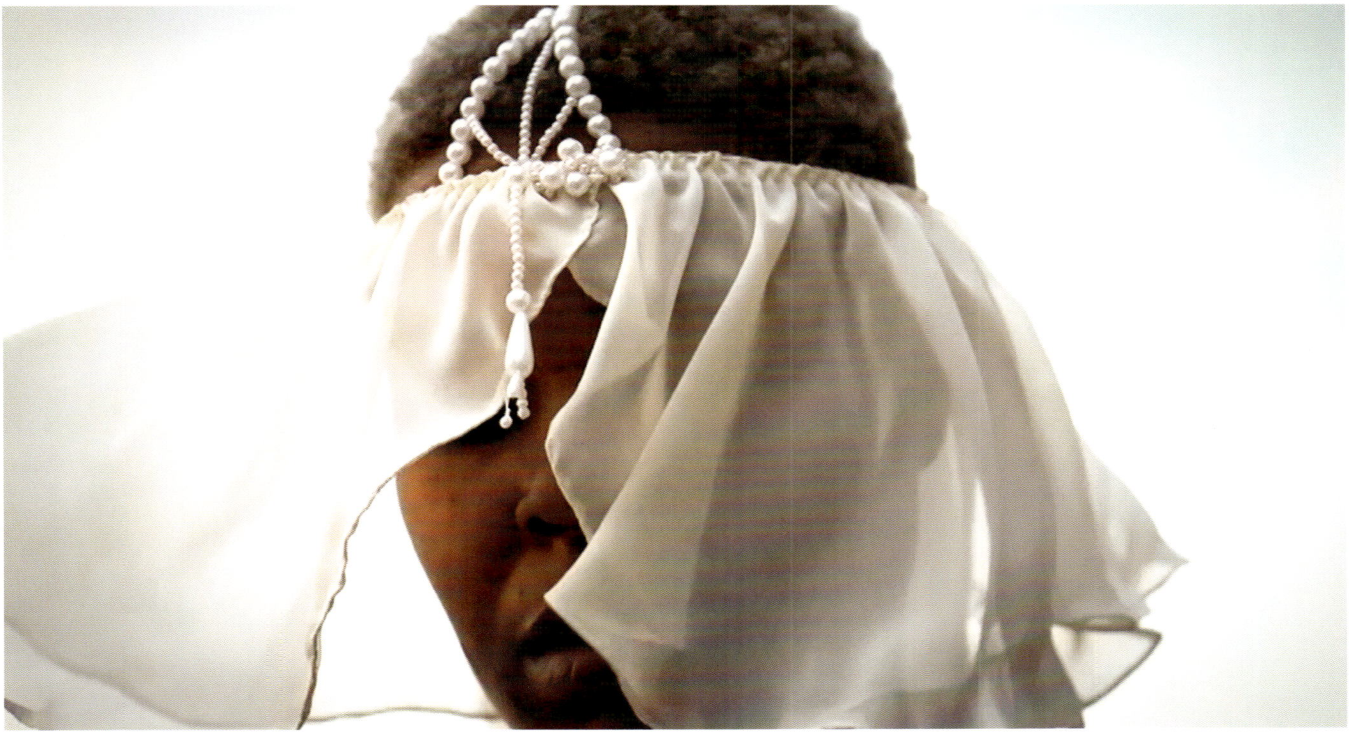

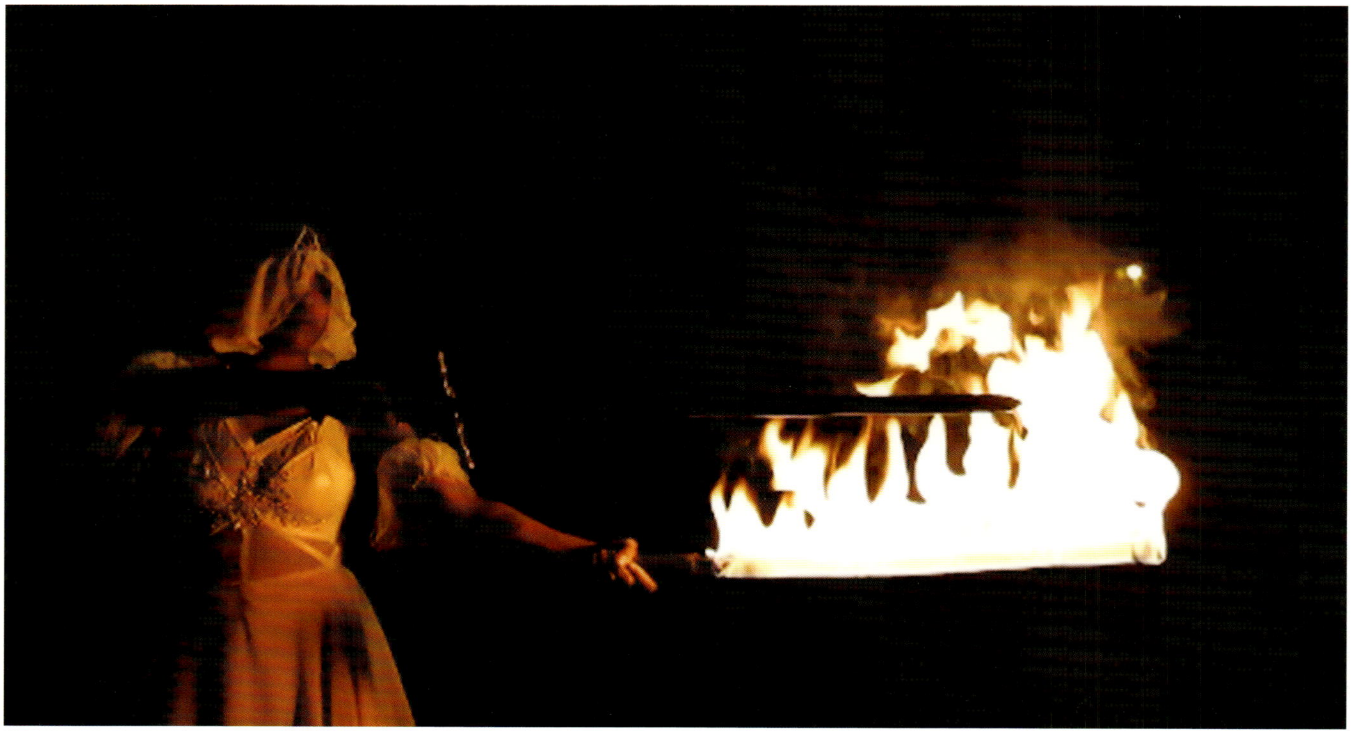

Left and right
JEFFERSON PINDER
Overture, 2013
Video, 2-channel projection; 8 minutes
(video stills)

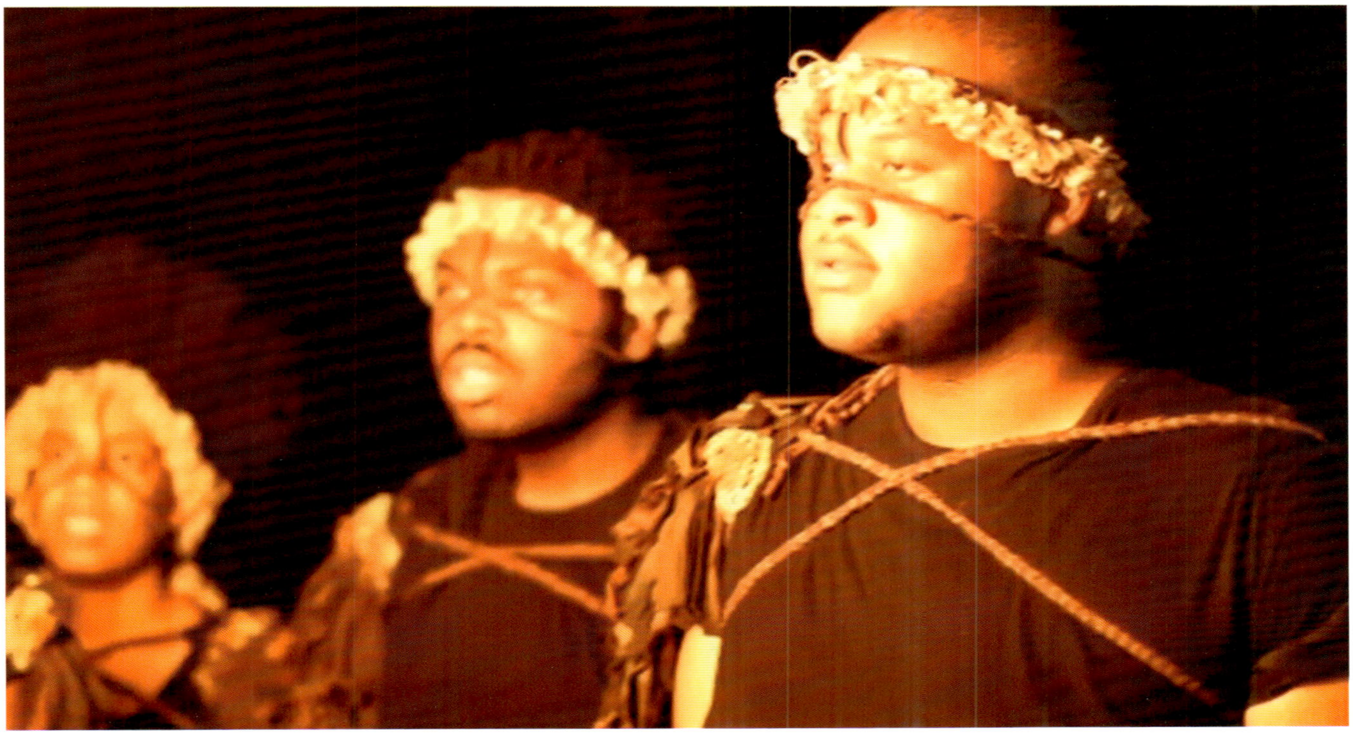

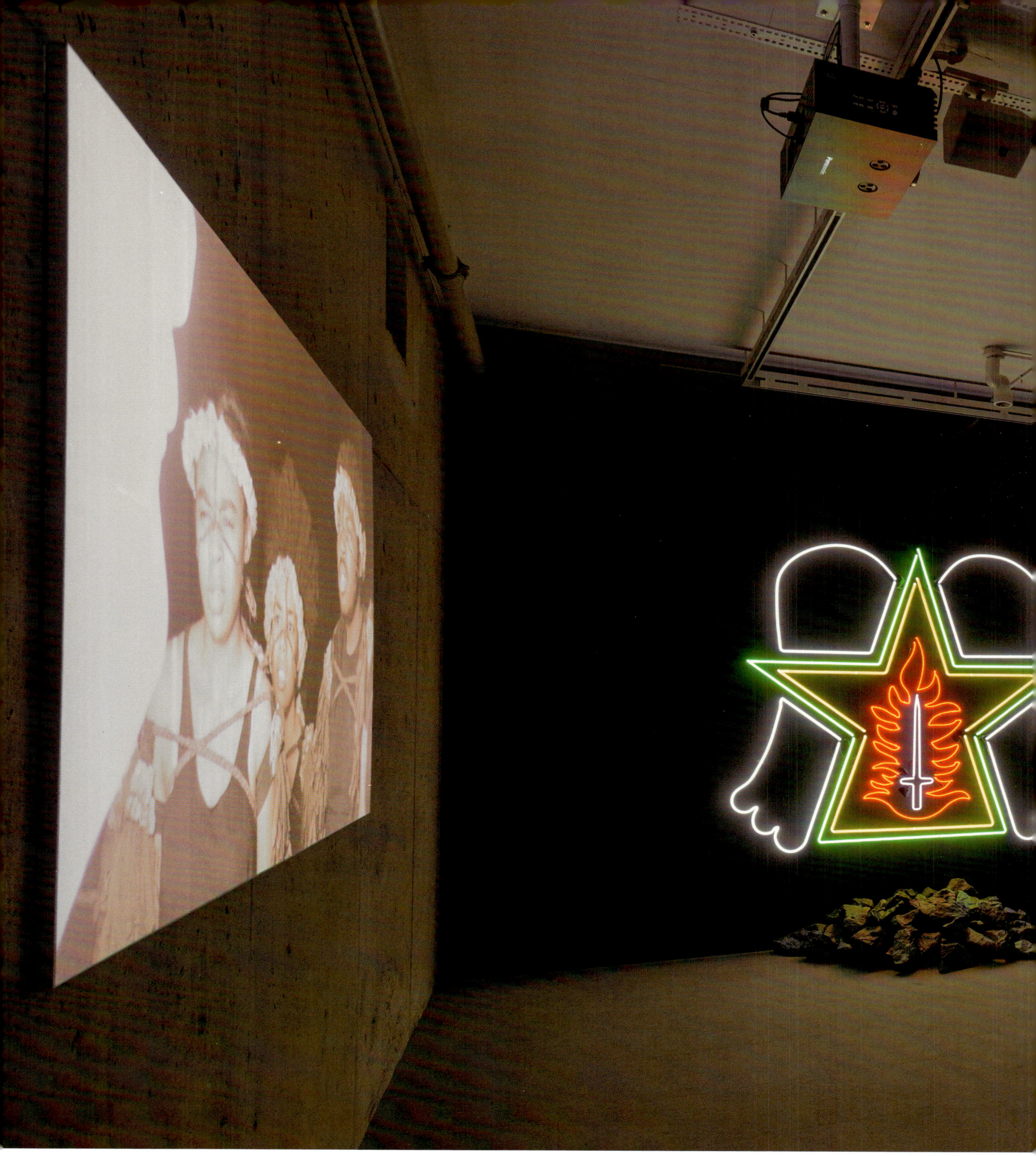

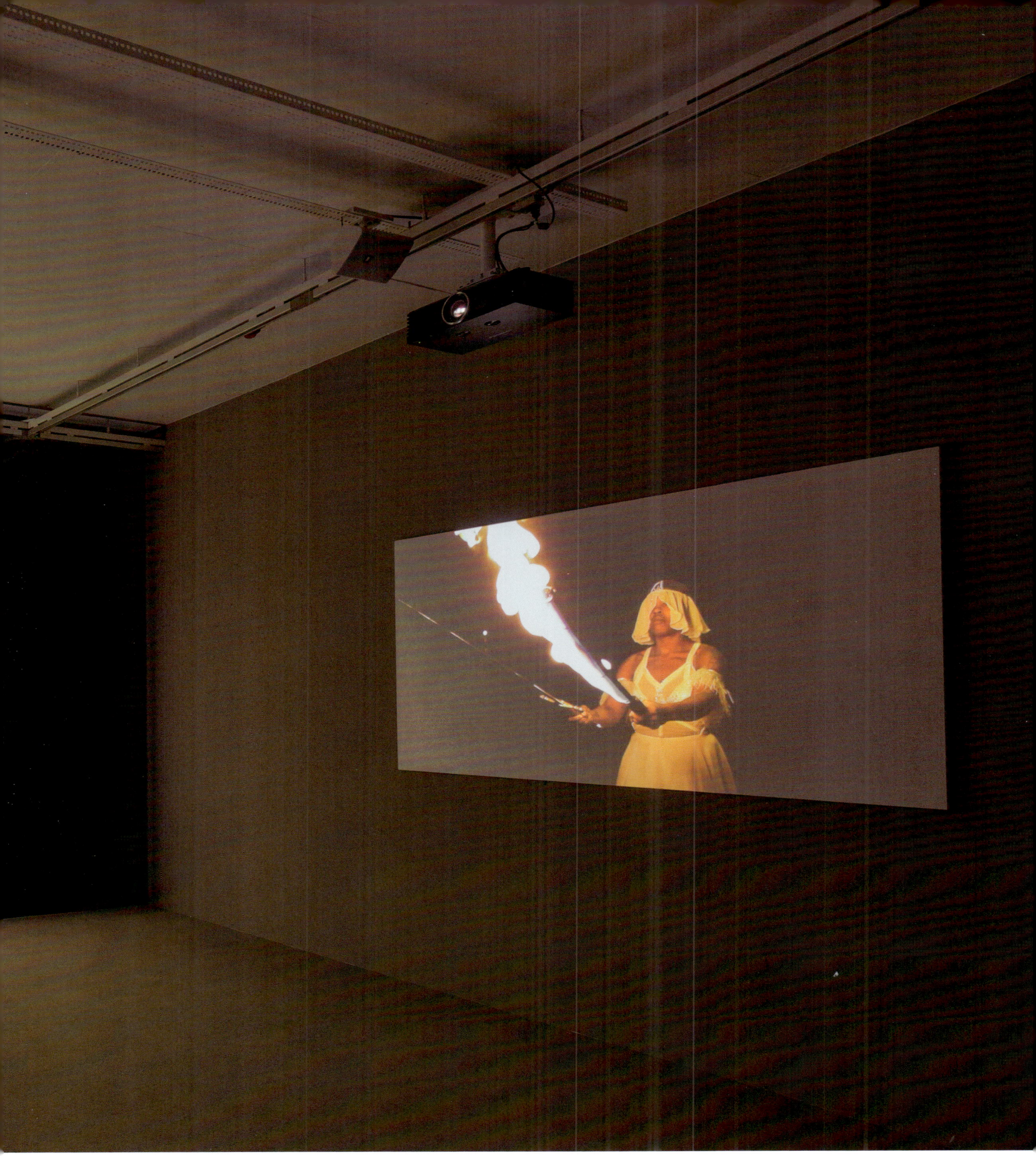

JEFFERSON PINDER
Installation view

TIM ROLLINS & K.O.S.

TIM ROLLINS & K.O.S.
DARKWATER (after W.E.B. Du Bois), 2013
Furnace black watercolor, gold acrylic on vintage book pages on panel
24 elements, each 7" x 5"
Courtesy of Studio K.O.S. and Lehmann Maupin, New York and Hong Kong
With students from the Renaissance School, Springfield, Massachusetts: Dawell Bautista, Alexandria Belhumeur, Jaqueline Clark-Harris, Korey Collazo, Michael DeAngelo, Cervante Golden, Marcus Martinez, Michael Mascaro, Damahya Mongroo, Tracy Nguyen, Roderick Sellars, Alice Swan, Cora Swan, Mercy Togba, Kassandra Velez

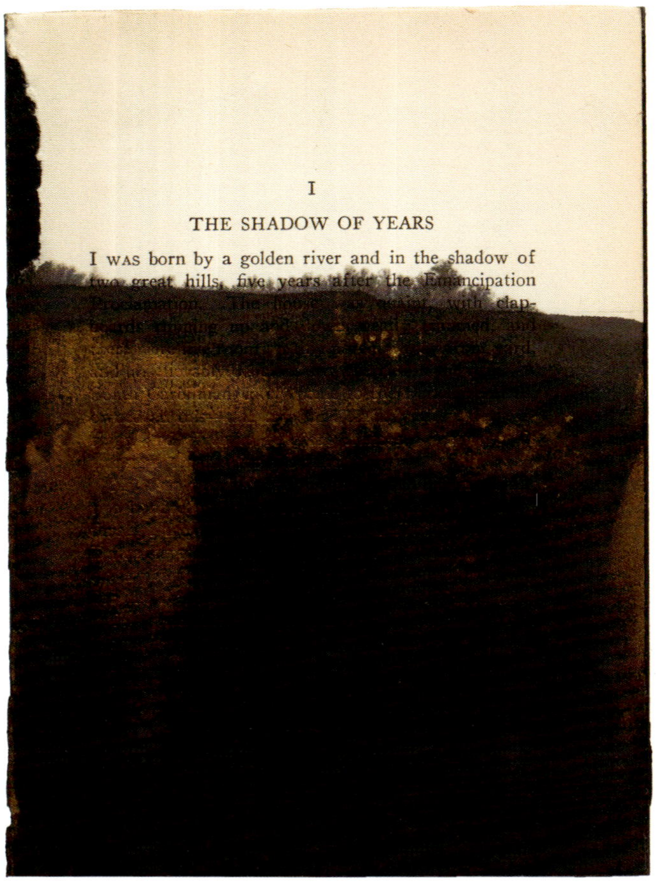

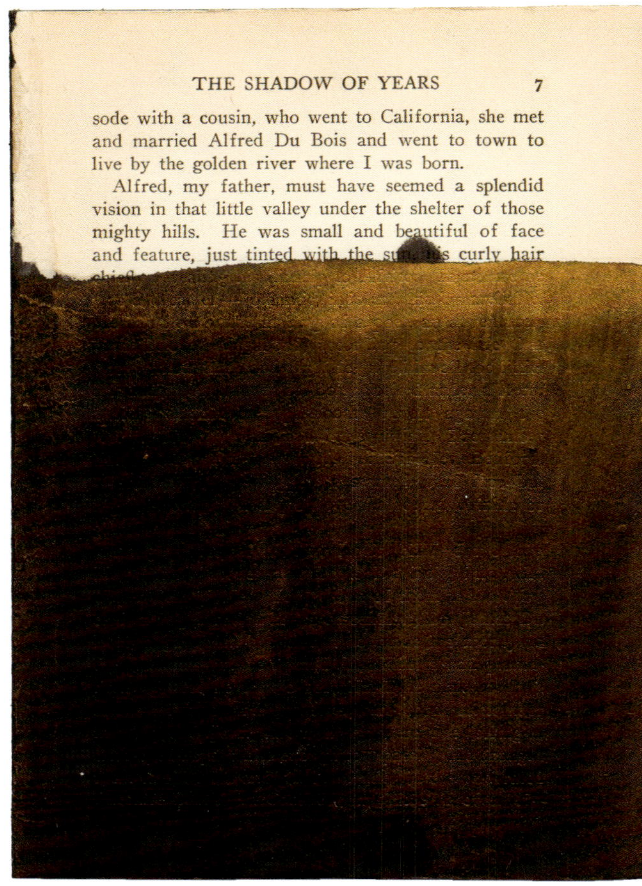

Left and right

TIM ROLLINS & K.O.S.

DARKWATER (after W.E.B. Du Bois), 2013 *(details)*

Furnace black watercolor, gold acrylic on vintage book pages on panel

24 elements, each 7" x 5"

Courtesy of Studio K.O.S. and Lehmann Maupin, New York and Hong Kong

With students from the Renaissance School, Springfield, Massachusetts

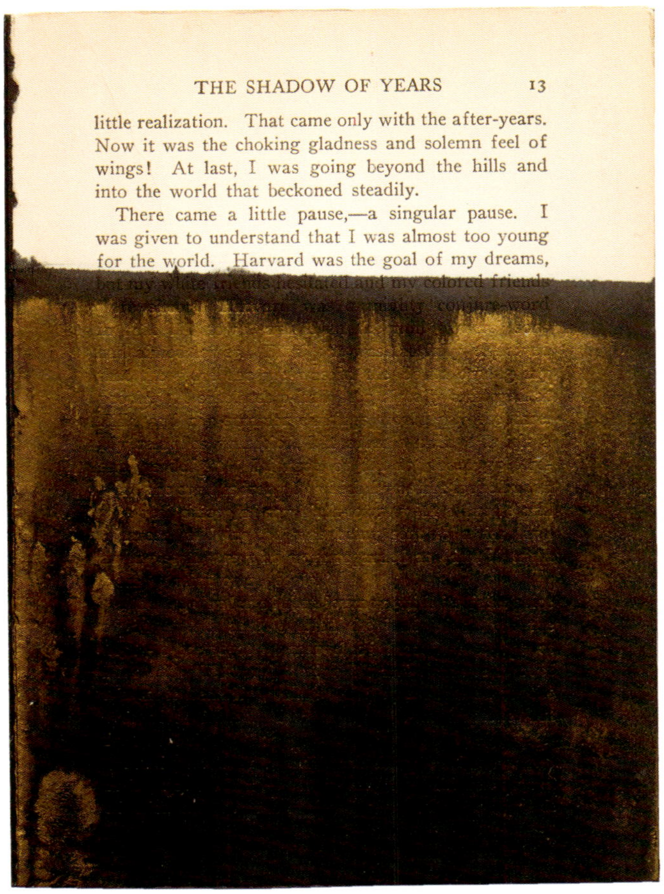
THE SHADOW OF YEARS 13
little realization. That came only with the after-years.
Now it was the choking gladness and solemn feel of
wings! At last, I was going beyond the hills and
into the world that beckoned steadily.
There came a little pause,—a singular pause. I
was given to understand that I was almost too young
for the world. Harvard was the goal of my dreams,

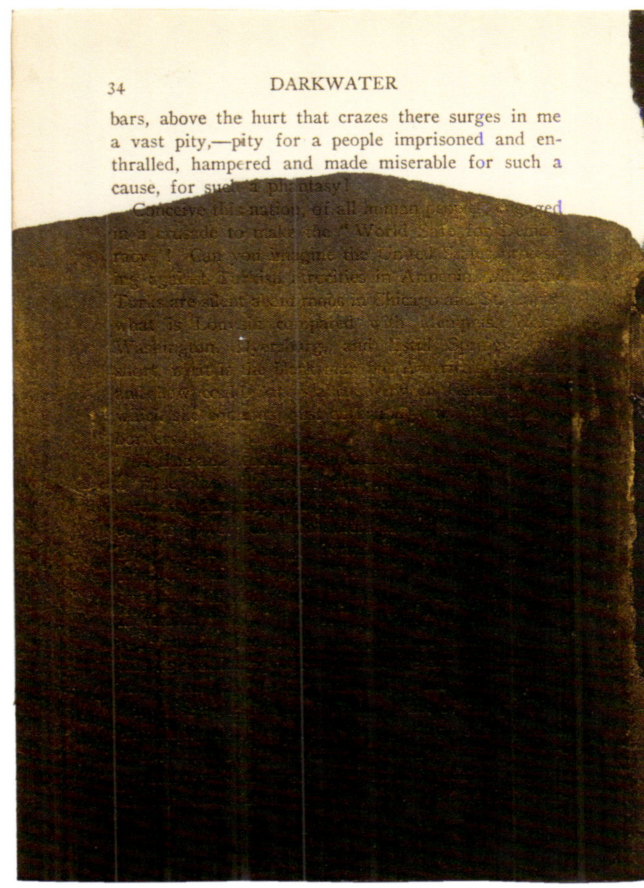
34 DARKWATER
bars, above the hurt that crazes there surges in me
a vast pity,—pity for a people imprisoned and en-
thralled, hampered and made miserable for such a

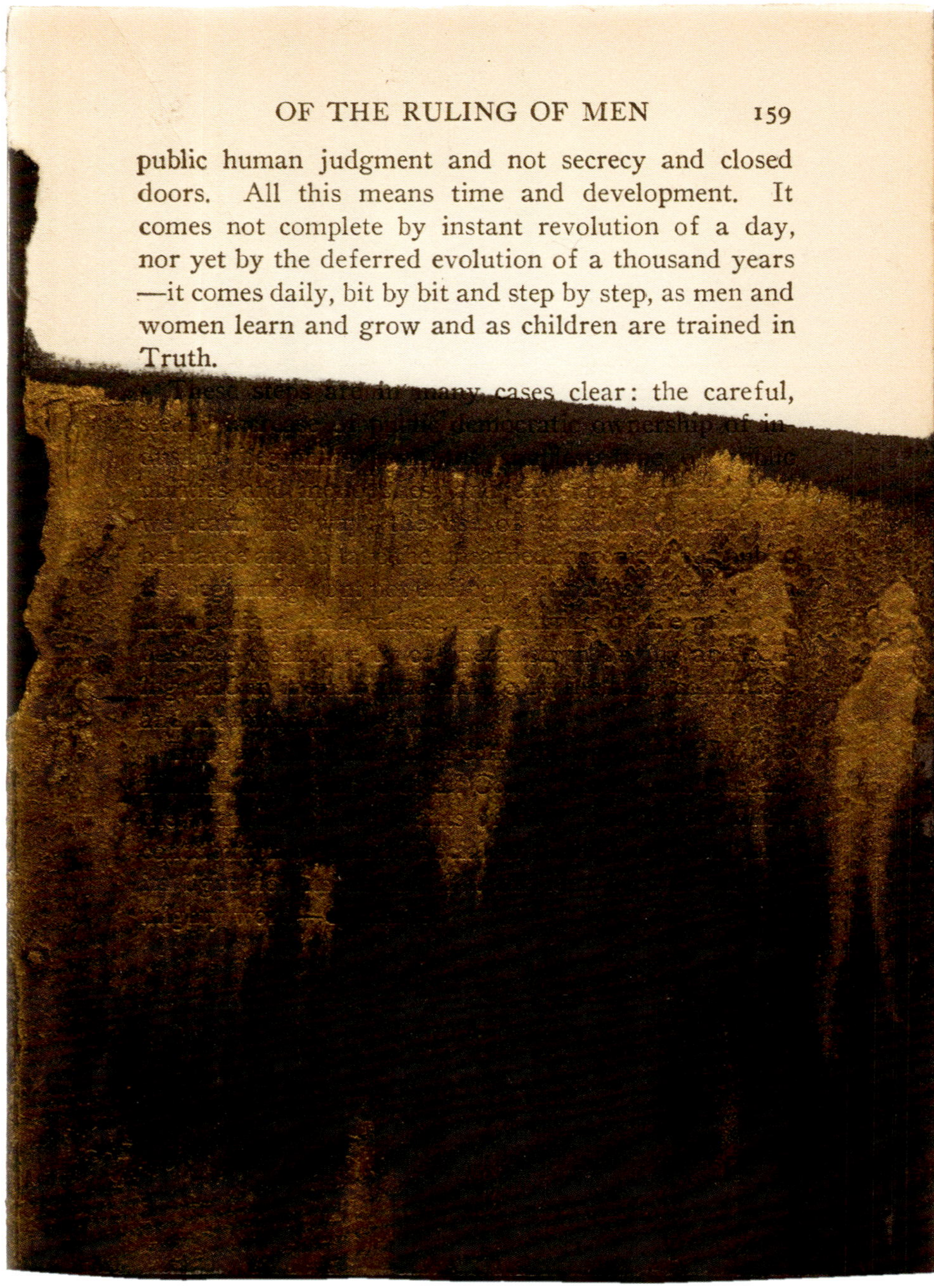

Left and right
TIM ROLLINS & K.O.S.
DARKWATER (after W.E.B. Du Bois), 2013 *(details)*
Furnace black watercolor, gold acrylic on vintage book pages on panel
24 elements, each 7″ x 5″
Courtesy of Studio K.O.S. and Lehmann Maupin, New York and Hong Kong
With students from the Renaissance School, Springfield, Massachusetts

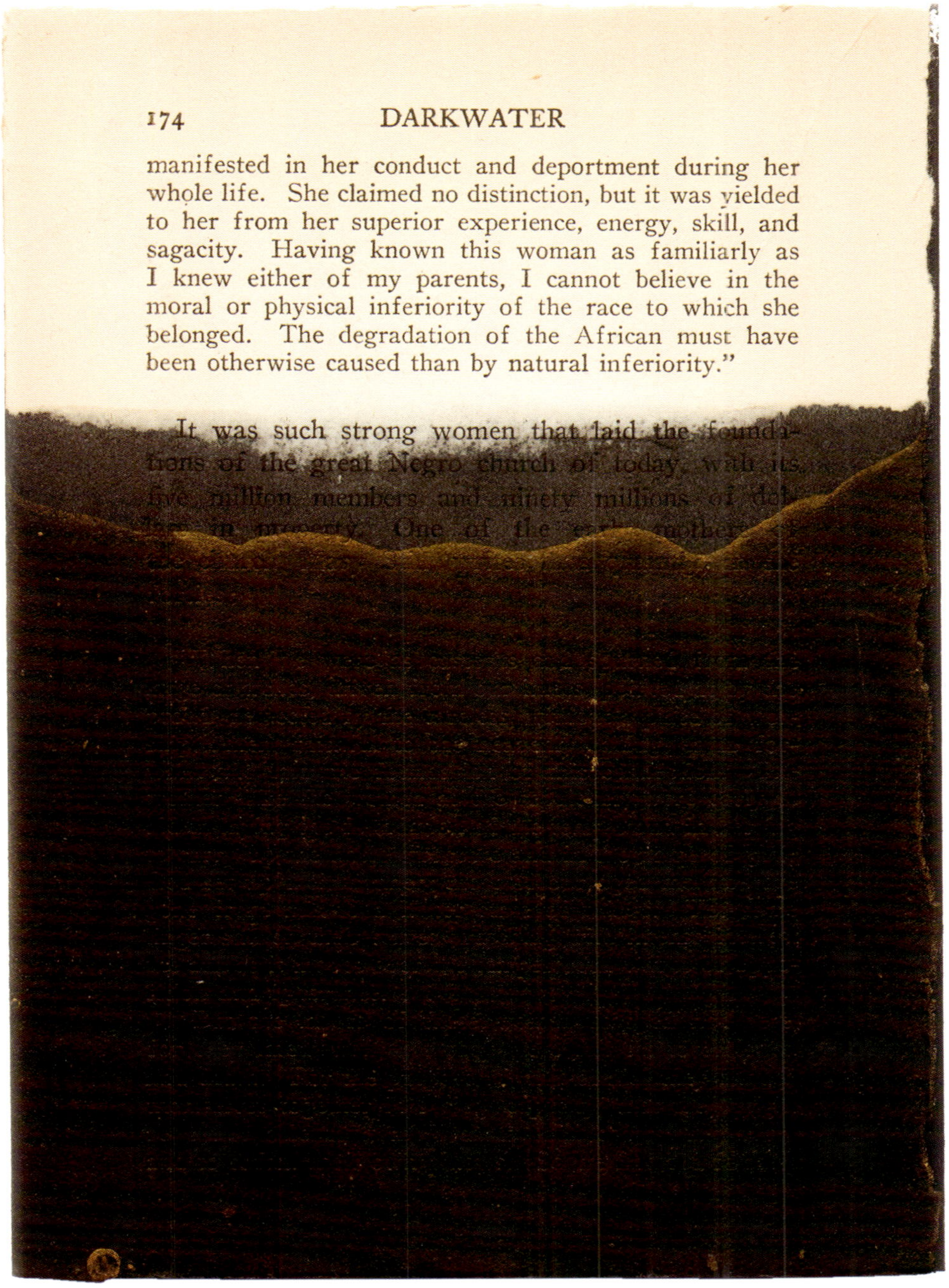

174 DARKWATER

manifested in her conduct and deportment during her whole life. She claimed no distinction, but it was yielded to her from her superior experience, energy, skill, and sagacity. Having known this woman as familiarly as I knew either of my parents, I cannot believe in the moral or physical inferiority of the race to which she belonged. The degradation of the African must have been otherwise caused than by natural inferiority."

It was such strong women that laid the foundations of the great Negro church of today, with its five million members and ninety millions of dollars in property. One of the

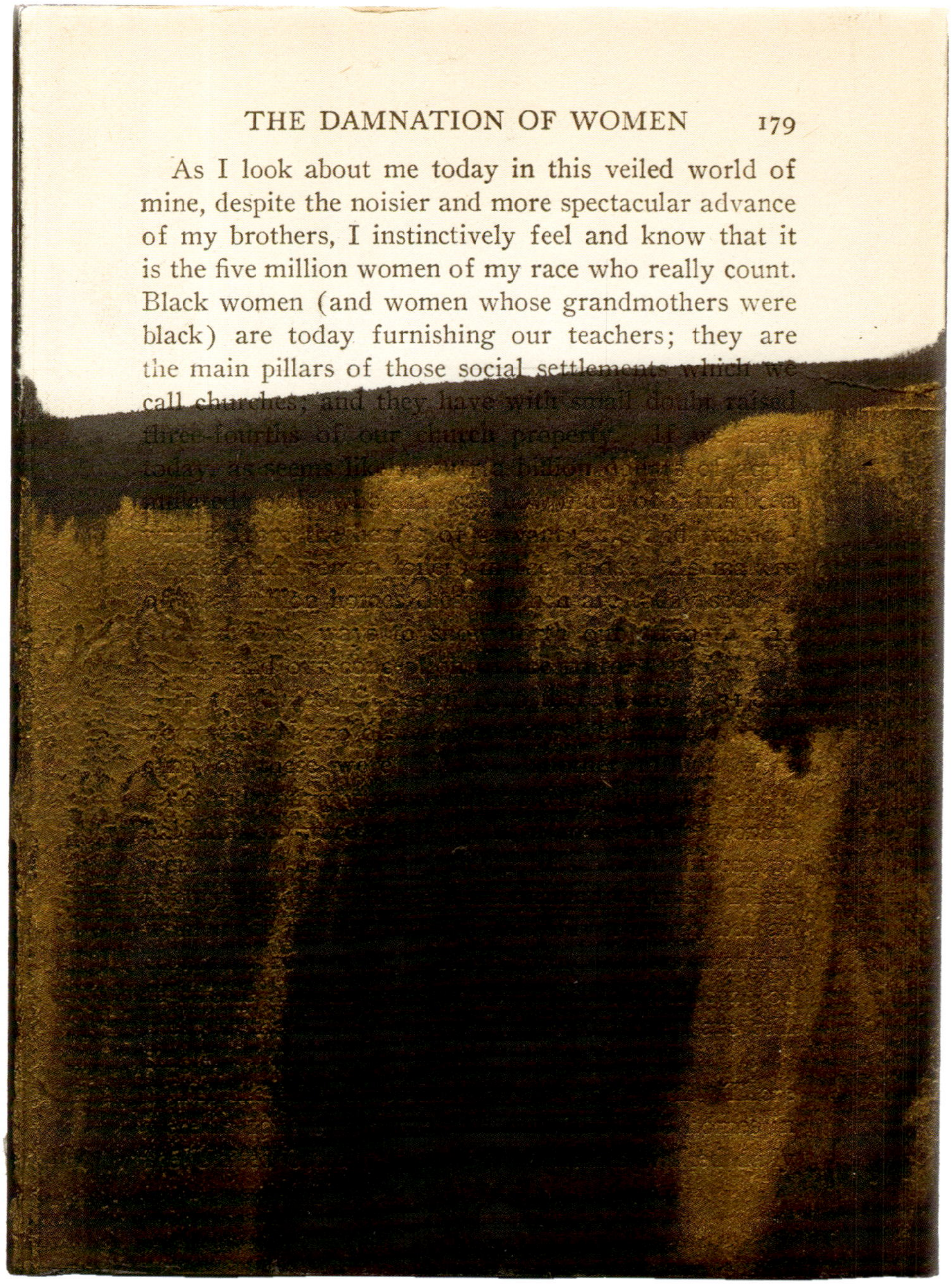

Left and right
TIM ROLLINS & K.O.S.
DARKWATER (after W.E.B. Du Bois), 2013 *(details)*
Furnace black watercolor, gold acrylic on vintage book pages on panel
24 elements, each 7″ x 5″
Courtesy of Studio K.O.S. and Lehmann Maupin, New York and Hong Kong
With students from the Renaissance School, Springfield, Massachusetts

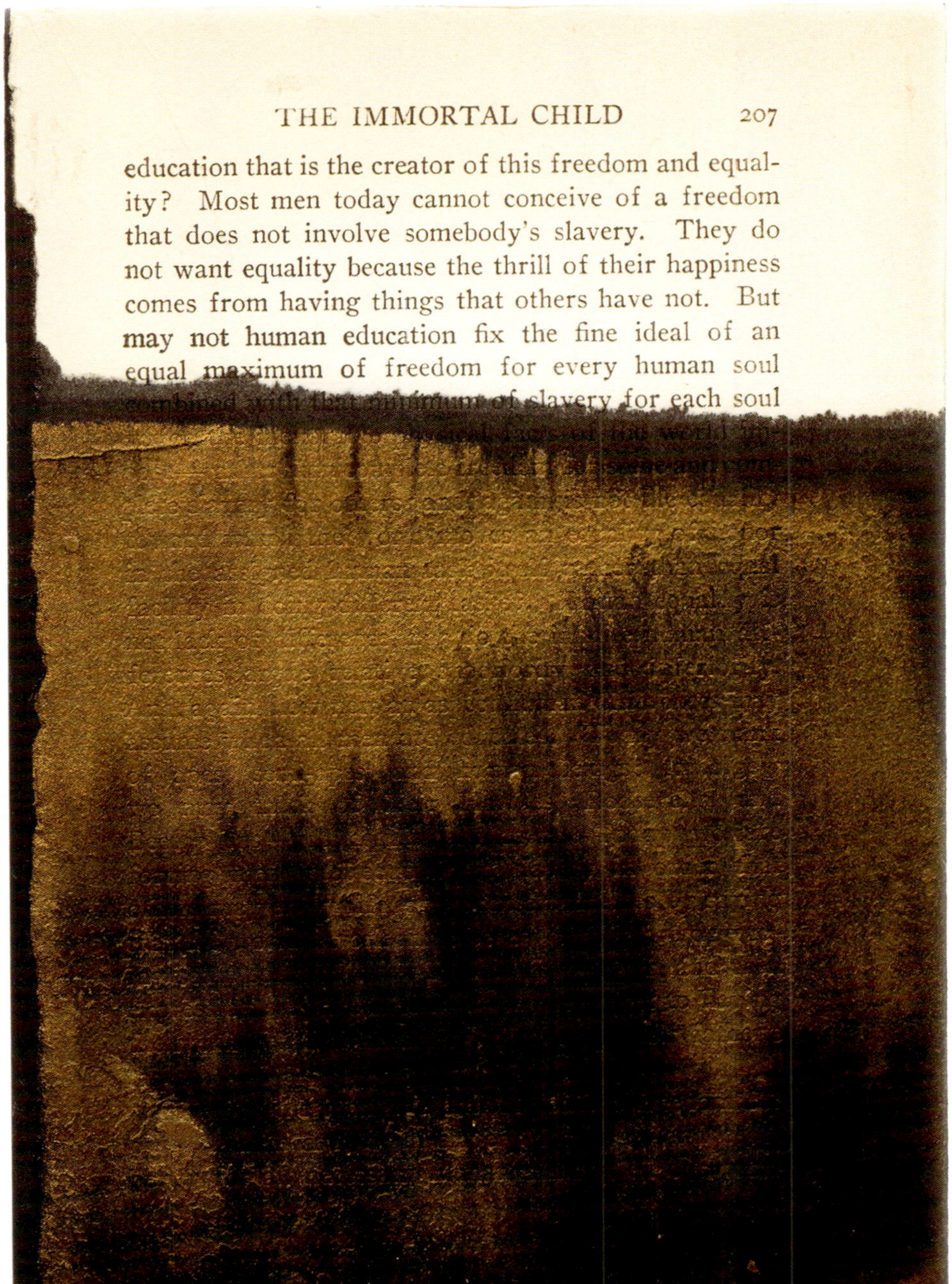
THE IMMORTAL CHILD 207
education that is the creator of this freedom and equal-
ity? Most men today cannot conceive of a freedom
that does not involve somebody's slavery. They do
not want equality because the thrill of their happiness
comes from having things that others have not. But
may not human education fix the fine ideal of an
equal maximum of freedom for every human soul
combined with that minimum of slavery for each soul

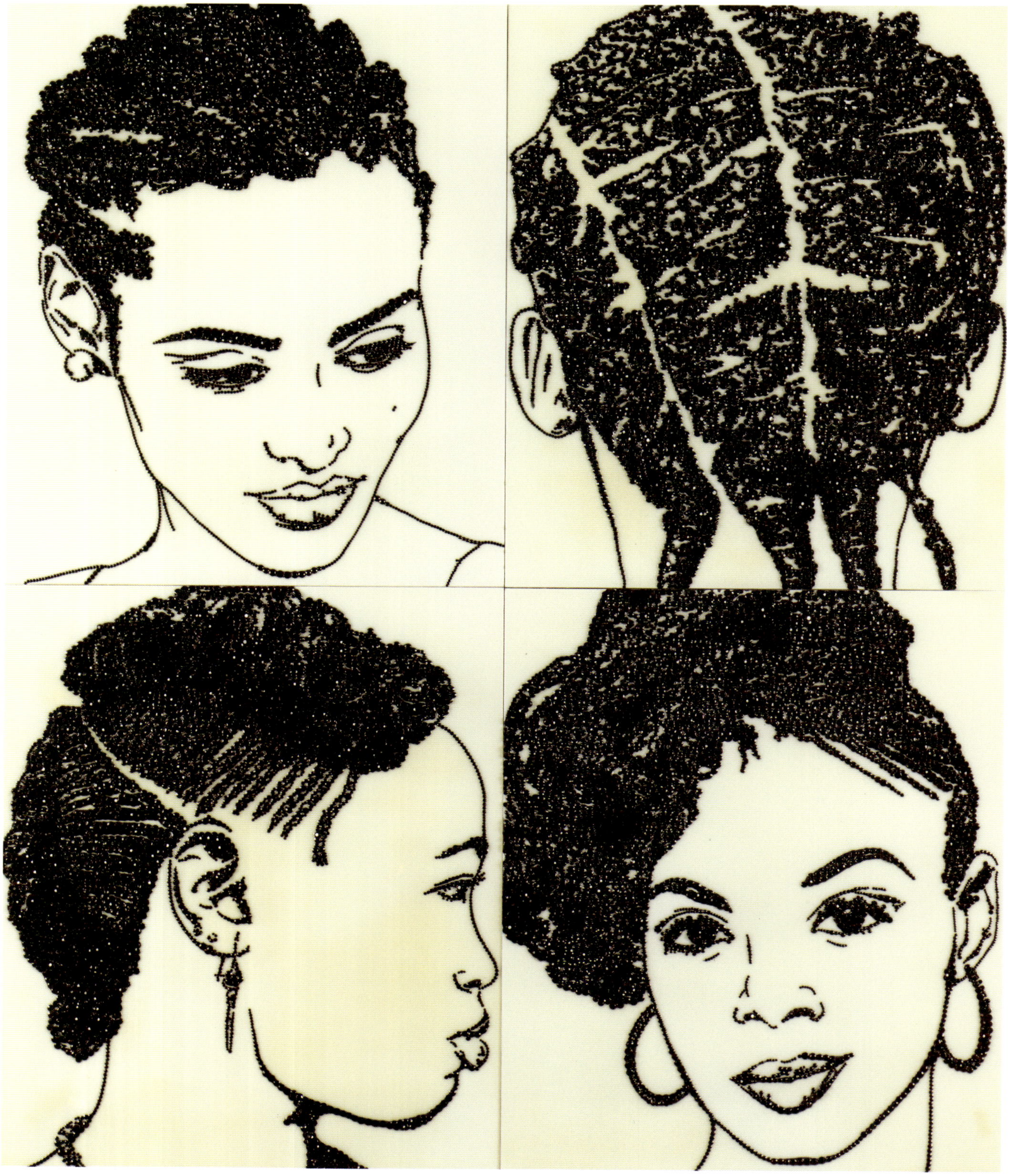

Above
MICKALENE THOMAS
Hair Portraits, 2013 *(details)*
Rhinestones and acrylic on wood panel,
24 panels, each 24″ x 20″,
installation 48″ x 240″
Courtesy of Melva Bucksbaum and Raymond Learsy, Mickalene Thomas, and Lehmann Maupin, New York and Hong Kong

MICKALENE THOMAS

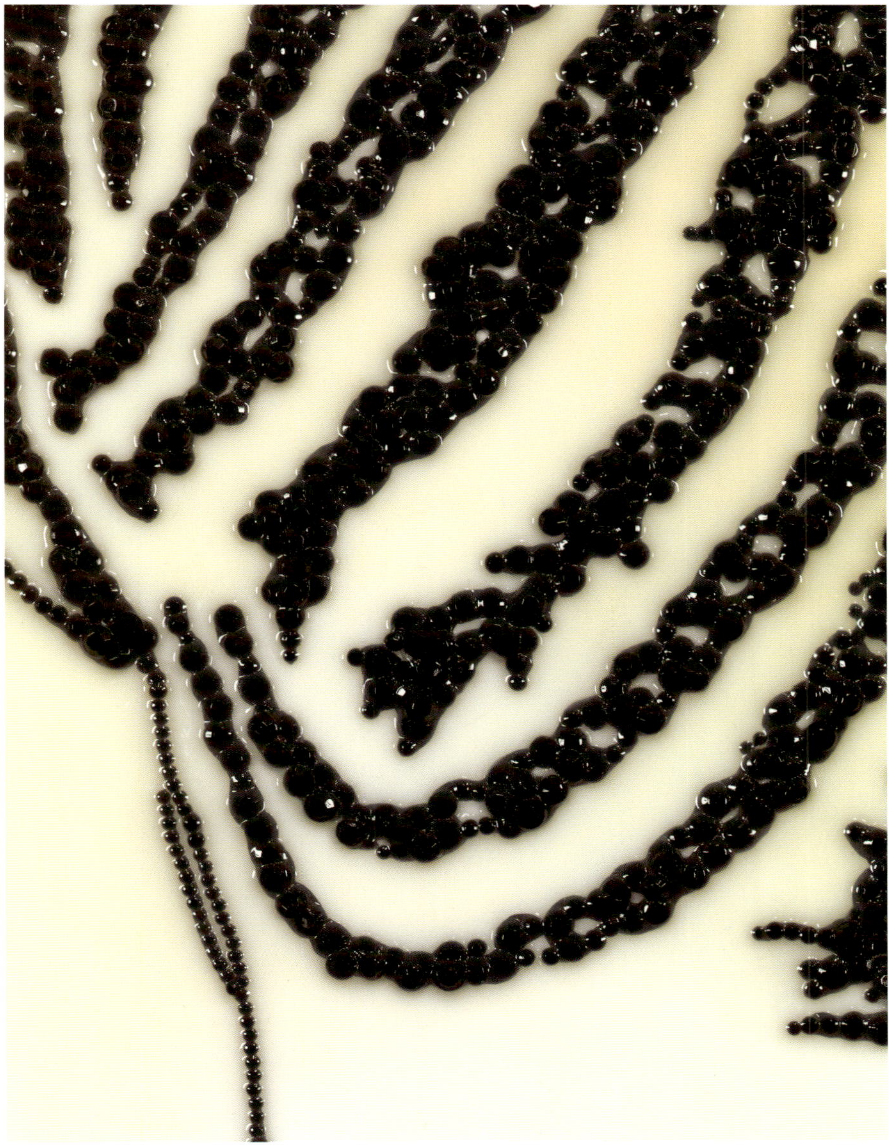

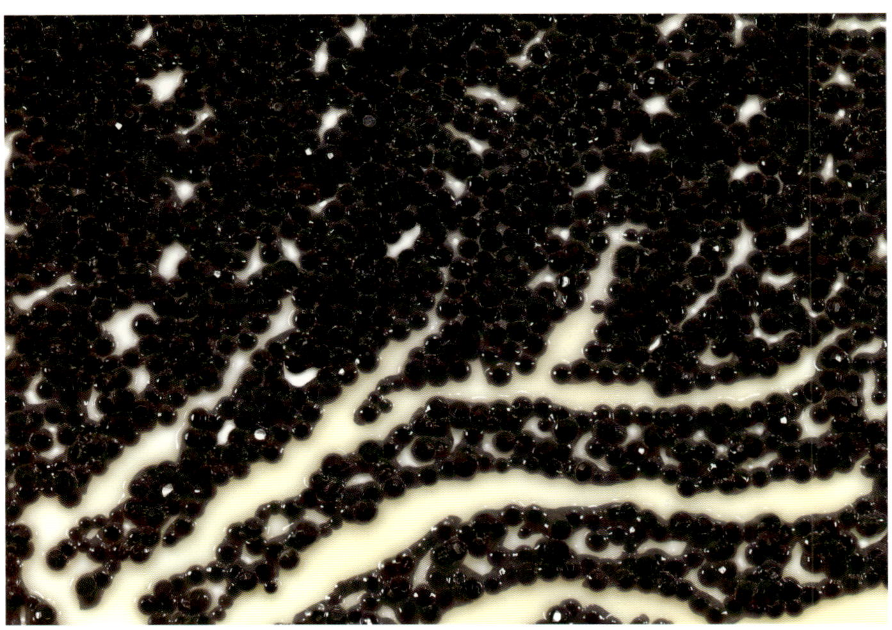

Above and below:
MICKALENE THOMAS
Hair Portraits (details), 2013
Rhinestones and acrylic on wood panel,
24 panels, each 24″ x 20″,
installation 48″ x 240″
Courtesy of Melva Bucksbaum and Raymond Learsy, Mickalene Thomas, and Lehmann Maupin, New York and Hong Kong

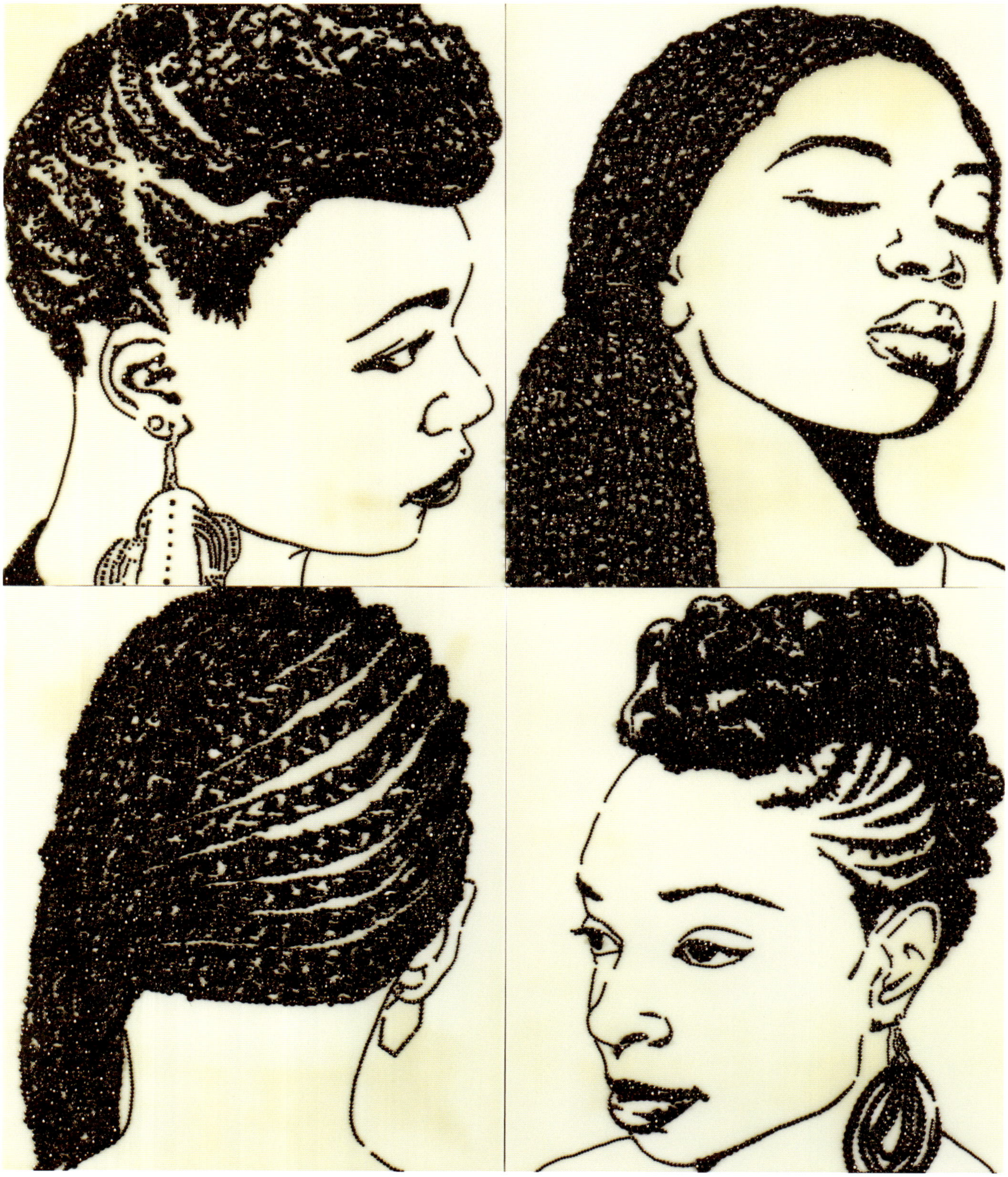

Left and right
MICKALENE THOMAS
Hair Portraits, 2013 *(details)*
Rhinestones and acrylic on wood panel,
24 panels, each 24″ x 20″,
installation 48″ x 240″
Courtesy of Melva Bucksbaum and Raymond Learsy, Mickalene Thomas, and Lehmann Maupin, New York and Hong Kong

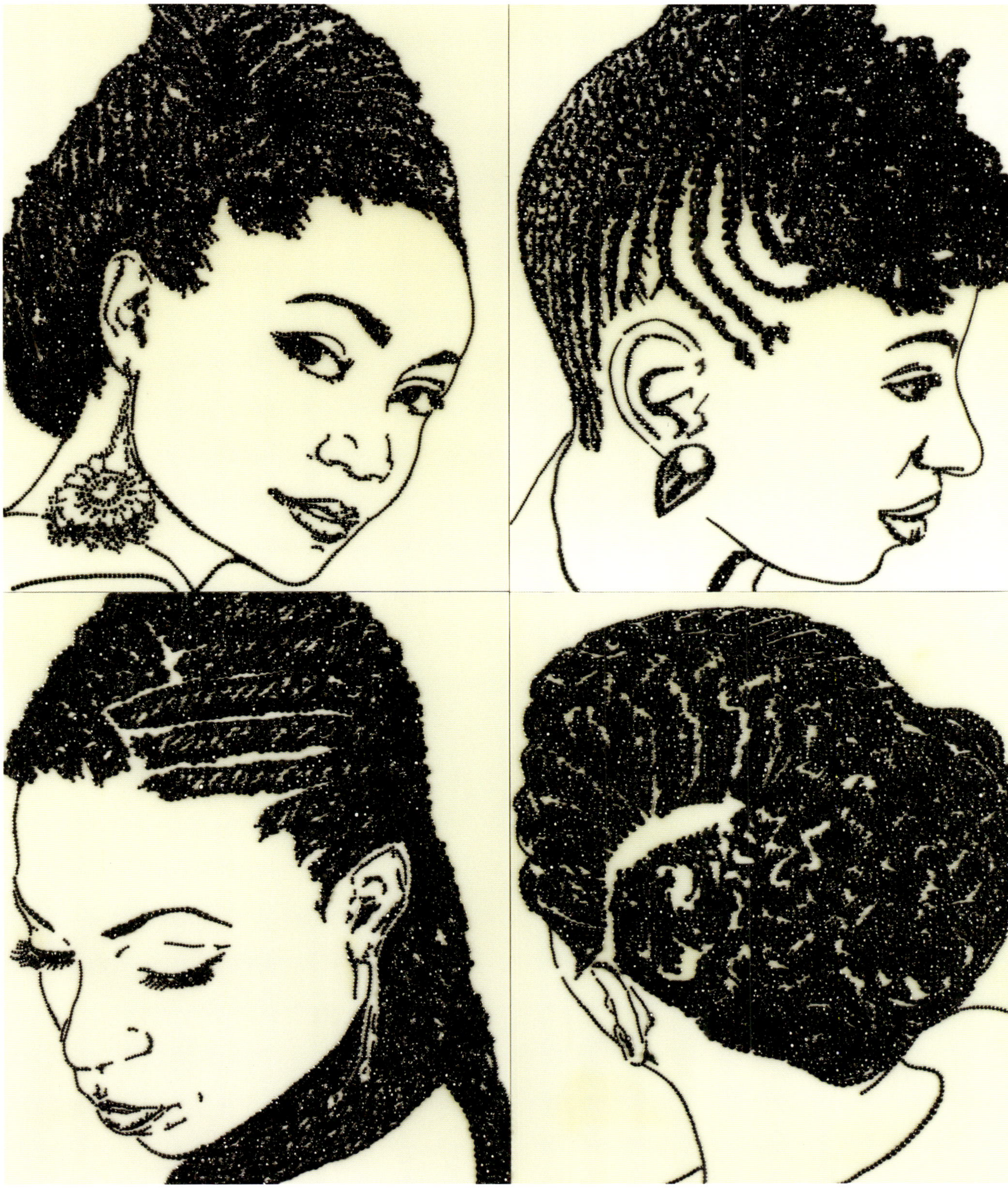

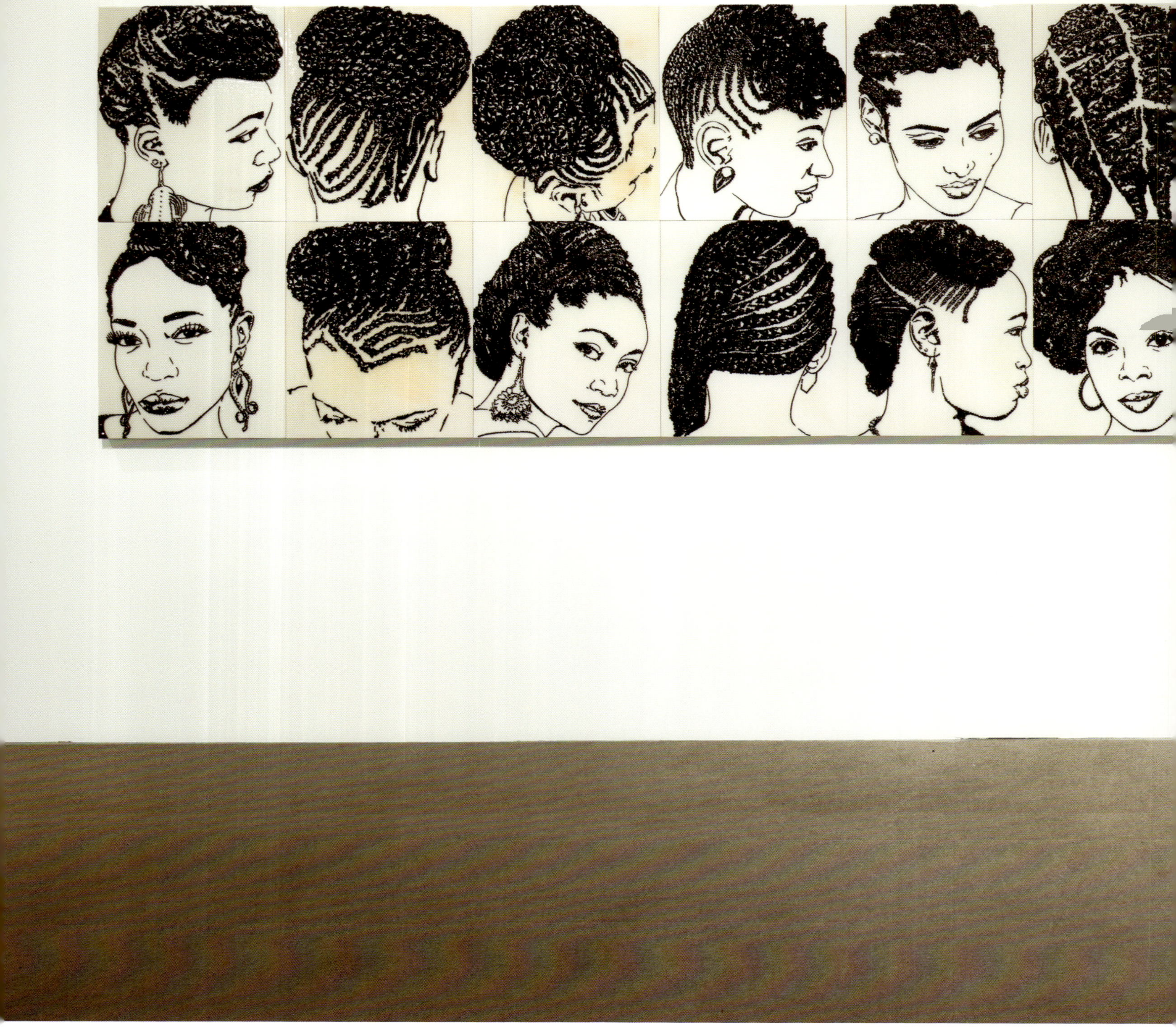

MICKALENE THOMAS
Hair Portraits, installation view, 2013
Rhinestones and acrylic on wood panel,
24 panels, each 24" x 20",
installation 48" x 240"
Courtesy of Melva Bucksbaum and Raymond Learsy, Mickalene Thomas, and Lehmann Maupin, New York and Hong Kong

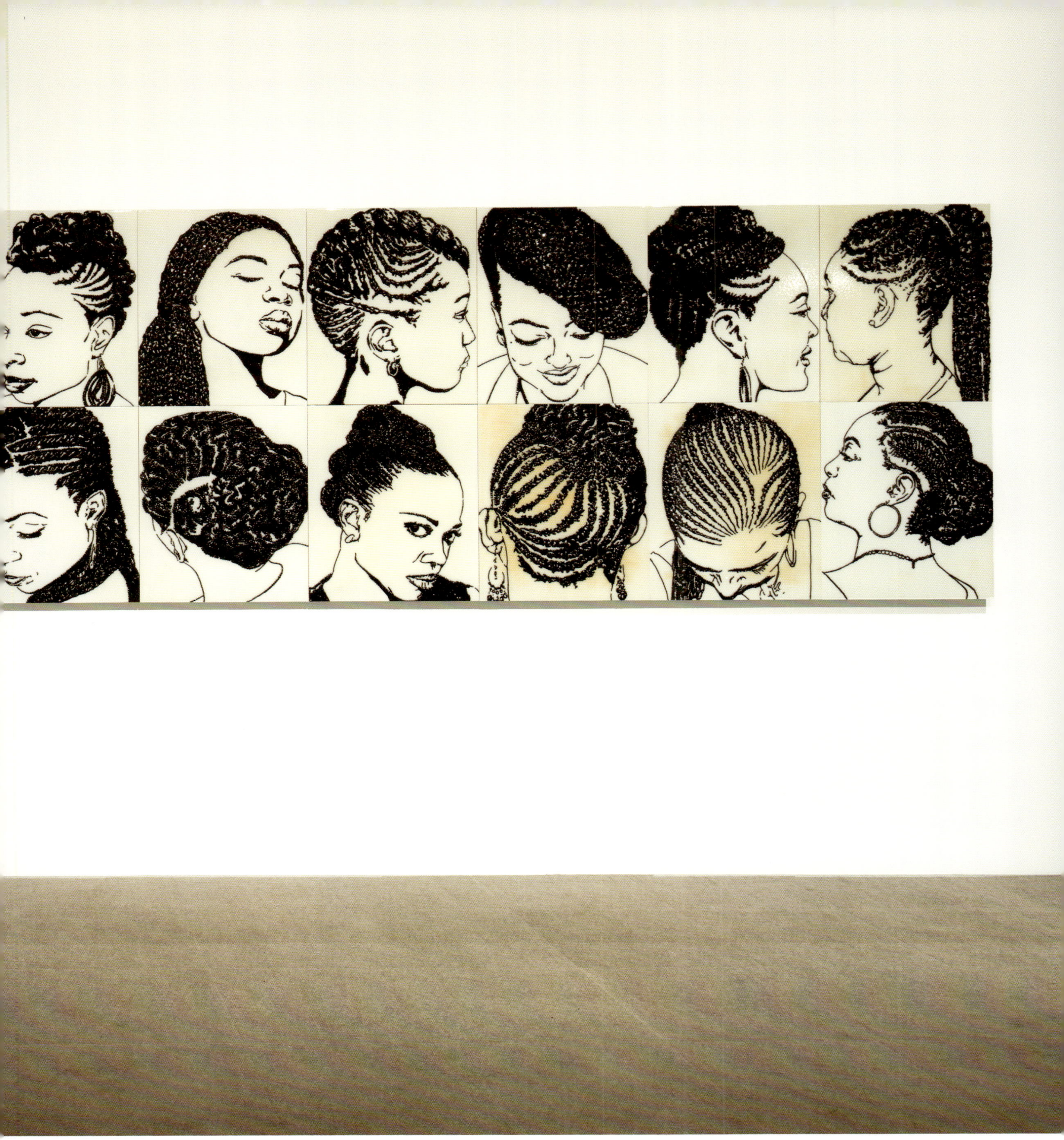

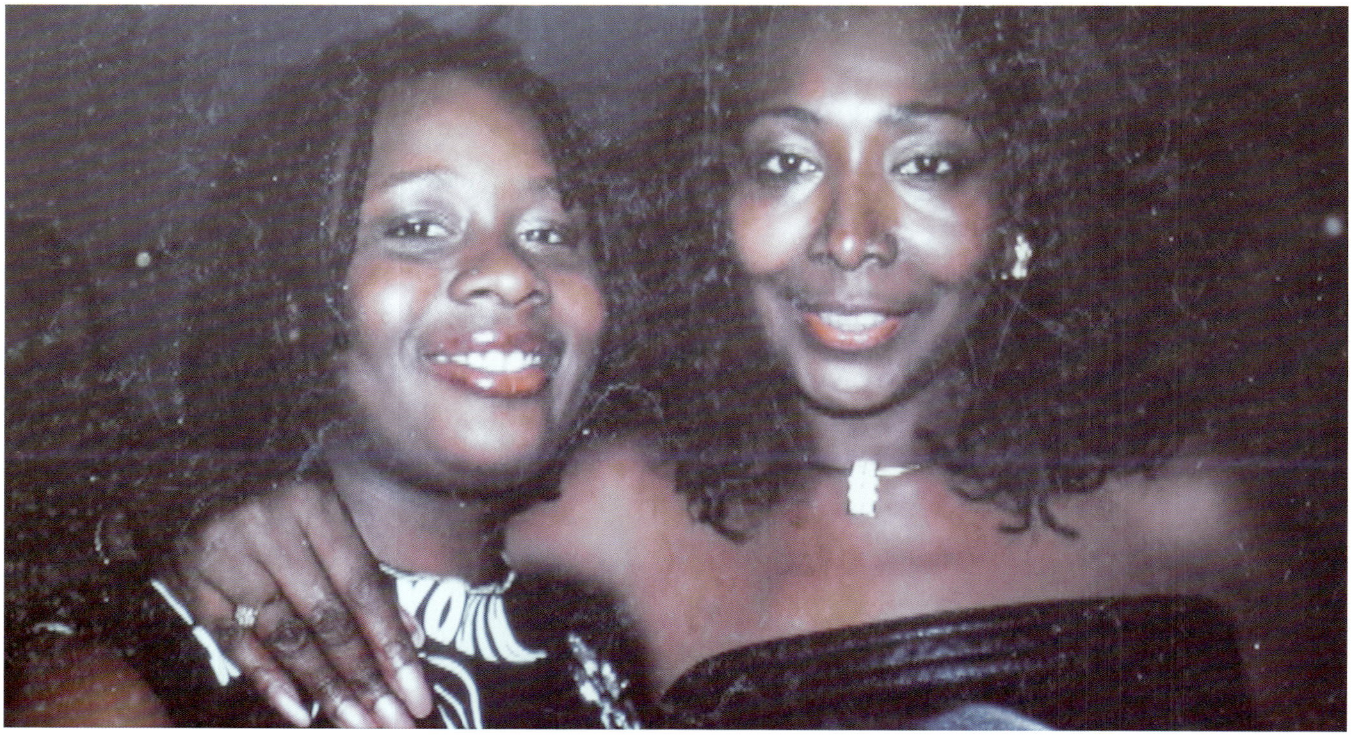

Left and right
MICKALENE THOMAS
Video stills from *Happy Birthday to a Beautiful Woman*, 2013

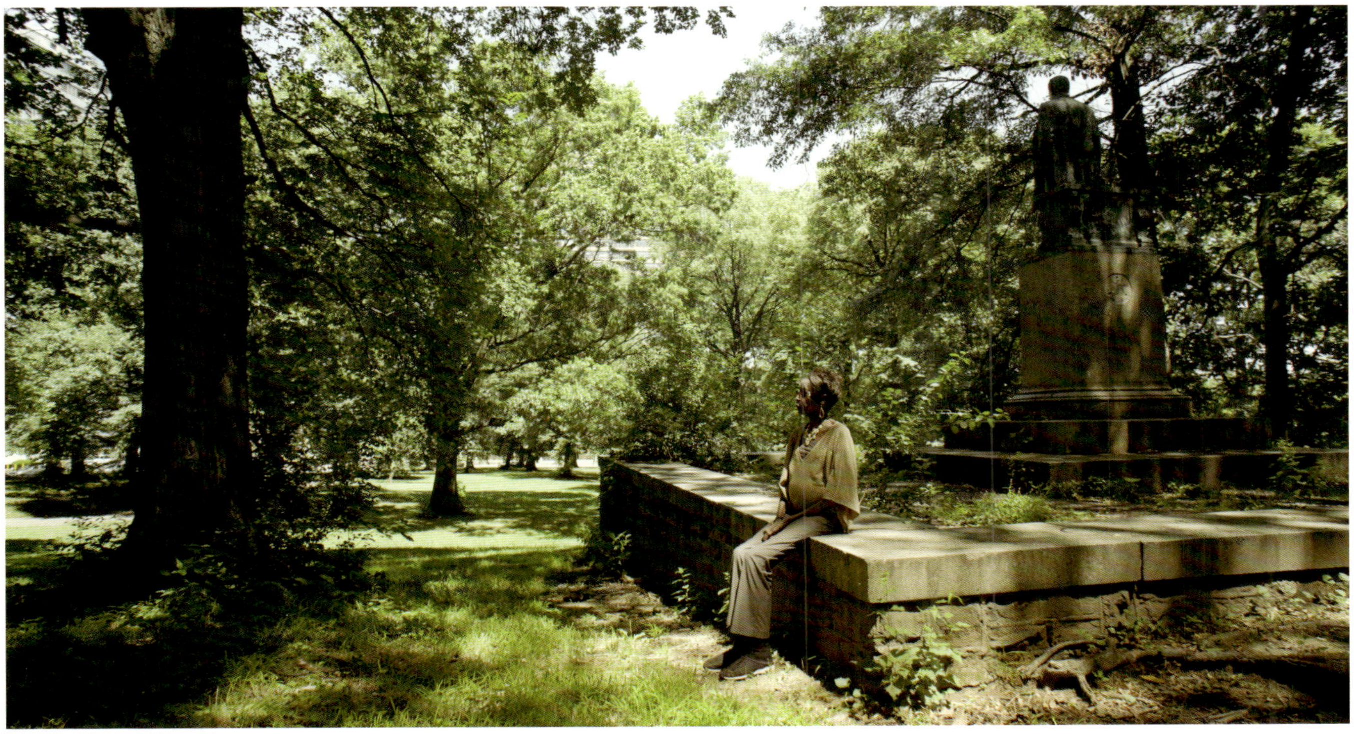

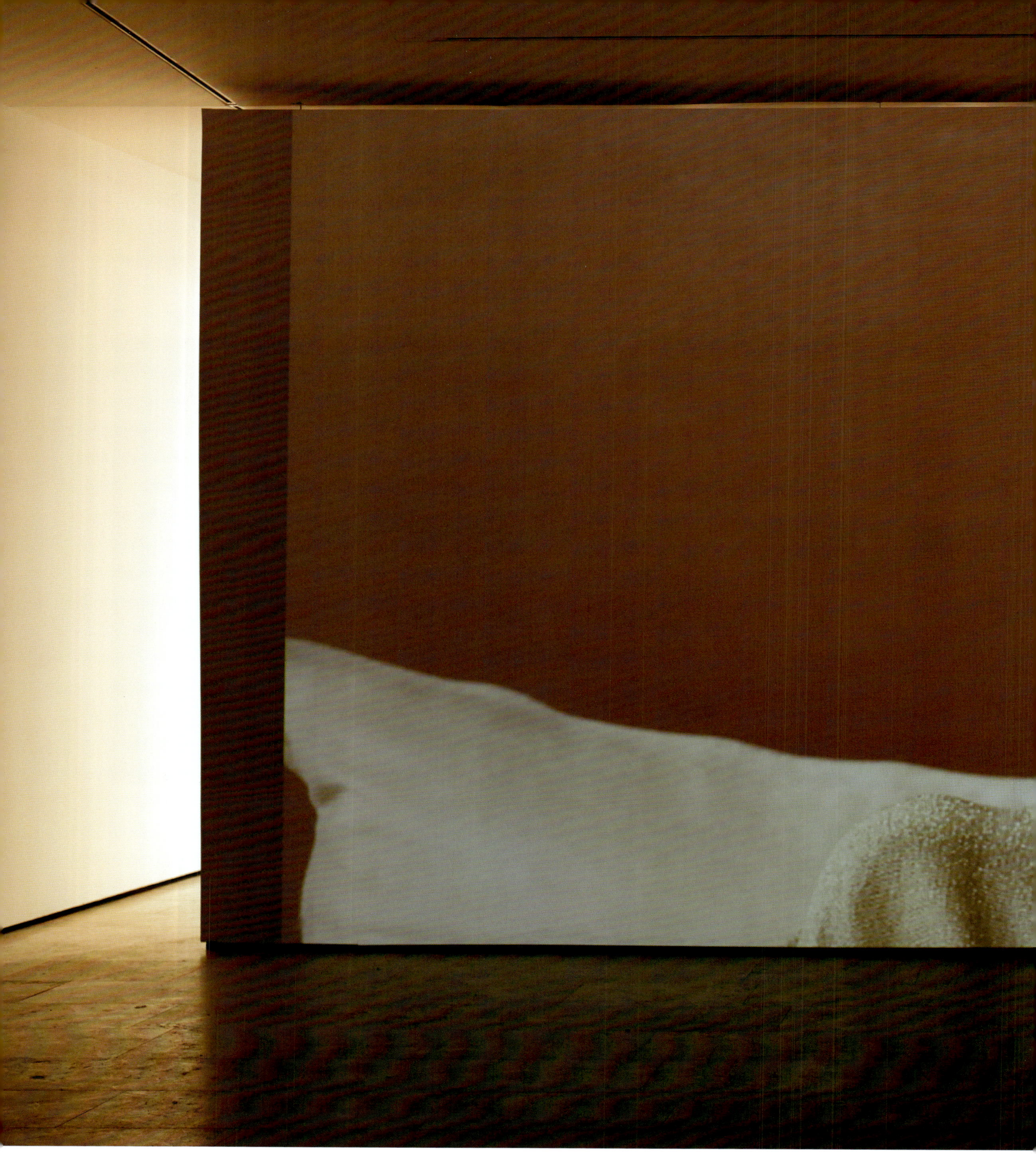

MICKALENE THOMAS
Video still from *Happy Birthday to a Beautiful Woman*, 2013
Installation view

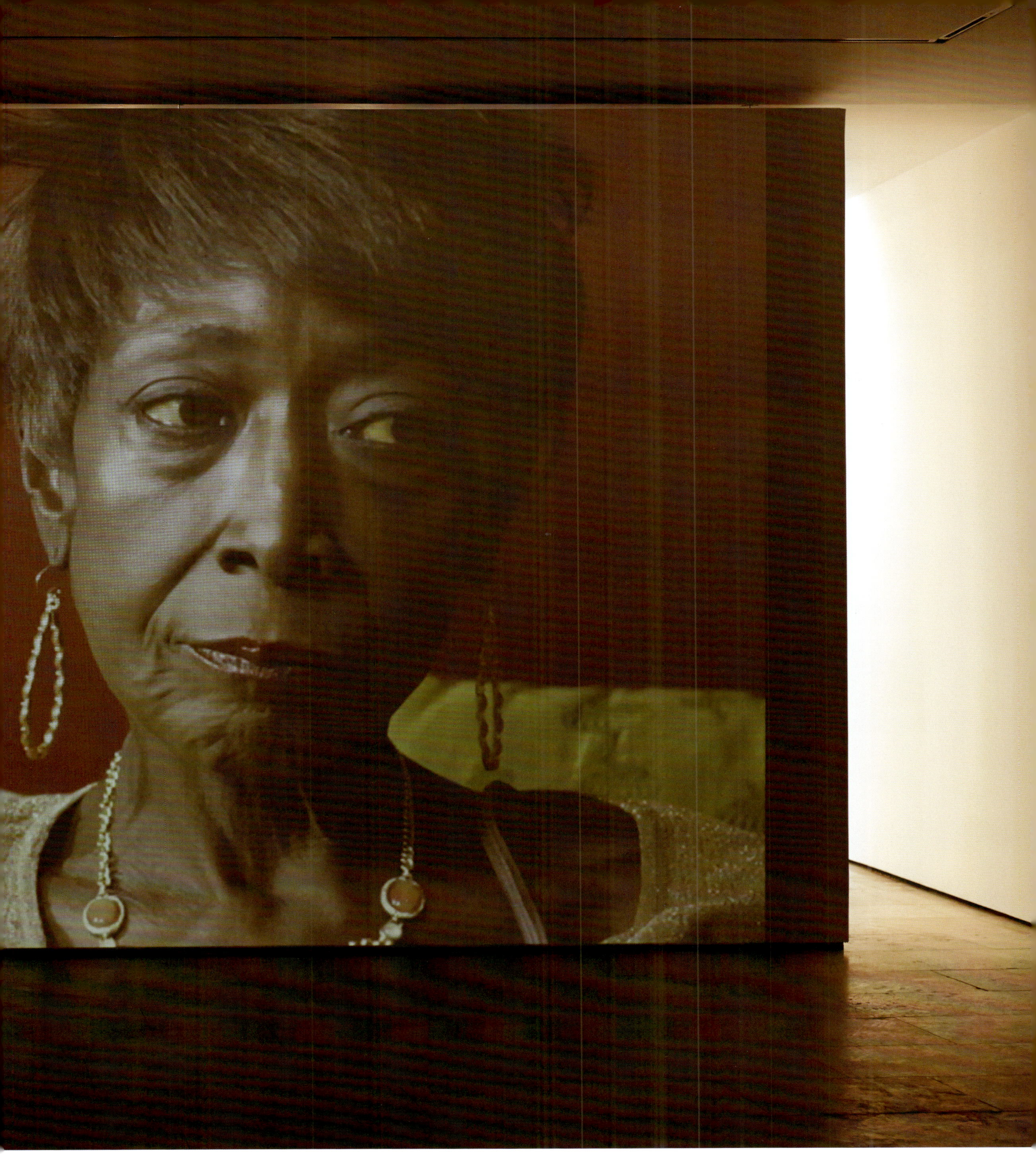

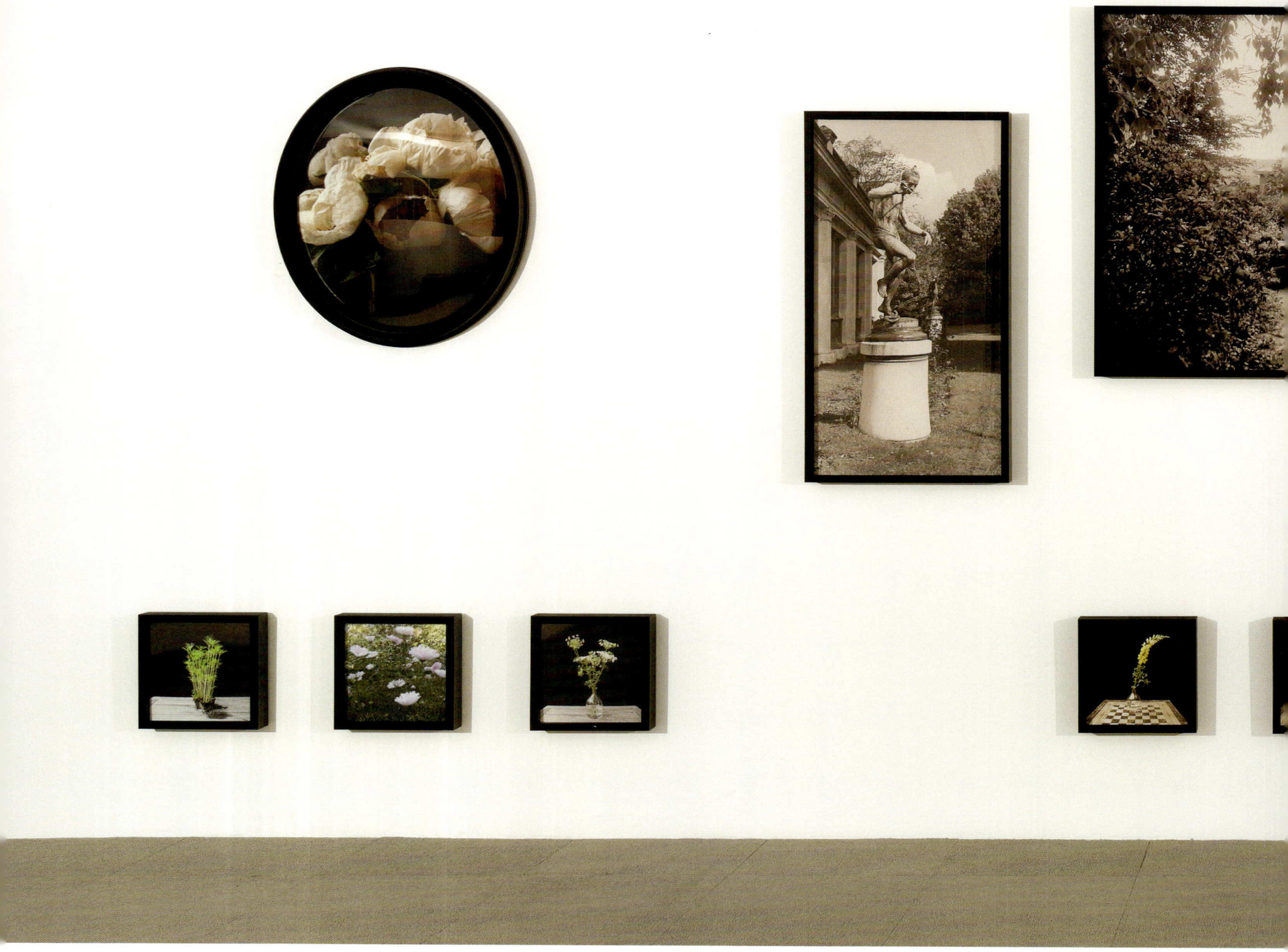

CARRIE MAE WEEMS
Peony of Hope
2013
Installation view

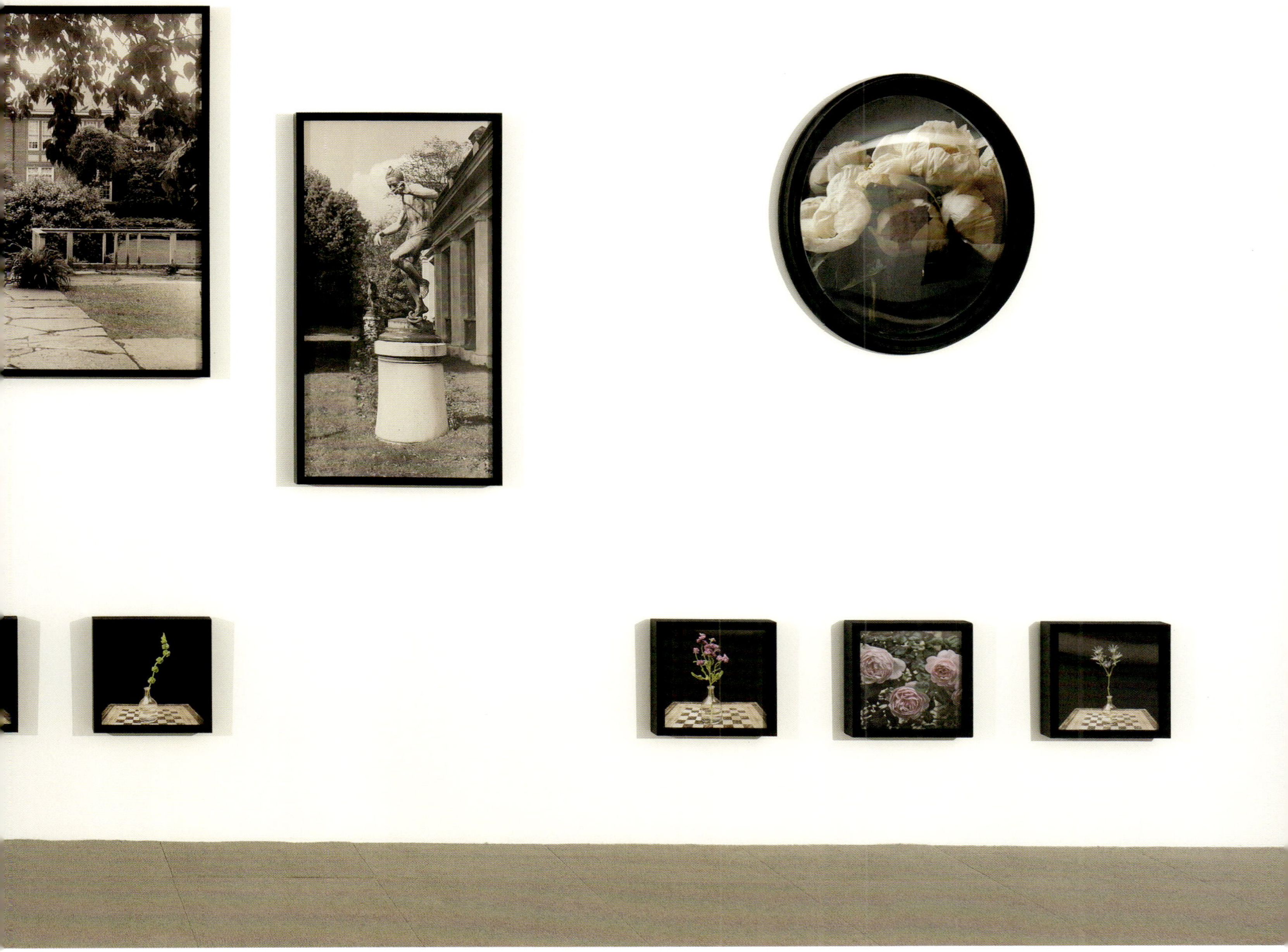

CARRIE MAE WEEMS

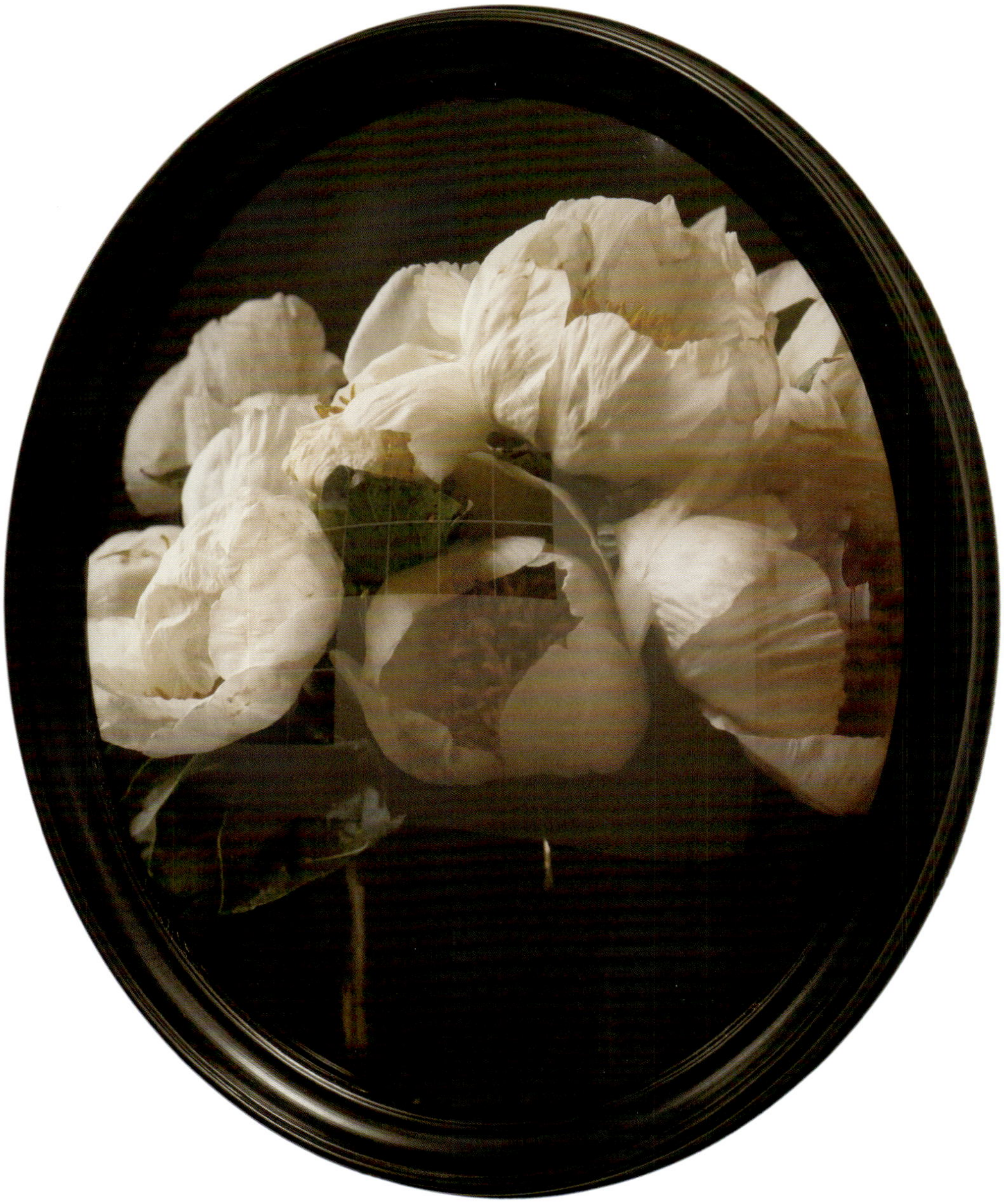

CARRIE MAE WEEMS
The W.E.B. Du Bois Peony, 2013
24″ x 22″
Archival inkjet print on rag paper

Opposite top
CARRIE MAE WEEMS
The Garden Space, 2013
22″ x 45″
Archival inkjet print on rag paper

Opposite below
CARRIE MAE WEEMS
A Considered Space, 2013
35″ x 45″
Archival inkjet print on rag paper

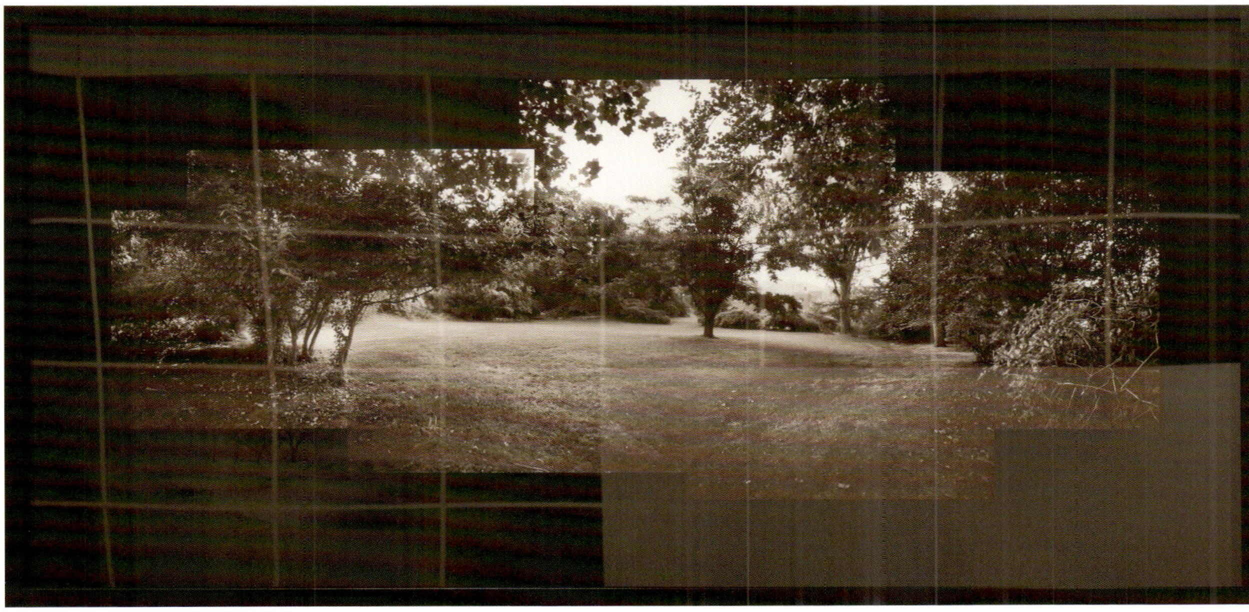

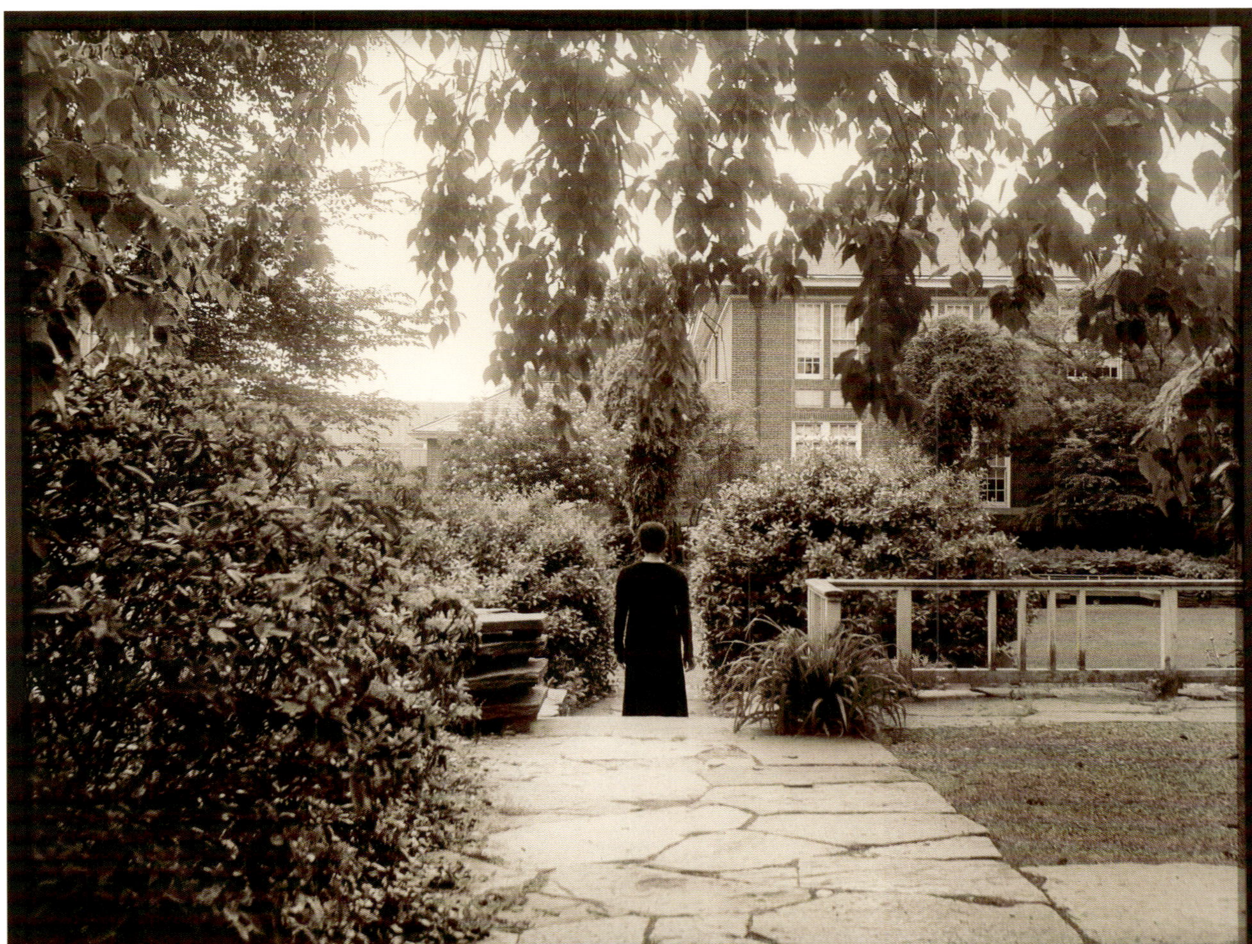

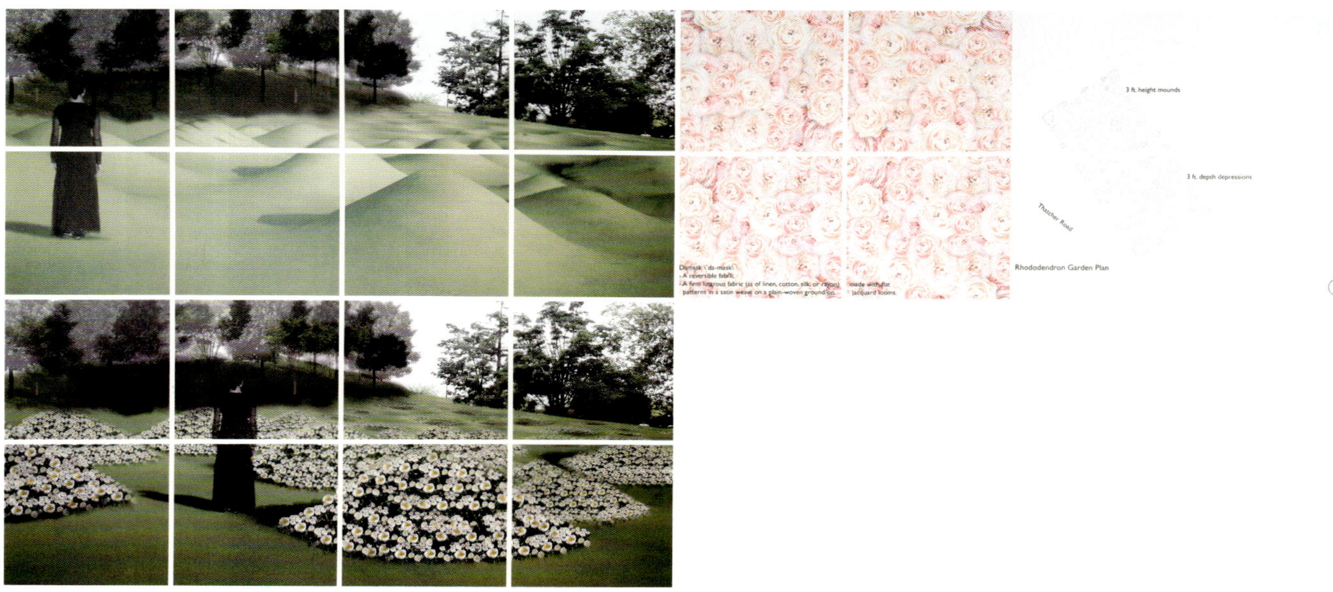

Left and right
CARRIE MAE WEEMS AND WALTER HOOD
2013 Proposal for W.E.B. Du Bois Garden,
University of Massachusetts Amherst
Site model and digital renderings
Courtesy of Hood Design Studio

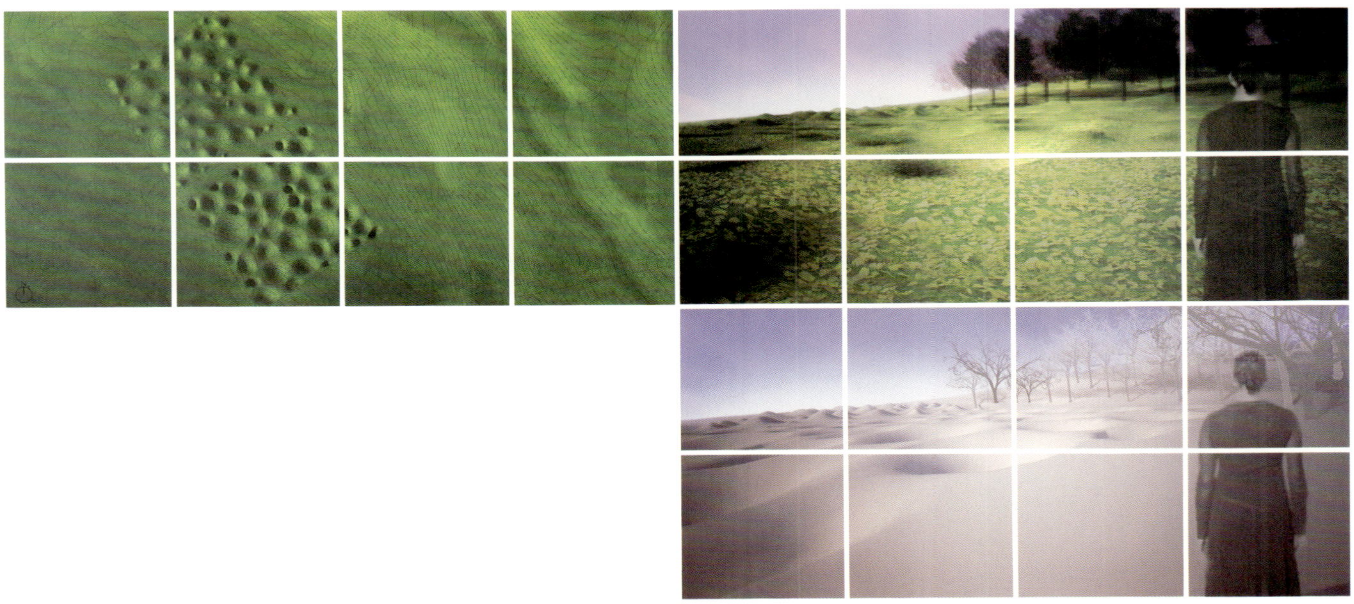

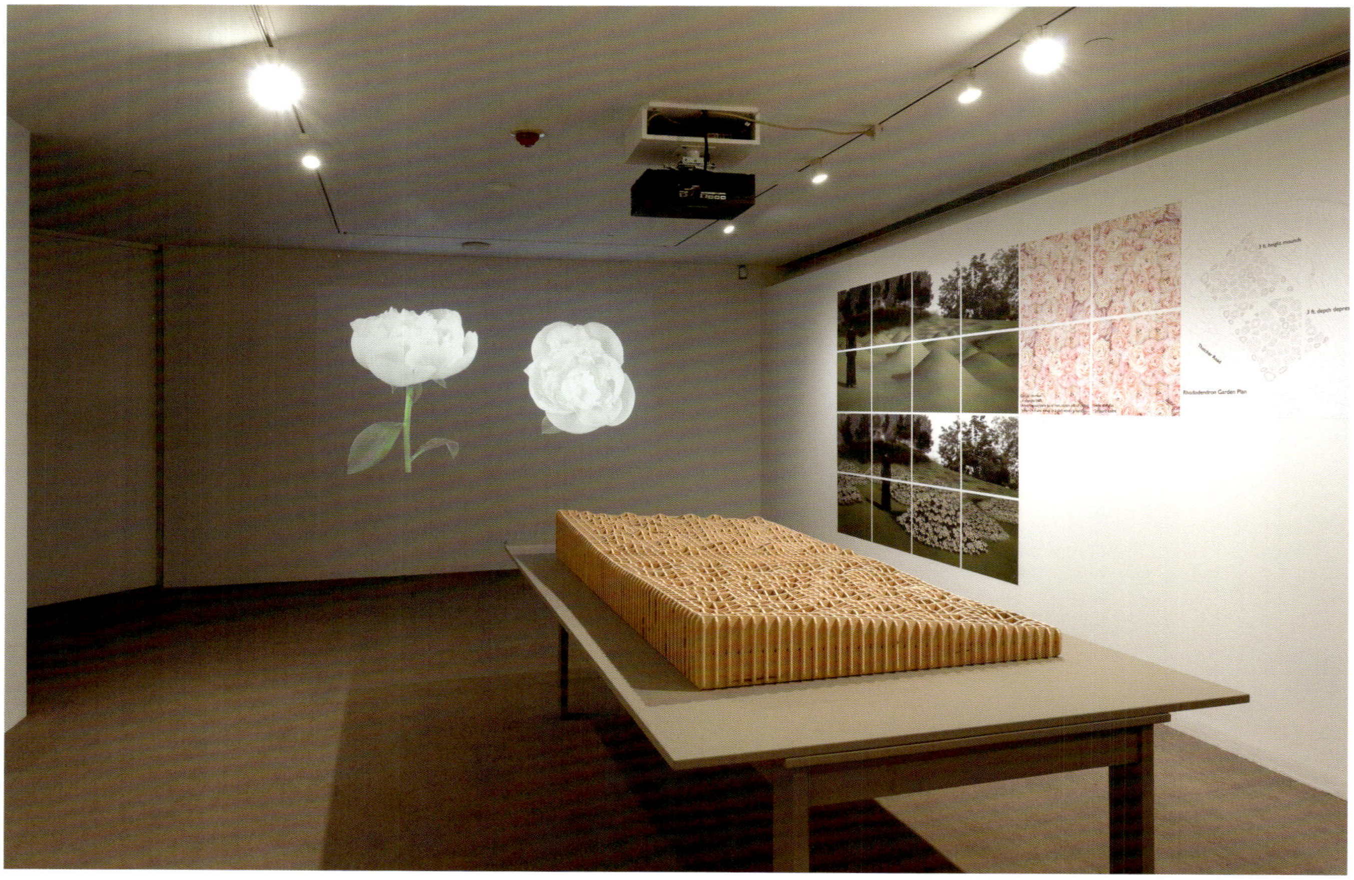

Above
CARRIE MAE WEEMS AND WALTER HOOD
2013 Proposal for W.E.B. Du Bois Garden,
University of Massachusetts Amherst
Site model and digital renderings
Courtesy of Hood Design Studio
Zygimantas Cepaitis
Peony time-lapse video, 1 minute, color-
Copyright © Zygimantas Cepaitis, Zygistudio

Left above
CARRIE MAE WEEMS
Du Bois in China, 2013
Video, 9 minutes, 46 seconds, sound; reworking of original Chinese government 16mm color film footage from 1959. *Source film courtesy of W.E.B. Du Bois Library Special Collections and University Archives. Courtesy of the artist and Jack Shainman Gallery, New York*

Left below
CARRIE MAE WEEMS

Top: all archival inkjet prints on rag paper, from left:
The Garden Space, 2013, 22" x 45"
The W.E.B. Du Bois Peony, 2013, 24" x 22"
Flute Player, 2013, 35" x 16"
A Considered Space, 2013, 35" x 45"
Flute Player, 2013, 35" x 16"
The W.E.B. Du Bois Peony, 2013, 24" x 22"
The Garden Space, 2013, 22" x 45"

Bottom: all archival inkjet prints on rag paper, 10" x 10", from left:
Floral Study (Spikes), 2013
Floral Study (Cherry), 2013
Floral Study (Poppy), 2013
Floral Study (Du Bois Study 7 with Table), 2013
Floral Study (Cosmos), 2013
Floral Study (Wildflower), 2013
Floral Study (Queen Anne's Lace), 2013
Floral Study (Du Bois Study 5 with Table), 2013
Floral Study (Du Bois Study 4 with Table), 2013
Floral Study (Du Bois Study 2 with Table), 2013
Floral Study (Du Bois Study 1 with Table), 2013
Floral Study (Roses for Yolanda), 2013
Floral Study (Du Bois Study 3 with Table), 2013
Floral Study (Du Bois Study 12 with Table), 2013
Floral Study (Zinnia), 2013
Floral Study (Pompoms), 2013
Floral Study (Lilies), 2013

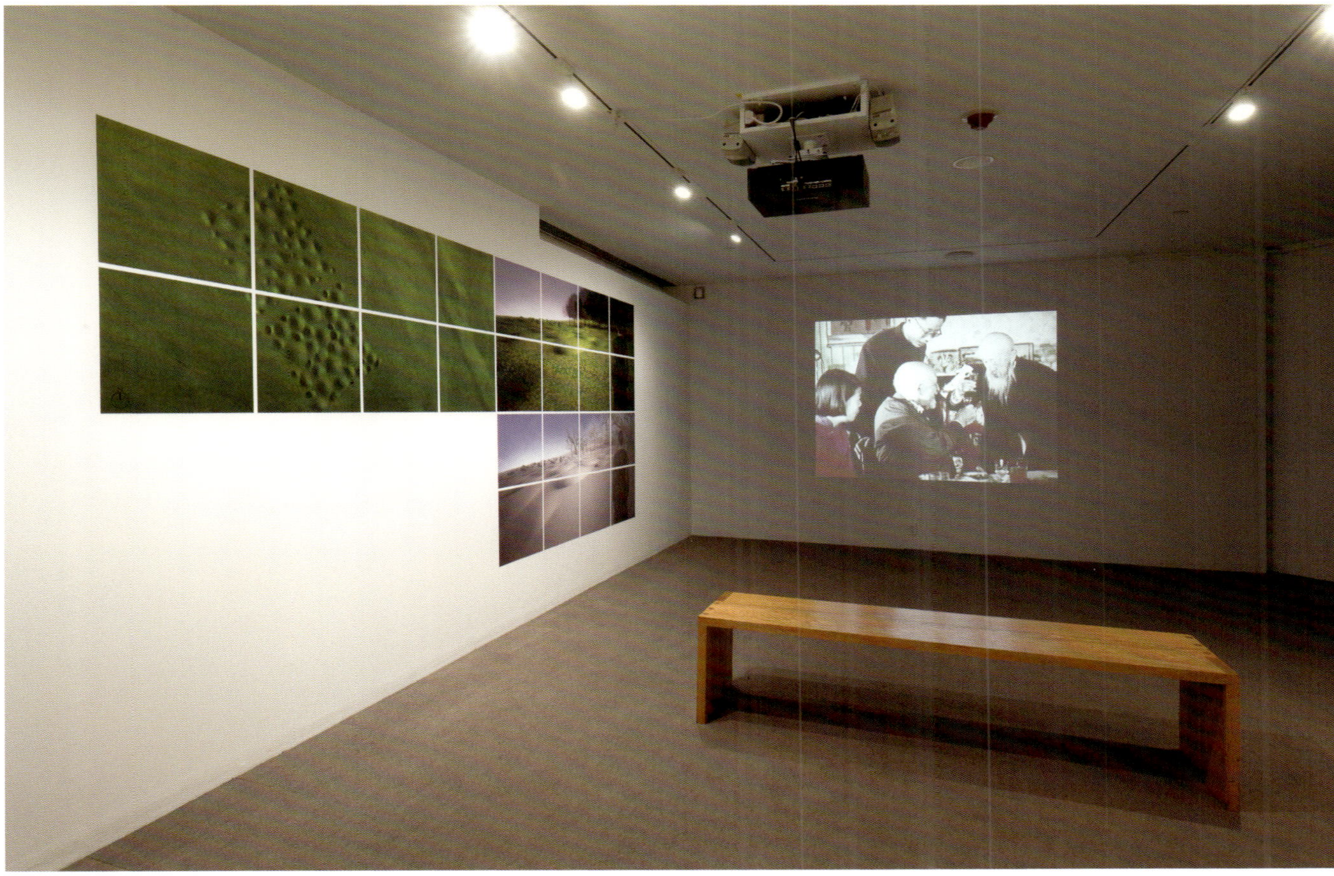

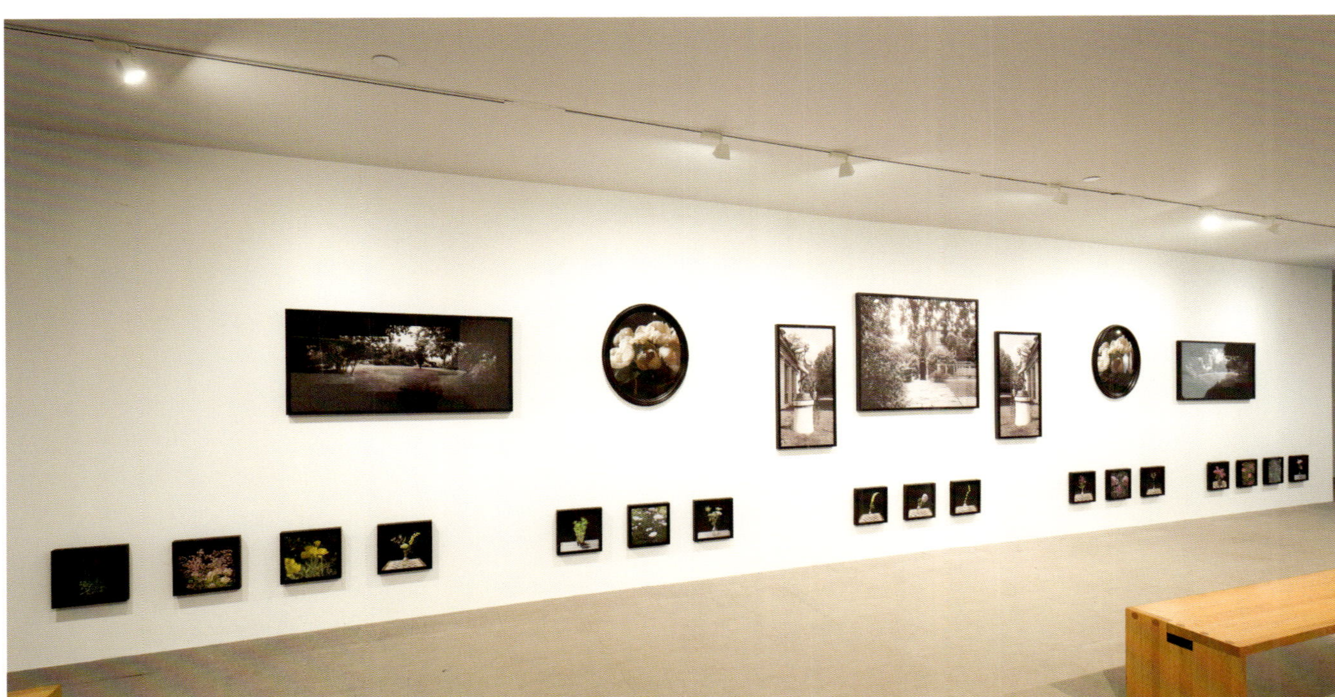

ARTIST STATEMENTS
AMHERST ARTISTS

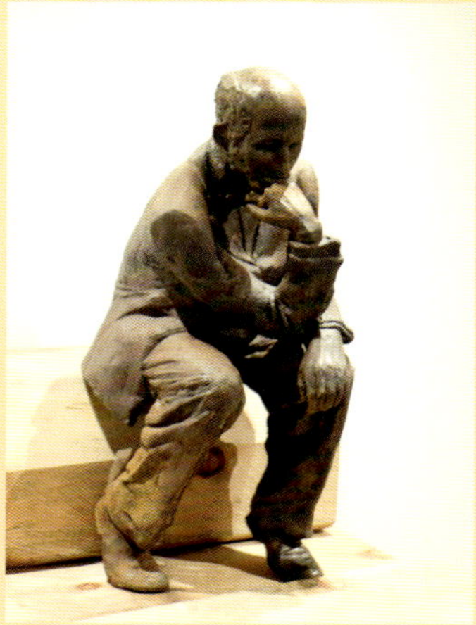

RADCLIFFE BAILEY

MY EARLY THINKING on W.E.B. Du Bois was one of respect and admiration for an African American freedom fighter whose excellence placed him in an international pantheon of human rights activists. This was the Du Bois of school reports and Black History programs. Du Bois's prediction of struggle along the color line during the twentieth century seemed like a foregone conclusion, so accurately had it played out.

The W.E.B. Du Bois that I personally make use of came gradually into view as I began to grasp the incredible creativity of his fertile mind. Du Bois possessed a mind so creative that in whatever situation or endeavor he placed himself, he was capable of taking in information and fashioning new and original thinking constructs — striking perspectives on history, sociology, culture, and art that others with the same information had not produced.

William E.B. Du Bois's assertion that one should be able to be African and American is simply good sense. Art is likewise particular and universal simultaneously. I too am "a co-worker in the kingdom of culture," striving to create art that genuinely articulates my message to African Americans and the art world.

Du Bois had definite points of view on art and its uses, proclaiming on one occasion, "I do not care a damn for any art that is not used for propaganda," when he felt the Harlem Renaissance was veering off track. I share his value of art that is authentic and culturally excellent in its execution.

I enjoy combining African and African American cultural motifs with modern art concerns in order to send messages to multiple recipients. I am using Rodin and Thomas Day as springboards for a statement about W.E.B. Du Bois. I think Du Bois would approve of the Republican Socialist leanings that inspired Rodin's *Thinker* as well as the excellence of African American furniture craftsman Thomas Day.

MARY EVANS

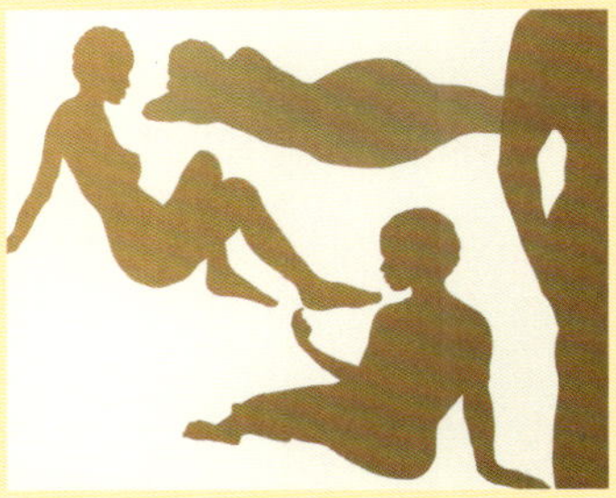

W.E.B. DU BOIS and I share a birthday, February 23! I was born in Lagos, Nigeria, in 1963, just down the coast from where he died in Accra. I first made these realizations when I visited his tomb and museum in Accra in 2005 during a visit to Ghana and ever since have felt a pull toward him and an urge to make these coincidences manifest in some way.

Du Bois migrated to Africa and ended his days in the land of his ancestors during a period when many Africans, myself included, were migrating to Europe and America. Even though my migration was for family reasons and Du Bois's migration was for work reasons, neither of our personal migrations were untouched by the political, cultural, and imperial influences of the time.

An all-encompassing thematic of my practice is the legacy of the African diaspora whether through force or emigration. Much of my work seeks to engage with the *Souls of Black Folk* either lost in the Atlantic or haunting the old European forts in West Africa.

In this passage from *The Souls of Black Folk* Du Bois's questioning of the value of human life is at once lamentable and hopeful.

> My journey was done, and behind me lay hill and dale, and Life and Death. How shall man measure Progress there where the dark-faced Josie lies? How many heartfuls of sorrow shall balance a bushel of wheat? How hard a thing is life to the lowly, and yet how human and real! And all this life and love and strife and failure, — is it the twilight of nightfall or the flush of some faint-dawning day?

W.E.B. Du Bois, "Of the Meaning of Progress," *The Souls of Black Folk*

BRENDAN FERNANDES

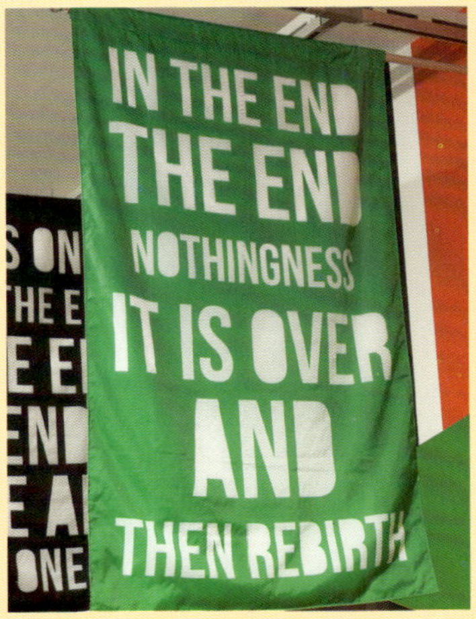

THE TEXTS OF DU BOIS have influenced the work I am exhibiting in this show by shaping my ideas on solidarity and utopia. Du Bois's goal of seeking a place for Pan-Africanism brings into light ideas of solidarity among minorities around the globe, particularly Africans and Asians who have sought to define their nations and selves after colonialism and imperialism. I am investigating Du Bois's inquiries into race and class, as well as exploring Du Bois's attempts to unify and emancipate African Americans and Africans, through the desire to create the *Encyclopedia Africana*. This book for Du Bois aimed to define the Negro and Africans, but it could never in principle be realized. I further found inspiration in the apocalyptic tale "Dark Water," in which two individuals of two races survive the end of the world, and unify for a moment before realizing the world still exists. In part my work will take the form of a performance in which the University Color Guard will march from the Du Bois Library to the museum, carrying a symbolic version of the *Encyclopedia Africana*, as well as flags and banners, while reciting a poem written by me that speaks of finding utopia in an ending. A flag and banner installation will also exist in the museum.

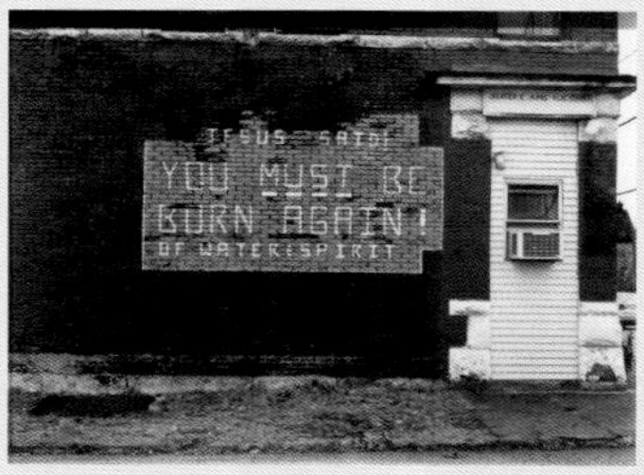

LATOYA RUBY FRAZIER

ON JULY 21, 1930, W.E.B. Du Bois gave a speech that addressed man's relation to the Housatonic River and its condition. Du Bois described the Housatonic River as *the center of the picture*. Yet the valley of Great Barrington turned away and used the Housatonic as "a sewer, a drain, a place for throwing waste." In 1982, similar to Du Bois, I was born next to another river, the Monongahela, in Braddock, Pennsylvania. Andrew Carnegie's nineteenth-century steel mill, railroads, and bridges dissect and erode the waters. One night the river flooded. Crossing through miles of man-made manufactures, contaminated soils, and debris, it filled the basement and soaked the floors of my childhood home on Washington Avenue, in the area historically known as The Bottom. Growing up there has made me realize that, if seventy percent of the world is covered with water and more than fifty percent of our bodies are comprised of water, then the properties found in waters that surround our artificial environments reflect not only a physical condition, but a spiritual condition in which we exist. Through a series of aerial photographs of the Mon-Valley Braddock region, *A Despoliation of Water: From the Housatonic to Monongahela River (1930 – 2013)* will reveal that Du Bois's words resonate with the current environmental crisis along the Monongahela River in Braddock, Pennsylvania.

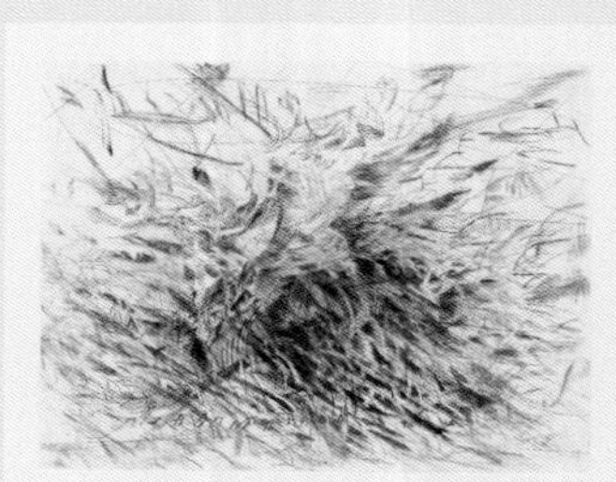

JULIE MEHRETU

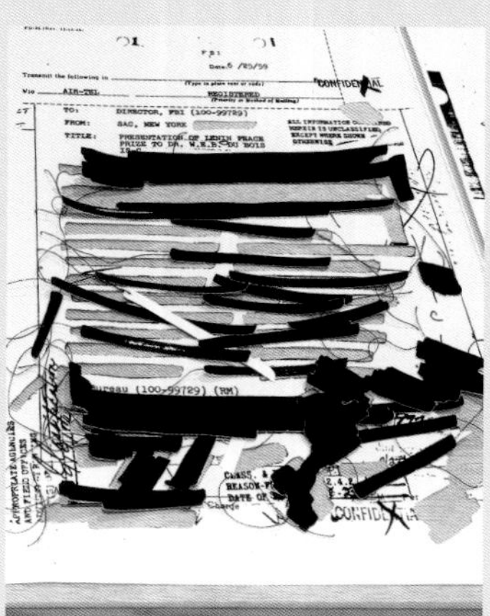

ANN MESSNER

I RESPOND TO THINGS that I do not understand; my work as an artist is a process of coming to terms with what I otherwise am unable to reconcile. In reading *The Autobiography of W.E.B. Du Bois* I met such a situation:

In 1950 at the age of eighty-three, Du Bois (along with four colleagues from the Peace Information Center) was indicted by the Department of Justice for refusing to register as "agents of a foreign principal." The defendants were acquitted on the basis that the prosecution failed to support the allegations, but not without the personal trauma of being accused and the burden of public scrutiny caused by the trial. I was struck by the Cold War rhetoric and the demonization of a man who should instead have been celebrated *for a lifetime commitment to the advancement of the lives of peoples of African descent*, but more importantly how, despite the realities of age, Du Bois persisted in the face of nonsensical opposition to labor for what he believed to be just into his final years.

This project began by gathering what I knew — the chronicles of spoken word and song. The aural has a way of claiming space, of moderating and soothing what cannot otherwise be assuaged. It summons you to listen. The FBI files were something I came upon by chance (if there is such a thing). These, at times heavily, redacted files offer witness, what is removed forms a tale of its own of elegiac proportion, evidence of persisting secrets and forbidden truths.

My resolute *removal of the removal*, the cutting out to cancel, to void the space of redaction, perhaps an act of futility, nevertheless stands as a small gesture, a nod in recognition of what we lose when we do not allow the space for dissent, when we condemn to silence what is different.

JEFFERSON PINDER

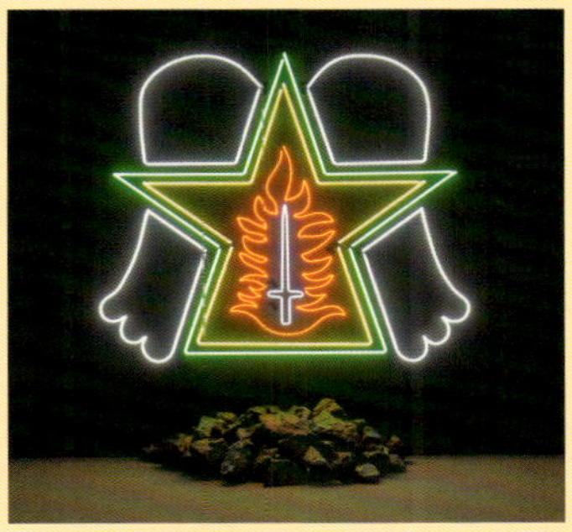

IN 1913 W.E.B. Du Bois successfully tried his hand at making a theatrical work about the ten-thousand-year history of the black race. His pageant, titled *The Star of Ethiopia*, gave the world yet another way of looking at his genius. Mixing inspiration from opera and classical theater with the stylization of spirituals, Du Bois set out to unabashedly educate the masses about the proud and complex history of the black race.

My installation begins with the limited extant photo documentation of the four pageant productions. Taking cues from the multiple *Star of Ethiopia* scripts found in the University of Massachusetts *Credo* web database, and flowing with the theme of the exhibition *Du Bois in Our Time*, I created multiple abstract video shorts of iconic moments found in the pageant. They focus primarily on the characterization of the "Veiled Woman" (Du Bois's iconic representation of "Negro Womanhood") and her quest to lead the untamed people of Africa to civilization.

Using some of the music performed in the pageant (as well as a contemporary score), I am seeking to offer colorful interpretations of moments taken from Du Bois's most creative and ambitious work.

TIM ROLLINS & K.O.S.

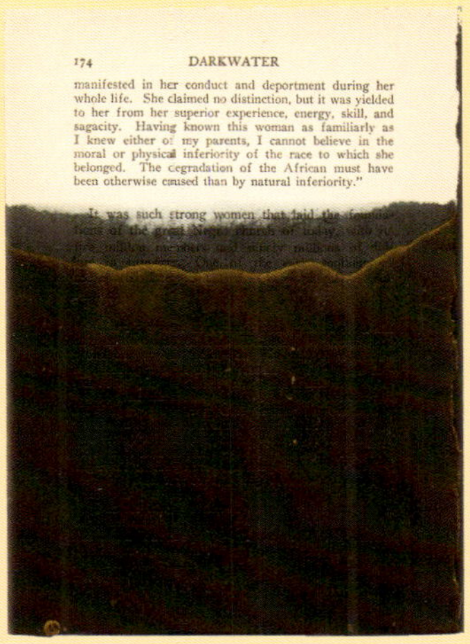

OF ALL OF THE WRITINGS of W.E.B. Du Bois, what draws us to his *Darkwater*?

Over ninety years ago, W.E.B. Du Bois writes of being born by a golden river in the Berkshire Hills of Massachusetts, a mother with a face of dark shining bronze, a tall black landlord with golden earrings.

Du Bois believes in a "God who made of one blood all nations that do dwell on earth." All throughout *Darkwater* he insists that art is a form of perpetual prayer and patience. He believes in educating children toward beauty, truth, even grandeur. Education is "the problem of problems." This son of Great Barrington generates a lyrical essay and instrumental poetry.

Again, what's the attraction to the visage, life, legacy, and model of Du Bois? Maybe it's because as a young scholar on his summers off at Fisk University he taught poor kids at the Wheeler School in Wilson County in rural Tennessee. Maybe this was the simple but revolutionary learning experience that changed his life and predestined his future thought and activism.

He writes of "The Immortal Child" and the life and music of a Samuel Coleridge-Taylor and soon we are often playing a recording of the "American Negro Melodies" in our studio while working.

Golds, furnace-black rivers, eternal flowing, movement, veils, baptism, chance, and, always, Patience. We study, admire, and emulate Du Bois, but, moreover, we *feel* him.

We find ourselves in March of 2013 visiting the Renaissance School in Springfield, Massachusetts, and a diverse group of 6th, 7th, and 8th-grade students. In a brightly lit classroom we are all reading *Darkwater* together beginning with the great "Credo." The young participants then write their own personal credos. Then they illustrate them.

Soon we are literally baptizing pages rent from a first edition of *Darkwater* deeply embossed in old letterpress and golden with ninety-three years of age. One by one, each young artist dips a page they have personally selected in a pool of furnace-black ink laced with gold pigment. What happens happens . . . and what is happening? A painting that painted itself — something supernatural. It's an old-fashioned New England seance with all of us focused together at the table. Art is our medium. It's not long before the fiercely loving ghost of W.E.B. Du Bois has been summoned and is fully present in a Springfield public school.

Du Bois speaks, whispers, lectures, and even sings to us while we make our own dark and gold rivers of veils, chances, and changes.

— *Tim Rollins, Studio K.O.S.*

IN *DARKWATER*, W.E.B. Du Bois writes, "In the treatment of the child the world foreshadows its own future and faith. All words and all thinking lead to the child, — to that vast immortality and the wide sweep of infinite possibility which the child represents."

The ethos of our collective practice resonates with Du Bois's belief in the immortal child and its countless possibilities. We believe in the importance of all measures that help cultivate and further those possibilities. Du Bois's strategy for transcendence lives within the child itself. We celebrate this spirit of change, examining our lives on a daily basis and through the process knocking through walls: walls meant to categorize, compartmentalize, segregate, separate, and repress. We are the immortal child pressing forward in this continued fight.

— *Angel Abreu, Studio K.O.S.*

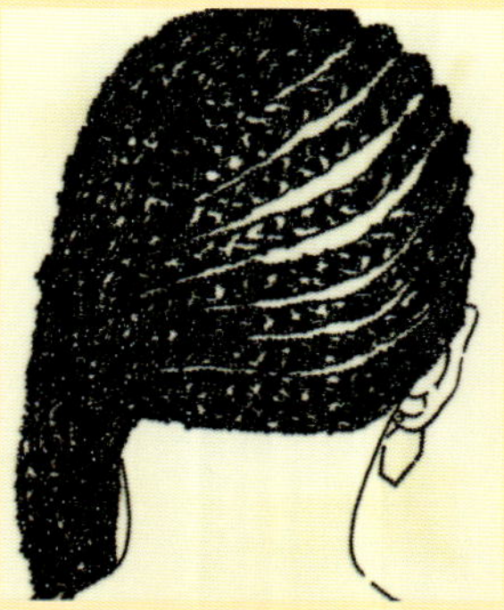

MICKALENE THOMAS

CARRIE MAE WEEMS

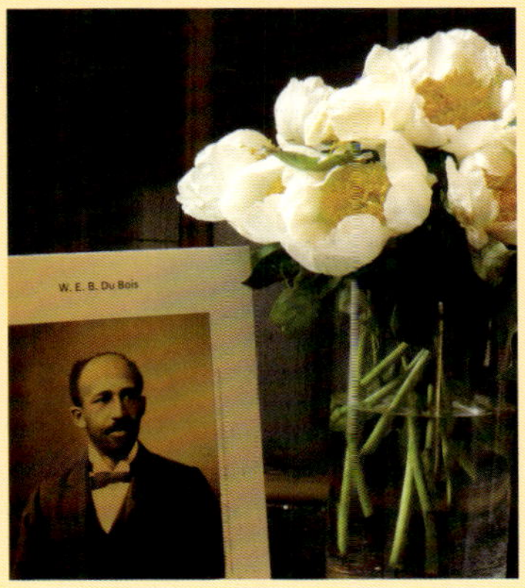

The William E.B. Du Bois peony is now available at **www.hollingsworthpeonies.com** for distribution.

Concerned with stepping out of the gallery and interested in reaching a broader public, what started as the naming of a flower for Du Bois has blossomed into *A Proposal for The Du Bois Memorial Garden*.

For their project, visual artist Carrie Mae Weems and landscape architect Walter Hood have created a proposal for the design of a Du Bois Memorial Garden on the campus of the University of Massachusetts at Amherst. In this exhibition they consider the planned site, its surrounding landscape, and its meaning.

Consisting of drawings, large-scale photographs, small floral studies, and a video projection, the project suggests the possible directions for the final garden and considers types of gardens: formal, casual, floral, sculptural, and even vertical gardens.

While Weems made the photographs and crafted the video projection based on Du Bois's trip to China, Hood produced a series of imaginative drawings invoking the possible aesthetic dimensions of a contemplative garden space.

Working closely with Hollingsworth Farms and the American Peony Society, Weems has named a new variety of peony in honor of Du Bois. This flower, which she calls the Peony of Hope, will anchor the garden. It will become available to the general public in September 2013, thereby allowing thousands of garden enthusiasts to engage in a lasting and sustained memory of Du Bois.

THE WILLIAM E.B. DU BOIS PEONY IS NOW AVAILABLE ONLINE: www.hollingsworthpeonies.com for distribution.

DU BOIS IN OUR TIME: *SYMPOSIUM*

THE SYMPOSIUM *Du Bois in Our Time* brought together historians, social scientists, artists, political activists, writers, curators, and students as panelists and audience to share their understandings of the connections of W.E.B. Du Bois to the twenty-first century on the occasion of the fiftieth anniversary of his death in 1963. The purpose of the symposium was to experiment in pushing the boundaries of these disparate modes of understanding. Nothing honored the multiple talents, the broad vision, and creativity of Dr. Du Bois more than the idea of using his life's work to convene a new way to define and exemplify interdisciplinary imagination.

Symposium panelists asked what happens to an artist who has the opportunity to try out ideas through a dialogue with scholars who have studied, taught, and written about Du Bois's work for decades. In turn, what happens to a scholar whose work goes through the process of collaborating with such artists? What kind of new understanding occurs when a student of history or literature is a firsthand witness to the crucible of artistic creativity? How does artistic expression serve as a method of scholarly research and discovery? This symposium investigated new territory and helped open the doors to new ideas which will become increasingly relevant in the years to come.

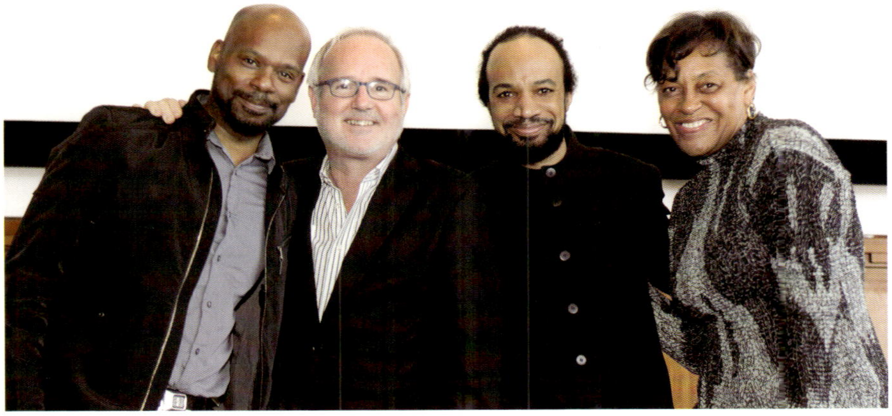

Jefferson Pinder, Tim Rollins, Reiland Rabaka, and Carrie Mae Weems

WATCH THE SYMPOSIUM VIDEOS ONLINE: https://fac.umass.edu/UMCA/Online/DuBoisInOurTimeSympoiumVideos

FEATURED SPEAKER
DR. JOHNNETTA BETSCH COLE

In 2009 Dr. Cole assumed the position of director of the Smithsonian's National Museum of African Art. She was the first African American woman to serve as president of Spelman College (1987–1997), and she also served as president of Bennett College for Women (2002–2007). She was a faculty member at UMass Amherst from 1970 to 1983, with appointments in the W.E.B. Du Bois Afro-American Studies Department and the Department of Anthropology; she also taught courses in Women's Studies and from 1981 to 1983 served as associate provost for undergraduate education.

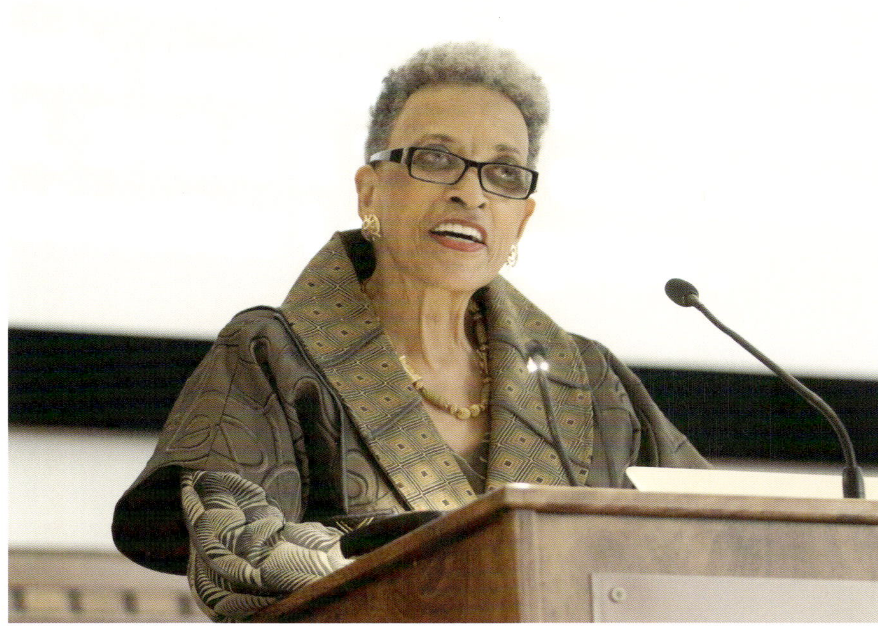

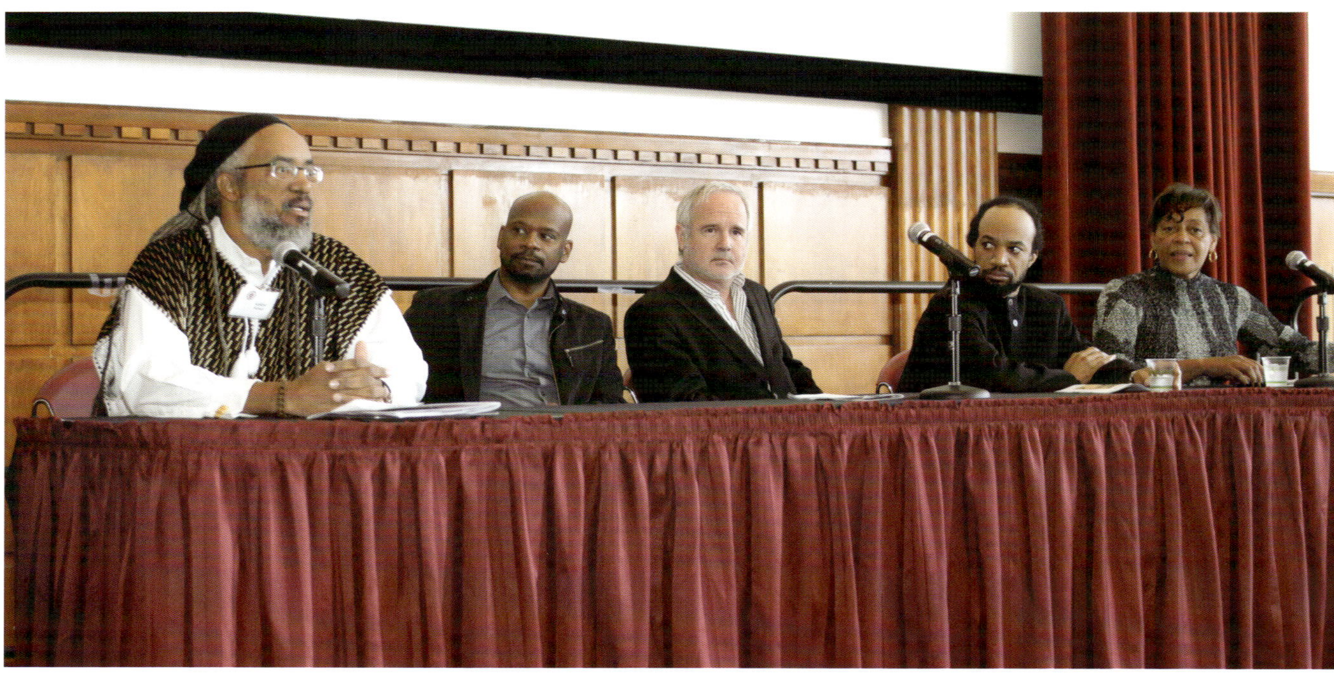

THE LITERARY MAN

Moderator: Professor **Amilcar Shabazz** (Afro-American Studies, UMass) — with Professor **Reiland Rabaka** (Africana Studies, Women and Gender Studies, University of Colorado Boulder) and artists **Jefferson Pinder**, **Tim Rollins**, and **Carrie Mae Weems**

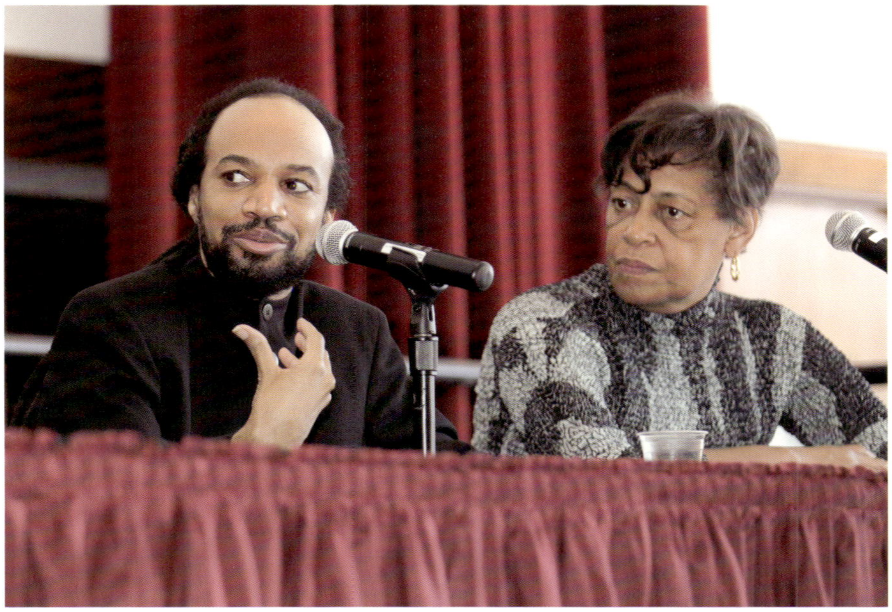

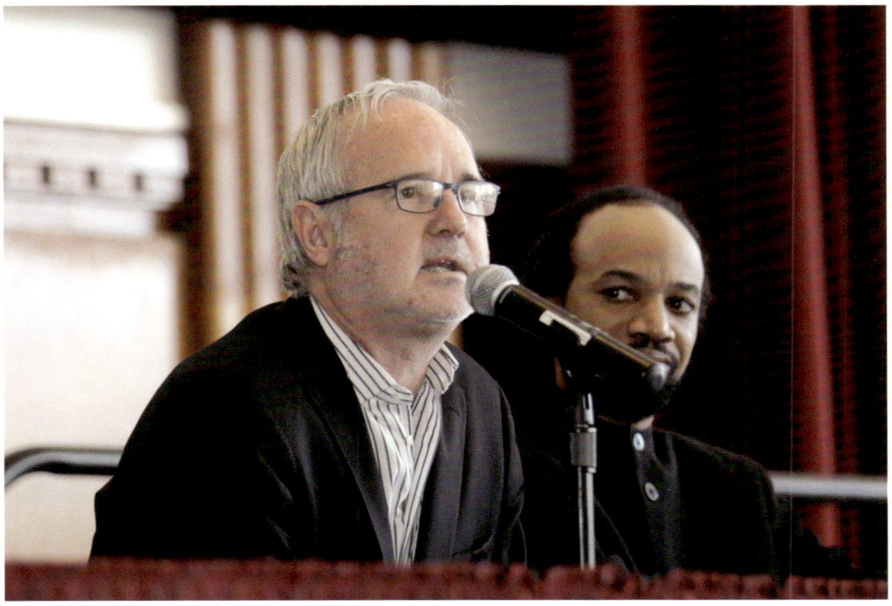

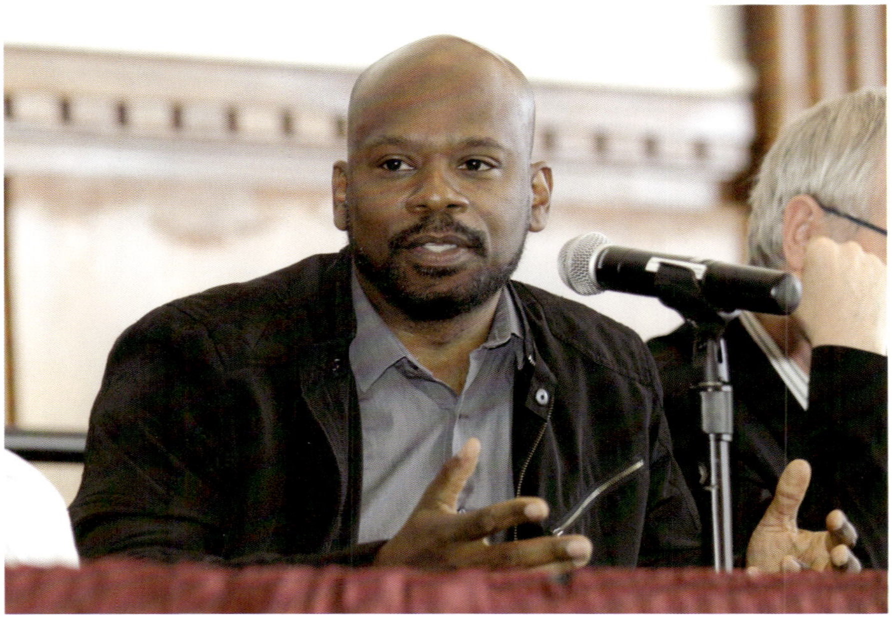

ART AND POLITICS

Moderator: Professor **Susan Jahoda** (Art, UMass)— with Professor **Bill Strickland** (Afro-American Studies, UMass) and artists **Ann Messner** and **LaToya Ruby Frazier**

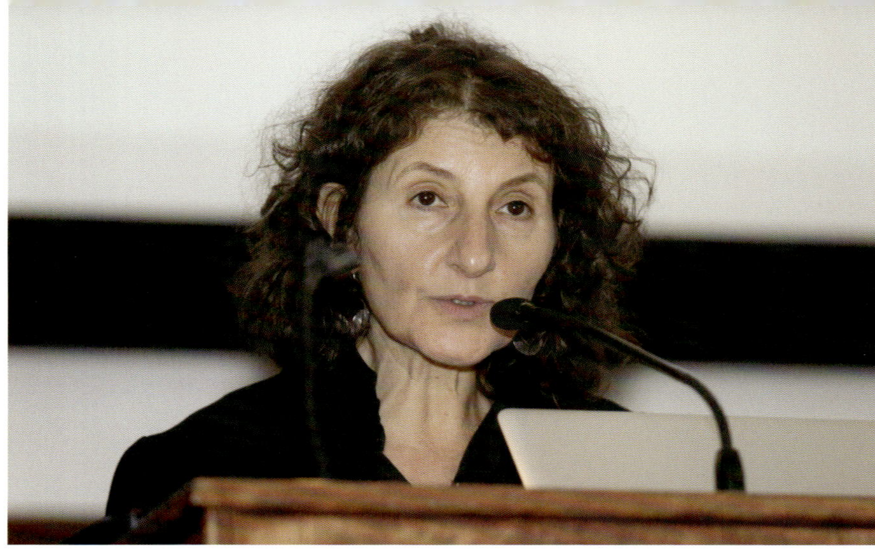

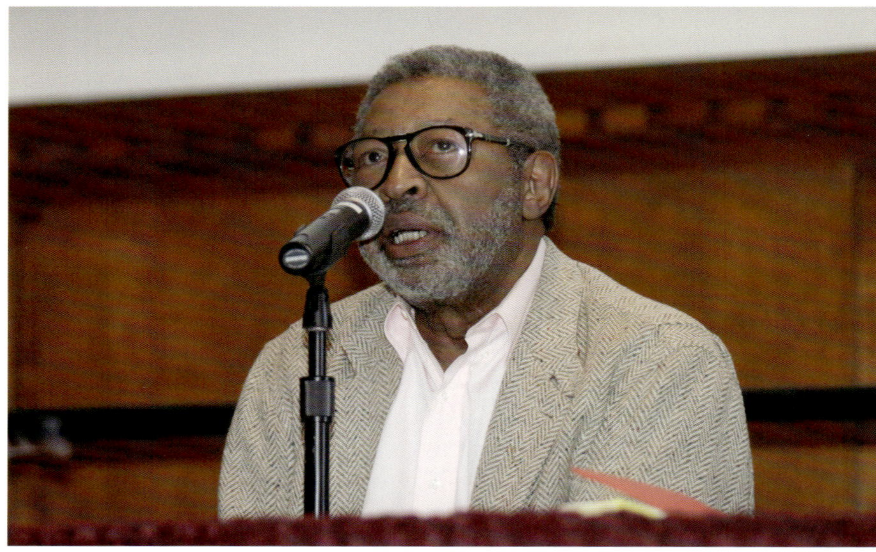

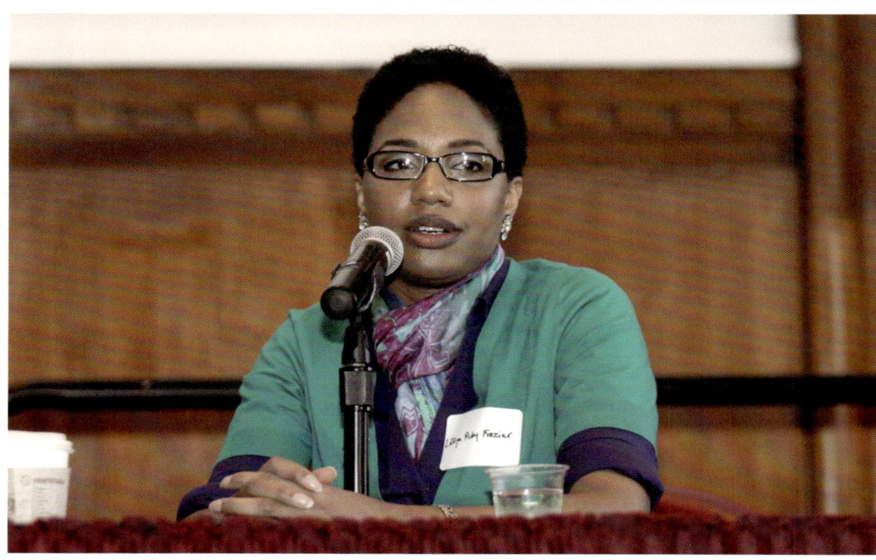

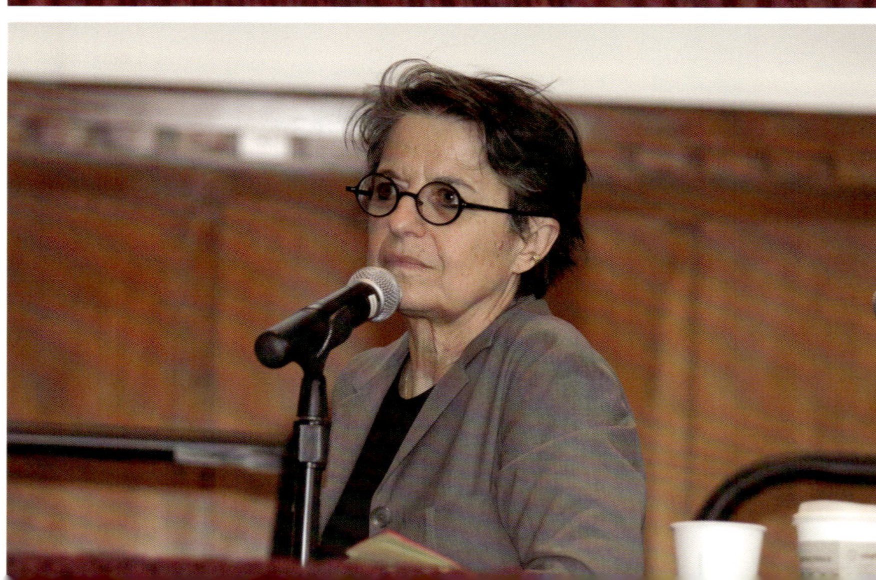

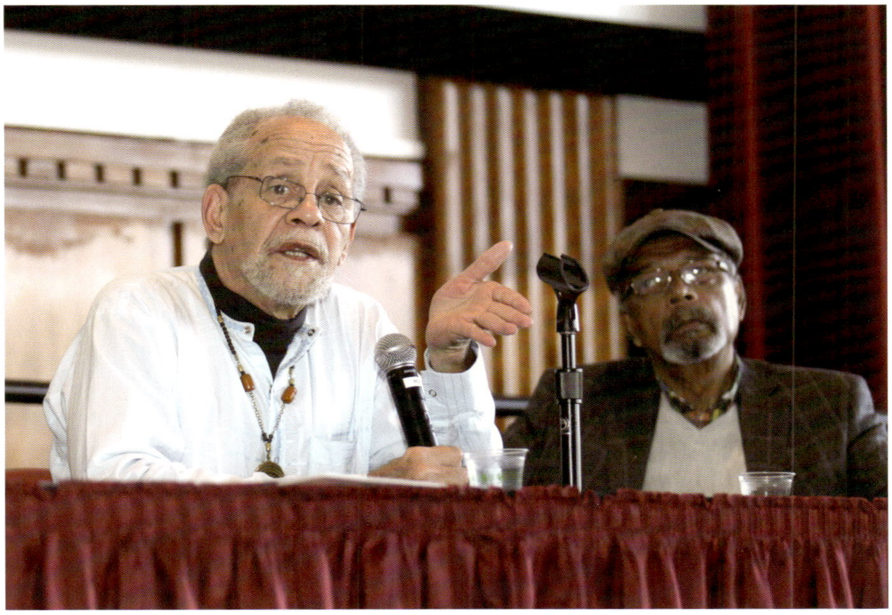

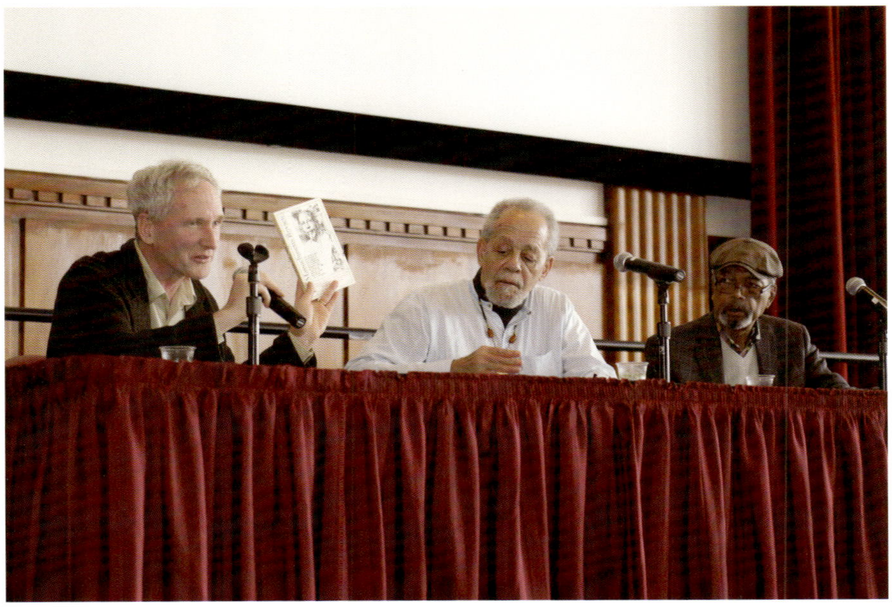

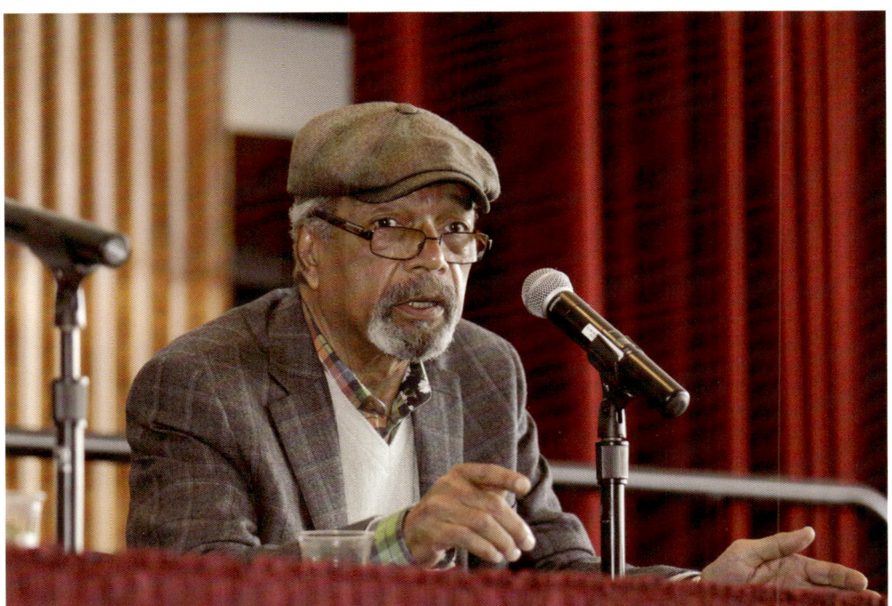

UMASS AND DU BOIS

Emeritus Professor **Ekueme Michael Thelwell** (Afro-American Studies, UMass) and artist and Professor of Art Emeritus **Nelson Stevens** in dialogue, as witnesses to the connection and deep roots between Du Bois and UMass in the past fifty years

RACIAL PERSPECTIVE

Moderator: Professor **Manisha Sinha** (Afro-American Studies, UMass) — with Professor **Saidiya Hartman** (English and Comparative Literature, and director of the Institute for Research on Women and Gender, Columbia University) and artists **Mickalene Thomas** and **Radcliffe Bailey**

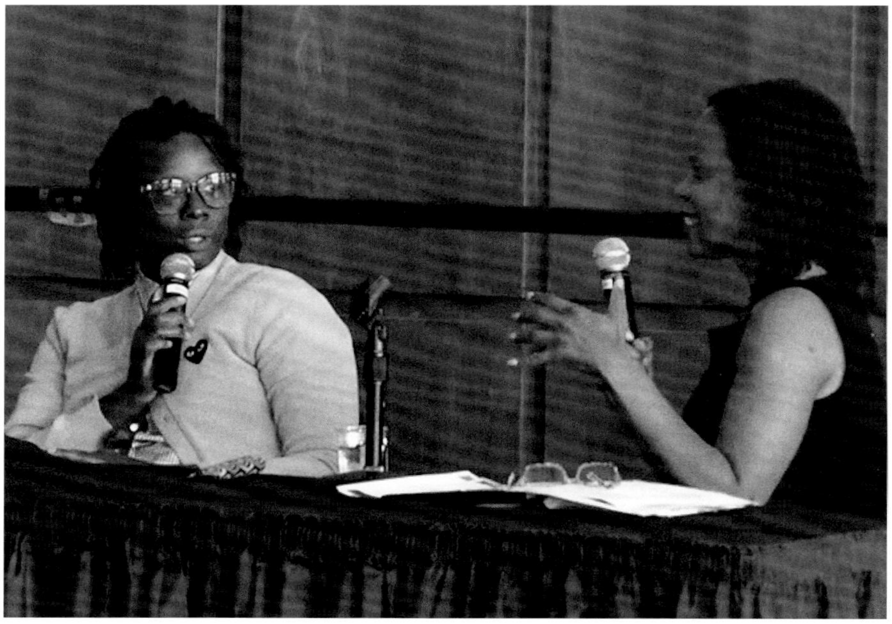

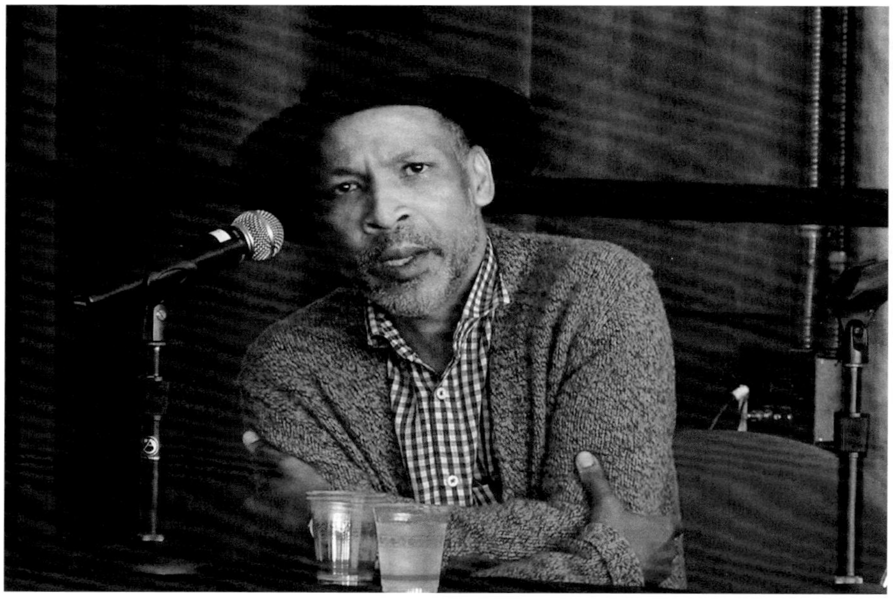

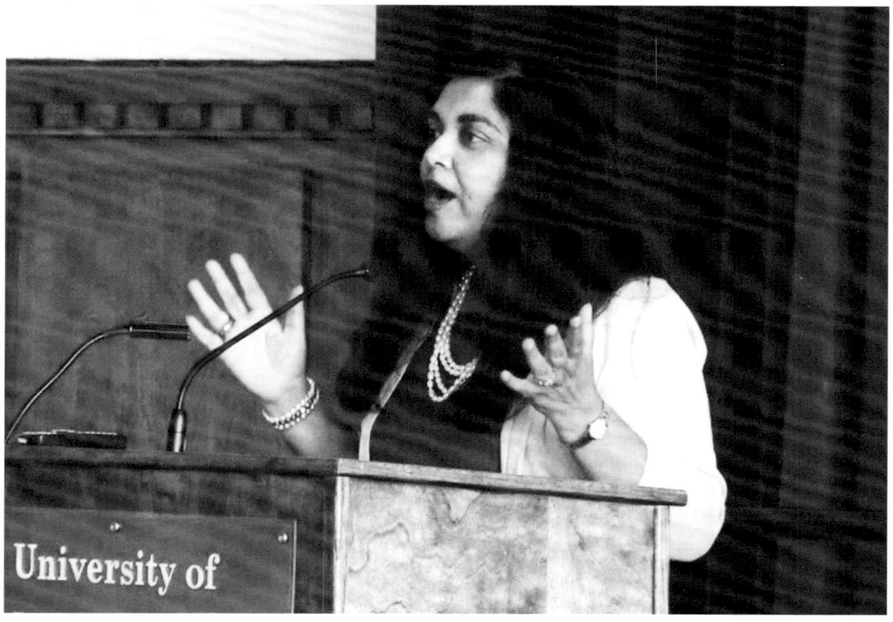

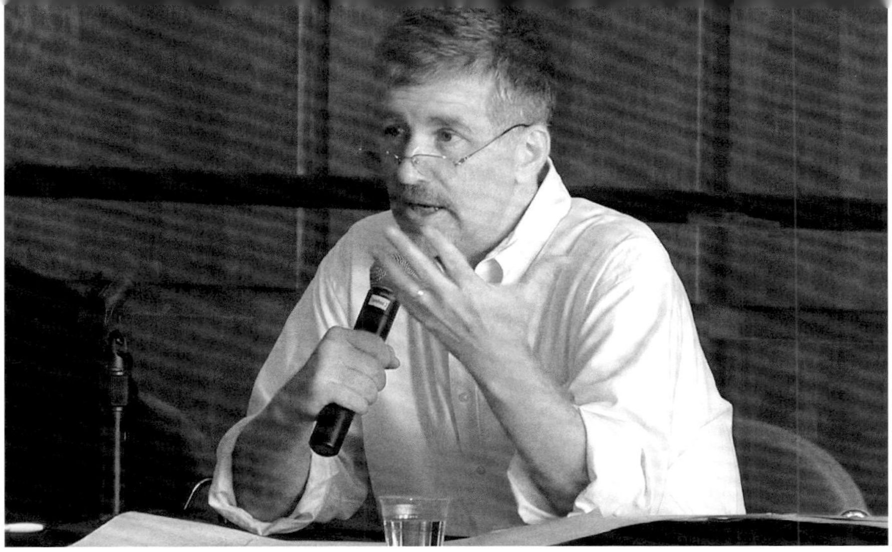

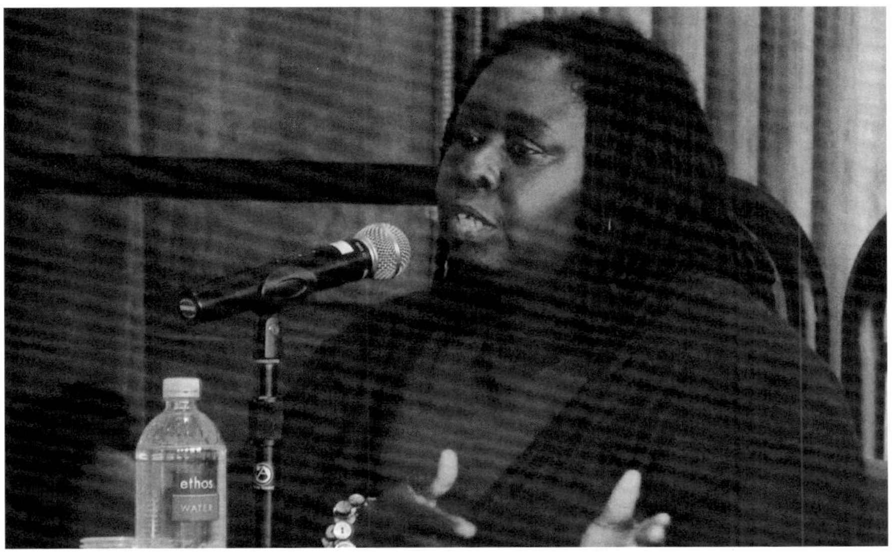

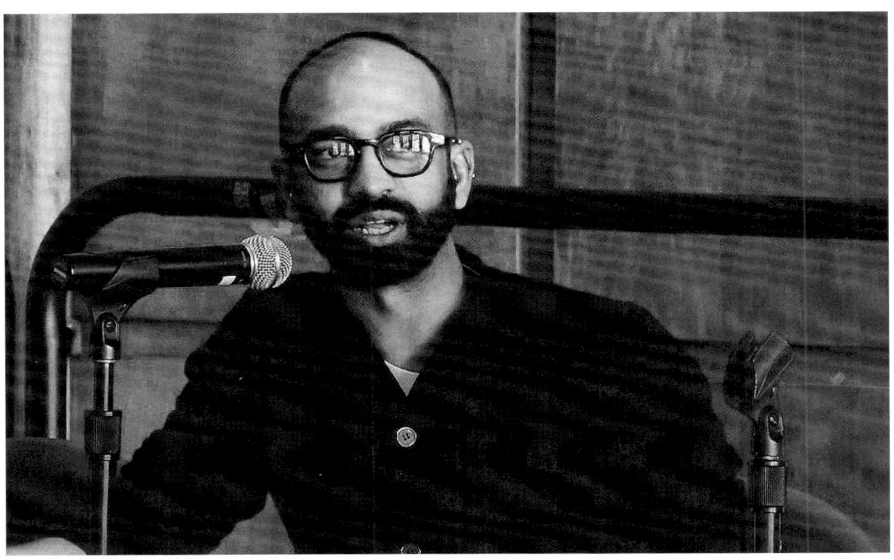

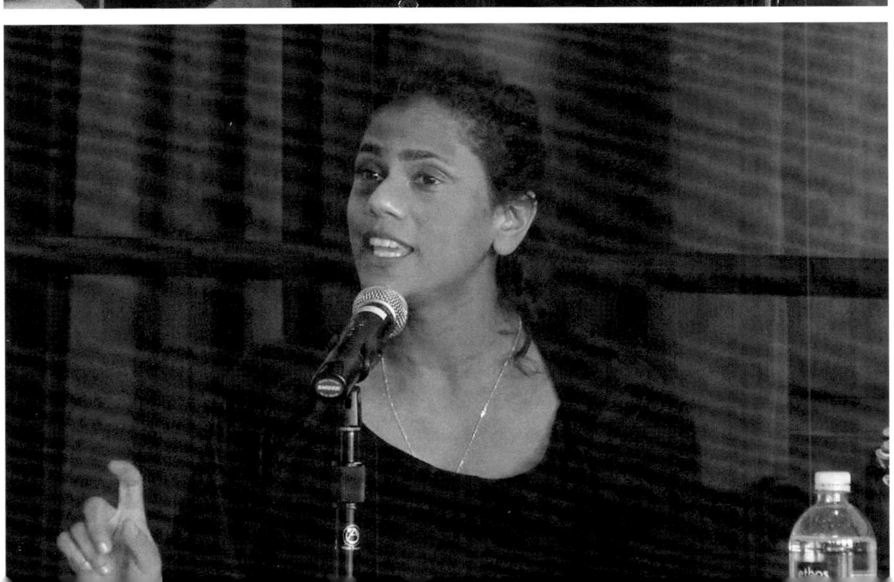

GLOBAL LEGACY

Moderator: Professor **Tanya Fernando** (English and Comparative Literature, UMass) — with Professor **James Campbell** (History, Stanford University) and artists **Mary Evans** and **Brendan Fernandes**

DU BOIS IN OUR TIME:
LECTURES, PANEL DISCUSSIONS, PERFORMANCES, AND RESIDENCIES

Held throughout Fall 2013

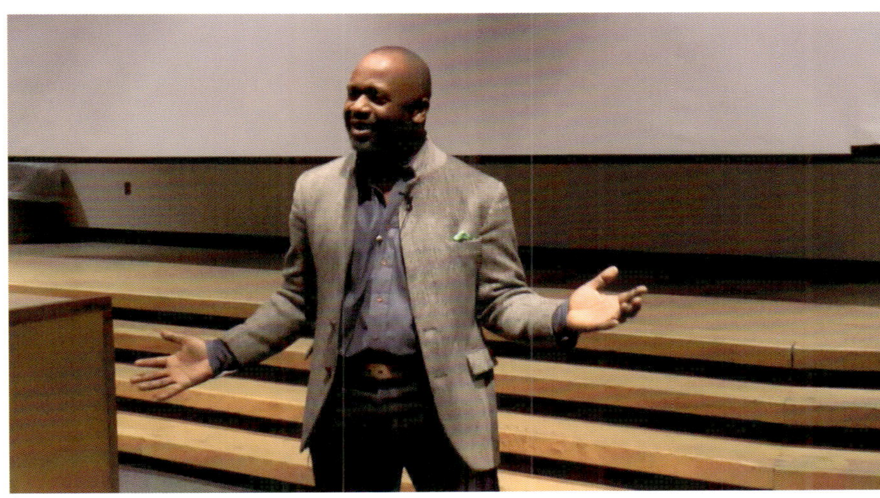

Lecture by artist and urban planner Theaster Gates

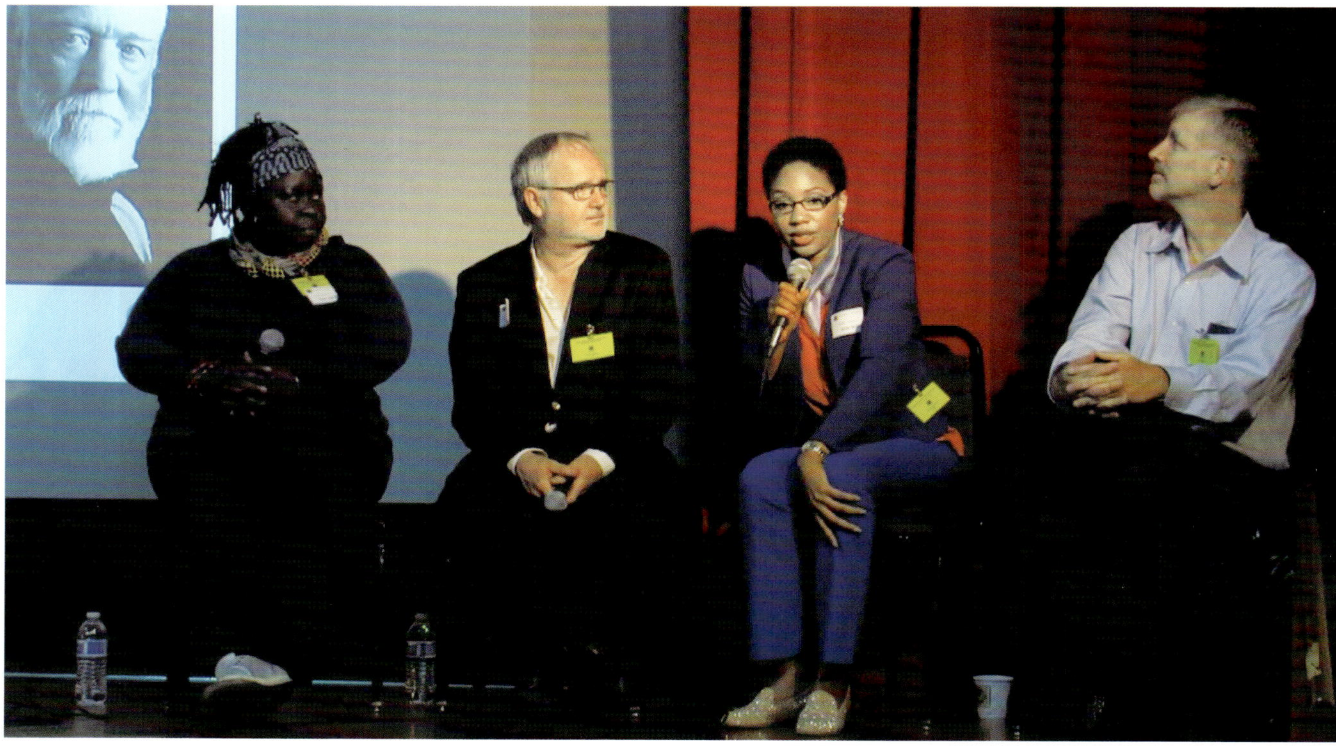

DU BOIS *AND ART* IN OUR TIME

A conversation with artists Mary Evans, LaToya Ruby Frazier, Tim Rollins, and James Campbell, Professor of U.S. History, Stanford University
Held at the Springfield Museums

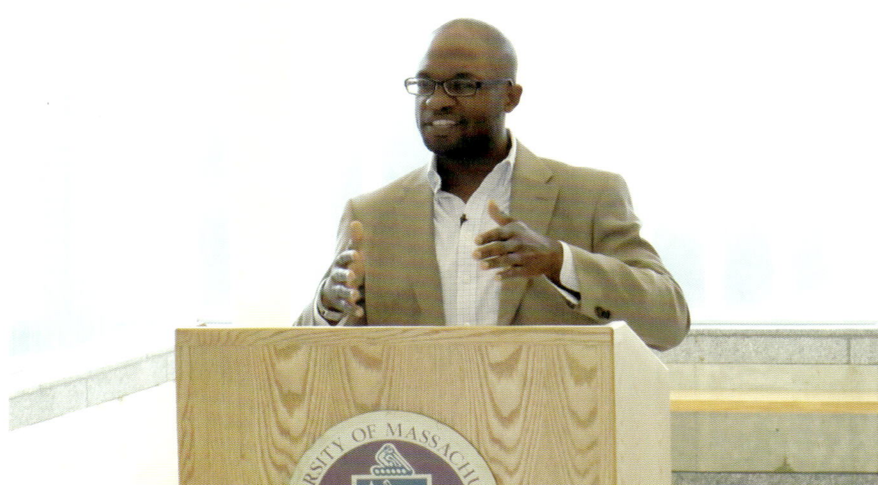

OCTOBER 8

ETHICS OF BEAUTY: DU BOIS AND THE IMPORTANCE OF PHOTOGRAPHY

Public lecture by W.E.B. Du Bois Library Fellow Horace D. Ballard Jr., Ph.D. candidate, Brown University

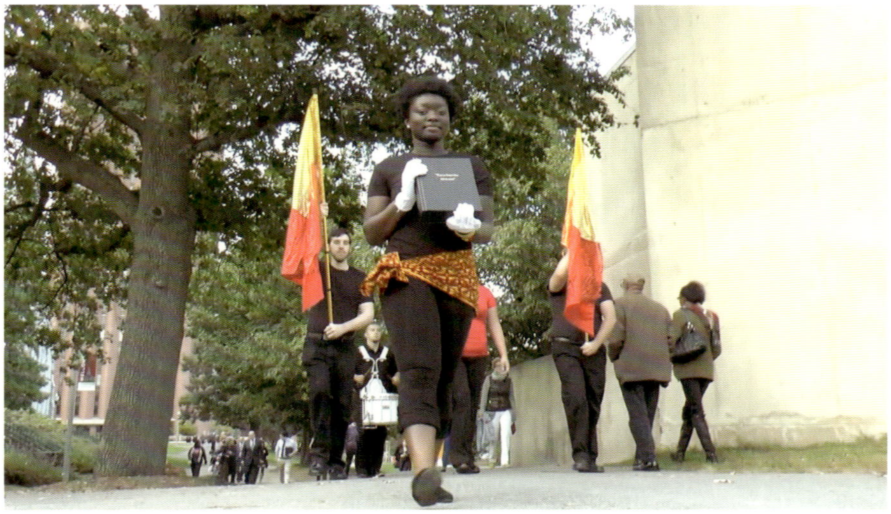

SEPTEMBER 27

W.E.B. DU BOIS LIBRARY TO UMCA

Performance by Brendan Fernandes and the UMass Color Guard

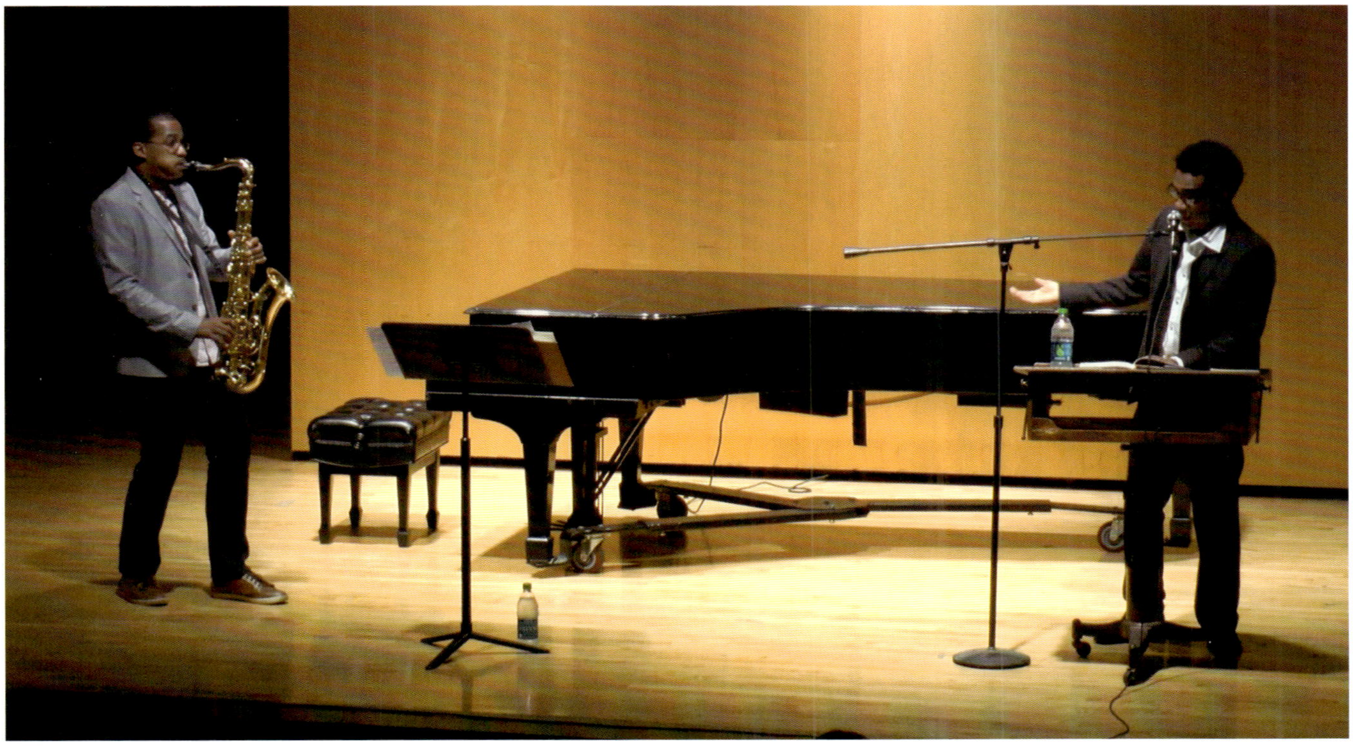

OCTOBER 15

THE SUPPRESSION OF SOUND

An evening with poet Thomas Sayers Ellis and saxophonist James Brandon Lewis

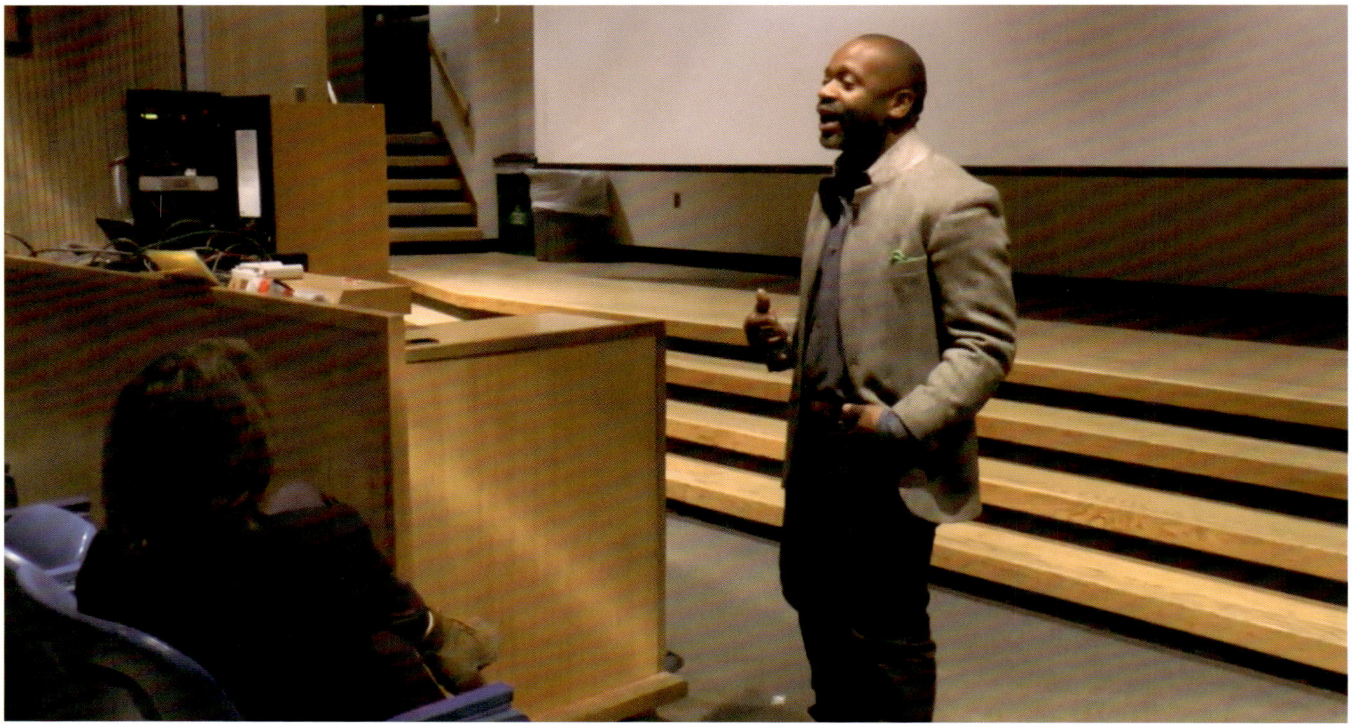

NOVEMBER 4

DU BOIS: THE EARLY SOCIAL PRACTITIONER

Lecture by artist and urban planner Theaster Gates

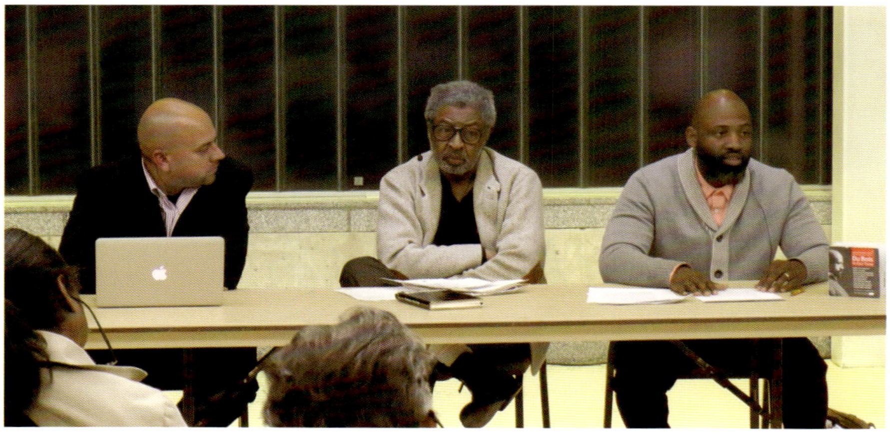

NOVEMBER 13

COLOR LINES OF EDUCATION

A conversation about Du Bois's views on education and the realities of educational opportunities today for students of color. Three educators reflect on the educational and social system in the United States — Chris Tinson, professor of African American Studies, Hampshire College; Bill Strickland, professor of Afro-American Studies, UMass Amherst; and Jason G. Irizarry, director of Urban Education, associate professor Department of Teacher Education and Curriculum Studies, UMass Amherst

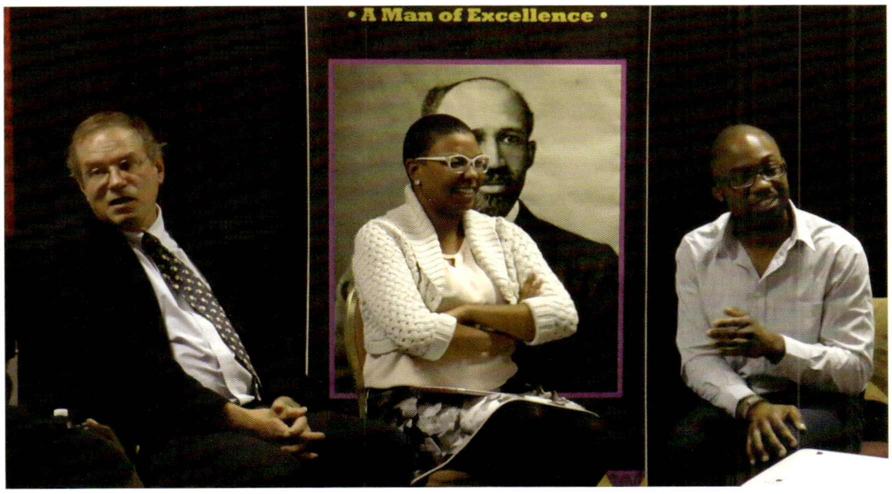

NOVEMBER 16

OPEN YOUR EYES

A conversation on African American Art since Du Bois with James Smethurst, professor of Afro-American Studies, W.E.B. Du Bois Library Fellow Horace D. Ballard Jr., Ph.D. candidate, Brown University, and Kelli Morgan, Ph.D. candidate, UMass Amherst. Held at PAHMUSA (Pan African History Museum USA), Springfield, Massachusetts

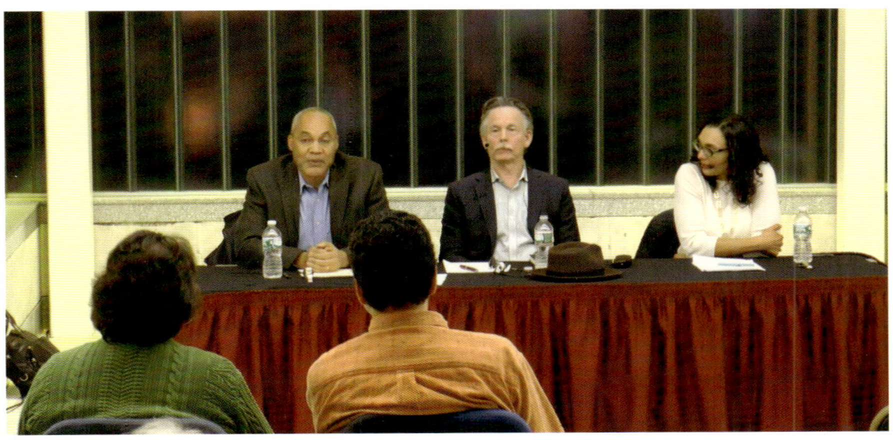

NOVEMBER 20

VOICES OF PROTEST

A conversation about Du Bois and social movements of his time with Barbara Krauthamer, professor of History, UMass Amherst; Nick Bromell, professor of American Studies, UMass Amherst; and Preston H. Smith II, professor of Politics and chair of Africana Studies, Mount Holyoke College

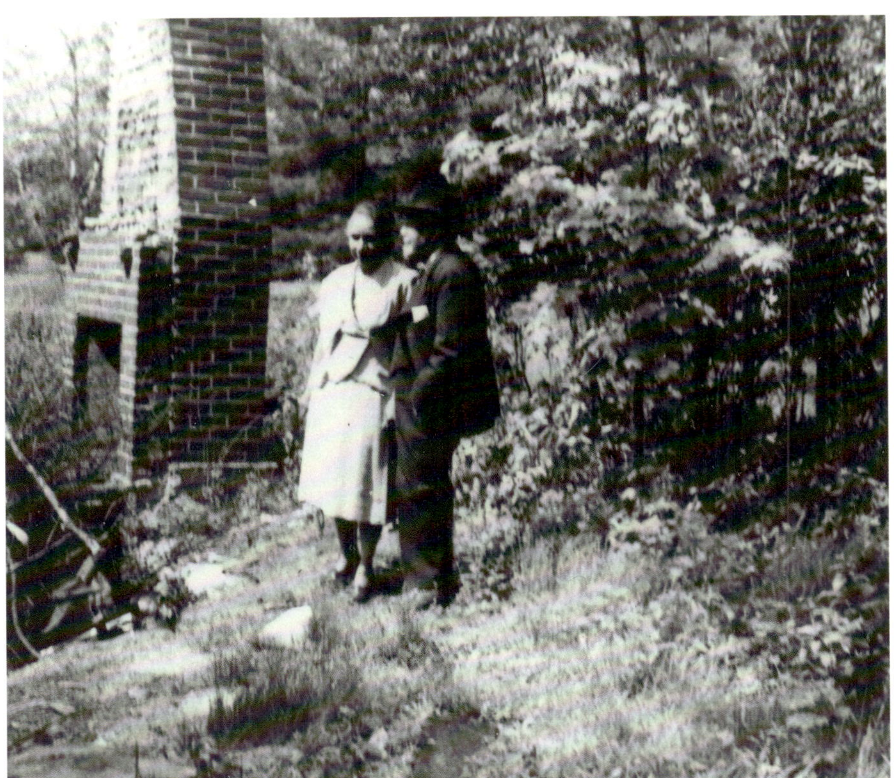

OCTOBER 19

BUS TRIP: GUIDED TOUR OF THE W.E.B. DU BOIS HOMESITE, GREAT BARRINGTON, MASSACHUSETTS

Courtesy of W. E. B. Du Bois Papers, Special Collections and University Archives, University Libraries, University of Massachusetts Amherst

TIM ROLLINS & K.O.S. AT THE RENAISSANCE SCHOOL IN SPRINGFIELD, MASSACHUSETTS

From March 27 to 29, 2013, Tim Rollins and Angel Abreu, a member of his collective (Kids of Survival), visited the Renaissance School in Springfield, Massachusetts, as part of an artist-in-residence program sponsored by the UMCA. Tim Rollins and Angel Abreu collaborated with middle school students and teachers on a project that combined lessons in reading and writing with the production of works of art. In a process they call "jammin'," Rollins and one of the students read aloud from the selected texts, "Credo" and "The Immortal Child" from *Darkwater: Voices From Within the Veil*, while the other members of the class drew and related the stories to their own experiences. The results of this collaborative workshop/residency were featured in the exhibition *Du Bois in Our Time*.

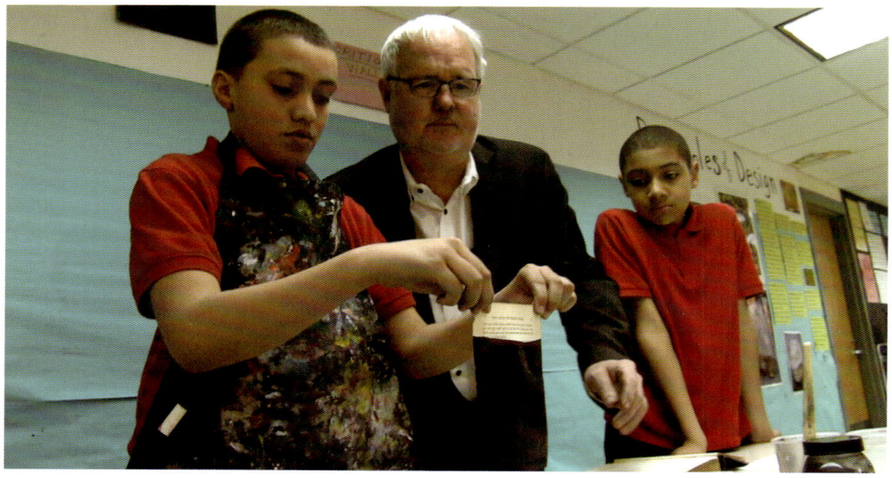

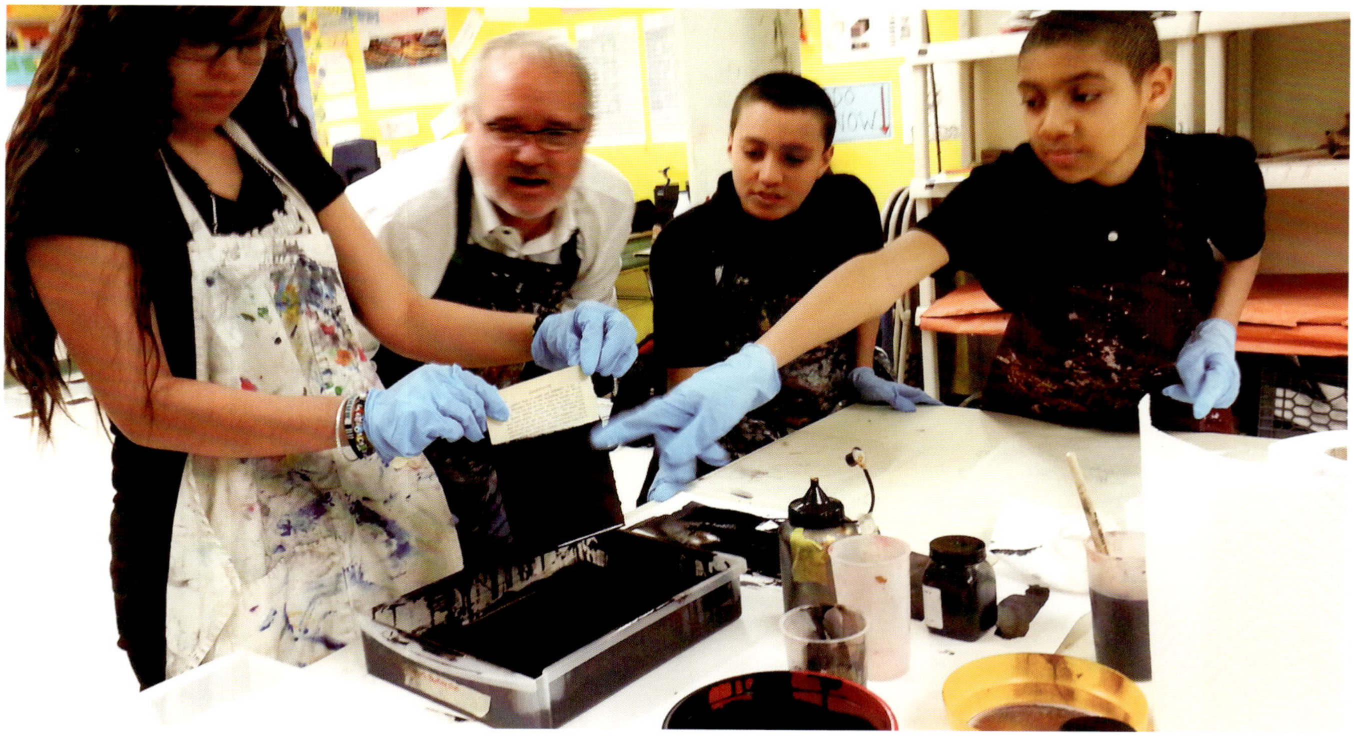

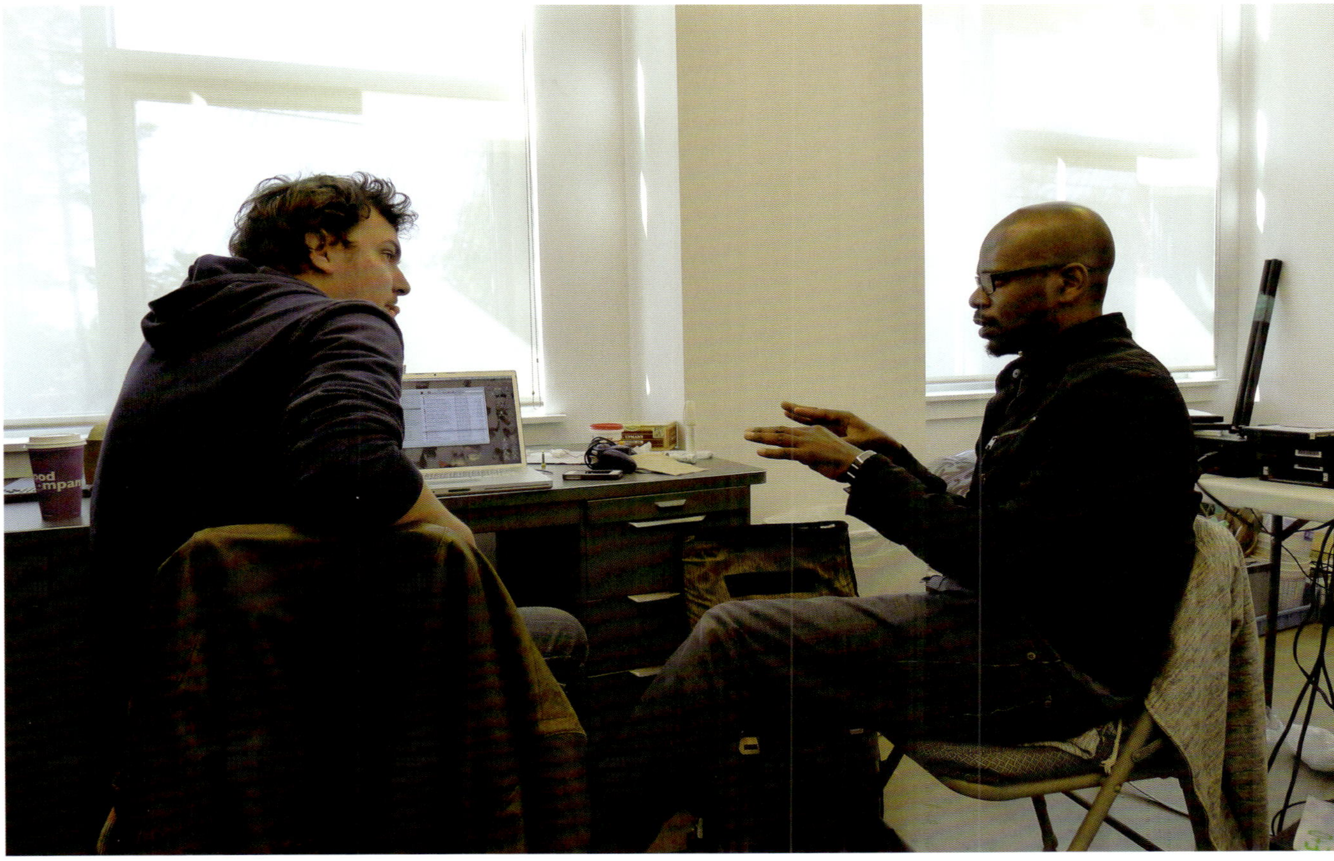

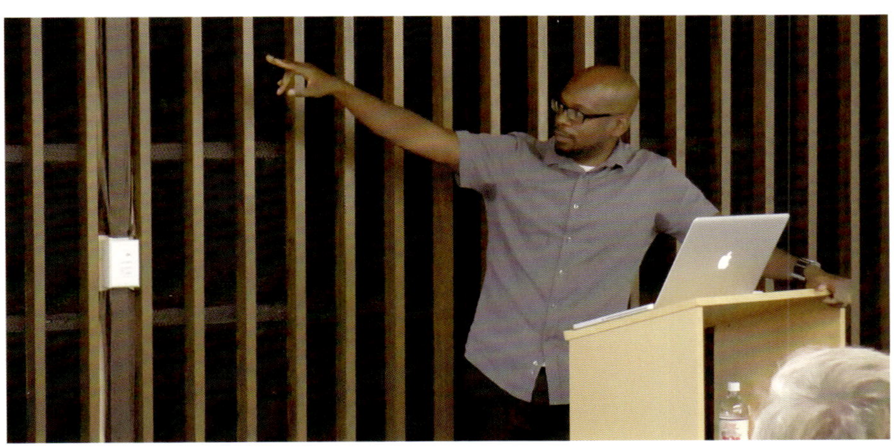

JEFFERSON PINDER RESIDENCY AT UMASS AMHERST

Jefferson Pinder conducted a highly successful week-long residency at UMass Amherst, October 7–11, 2013, with a unique multidisciplinary focus, thanks to the support of the Class of 1961 Artists Residency Program. UMass students were provided with direct access to the artist who offered a teaching and mentorship role through one-on-one critique sessions with M.F.A. students in Studio Art; interaction with a Performance Workshop class; and participation in seminar discussions integrating the arts and humanities. In addition he gave a public lecture titled "Making Art and Making History." Jefferson Pinder's residency enlivened the cultural life of the campus, enhanced and supplemented educational opportunities, and brought the artist together with a wide spectrum of people — students, faculty, and community members.

A DISTINCT BUT RELATED EXHIBITION, *Du Bois in Our Time/Accra,* premiered in March 2014 at the Nubuke Foundation and the Du Bois Centre, both in Accra, Ghana. This was timed to coincide with Ghana's Independence Day celebration. Acknowledging the breadth of Du Bois's influence and his role in the Pan-African movement, *Du Bois in Our Time/Accra* reintroduced Du Bois back into the consciousness of today's West Africa. By engaging African artists, writers, and scholars in dialogue, the aim was to revitalize the legacy of Du Bois and make it more accessible to a wider audience. Programming included lectures, open discussions, workshops, and an exhibition of contemporary art. *Du Bois in Our Time/Accra* was organized by Odile Tevie, director of the Nubuke Foundation, with guest curator Tayo Ogunbiyi.

DU BOIS
IN OUR TIME/ACCRA

ON MARCH 6 THE CHIEFS OF FANTE signed the Bond of 1844 with the British-appointed governor of the coastal states. The chiefs had ceded authority over some judicial matters to British officials. This relationship gradually became one of dependency and protection at the time when the Fante were seeking respite from the incessant attacks of the Asante. The signing of the bond marked the beginning of the relationship that resulted almost 40 years later in the coastal states becoming part of the Crown Colonies in 1886. The metamorphoses of the relationship forced by other events like the Berlin Conference to partition the continent of Africa ushered in the beginnings of the colonial rule of many Western European states over several African countries.

Let us fast-forward 170 years later, to 2014 and 50 years after the death of W.E.B. Du Bois, a vocal and energetic civil rights leader whose writings, speeches, activism, and support of Pan-Africanism drew Kwame Nkrumah into his circle of friends. Ghana's first president came to understand more about the need to fight for the rights of the people of the then Gold Coast under the tutelage of W.E.B. Du Bois. The legacy of W.E.B. Du Bois cannot be looked at in the Ghanaian context without looking at the role he played during our independence struggle. Not be taken lightly is W.E.B. Du Bois's renunciation of his American citizenship for a Ghanaian one. There are quite a number of strands that have come into play with the *Du Bois in Our Time* project. The idea of this project was to employ a multiprismed lens to examine the legacy of W.E.B. Du Bois the man. Indeed just as a prism refracts light, those involved in the project — artists, academics, writers, scholars, Pan-African enthusiasts — would each from their own perspective relearn and reflect on his relevance and importance in present-day Ghana. There has been no limit to the information available about W.E.B. Du Bois, in Ghana at the Du Bois Centre and in his personal library, and, at Special Collections and University Archives, University Libraries, University of Massachusetts Amherst, access to his writings and correspondence through its archives and online resources.

DU BOIS IN OUR TIME/ACCRA ONLINE: http://www.pac-hub.com/

As the director of a foundation that is working against all odds to encourage nascent young talents in Ghana, I seldom see young artists invited to share a stage with internationally acclaimed artists and professionals. Additionally, this project presented a tempting opportunity for the artists to explore new mediums that they would ordinarily not have engaged.

This project has seen academic and artistic sifting through myriads of information, writing, poetry, objects, smells, pictures. . . . Several discussions, conversations, and workshops were held, and these continued during the opening events at the Du Bois Centre on March 5 and 6, 2014.

The project, which started at UMCA, at the University of Massachusetts Amherst in 2012, has culminated in a transatlantic exploration and sharing of our connection to the great mind of a legendary person. The University of Massachusetts Amherst is the largest repository — physical and online — of resources for W.E.B. Du Bois, and this includes his books, manuscripts, photographs, memorabilia, and correspondence. Through this collaboration we have provided platforms for dialogues to take place between and within several communities inside and outside Ghana. In September 2013, the *Du Bois in Our Time exhibition* commenced at UMCA following the commissioning of ten artists who presented their works and with several programs held around the launch of the exhibition. This included artists' talks and discussions and workshops. Similar events took place with the *Du Bois in Our Time/ Accra* program. We were lucky to have the full support of the Du Bois Centre in this project. The director, Mr. Keelson, gave the artists full access to the entire Du Bois archive in Ghana. It is no surprise, then, that with their final works, they have "moved in" and are feeling very comfortable in the home and personal space of Du Bois — his bedroom, library, living room. This "occupation" has been achieved, in my opinion, because of the medium we encouraged the eight Ghanaian artists to work in. The eight worked intensely with Jude Anogwih and Emeka Ogboh in a multimedia art workshop. While exploring this archive, the artists created works using new media platforms — sound, photography, and video.

Mary Evans, an internationally renowned artist, was commissioned to create works for the exhibition. Her site-specific work immerses and engages the audience within a two-dimensional time frame, drawing them into this dialogue using an everyday material — paper — to evoke memories, questions, answers . . . sometimes uncomfortable, sometimes optimistic.

The opening dates for the exhibition were chosen to challenge the consciousness of the audience. On the eve of Ghana's independence declaration on March 5, 1957, there was such a deep sense of hope and expectation among the people. The questions we are asking about the legacy of W.E.B. Du Bois today should be reflected upon very deeply by every Ghanaian. Kwame Nkrumah believed strongly that our struggles and subsequent emancipation could not be fully attained for our nation unless it was linked to the freedom of all African nations.

This exhibition goes a long way toward showing that this examination cannot end, and not until the envisaged freedom and emancipation are felt by all citizens of Ghana can we truly declare total freedom for everyone. If the struggle still continues, then what part shall you play?

Odile Tevie
Director, Nubuke Foundation

BERNARD AKOI-JACKSON

DU BOIS IN OUR TIME: REACHING AROUND THE BAOBAB TO MIRROR GLIMPSES OF OURSELVES AND A FUTURE

W.E.B. DU BOIS may be remembered as a subject, a man, or even an institution—for this, indeed, is what he must have been even before his death in 1963. He was, in mortal terms, the proverbial Adido of the "knowledge-like-a-baobab-tree" adage, so vast, so wide, so totally encompassing that one could not merely envelop him. His reach was, and continues to be, celestial. By "celestial," we do not seek to ascribe sacredness to the man, a mere mortal; we are quite certain Du Bois himself would have cringed at that thought. The celestial nature that I'm ascribing to him, then, navigates the expansive reach of his thought, beliefs, and aspirations that were encapsulated in his writings and poetry. These are the things that assume cosmic import, with the propensity to shoot across galactic skies, into the depths of a primordial blackness. His was a belief that all will eventually recognize and acknowledge the sanctity of the origins of humankind: Africa. It was his postulations, combined with the thoughts of others like Marcus Garvey, that planted the seeds of Pan-Africanism in the schemes of Dr. Kwame Nkrumah until they eventually became commonplace.

So how are we, as children of this moment, dialoguing with Pan-Africanism? What have been the prospects following the creation of the Organization of African Unity (OAU) and eventually the African Union (AU)? What impact have Du Bois's and Nkrumah's toils had on our collective psyche? How might we awake from our slumber of cultural amnesia and begin speaking across generations to a future that is bound to be bright? How are we preparing to handle our destinies in a manner that would be different from what has been and still be accountable to our histories? It is important that such questions and many more continue to burden our minds. By titling this exhibition *Du Bois in Our Time*, what do we insinuate? Do we posit a claim to contemporaneity with Du Bois the man? Can we? Must we? Dare we even dream it? Are we in any way his equals? Or is it that the organizers, in seeking to grapple with the variegated magnitude of his influence and its relevance in our present, have coined this phrase: "Du Bois in Our Time"?

And is it our coinage, really? And with "our," who do we imply? Is it "we," being the artists, researchers, and scholars, or the general public? Who are we? Are we children of a lost generation or are we the children Du Bois himself seeks to address in his 1920 poem "Children of the Moon"? What the artists and scholars have sought to do in this project, then, is to engage this vastness that Du Bois's ideas represent. This is done from various positions that must be duly acknowledged and appreciated. Each artist, for instance, has a personal methodological preference. But this notwithstanding, as time went on there was no doubt that collaborations would emerge, further pursuing the Pan-Africanist trajectory that any engagement with Du Bois would evoke. The intense debates, discussions, and research session that those few days in the W.E.B. Du Bois Centre in Accra engendered can only be cherished. Our chance encounter with Professor Gayatri Chakravorty Spivak and the Skype session with Professor Biodun Jeyifo brought about some focus for many of us.

Tema, 2014

Opposite:
BERNARD AKOI-JACKSON
Metaphor: A pun,[un]-intended, at the awakening thresholds of an epoch's dreaming yet.
2013
Video still

ARTIST STATEMENTS AND ARTWORKS

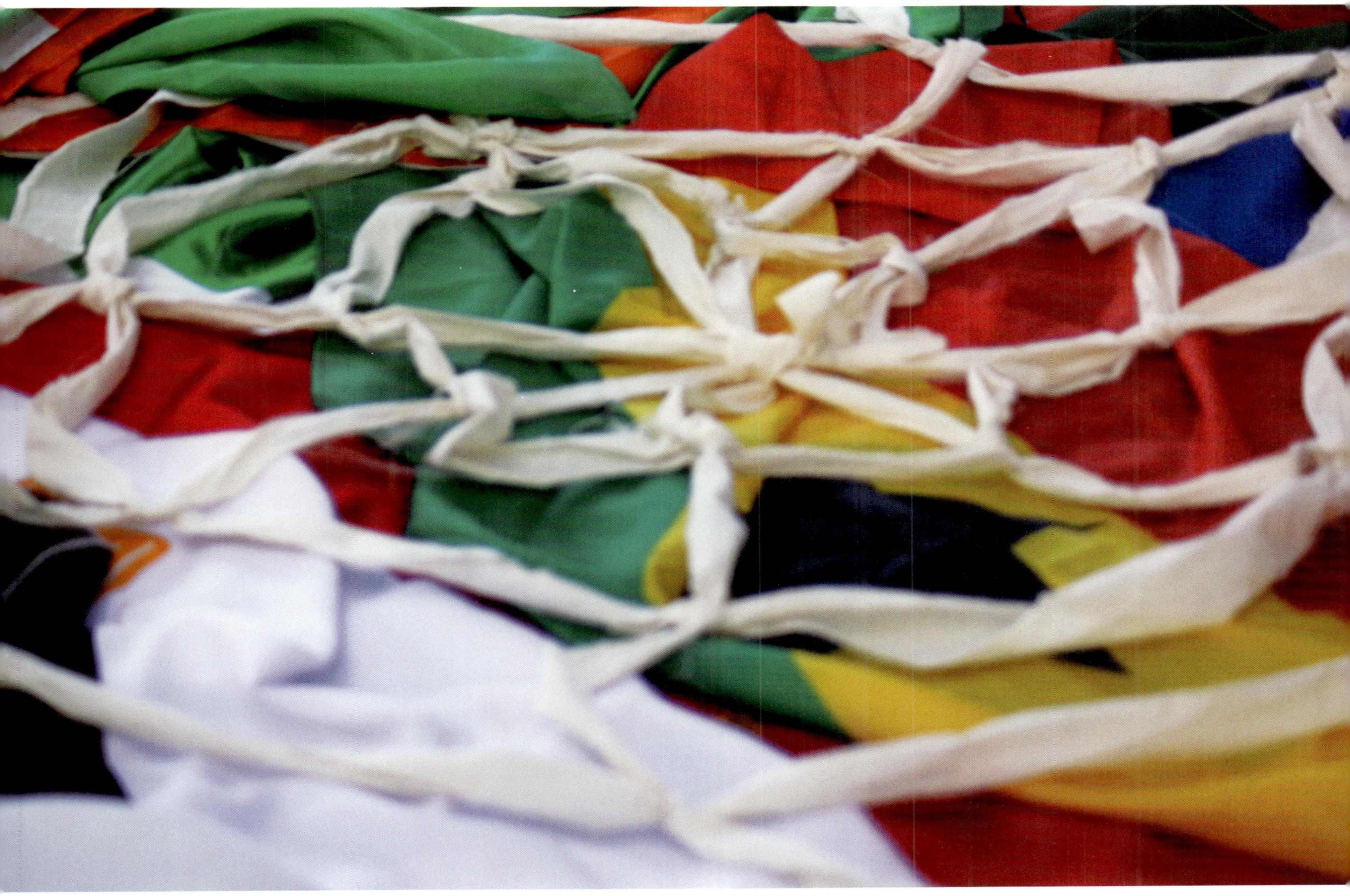

BERNARD AKOI-JACKSON

Du Bois described his maternal grandfather as "very dark," his maternal grandmother as a "Dutch African woman," and his mother as "dark shining bronze."
— E. M. Rudwick, *W.E.B. Du Bois, Propagandist of the Negro Protest*

One may posit the idea that W.E.B. Du Bois's life project spun forth from a site of hybridity. This deportment is akin to my own personality and artistic praxis. W[h]e inhabit[ed] and constantly engage[d] an analogous space of multiple culturalities populated by numerous places. This space presents many opportunities for tolerance, cooperation, agreement, and pacifism. But it is a potentially contested space too, potentiating contradictory others, like disagreement, crisis, and conflict. It is, however, usually pragmatic that one who indeed embodies such concepts of hybridity essentially becomes a catalyst to efforts toward unification with attendant pluralities. This does not imply the "blanket" unification that globalist capitalism propitiates; rather, a unification that operates on human[e] levels is what is sought.

When we consider W.E.B. Du Bois: his being, originally African American of distant Huguenot and "mulatto" stock with links in the Bahamas, mixed with myriad other racial heritages such as French and Dutch, to state but a few; his thought[s]; his combats and protests; his diverse emotional experiences; influences that wrought his theoretical, philosophical, ideological, and political trajectory; his fighting through discrimination and segregation in America, through further education in Germany and to his eventual adopted final home and resting place in Accra, Ghana — this is a life lived as though enmeshed. Entanglement in this context is not oppressive; it leads to an eventual emancipation premised on the concepts of networking and commun[al]ism[?]

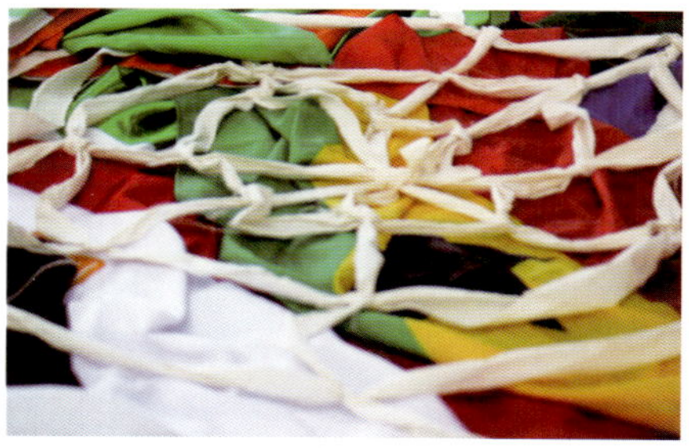

In this work we chart the course of a becoming, a seeking to question that state of inertia — inaction — so as to begin [a] journey[s] of [re-]discovery. Conceptually and materially, it becomes a *bricolage*; disparate elements and layered references intertwine to weave a narrative that, despite its simplicity, presents a complexity quite akin to the being of Du Bois himself. The central image becomes a large wall projection of my hands tying up strips of cloth to create a web, and therein lies the [un]intended pun "at the awakening thresholds of an epoch's dreaming yet." In bringing together disparate materials, forms, sounds, images and texts, *Metaphor* becomes an even richer tapestry of possibilities. The epoch is itself still dreaming. Is there any chance of an awakening for a people and a time that has so long been comfortably cocooned in rosy beds of cultural amnesia? How might this current generation and forthcoming ones access the voices of sages gone by, when much of our collective ethos is still couched in syncretic pseudoscientific models that are deficient culturally and spiritually?

In viewing the work, audience[s] is[are] expected to begin contemplating journeys. Journeys of discovery, re-discovery, or recovery.

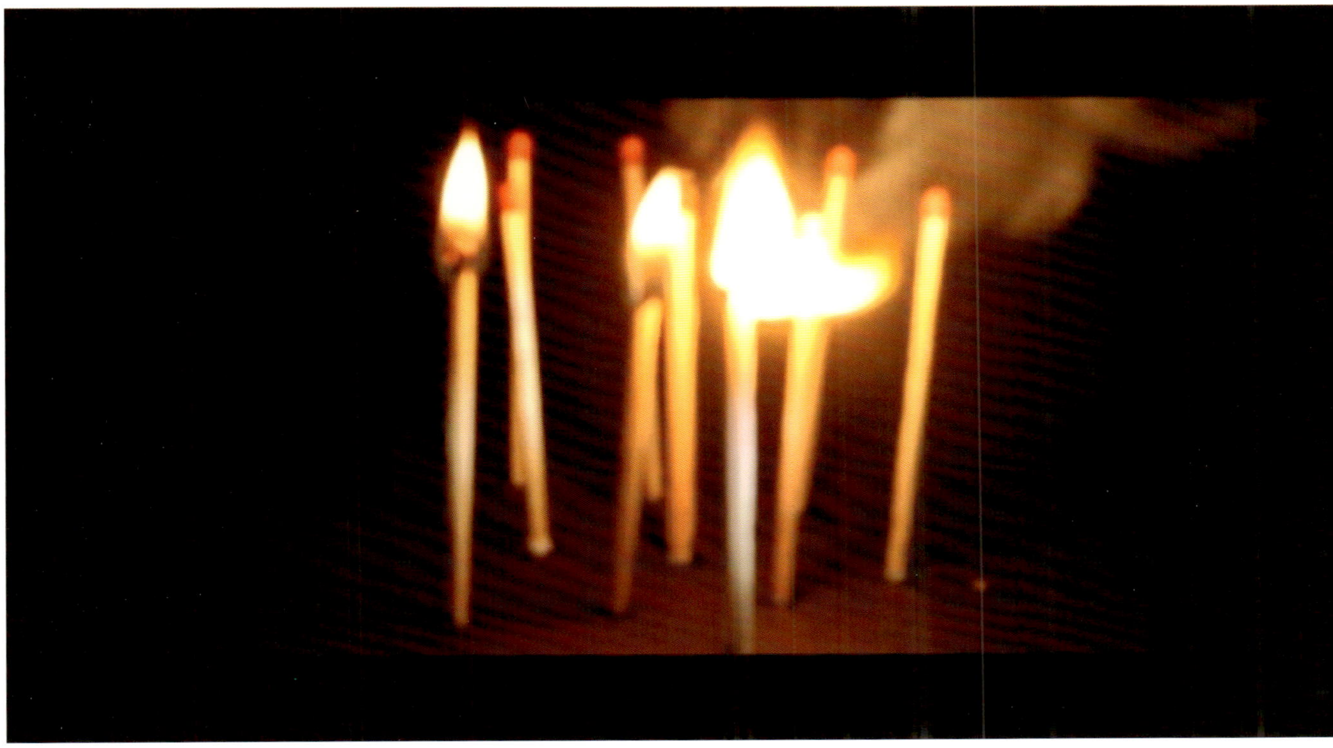

ADWOA AMOAH

The ability to be intelligent, have broad sympathy, knowledge of the world and of the relation of men to it was W.E.B. Du Bois's advocacy for higher intellectual education. The *Talented Tenth* employs light and fire to address issues of leadership, power, and knowledge, bringing to bear ideas of sharing and reconstruction.

The video begins with a single matchstick emerging from a dark background. The blurry element symbolizes the difficulty and struggle to build and achieve, to educate the best minds of a black race and disseminate them into the general population, thus allowing the general enlightenment of all.

ADWOA AMOAH
Talented Tenth
2013
Video still

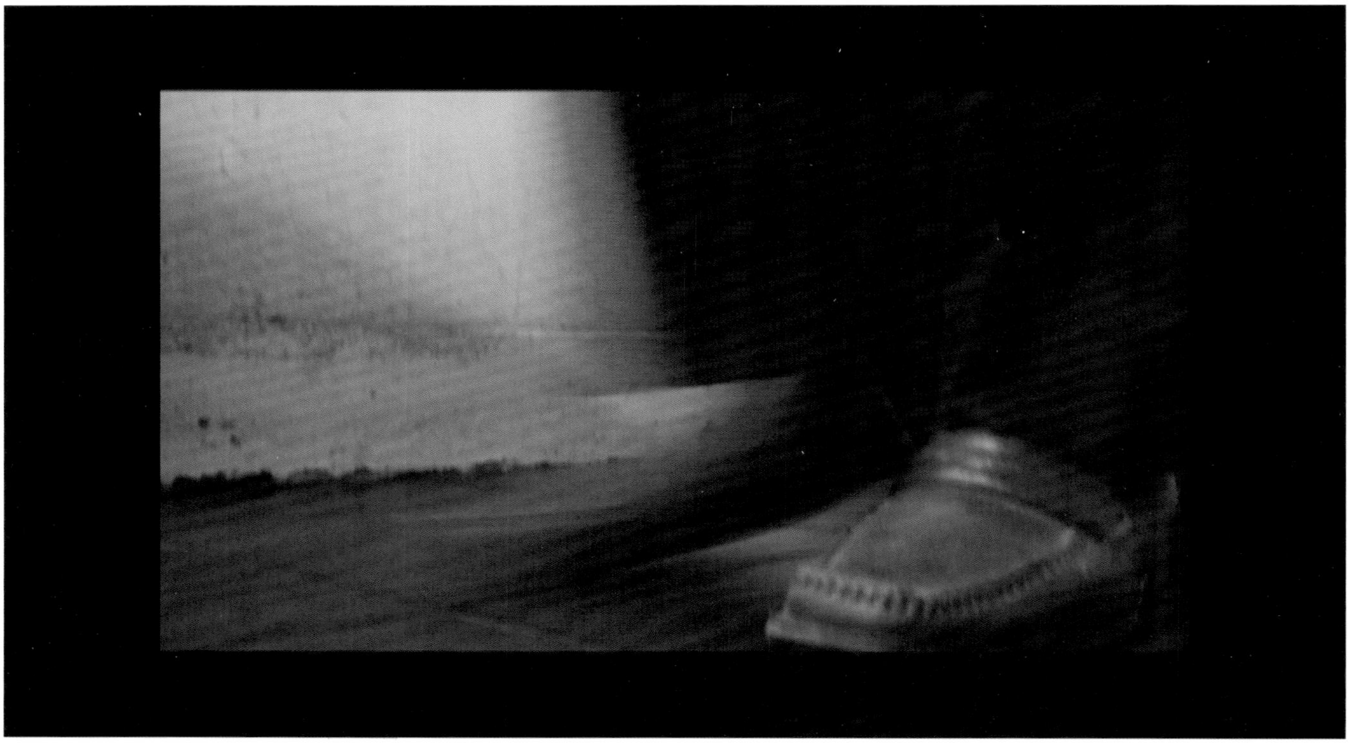

KWASI OHENE-AYEH
ATO ANNAN

This work explores the subjects of identity, geography, migration, and [dis] location of W.E.B. Du Bois from the perspective of two Ghanaian artists, I.U.B. and ato annan. The work investigates Du Bois from a personal and relational angle.

In the foreword of the Ghana University Press publication of *Selected Poems*, Kwame Nkrumah describes him as a "sensitive Fighter Poet who for three-quarters of a century struggled against the waves of Oppression, Misery and Woe which engulfed his people." In the same book, Shirley Graham states of his writing style that it "is always highly personal and is neither constant nor consistent." Furthermore, Graham states that "Du Bois wrote in awful isolation; an isolation at first imposed because of his color and later wholeheartedly embraced."

A passionate, vociferous intellectual of Du Bois's nature must have endured lengthy moments of angst — what Irit Rogoff terms psychic subjectivities — desire, compulsion, anxiety. Of course the context of Rogoff's terminologies derive from her deconstructionist theorization of geography, where she offers one (of four) definitions

KWASI OHENE-AYEH
ATO ANNAN
Exit Frame
2013
Video still

as "a site of collective national, cultural, linguistic and topographical histories." Du Bois's fight for equality, dignity, and justice must have stemmed from a belief in sacredness of identity or ethnicity or race. Therefore those moments of awful isolation spent writing in defense and in glorification and acceptance of his identity must have produced torturous moments for this Afro-American intellectual.

The project agrees with Rogoff's premise in its study of Du Bois, his writings, ideas, ideals, and vision as a conceptual structure or order of existing knowledge. It becomes far more legitimate when Du Bois's essence or life's meaning is studied with these far less obvious moments in mind, which may have worked together to define him and his struggle as a Pan-African advocate.

The video depicts a pensive character pacing back and forth, pondering what seems to be an ominous decision he must make. The subject is all too aware of the political implications his final decision would arouse and yet slams his passport as a final gesture that inevitably alters his citizenship status. Du Bois responds to his "Ghana Calls"...

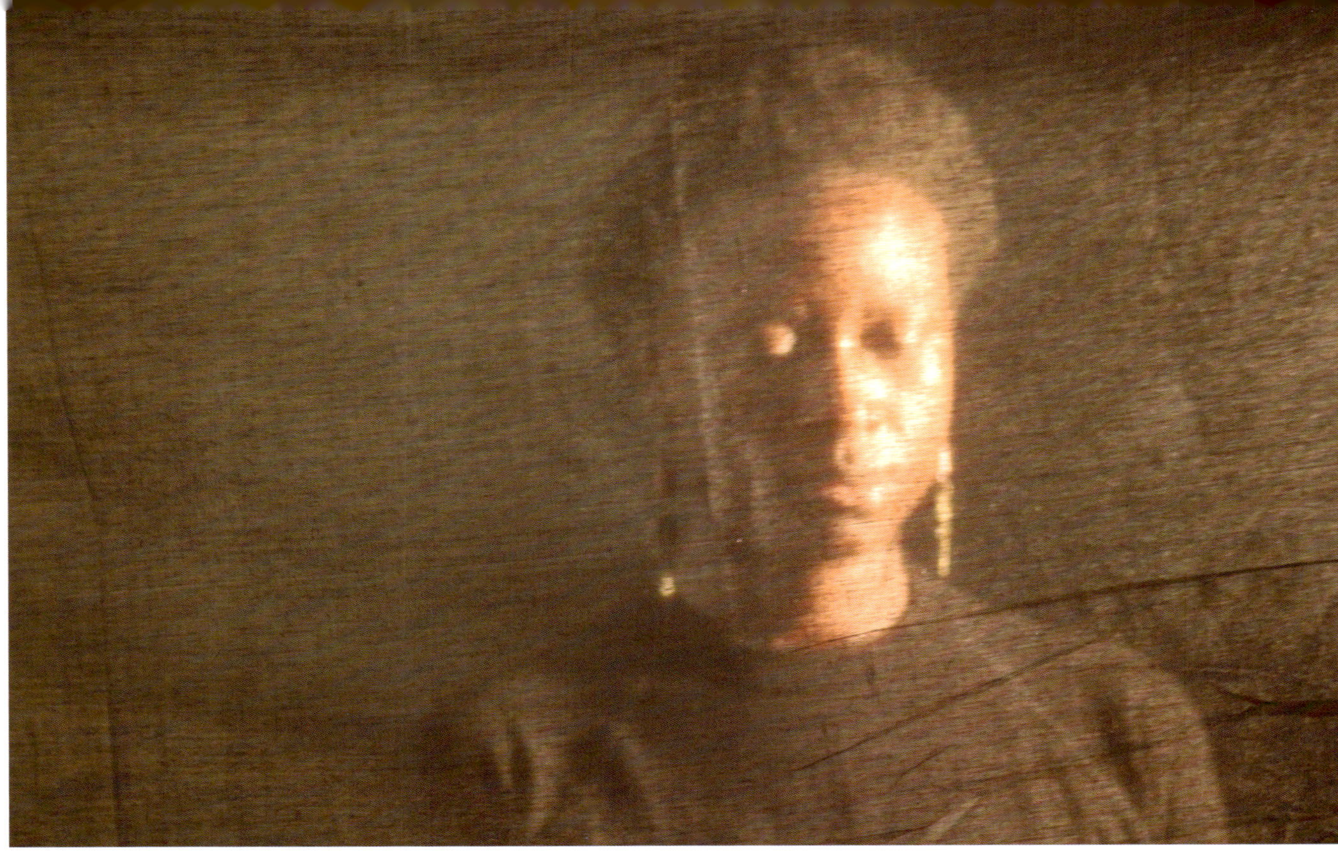

YAGANOMA BAATUOLKUU

YAGANOMA BAATUOLKUU
The Veil
2013
Video still

The Veil is a study and a juxtaposition of Du Bois's poetic essays, *The Souls of Black Folk*. In these essays Du Bois explores what he terms a "Veil" through which "white folk" viewed blacks. He discussed the perception that the Negro is a "seventh son." Looking back at my three years abroad, I experienced several instances of exclusion, where after my education I sought jobs: filling in application forms with such explicit racial segregatory indications such as: 1. Scottish; 2. White British; 3. Black British; 4. Asian British; 5. European; 6. Asian; 7. African; and 8. Other. All these categorizations made me realize that in general Western thought, the concept of the Negro as the "seventh son" had not changed since the time of Du Bois. I explore his ideology on the "veil" and what it means in our society today, searching within the various veils that exist within our society, the relevance of his ideologies in the framework of the twenty-first century. I do not analyze, interpret, or discuss who Du Bois was. I just engage the idea of the veil through this performance. I engage it in light of my own experiences, leaving its several modes of interpretation to the viewer.

"I have sought here to sketch, in vague, uncertain outline, the spiritual world. . . . I have tried to show what Emancipation meant, what was its aftermath. I have sketched in swift outline the two worlds within and without the Veil, and thus have come to the central problem of training men for life. I have stepped within the Veil, raising it that you may view faintly its deeper recesses — the meaning of its religion. I have ended with a tale twice told but seldom written and a chapter of song. . . some echo of haunting melody from the only American music which welled up from black souls in the dark past. And, finally, need I add that I who speak here am bone of the bone and flesh of the flesh of them that live within the Veil?"

(from W.E.B. Du Bois, "Forethought," *The Souls of Black Folk*)

SERGE ATTUKWEI CLOTTEY

The video explores notions of black and white identity, W.E.B Du Bois's prophetic genius and vast wisdom, and revolves around individuals who, challenged by simultaneous inhabitation of different races, perform through practicing, remembering, or reinventing themselves and subjecting the basic element color to multidisciplinary mutations, proliferations, and syntheses. In equally acting processes the feeling fit image transforms into sequences fused with bodies, space, sound, and text that expose the multiple identity of a complex superorganism. Ultimately interested in the idea that reality is our own construction, that we build it and that we create the reality we want in our life. There is not only one way of viewing reality. By combining its materials, symbolic origins, its influence on our sense of social reality, its sociopolitical implications and its future potentials, we are confronted primarily with a moral issue: whether we are going to treat our fellow races as we want to be treated. Let the world meet as men with men. Give utter justice to all. Extend democracy to all, and treat all men according to their individual deserts and different roles and meanings. They connect incompatible historical and geographical scenarios.

SERGE ATTUKWEI CLOTTEY
Colour Unfinished
2013
Video still

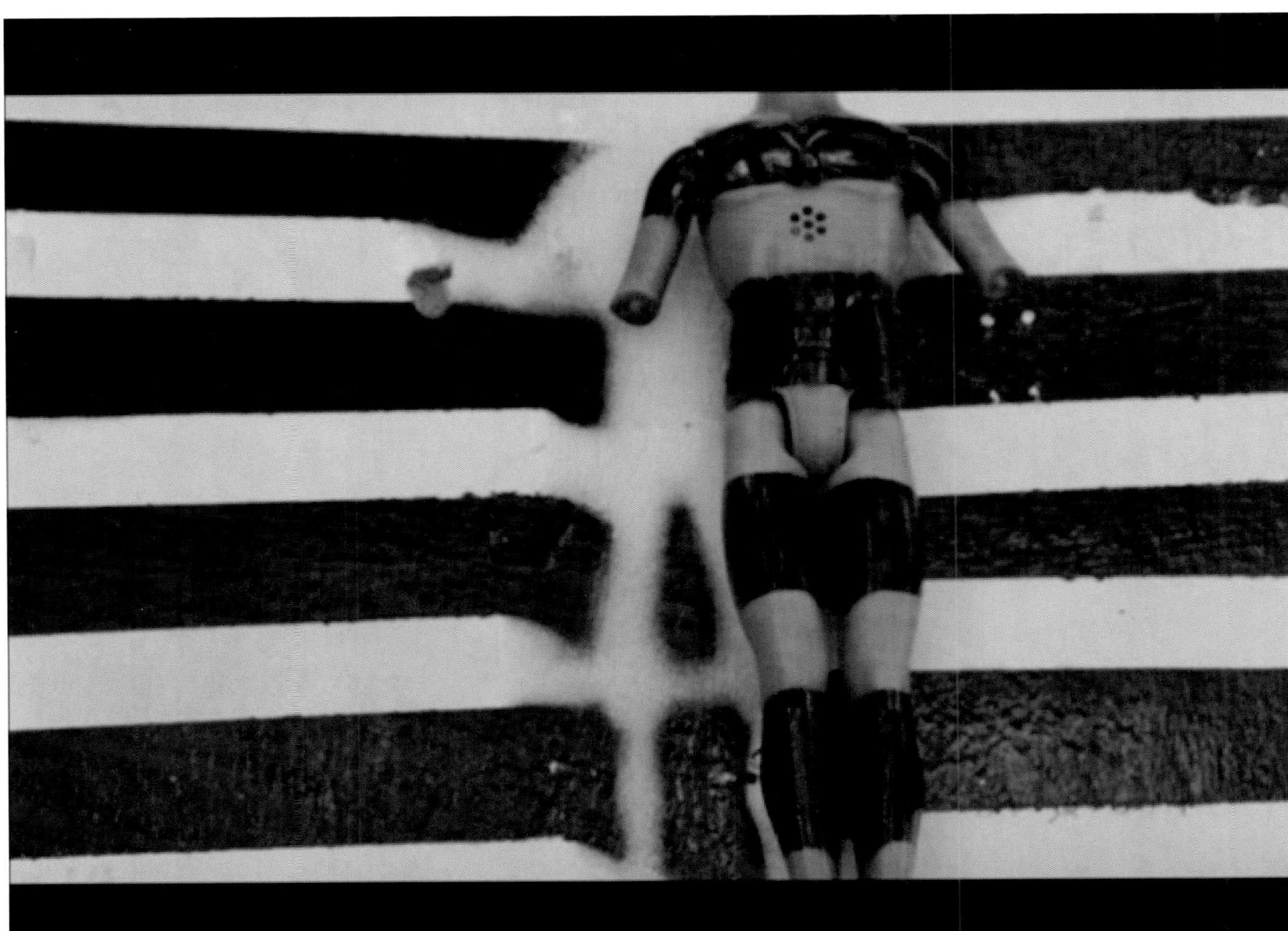

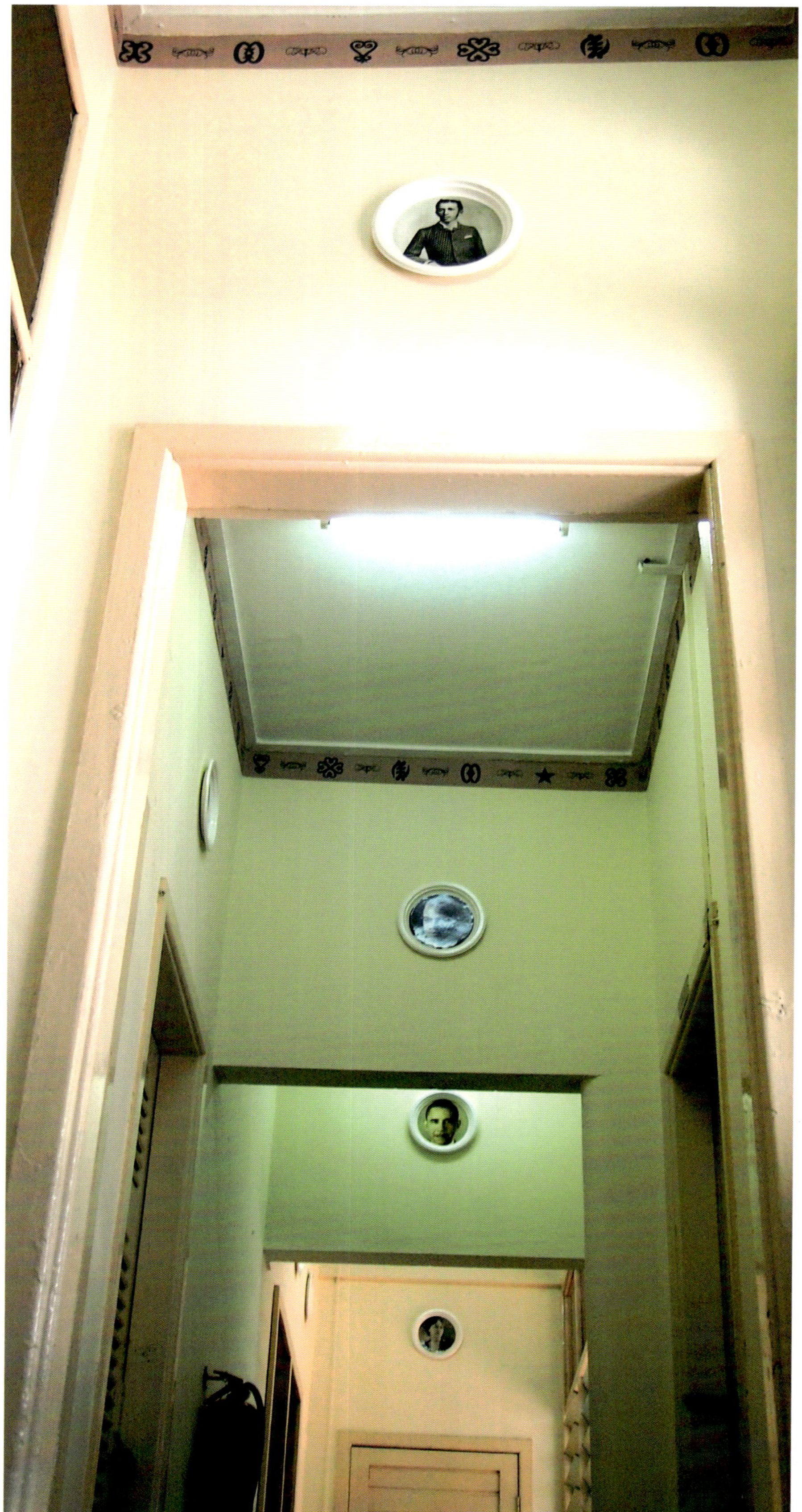

MARY EVANS

The title *Pantheon* for me situates the work in a couple of ways. Firstly it sites the work toward the ceiling in the Du Bois Centre — skywards and heavenwards. The viewer is compelled to look up to engage with the work. Secondly, the term "Pantheon" unites Du Bois and his fellow Pan-Africanists and modern thinkers in a firmament of significant figures and events. The Pantheon in ancient Rome was a collection of the ancient gods. I am not suggesting that Du Bois and his peers and the more contemporary figures are gods, but I do want to commemorate their achievements through this piece of work.

Pantheon is comprised of two elements. Firstly the portraits collaged onto painted paper plates hung above the doors and below the ceiling in the corridor of the Du Bois Centre. Secondly a decorative border of black pictographic images is printed on

MARY EVANS
Pantheon
2013
Mixed media installation

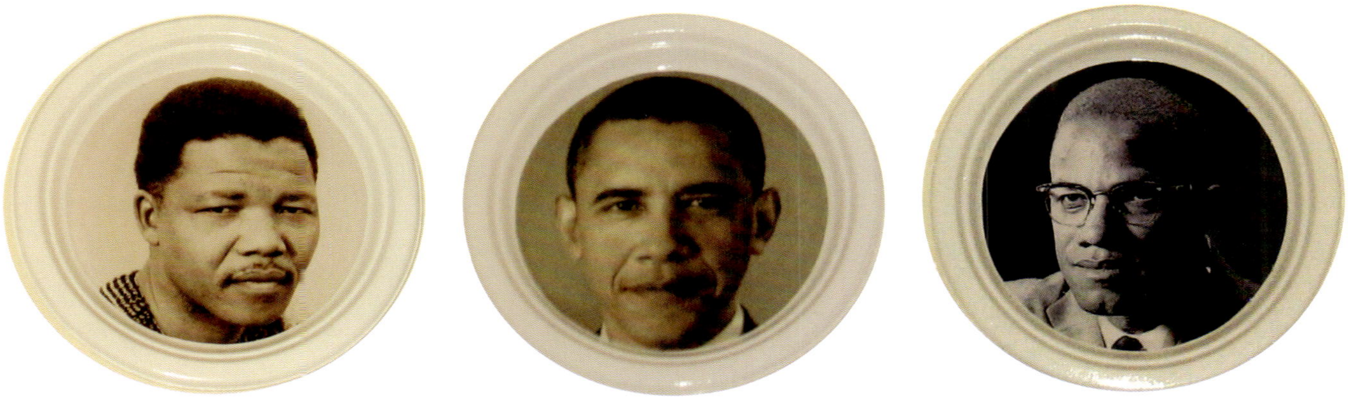

brown paper. This border "frames" the plates by being placed in two strips along the tops of the doors and under the ceiling.

My first impression of the Du Bois Centre in 2005 was the realization that it was Du Bois's home for the last couple of years of his life. The first objects that struck me were the photographs of Du Bois with his wife and the Nkrumahs in the first space of the house. I decided to use the plates as a site for the photographs, to tap into what I felt was the "domestic" ambience of the Du Bois Centre. I have read about Du Bois the Pan-Africanist and civil rights leader, but initially I really wanted to tap into Du Bois the family man, husband, friend, and father.

The contrast between the plates with their sepia-toned portraits and the graphic printed wallpaper border will be intriguing I think, and I hope will look as though it belongs in the domestic setting of the space. Du Bois was a Victorian gentleman, and the plates look as though they belong in a Victorian parlor. Even the very idea of a wallpaper border as a decorative device is Victorian in origin. The pictographic symbols printed onto the border will be in stark contrast to the plates depicting the pantheon of Pan-Africanists. The Pan-Africanists were learned, educated, and lettered people who wrote and campaigned for African unity, in contrast with the more ancient pictographic writings that have a completely different resonance. Du Bois and his peers, while striving and dreaming of a united continent, still, I think, held Africa's ancient traditions dear to them. Du Bois lived his final years in Ghana and died on African soil.

After the British Abolition of Slavery Act in 1807, commemorative plates and medallions were made to strengthen the abolitionists' cause. I am interested in how a decorative object such as a plate made from fine bone china could be a site for political and social propaganda. As this juxtaposition of the ornamental and the politically conscious is a common theme of my practice, I used the abolition as my starting point and decided to make a piece of work commemorating those who have not often been commemorated in this way. Some of the images on the plates are depictions of slaves, rebel slaves, abolitionists, African, African American, and Caribbean thinkers and radicals. Others are just black faces I wanted to see on that site. Using plates as a site anchors the portaits of Du Bois and his peers as well as more recent figures in a commemorative and decorative firmament of significant figures pictured during significant events.

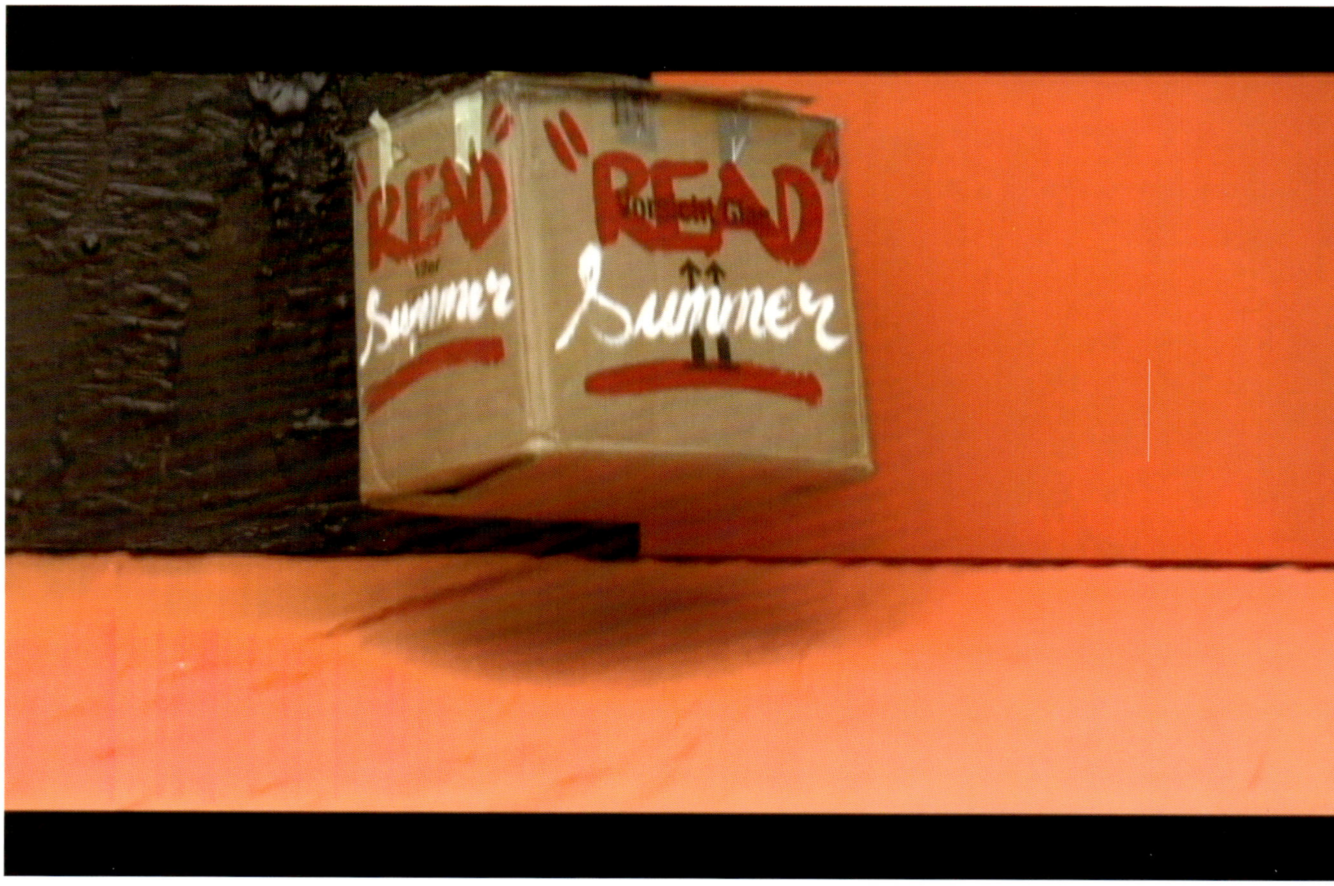

KELVIN HAIZEL

An amalgam of historical events during the 1920s and W.E.B. Du Bois's renunciation of capitalism and adoption of communism form the tenets of my experimental video.

The title is a pun on James Weldon Johnson's description of the 1920s as a "Red Summer." According to him, the era was characterized by brutish lynching on racial lines, arguably justified by "Jim Crow" laws and etiquette. At this time, Du Bois had renounced capitalism to adopt communism. Hear him speak: "I now state my conclusion frankly and clearly: I believe in communism. I mean by communism, a planned way of life in the production of wealth and work designed for building a state whose objective is the highest welfare of its people and not merely the profit of a part." (*Autobiography* 1968:57) He also later warns the free enterprise state, in an article in the *Pittsburgh Courier,* that it is doomed for self-destruction because it cannot reform itself. To relate this premise to my own experience, as a student currently reading a course in business and also practicing art, I feel caught up in some form of elitist familiarity of similar dimensions. Straddling these two spaces makes me notice their tendency to exclude the masses with regards to the possession of knowledge and material wealth. This greed of the capitalist few, as expressly stated by Du Bois, will grind to a halt by its very design. A case in point is the recent recession signaling the wearing-out of the global capitalist machinery.

KELVIN HAIZEL
"Read" Summer
2013
Video still

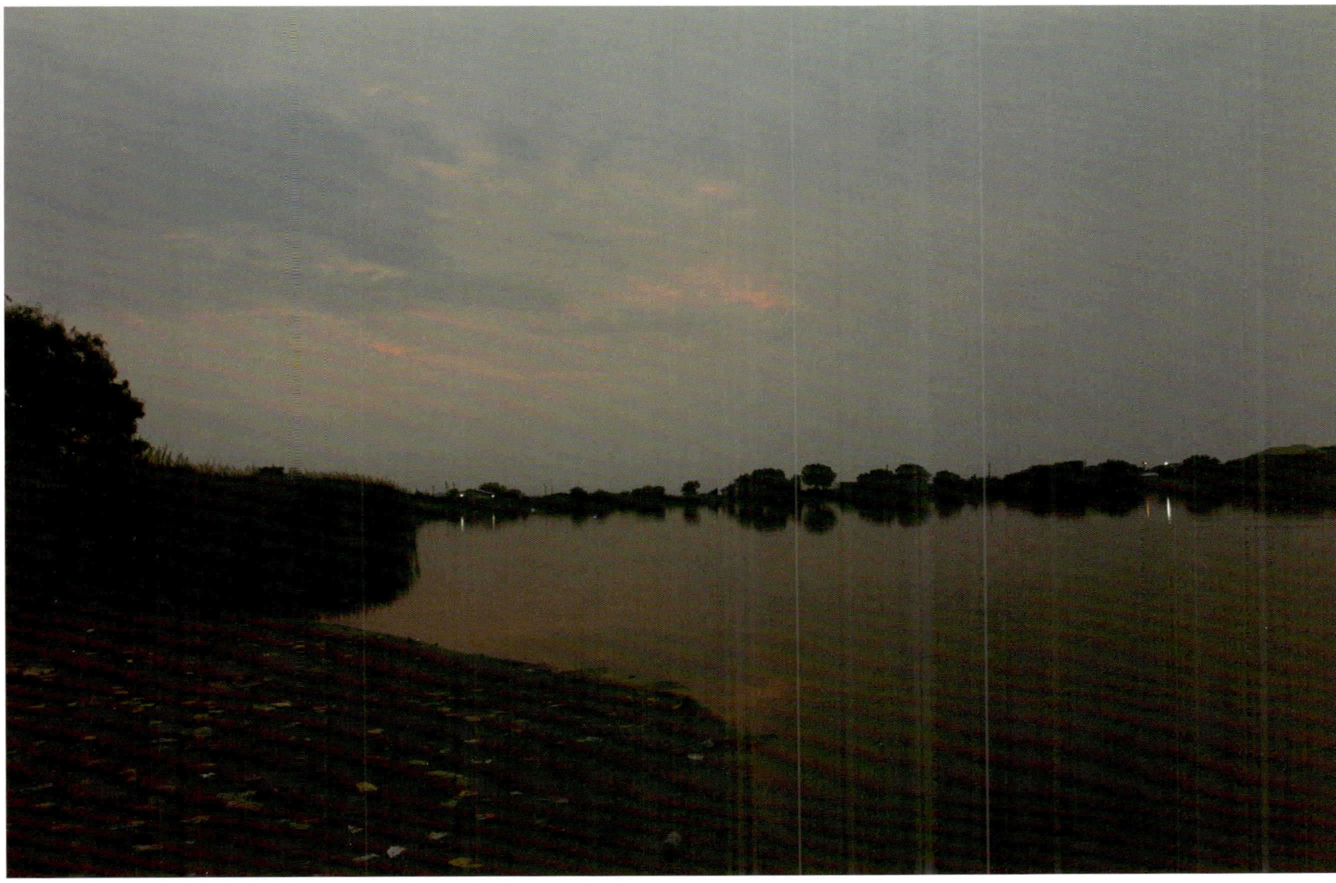

MAWULI KELLY TOFAH

The video *Equals* is a study of Du Bois's writing on equality in North America from 1960 to the 1980s. I look at the battle for equality, which was dominant in his writing. This study takes the form of viewing life through convergent diversity, in that inasmuch as we are different, the similarities continue to permeate all spheres of cultural and material life. Du Bois takes the view that there will never be "absolute equality of opportunity," thereby opening doors for debate, critique, and analysis of the term "equality" that is often used. Could terms such as "respect," "understanding," and "tolerance" be substituted here? If these words come to replace the fundamental right of humans for equality in light of what one is rightly entitled to, do we not lose the essence of equality? Interviews and still photography are used to produce a 3:13-minute video that explores those differences that can/do exist among both natural and man-made creations: opposites and complements.

MAWULI KELLY TOFAH
Equals
2013
Video still

CONTRIBUTORS
UMCA AMHERST ARTISTS

RADCLIFFE BAILEY

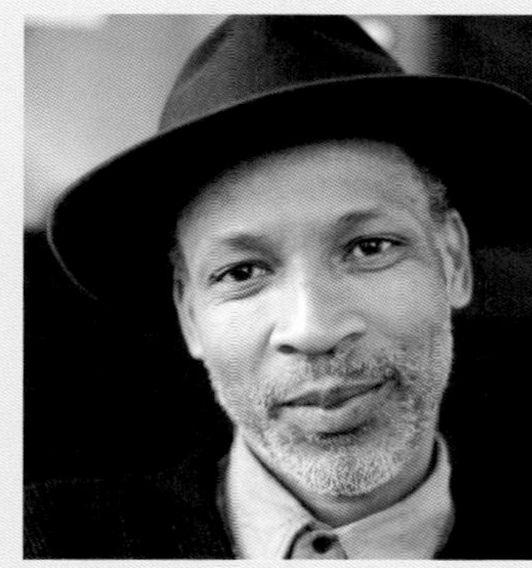

Radcliffe Bailey is a painter, sculptor, and mixed media artist who utilizes the layering of imagery, culturally resonant materials, and text to explore themes of ancestry, race, and memory. Bailey believes that by translating his personal experiences, he can achieve an understanding of and healing from a universal history. His work is often made from found materials and certain pieces from his past, including traditional African sculpture, tintypes of his family members, piano keys, and Georgia red clay.

In a 2013 interview with Lilly Lampe in BOMBlog, Bailey describes his creative process, "the day by day experience of art, even though my work may seem to have this layer of history, it is also a cover for what I'm dealing with on a day to day. It's very much about today. We were talking about where I go next: I'm still thinking about today and yesterday and what's coming in front of me tomorrow. It's my attitude to my studio practice."

Bailey was born in Bridgeton, New Jersey, in 1968, and grew up in Atlanta, Georgia, where he currently lives and works. Bailey received a B.F.A. in 1991 from the Atlanta College of Art.

In response to his show *Memory as Medicine* (2012), at the High Museum, the artist description notes: "Bailey harmonizes an intuitive balance of world history and familial memory. Through exploration of the past, the present, and the unknown, Bailey layers meaning into his art by layering objects. Combining two- and three-dimensional forms, he uses various mediums and scale to create a diverse and engaging collection of art that can be read together as pages of the same book."

His past exhibitions include *Memory as Medicine*, High Museum of Art, Atlanta (2011), which traveled to the Davis Museum and Cultural Center, Wellesley College, and the McNay Art Museum, San Antonio, TX; *New/Now: Radcliffe Bailey*, New Britain Museum of American Art, New Britain, CT (2004); *Neo-HooDoo*, organized by the Menil Collection, Houston, TX, at Miami Art Museum, FL (2009), and traveled to MoMA P.S.1, NY (2009). Bailey's work is in the collections of the Metropolitan Museum of Art, New York; the Smithsonian Museum of American Art, Washington, D.C.; The Corcoran Gallery of Art, Washington, D.C.; the Museum of Fine Arts, Houston, TX; the Nelson-Atkins Museum of Art, Kansas City, MO; and the High Museum of Art, Atlanta, GA, among others.

Jack Shainman Gallery has represented Bailey since 2002. Solo exhibitions in the gallery include *Maroons* (2014), *Outer Spaceways* (2011), *Altered Destiny* (2007), and *Meet Me by the River* (2002).

MARY EVANS

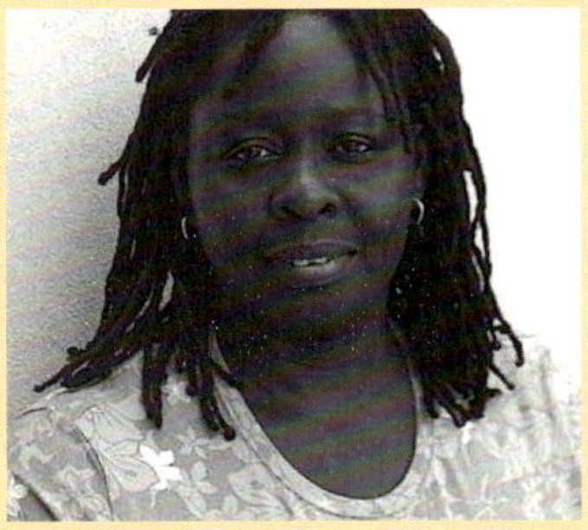

Mary Evans was born in Lagos, Nigeria, in 1963 and now lives and works in London, UK. Evans's interests are centred on the social, political, and historical frameworks of diaspora, migration, global mobility, and exchange. She endeavors to investigate how the social, cultural, and political dynamics of modern Britain are in many respects the legacy of Britain's imperial past. With a particular interest in historical representations of African people, Evans often employs stenciling and cutting techniques, using different shades of brown kraft paper to represent bodies against white backgrounds; the execution of her work tends towards the site-specific on a large scale. In 2012 Evans had a solo exhibition, *Cut and Paste*, at Tiwani Contemporary in London. She has been the recipient of numerous awards and grants, including the Arts Council England (Individual Grant), the Smithsonian Artists' Research Fellowship, and a Rockefeller Foundation Bellagio Centre residency. Evans is an associate lecturer at Central Saint Martins in London.

BRENDAN FERNANDES

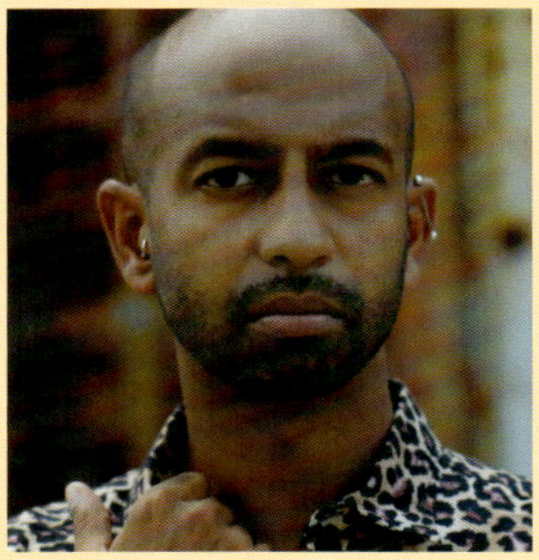

Brendan Fernandes is a Canadian artist of Kenyan and Indian descent. His work investigates the plasticity of personal identity, foregrounding in particular the process of migration. Migration defines identity via one's transformation of becoming something else through processes of loss and gain, forgetfulness and remembrance. In his newest work he draws on these explorations in order to look at the intimate relation between embodiment and identity, questioning how movement techniques are recalled in the body via muscle memory, and explores this phenomenon through cultural dance, ballet, and the language that prescribes directions for the dancer to move. He completed the Independent Study Program of the Whitney Museum of American Art (2007) and earned his M.F.A. (2005) from the University of Western Ontario and his B.F.A. (2002) from York University in Canada. He has exhibited widely, including exhibitions at the Solomon R. Guggenheim Museum, the Museum of Art and Design NY, Art in General, the Musée d'art Contemporain de Montréal, the National Gallery of Canada, the Art Gallery of Hamilton, the Studio Museum in Harlem, Mass MoCA, the Andy Warhol Museum, ZKM, the Art Gallery of York University, Deutsche Guggenheim, the Bergen Kunsthall, Manif d'Art: the Quebec City Biennial, the Third Guangzhou Triennial, the Western New York Biennial through the Albright-Knox Art Gallery, Sculpture Center, and the Stedelijk Museum. He was a finalist for the Sobey Art Award, Canada's preeminent award for contemporary art (2010), and was on the longlist for the 2013 prize. He is currently a recipient of a Robert Rauschenberg Residency Fellowship and will be included in upcoming exhibitions at the Seattle Art Museum and the Brooklyn Museum.

LATOYA RUBY FRAZIER

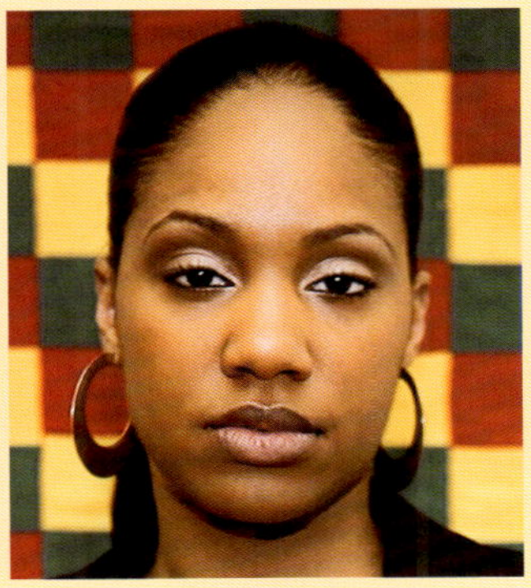

LaToya Ruby Frazier was born in1982, in Braddock, Pennsylvania, received her B.F.A. in applied media arts from Edinboro University of Pennsylvania (2004) and her M.F.A. in art photography from Syracuse University (2007). She also studied under the Whitney Museum of American Art Independent Study Program (2010–2011) and was the Guna S. Mundheim Fellow for visual arts at the American Academy in Berlin (2013–2014).

In 2014, Frazier accepted the assistant professor of photography position at the School of the Art Institute of Chicago. She has previously held academic and curatorial positions at Yale University School of Art, Rutgers University, and Syracuse University. Frazier lectures prolifically at academic and cultural institutions such as the International Center of Photography; Columbia University School of the Arts; Parsons the New School; Pratt Institute; Cooper Union; Tisch School of Arts, New York University; and the School of Visual Arts, all in New York City; Freie Universitat Berlin, Dahlem Humanities Center and Hamburger Bahnhof; and Tate Modern, London.

Frazier's work is exhibited widely in the U.S. and internationally, with notable solo exhibitions at Brooklyn Museum; Seattle Art Museum; Institute of Contemporary Art, Boston; and Contemporary Arts Museum Houston. Her work has also been featured in the following group shows: *The Generational Triennial: Younger Than Jesus* (2009), New Museum, New York; *Greater New York* (2010), MoMA PS1, New York; *Commercial Break, Garage Projects* (2011), 54th Venice Biennale; *Gertrude's/ LOT* (2011), Andy Warhol Museum, Pittsburgh; *Empire State* (2013), Palazzo delle Esposizinoi, Rome; and *The Way Of The Shovel: Art as Archaeology (2013),* Museum of Contemporary Art, Chicago, among many others

Her work has been exhibited in the following biennials: the Whitney Museum of American Art Biennial (2012), New York, *Recycling Memory: Recapturing the Lost City* (2014), 11th Nicaraguan Visual Arts Biennial, Managua; *Mom, am I barbarian?* (2013),13th Istanbul Biennial; and Busan Biennale (2014), South Korea.

Frazier is the recipient of many awards, including a fellowship from the John Simon Guggenheim Memorial Foundation (2014), Gwendolyn Knight and Jacob Lawrence Prize of the Seattle Art Museum (2013), the Theo Westenberger Award of the Creative Capital Foundation (2012), the Louis Comfort Tiffany Foundation Award (2011), and Art Matters (2010)

Her work can be found in public and private art collections such as the Brooklyn Museum; Carnegie Museum, Pittsburgh; Centre National Des Arts Plastiques, France; JP Morgan Chase Collection, Library of Congress, Washington, D.C.; Museum of Contemporary Art, Chicago; Museum of Contemporary Photography, Columbia College, Chicago; Nacher Museum at Duke University, Durham, N.C.; Spelman College Museum of Fine Art, Atlanta; Whitney Museum of American Art, New York; Zabludowicz Collection, London, and Pomeranz Collection, Vienna, among others.

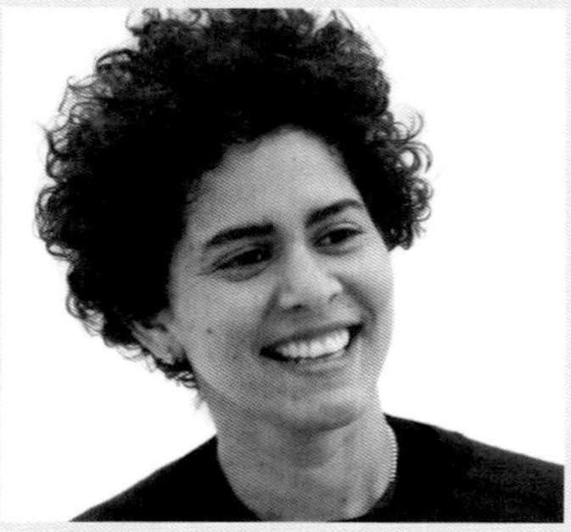

JULIE MEHRETU

Julie Mehretu was born in 1970 in Addis Ababa, Ethiopia. She studied at Kalamazoo College in Michigan (B.A., 1992) and at the Université Cheikh Anta Diop in Dakar, Senegal (1990–91). She received an M.F.A. in painting and printmaking from the Rhode Island School of Design in 1997. She has received numerous awards, including the MacArthur Award (2005), the American Art Award granted by the Whitney Museum of American Art (2005), the 2002 Penny McCall Award, the Rhode Island School of Design Alumni Council Artistic Achievement Award (2006), and the Berlin Prize: Guna S. Mundheim Fellowship at the American Academy in Berlin, Germany (2007). She has participated in numerous international exhibitions and biennials, including Documenta 13 (2012), the New Orleans Biennale (2008), the 15th Biennale of Sydney (2006), and the Whitney Biennial, Whitney Museum of American Art (2004). She has had solo exhibitions at such institutions as the Guggenheim Museum, New York (2010), the Museo de Arte Contemporáneo de Castilla y León, Spain (2006), and the Walker Art Center, Minneapolis (2003). Mehretu now lives and works in New York and Berlin.

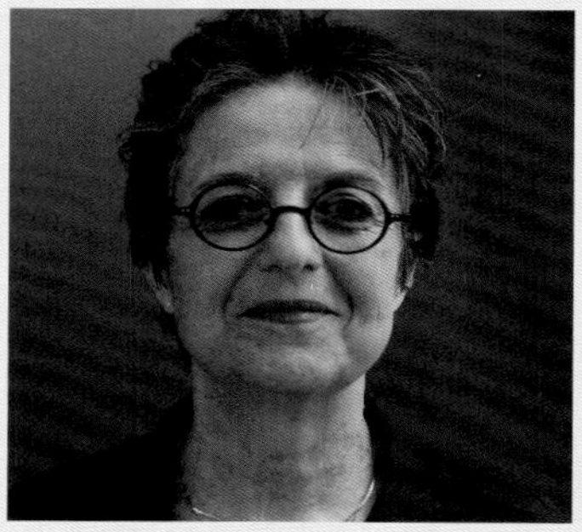

ANN MESSNER

New York–based artist Ann Messner has focused her work since the 1970s on an investigation of the intersections between private life/space and public/civic experience, concentrating on the relationship between the individual and the larger social body as encountered within public space or discourse. Her projects have traversed boundaries between the directly political and cultural, blurring mistaken distinctions between the two.

Ann was the creative director for *disarming images,* produced and distributed by the collective Artists Against the War, 2005. Other individual projects include *oracle*, Wesleyan University, 2005; *outpost*, a public installation, New York, 2008–2009; and the tabloids *penitentiary*, distributed at Eastern State Penitentiary, Philadelphia, 2006; and *the disasters of war*, Center for the Arts, Wesleyan University, 2006 and The Renaissance Society, University of Chicago, 2008.

Recent group exhibitions include *The Real Estate Show: Was Then 1980, What Now? 2014,* Fuentes and Cuchifritos Galleries, New York; *Petites Résistances,* Hans-Peter-Zimmer Foundation, Dusseldorf, Germany; *Women Choose Women (Again),* Visual Arts Center of New Jersey; *Act/OUT*, Onomatopee, Eindhoven, Netherlands; *Global Fight Club: Aspects of Terror in Contemporary Art*, Meinblau, Berlin; and *Art, Access & Decay: New York 1975–1985*, Subliminal Projects, Los Angeles.

Ann is a recipient of numerous awards, including a Guggenheim Fellowship, a Gottlieb Foundation Fellowship, the Anonymous Was a Woman Award, a Henry Moore International Fellowship, an NEA and two New York Foundation for the Arts awards in sculpture. She was a Bunting Fellow at the Radcliffe Institute for Advanced Study, Harvard University, and was appointed a Senior Fellow at the Princeton University Council on the Humanities. Ann has taught at MIT's Visual Arts Program, Hunter College, and Maryland Institute of Art. She is currently a full professor and coordinator of MFA Integrated Practices at Pratt Institute.

JEFFERSON PINDER

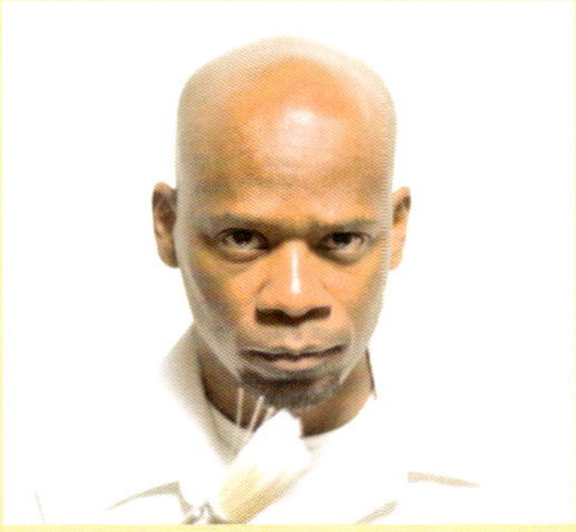

Jefferson Pinder, a Chicago-based video/performance artist, seeks to find identity through the most dynamic circumstances. His experimental videos and films feature minimal performances that reference music videos and physical theater. Pinder's work provides personal and social commentary in accessible and familiar format. Inspired by soundtracks, he utilizes hypnotic popular music and surreal performances to underscore themes dealing with Afro-Futurism, physical endurance, and blackness.

His work has been featured in numerous group and solo shows, including exhibitions at the Studio Museum in Harlem; the Wadsworth Athenaeum Museum of Art in Hartford, Connecticut; Showroom Mama in Rotterdam, Netherlands; the High Museum in Atlanta, Georgia; and the Zacheta National Gallery in Warsaw, Poland. Pinder's work was featured at the Smithsonian's National Portrait Gallery exhibition *Recognize*. In the spring of 2012 his action-packed endurance performance *Ben-Hur* was featured at the Corcoran Gallery of Art, Washington, D.C. Most recently he's been grappling with segregation and music in Alabama with a large-ensemble performance titled *Belly of the Beast* in downtown Birmingham, a commission sponsored by the Birmingham Museum of Art.

Jefferson received his B.A. in theater from the University of Maryland and studied at the Asolo Theatre Conservatory in Sarasota, Florida. In 2001, Jefferson returned to the University of Maryland to receive his M.F.A. in mixed media. Currently he is an associate professor in the Contemporary Practices department at the School of the Art Institute of Chicago.

TIM ROLLINS & K.O.S.

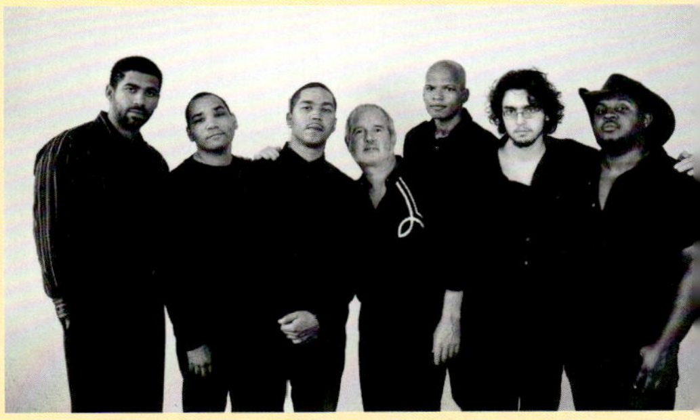

Tim Rollins studied fine art at the University of Maine and earned a B.F.A. from the School of Visual Arts in New York. After graduate studies in art education and philosophy at New York University, Rollins began teaching art for special education middle school students in a South Bronx public school. In 1984, he launched the Art and Knowledge Workshop in the Bronx together with a group of at-risk students who called themselves K.O.S. (Kids of Survival). In 1997, the documentary *Kids of Survival: The Art and Life of Tim Rollins & K.O.S.*, was well received at the London Film Festival; Cinema de Real, France; and the Hamptons International Film Festival.

Since its inception, the group has exhibited extensively worldwide, including Smithsonian American Art Museum, Washington, D.C. (2011); Galleria d'Arte Moderna e Contemporanea, Bergamo, Italy (2011); Museum fur Gegenwartskunst, Basel, Switzerland (2012); and Hayward Gallery, London (2012). In 2006, Tim Rollins & K.O.S. were included in the Whitney Biennial. A retrospective of the group's twenty-year career opened at the Tang Teaching Museum and Art Gallery at Skidmore College in 2009 and traveled to the Frye Museum in Seattle and the ICA Philadelphia later that year. A fully illustrated hardcover catalogue, copublished by the Tang Museum and MIT Press, accompanied the exhibition. The group's work is represented in prestigious public and private collections, including the Dallas Museum of Art, Texas; Museum of Modern Art, New York; Hirshhorn Museum of Art, Washington, D.C.; Tate Modern, London; and Smithsonian Museum of American Art, Washington, D.C. Tim Rollins & K.O.S. are based in New York City.

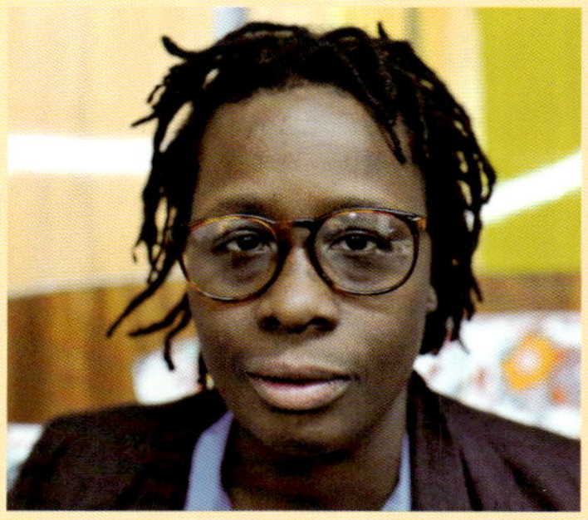

MICKALENE THOMAS

Mickalene Thomas was born in New Jersey and now works in Brooklyn, New York. She is a distinguished multidisciplinary visual artist best known for combining art-historical, political, and pop-cultural references to create striking figurative and nonfigurative paintings. Thomas introduces complex notions of femininity and challenges common definitions of beauty and aesthetic representation. Her work stems from her long study of art history and classical genres of portraiture and landscape.

Inspired by various sources that range from the nineteenth-century Hudson River School to Édouard Manet, Alice Neel, and Romare Bearden, she has created a true signature style and continues to explore notions of beauty from a contemporary perspective infused with influences of popular culture and pop art, redefining contemporary ideas of portraiture. In combining traditional genres with African American female subjects, Thomas makes a case for opening up the conventional parameters of art history and culture. Thomas's layered process of fragmentation, in which she begins with a photographic portrait and moves to collage and then on to painting, is the result of discreet borrowings from our twenty-first-century language of mass culture. Strategically placed objects in her photographs come into sharper relief during the collage stage as deliberately exposed tape and abrupt lines between forms frame our perspective, focusing us on the distinct cultural languages that she puts on view. Thomas is represented by Lehmann Maupin in New York, Suzanne Vielmetter Los Angeles Projects, Galerie Nathalie Obadia in Paris, and Kavi Gupta Gallery in Chicago.

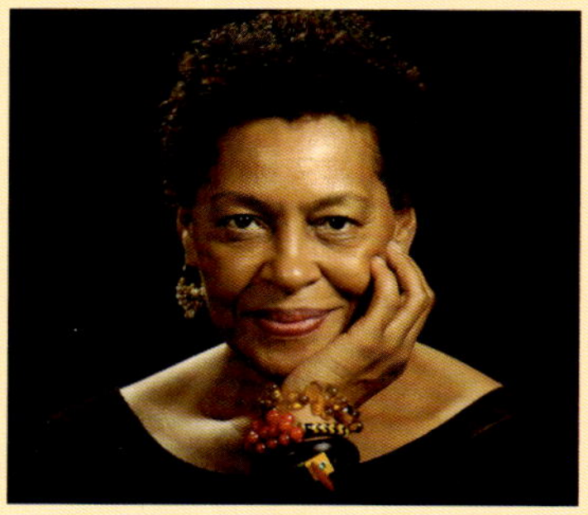

CARRIE MAE WEEMS

Carrie Mae Weems has worked toward developing a complex body of art that has employed photographs, text, fabric, audio, digital images, installation, and video over the past thirty years. Her work has led her to investigate family relationships, gender roles, the histories of racism, sexism, class, and various political systems. Weems has participated in numerous solo and group exhibitions at major national and international museums, including the Whitney Museum, the Museum of Modern Art, and the Metropolitan Museum of Art. Most recently, her work was the focus of a major retrospective, *Carrie Mae Weems: Three Decades of Photography and Video*. The exhibition began its run at the Frist Center for Visual Arts in Nashville, and ended its five-museum tour at the Solomon R. Guggenheim Museum, New York, in May 2014. Weems has received numerous awards, grants, and fellowships, including the prestigious Prix de Roma, the National Endowment for the Arts, the Alpert, the Anonymous was a Woman, and the Tiffany Awards. In 2012, Weems was presented with one of the first U.S. Department of State's Medals of Arts in recognition of her commitment to its Art in Embassies program. In 2013 Weems was a recipient of the MacArthur "Genius Grant" and the Congressional Black Caucus Foundation's Lifetime Achievement Award. In 2014 she received the BET Honors Visual Artist award. She is represented in public and private collections around the world, including the Metropolitan Museum of Art and the Museum of Modern Art, New York; the Museum of Fine Arts, Houston; and the Museum of Contemporary Art, Los Angeles. Weems has been represented by Jack Shainman Gallery since 2008.

SCHOLARS

JAMES T. CAMPBELL

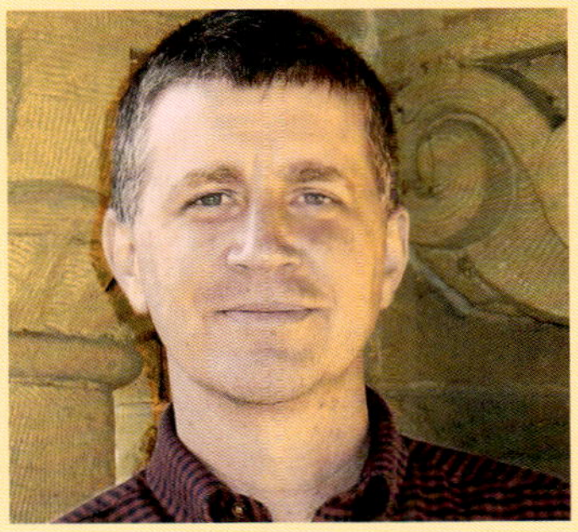

JAMES T. CAMPBELL is the Edgar E. Robinson Professor in United States History at Stanford University and specializes in African American history and the history of the black African slave trade. His research spans the history of the American slave trade with Africa, the Harlem Renaissance, and the civil rights movement.

Professor Campbell received his B.A. from Yale University, and his M.A. and Ph.D. from Stanford University. He was a professor of Africana Studies and American Studies at Brown University, where he also served as chair of the Brown University Steering Committee on Slavery and Justice from 2003 to 2006. He has held teaching positions and fellowships at Northwestern University and Harvard University. James Campbell has worked as a consultant for the History Channel, the United States Department of Education Teaching American History Grants, the Civil Rights Living Memorial Project as well as the 2003 PBS film series *This Far by Faith: African-American Spiritual Journeys*. He has contributed to projects related to black history such as "Freedom Now!," a website about the history of the Mississippi Freedom Movement. His current research interests fall in the area of "public history," examining the ways in which societies document and tell stories about their past, not only in textbooks and academic monographs, but also in the context of museums, historic sites, movies, and political movements.

Campbell's publications include *Race, Nation, and Empire in American Life* (University of North Carolina Press, 2007) (co-edited with Matthew Guterl and Robert Lee, 2007); *Middle Passages: African American Journeys to Africa, 1787–2005* (Penguin Press, 2006); and *Songs of Zion: The African Methodist Episcopal Church in the United States and South Africa* (Oxford University Press, 1995). In 2006, *Middle Passages* was awarded the Mark Lynton History Prize from the Columbia School of Journalism and the Nieman Foundation at Harvard University, and the Lois P. Rudnick Prize from the New England American Studies Association. Campbell's first book, *Songs of Zion*, was awarded the Carl Sandburg Literary Award for Nonfiction and the Organization of American Historians' Frederick Jackson Turner Prize. Campbell has written numerous articles and essays, and is currently writing on the history of the "Americanization" of South Africa and on the role of Africa in the life and scholarship of Du Bois.

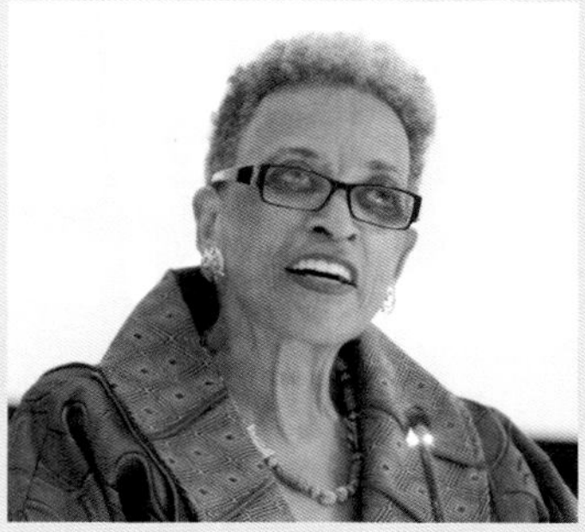

JOHNNETTA BETSCH COLE

Dr. Johnnetta Betsch Cole was appointed director of the Smithsonian National Museum of African Art (NMAfA) in March 2009. The museum's collection of over 10,000 objects represents nearly every area of the continent of Africa and contains a variety of media and art forms. NMAfA also has an extensive education program. Since the mid-1980s, Dr. Cole has worked with a number of Smithsonian programs. She currently serves on the Scholarly Advisory Board for the Smithsonian's National Museum of African American History and Culture, the construction of which will be completed on the National Mall by 2015.

Before assuming her current position, Johnnetta Cole had a long and distinguished career as an educator and humanitarian. Through her work as a college president, university professor, and through her published works, speeches, and community service she has consistently addressed racial, gender, and all other forms of inequality.

Dr. Cole served as president of Spelman College and Bennett College for Women. She is also Professor Emerita of Emory University, from which she retired as Presidential Distinguished Professor of Anthropology, Women's Studies, and African American Studies.

After one year in an early entrance program at Fisk University and completing her undergraduate studies at Oberlin College, Johnnetta Cole earned a master's degree and a Ph.D. in anthropology from Northwestern University with a focus on African Studies. Dr. Cole made history in 1987 when she became the first African American woman to serve as president of Spelman College.

Dr. Cole has conducted research in Africa, the Caribbean, and the United States, and she has authored and edited several books and scores of scholarly articles. She is a fellow of the American Anthropological Association and the American Academy of Arts and Sciences. She is a member of the board of trustees of the American Association of Art Museum Directors and Gregory University, in Uturu, Nigeria. She is also a member of the Toni Morrison Society.

Johnnetta Cole has been awarded sixty-one honorary degrees, and she is the recipient of numerous awards. In 2010, *Ebony* magazine listed her among the 100 most influential African Americans, and in 2011 *Washingtonian* magazine listed her among Washington, DC's most powerful women. On December 8, 2012, in Uturu, Nigeria, an Igbo Chieftaincy title of ADAOHA (Daughter of All) was conferred on Dr. Cole by His Royal Highness Eze Cyril Ibe, Eze Ogbonnaya Uwadiegwu, and Eze Chimezie.

Dr. Cole currently chairs the board of the National Visionary Leadership Project, and she is on the board of KaBOOM! She is on the Advisory Committee of America's Promise and Points of Light Foundation. Dr. Cole is a member of Delta Sigma Theta Sorority, Inc., The Links, Inc., and the National Council of Negro Women.

Dr. Cole is married to James D. Staton Jr. She is the mother of three sons and one stepson, and she has three grandchildren. Dr. Cole is also a mentor to many young women and men.

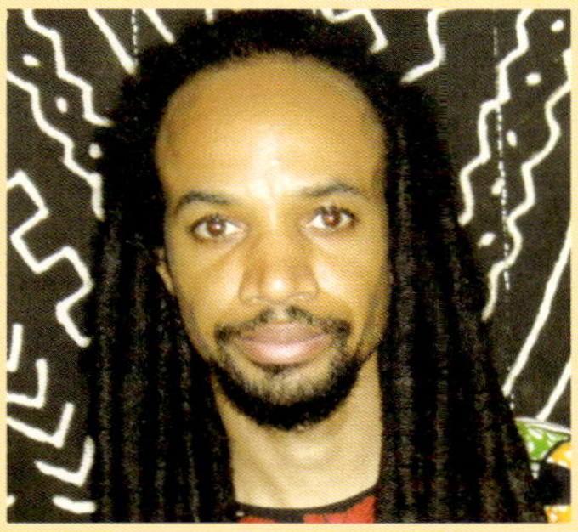

REILAND RABAKA

Reiland Rabaka is Professor of African, African American, and Caribbean Studies in the Department of Ethnic Studies at the University of Colorado at Boulder, where he also has affiliations with the Women and Gender Studies Program, Humanities Program, Graduate Program in Critical Theory, Center for Studies of Ethnicity and Race in the Americas (CSERA), School of Education, and College of Music. He is the author of more than fifty scholarly articles and book chapters, as well as twelve books, including: *Du Bois's Dialectics*; *Africana Critical Theory*; *Against Epistemic Apartheid: W.E.B. Du Bois and the Disciplinary Decadence of Sociology*; *Forms of Fanonism: Frantz Fanon's Critical Theory and the Dialectics of Decolonization*; *Concepts of Cabralism: Amilcar Cabral and Africana Critical Theory*; *The Negritude Movement*; *Hip Hop's Inheritance*; *Hip Hop's Amnesia*; and *The Hip Hop Movement*. Rabaka's research has been recognized with several awards, including funding from the National Endowment for the Humanities, the National Endowment for the Arts, the National Science Foundation, the Eugene M. Kayden Book Award, the Cheikh Anta Diop Book Award, and the National Council for Black Studies' W.E.B. Du Bois–Anna Julia Cooper Career Award. Rabaka's cultural criticism, social commentary, and political analysis has been featured in print, radio, television, and online media venues such as NPR, PBS, BBC, CNN, ABC, NBC, CBS, MTV, BET, VH1, *The Huffington Post*, *The Denver Post*, *The Dallas Morning News*, *The Houston Chronicle*, and *USA Today*, among others. He is also a published poet, spoken-word artist, and musician.

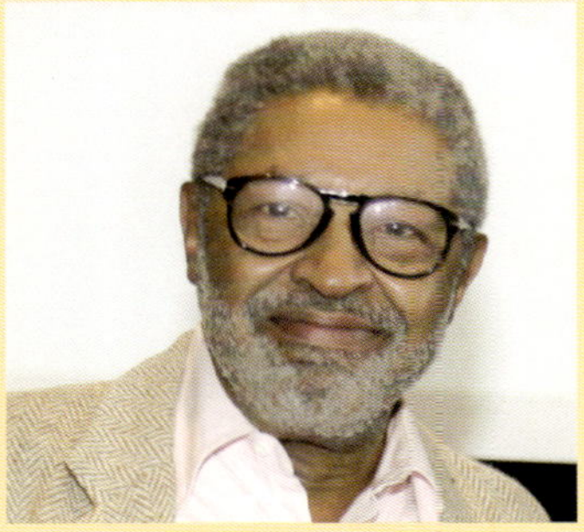

BILL STRICKLAND

Bill Strickland is Professor Emeritus in the W.E.B. Du Bois Department of Afro-American Studies at the University of Massachusetts Amherst, where he taught political science and is the Director of the Du Bois Papers Collection. The Du Bois Papers are housed at the University of Massachusetts library, which is named in honor of this prominent African American intellectual and Massachusetts native. Professor Strickland is a founding member of the independent black think tank the Institute of the Black World, headquartered in Atlanta, Georgia. Strickland was a consultant to both series of the prizewinning documentary on the civil rights movement, *Eyes on the Prize*, and the senior consultant on the PBS documentary *Malcolm X: Make It Plain*. He also wrote the companion book. More recently, Professor Strickland was a consultant on the Louis Massiah film about W.E.B. Du Bois, *W.E.B. Du Bois: A Biography in Four Voices*.

ACCRA ARTISTS

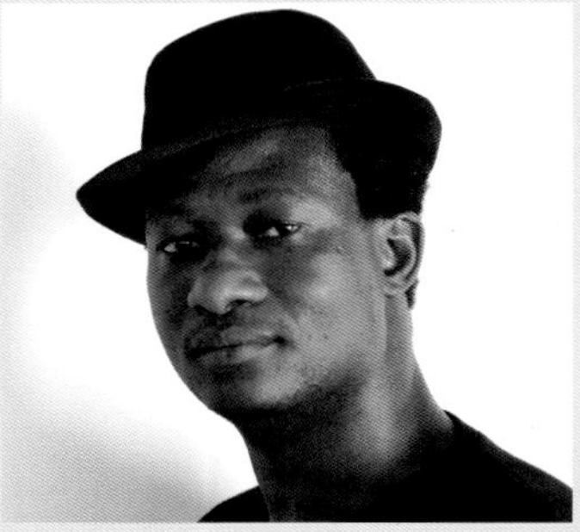

BERNARD AKOI-JACKSON

Bernard Akoi-Jackson is an artist and writer who interrogates hybrid postcolonial African identities through ephemeral, makeshift memorials and performative rituals of the mundane. He graduated with an M.F.A. from the College of Art, Kwame Nkrumah University of Science and Technology, Kumasi, in 2006. Using critical absurdity, he moves between genres — dance, poetry, installation, photography, and video — to confront the complexities of his specific cultural moment. In Akoi-Jackson's work, "jest" is as serious and profound as "clout," so that a balanced dose of these become the crux of his expression. His work has been shown in group and solo exhibitions in venues across Ghana and internationallly. In 2012 his one-minute video *Marking Time* was featured in a group show at the Slade Research Centre, Slade School of Fine Art, in London. His writing tracks the development of contemporary Ghanaian and African visual art and culture. He has contributed regularly to *ArtFOCUS*, and has written essays for several exhibition catalogues. Since 2006, Akoi-Jackson has facilitated workshops in Ghana and Germany. He lives and works in Tema, where he also teaches art at the Tema International School.

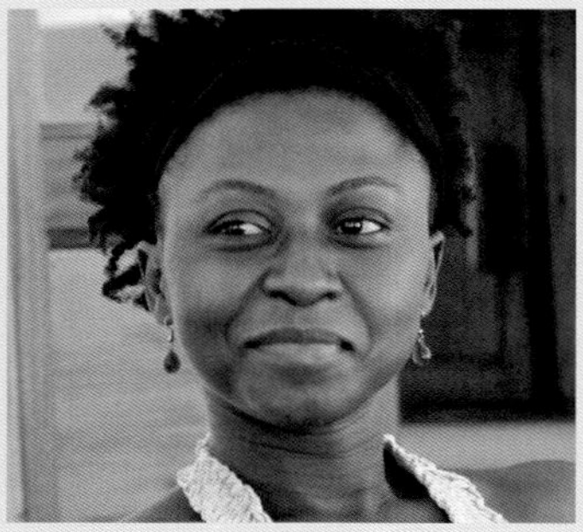

ADWOA AMOAH

Adwoa Amoah received her B.F.A. from the College of Art, Kwame Nkrumah University of Science and Technology, Kumasi, in 2003. Through painting and installation, Amoah observes the exchange and dissemination of public information and ephemera in Ghana using newspaper and street conversations. By stitching, gluing, painting, knotting, drilling and screwing metal, magazines, newspaper, canvas, plywood, and thread, she works metaphorically with parts of the eye, presenting an index of people's varied opinions and public information. She relies on macramé as both a process and a symbol of human exchange and connectivity. Amoah's work has been exhibited throughout Ghana and internationally. She has participated in a number of workshops and has curated many public art projects. In her current role as co-director of the Foundation for Contemporary Art, Ghana, she has coordinated the smARTpower Laboratory workshop, an initiative of the U.S. State Department, administered by Bronx Museum of the Arts. Amoah serves as a facilitator for the Global Crit Clinic, a professional development clinic based in the Fine Arts pedagogical studio critique, along with faculty from Parsons The New School for Design, New York. In 2012 she hosted the pilot clinic for Ghana at the Foundation for Contemporary Art, Ghana, which culminated in a public panel titled *From Inside to Outside; Interrogating Public Space and Exchange Structures in the Context of Contemporary Africa* and in May 2013 she hosted and served as project associate curator at the third International Art Residency Program, "The Archive: Static, Embodied, Practiced," with Nigerian International curator Bisi Silva, Centre for Contemporary Art, Lagos.

YAGANOMA BAATUOLKUU

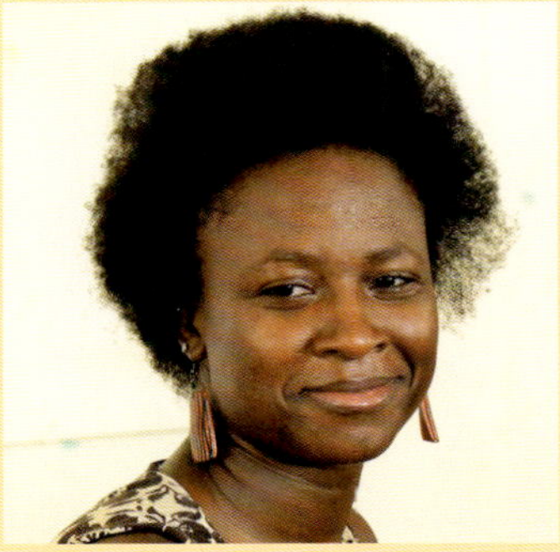

Yaganoma Baatuolkuu graduated from the College of Art, Kwame Nkrumah University of Science and Technology, Kumasi, in 2005 with a B.F.A. in Sculpture and then was granted an M.Litt. in Managing Creative Industries (Social Dynamics in Networking) from the University of St. Andrews, Scotland. Having left visual art for some time, she now seeks to reestablish herself through the exploration of experiential dialogues, mainly poetry. Her poetry currently explores experiences and their effect on life choices. She is working on her first poetry book.

SERGE ATTUKWEI CLOTTEY

Serge Attukwei Clottey has taken art in Ghana to a new level. Born and raised in La, located in Accra, Attukwei has known he wanted to be an artist since he was in primary school. His father is a nationally famous artist, and so he derived some of his passion for art that way, but he found a new way to articulate his vision for art and social justice in the world.

His artwork grapples with issues of environmental, political, and cultural concern within Ghana, both his mixed-media sculptures and his paintings. After graduating from junior high school, he spent three months in an electronics apprenticeship, and later attended Ghanatta College of Art and Design, where he completed his four years with a diploma in fine art. In 2006, Attukwei was offered a sponsored opportunity to study art in Brazil and came back with a new attitude toward his art and a renewed appreciation for everything in life. For him, art has always come first — at times even before feeding himself. He eats, sleeps, and breathes his artwork; it is as much a part of him as his skin.

> "My work combines activism and art, addressing cultural, political, combining science with the arts and economic inadequacies in the world. The art implicates both the individual and the government. It urges people into action and attempts to rectify the current state of ignorance. The issues affect the entire world; change starts with the individual. I follow the mantra 'Think globally, act locally.'"

MARY EVANS

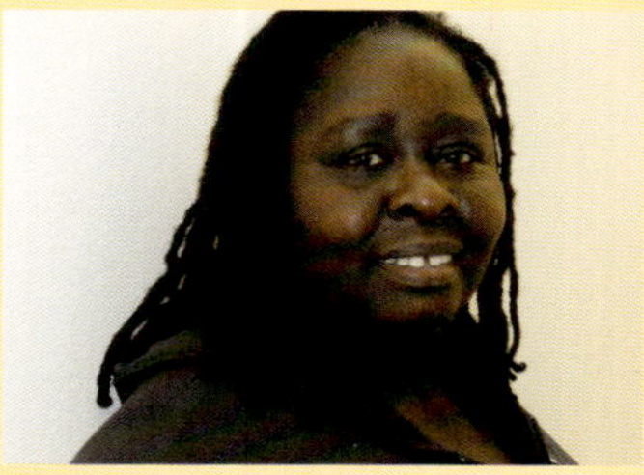

Mary Evans was born in Lagos, Nigeria, and received her B.A. from Gloucestershire College and M.A. from the University of London Goldsmiths College, followed by postgraduate work at the Rijksakademie in Amsterdam. Her work has appeared in the UK, Netherlands, United States, China, Canada, Mexico, and Dubai. She is the recipient of numerous grants and awards, including a Smithsonian Artist Research Fellowship. In addition to acting as a workshop presenter, she has been a lecturer at numerous colleges in the UK and the Netherlands.

She says, "Pattern is a strong leitmotif in my work. I am interested in pattern as ornament as well as pattern as standardization. However, the work is rarely pure ornament, but often reveals the historical, architectural, or social threads of its source. I use pattern and ornament as an aesthetic device through which the viewer can access the work. The intention is to look beyond the façade of ornament to see what lurks there.

"My research interests are centered on the social, political, and historical frameworks of diaspora, migration, global mobility, and exchange. I endeavor to investigate how the social, cultural, and political dynamics of modern Britain are in many respects the legacy of Britain's imperial past. I am fascinated by the circuitous route via which people arrive and settle somewhere through emigration and diaspora, whether willingly or by force; what affects people on those journeys, what they are forced to learn, and relearn, what they choose to remember and forget, and how they are irrevocably changed."

KELVIN HAIZEL

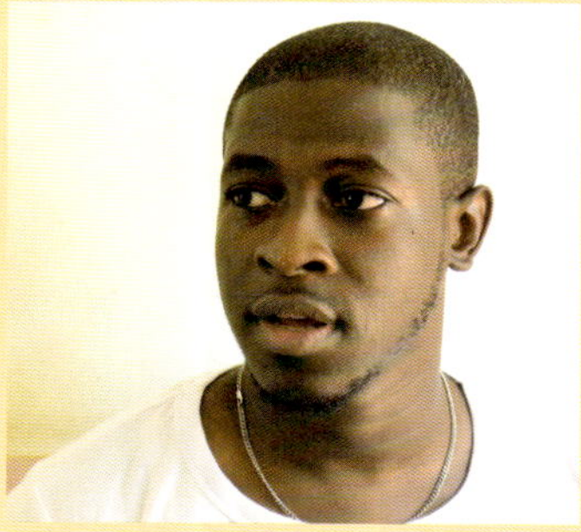

Kelvin Haizel graduated with a B.F.A. (Painting and Sculpture) from the college of Art and Sciences, Kwame Nkrumah University of Science and Technology, Kumasi, in 2010. He uses paintings, performance, interactive installations, and mixed media art as a way to engage spectators. His body of work elicits response pertaining to trance, simultaneous existence, and mass/consumed culture; these concerns are hidden in pseudomask imagery that he uses to question how loose, yet crafty, our social orientation tends to be. His most recent work deals with presenting just "specific material."

His practice seeks to evoke a response to questions embedded in the body of work as opposed to the omniscience of "the artist." As he is quick to tell you, "I have possession of few answers, and a lot of questions."

KWASI OHENE-AYEH

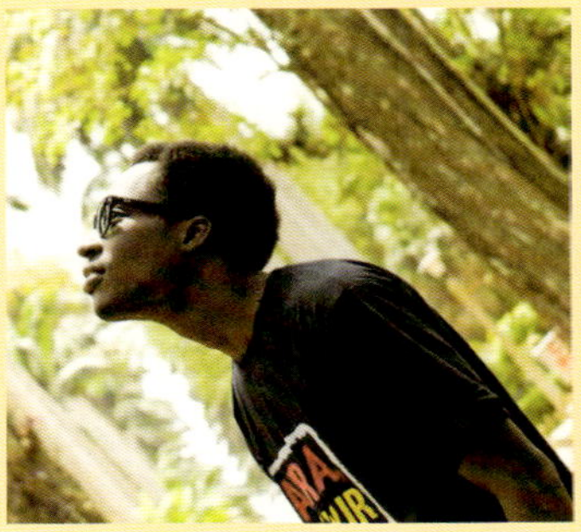

Kwasi Ohene-Ayeh (I.U.B.) graduated from the College of Art, Kwame Nkrumah University of Science and Technology, Kumasi, with a B.F.A. in Painting, and creates works influenced by the interrelated genres of poetry, music, dance, theater, sculpture, painting, and texts. He is also a cultural events organizer and co-organizer of the foremost open mic poetry event in Ghana, known as EHALAKASA. Born in Accra, Kwasi works in his home country while collaborating with a diverse mix of artists. In 2009, his fourth year in college, he had his first major art exhibition at the Alliance Francaise gallery in Ahodwo, Kumasi. This was a joint exhibition with French artist Charles Sauvat. Both artists showed sketches made over a period of ninety days, and Sauvat's sculptures inspired Kwasi to explore the idiom of "installations." Since then, the artist has been fascinated with situating objects in space to illustrate his ideas. Another major influence for the artist comes from his interactions with proponents of performance-based art in Ghana.

ATO ANNAN

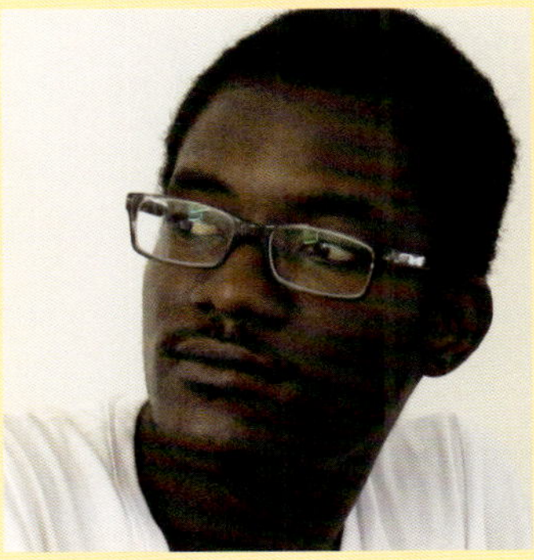

Ato Annan is a Ghanaian artist whose work consists of creating multilayered portraits of contemporary society. His work interrogates the alternating/shifting identities of people, particularly in Ghana and Africa. He uses painting, collage, installations, performative rituals of the mundane, video or sound, to confront the intricate cultural conditions of his contemporary society. His works have been exhibited in Africa, Europe, India, and the United States. Annan is currently projects coordinator at the Foundation for Contemporary Art, Ghana.

MAWULI KELLY TOFAH

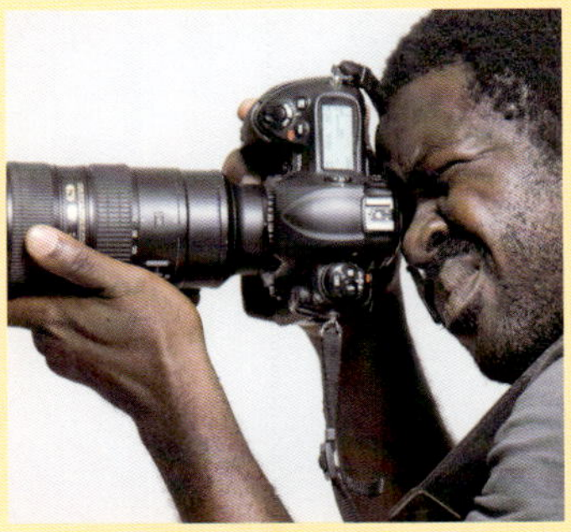

Mawuli Kelly Tofah was born in Keta, in the Volta region of Ghana, and raised in Swaziland in its capital, Mbabane, and in South Africa in the period of the apartheid. His passion for photography and sound grew during his childhood and through high school on his return to Ghana. Mawuli enrolled at Ghana's National Film and Television Institute, which provided him with enriching opportunities that helped develop his skills in photography, filmmaking, and sound production. He graduated in 2005 with a B.F.A. in Film Sound Production.

Since graduation he has worked with New York University, Accra, in the Department of Art and Art Professions as a teaching assistant for the Projects in Photography and Post Colonial Practice in studio arts. He has simultaneously been a freelance photographer for Courier International (Spain) and the Sunday *Times* in the UK. In addition, he has worked as a film sound engineer and filmmaker in Ghana and abroad. In 2012 and 2013 Mawuli was nominated for the Ghana movie awards in the category of sound mixing and editing.

ARTWORKS
UMCA AMHERST ARTISTS

RADCLIFFE BAILEY

Untitled, 2013, bronze, wood, 42″ x 24¼″ x 17″
Double Consciousness, 2013, steel, wax, 48″ x 48″ x 17″

MARY EVANS

Held, February 23, 2013, Kraft paper, dimensions variable

BRENDAN FERNANDES

In The End, 2013, screen-printed flags, painted wall mural, flags – 5′ x 3′, Mural – 11′ 4″ x 18′ 5″
The Encyclopedia Africana, 2013, hand-bound book, gold foil stamping, and black linen paper, 12″ x 9″ x 3″
Du Bois in Our Time, Encyclopedia Africana Performance, performance piece by Brendan Fernandes at the UMass campus as part of the symposium and exhibition *Du Bois in Our Time*. The *Encyclopedia Africana* is carried in a procession with the UMass Amherst Color Guard from the W.E.B. Du Bois Library to the University Museum of Contemporary Art, where it is placed in a niche. The book is part of the exhibition.

LATOYA RUBY FRAZIER

A Despoliation of Water: From the Housatonic to Monongahela River (1930–2013)
Born by Water and Spirit, Ninth and Washington Avenue, 2009, Gelatin silver print, 30″ x 40″
United States Steel Edgar Thomson Steel Works and Monongahela River, 2013 Gelatin silver print, 48″ x 58″
United States Steel Edgar Thomson Steel Works, Monongahela River and 1755 Battle of the Wilderness, 2013, duratrans, 27¼″ x 38¼″
Washington Avenue and Monongahela River, 2013, duratrans, 27¼″ x 38¼″
Monongahela River, bridges and shipping containers, 2013, duratrans, 27¼″ x 38¼″
Eighth and Washington Avenue, Specialty Steel Production Inc. Braddock Plant and My Childhood Home, 805 Washington Avenue, 2013 Duratrans, 27¼″ x 38¼″
Ninth and Talbot, BOC Gases, Talbot Towers, The Bottom and The Bunn Family House, 2013, duratrans, 27¼″ x 38¼″
The Waterfront and Courtyard Marriott, Homestead Steel Works and 1892 Homestead Steel Strike, 2013, duratrans, 27¼″ x 38¼″
United States Steel Clairton Coke Works and Clairton, PA, homes, 2013, duratrans, 27¼″ x 38¼″
United States Steel Clairton Coke Works, C.I.T.E. and Monongahela River, 2013, duratrans, 27¼″ x 38¼″

JULIE MEHRETU

Untitled, 2012, graphite and acrylic on canvas 25″ x 36″ x 2″

Algorithms, Apparitions and Translations, 2013, a series of five multiplate etchings with aquatint, spit bite, soft ground, hard ground, drypoint, and engraving, printed on Hahnemühle copperplate paper in an edition of 35, bon à tirer, plate size 23″ x 30″, paper size, 31¼″ x 37¼″

ANN MESSNER

Du Bois: The FBI Files, 2013, installation consisting of 447 running foot–incised digital scroll (hand-cut stenciled redaction), printed on Hahnemühle FA paper; 22-foot table inset with 6 in-wall MP5 Niles speakers, CD players, 4 CDs (audio component of the installation)

Installation accompanied by 44-page tabloid, edition of 5,000, distributed free throughout campus

JEFFERSON PINDER

Star of Ethiopia, 2013, neon, basalt stone, 72″ x 84¼″ x ⅝″

Overture, 2013, video, 2-channel projection; 8 minutes

TIM ROLLINS & K.O.S.

DARKWATER (after W.E.B. Du Bois), 2013, furnace black watercolor, gold acrylic on vintage book pages on panel, 24 elements, each 7″ x 5″, with students from the Renaissance School, Springfield, Massachusetts

MICKALENE THOMAS

Hair Portraits, 2013, rhinestones and acrylic on wood panel, 24 panels, each 24″ x 20″, installation 48″ x 240″

Happy Birthday to a Beautiful Woman: A Portrait of My Mother, 2010, video, 23 minutes, 6 seconds

CARRIE MAE WEEMS

The Garden Space, 2013, archival inkjet print on rag paper, 22″ x 45″

The W.E.B. Du Bois Peony, 2013, archival inkjet print on rag paper, 24″ x 22″

Flute Player, 2013, archival inkjet print on rag paper, 35″ x 16″

A Considered Space, 2013, archival inkjet print on rag paper, 35″ x 45″

Flute Player, 2013, archival inkjet print on rag paper, 35″ x 16″

The W.E.B. Du Bois Peony, 2013, archival inkjet print on rag paper, 24″ x 22″

The Garden Space, 2013, archival inkjet print on rag paper, 22″ x 45″

Floral Study (Spikes), 2013, archival inkjet print on rag paper, 10″ x 10″

Floral Study (Cherry), 2013, archival inkjet print on rag paper, 10″ x 10″
Floral Study (Poppy), 2013, archival inkjet print on rag paper, 10″ x 10″
Floral Study (Du Bois Study 7 with Table), 2013, archival inkjet print on rag paper, 10″ x 10″
Floral Study (Cosmos), 2013, archival inkjet print on rag paper, 10″ x 10″
Floral Study (Wildflower), 2013, archival inkjet print on rag paper, 10″ x 10″
Floral Study (Queen Anne's Lace), 2013, archival inkjet print on rag paper, 10″ x 10″
Floral Study (Du Bois Study 5 with Table), 2013, archival inkjet print on rag paper, 10″ x 10″
Floral Study (Du Bois Study 4 with Table), 2013, archival inkjet print on rag paper, 10″ x 10″
Floral Study (Du Bois Study 2 with Table), 2013, archival inkjet print on rag paper, 10″ x 10″
Floral Study (Du Bois Study 1 with Table), 2013, archival inkjet print on rag paper, 10″ x 10″
Floral Study (Roses for Yolanda), 2013, archival inkjet print on rag paper, 10″ x 10″
Floral Study (Du Bois Study 3 with Table), 2013, archival inkjet print on rag paper, 10″ x 10″
Floral Study (Du Bois Study 12 with Table), 2013, archival inkjet print on rag paper, 10″ x 10″
Floral Study (Zinnia), 2013, archival inkjet print on rag paper, 10″ x 10″
Floral Study (Pompoms), 2013, archival inkjet print on rag paper, 10″ x 10″
Floral Study (Lilies), 2013, archival inkjet print on rag paper, 10″ x 10″
2013 Proposal for W.E.B. Du Bois Garden, University of Massachusetts Amherst, 2013, Site model and digital renderings, with Walter Hood, *Courtesy of Hood Design Studio,* Zygimantas Cepaitis, Peony time-lapse video, 1 minute, color, Copyright © Zygimantas Cepaitis, Zygistudio
Du Bois in China, 2013, Video, 9 minutes, 46 seconds, sound; reworking of original Chinese government 16mm color film footage from 1959. *Source film courtesy of W.E.B. Du Bois Library Special Collections and University Archives*

ACCRA ARTISTS

BERNARD AKOI-JACKSON

Metaphor, 2013, video, 00:38,

ADWOA AMOAH

Talented Tenth, 2013, video, 02:30

KWASI OHENE-AYEH AND ATO ANNAN

Exit Frame, 2013, video, 00:58

YAGANOMA BAATUOLKUU

The Veil, 2013, video, 01:36

SERGE ATTUKWEI CLOTTEY

Colour Unfinished, 2013, video, 01:45

MARY EVANS

Pantheon, 2013, mixed media installation

KELVIN HAIZEL

"Read" Summer, 2013, video, 01:35

MAWULI KELLY TOFAH

Equals, 2013, video, 03:13

PHOTOGRAPHY CREDITS

TOM ADAMS, REELIFE PRODUCTIONS: (stills from video): 3, 4, 80 (bottom left and right), 81 (bottom left), 156, 157, 159, 160 (2), 161 (2), 162 (2), 163 (top and center), 164 (2),165 (bottom)

ED COHEN: 6, 151, 152 (2), 153 (3), 154 (4), 155 (3)

JUSTIN GRISWOLD: 80 top, 81 top

MITRO HOOD: 23

YOUNG MIN MOON: 165 top

STEPHEN PETEGORSKY: 11, 38, 39, 44, 45 (2), 46, 47, 59, 60, 64, 65, 66, 67, 68-69, 70, 71, 72-73, 74, 75 (2), 76-77, 78-79, 81 (bottom right), 82, 83, 84, 85, 86-87, 88, 89, 90, 91, 902, 93, 94, 95, 97, 98, 99, 100, 101, 102, 103, 104-105, 106, 107 (2), 109, 110-111, 112, 116-117, 120, 121, 122, 123, 124, 125, 127 (2), 130-131, 132, 136-137, 138, 139 (2), 140, 141, 142, 143 (2)

THE UNIVERSITY MUSEUM OF CONTEMPORARY ART
GRATEFULLY ACKNOWLEDGES SUPPORT FROM

ART WORKS.
arts.gov

ART MENTOR FOUNDATION LUCERNE

The Andy Warhol Foundation for the Visual Arts

NUBUKE FOUNDATION

ELIZABETH FIRESTONE GRAHAM FOUNDATION

MCC
massculturalcouncil.org

massHUMANITIES

ISI interdisciplinary studies institute

SC UMASS AMHERST LIBRARIES
scua.library.umass.edu

ART ANGELS
Community Foundation of Western Mass

UMASS CLASS OF 1961
Artists Residency Program

UMassAmherst
FINE ARTS CENTER